P9-AGL-372
DISCARD

Ivan Sanderson's Book of Great Jungles

Copyright by Philippe Halsman, courtesy of New York Botanical Societ

Ivan T. Sanderson.

574.90952

IVAN SANDERSON'S BOOK OF GREAT JUNGLES

BY

IVAN T. SANDERSON with DAVID LOTH

JULIAN MESSNER
Division of Pocket Books, Inc.
New York

WEST HILLS COLLEGE LIBRARY
COALINGA, CALIFORNIA

OCT 28 '70

Published by Julian Messner
Division of Pocket Books, Inc.
8 West 40 Street, New York 10018

© Copyright 1965 by Pocket Books, Inc.

Endpaper illustration: South American Indians
on upper Paraguay river in north Matto Grosso. Pix, Inc.

Printed in the United States of America

Library of Congress Catalog Card No. 65-23223

Acknowledgments

The photograph of the author on the jacket was taken by Philippe Halsman at the New York Botanical Garden. The animal shown with Ivan Sanderson is not a jungle animal but has been his personal pet and close companion for twelve years and has always traveled with him. It is a male Ring-tailed lemur from southern Madagascar, and is the sole survivor of a disastrous fire in which all of Mr. Sanderson's private collection of over two hundred rare animals were killed. "Katta," as this pet is named, is trained to assist in the collection of insects and other small animals in the field and has appeared on dozens of television shows.

Ylla from Rapho Guillumet

Gibbons.

Contents

Part V THE JUNGLE PEOPLES

Part VI DISCOVERERS AND EXPLORERS

Illustrations

Foreword

Foreword

My earliest recollection is having had a craving for living, growing green things. Perhaps this was a natural reaction to the somewhat dreary aspect of the city where I happened to have been born —Edinburgh, Scotland, and near which I spent the first five years of my life. I understand that in Iceland, an almost treeless and much more austere land, there are more potted plants in houses than anywhere else on earth. But Scotland is a comparatively lush country, especially on the west coast where my fisherman ancestors resided for, it seems, millennia. So how is it that an even more intense craving for the tropics possessed me from an early age? I don't remember having been shown even a picture of a coconut palm or a banana tree, but when my family moved to France, somebody must have told me about things called jungles. That did it!

There was something about the South of France, the ancient Provincia of Rome now called 'Provence,' that smelled right to me as a kid. The Mistral would blow over from North Africa hazing the sun; there were palms growing outside all year; there was early morning dew on the grapes, and the beaches—this was long before the Bikini Age—were pristine white sand with an occasional gaily painted fishing boat beached between piles of nets and old casks. The smell of the winds drifting up from the south seemed to grasp me like the writhing tendrils of tropical vines. It took me more than twice as long as the average child to learn how to read, so I was a bit late in getting on with the normal process of education. However, an uncle of mine who had spent twenty-five years in the tropics gave me a book entitled *The Malay Archipelago* by one Alfred Russel Wallace. I learned to read very quickly indeed after that.

Foreword

This is all so far away and long ago that I can no longer remember the true sequence of events. But, frankly, I don't really much care about the whys or the wherefores because, inexorably, I tramped through my young life with but one goal in view—The Jungles.

I spent my seventeenth birthday on the top of the great pyramid of Cheops because my guide got drunk—it was *Ramadan,* and he had bottles under his burnoose—and I first hit a jungle two months later in Ceylon. I was gone for eighteen months, wandering the East Indies with a young friend of my own age from Achi in northern Sumatra; walking from Saigon to Canton with another young friend, a Cantonese who just wanted to go home; flitting through the Pacific islands, and landing up in America. Then I had to hustle home, not an easy achievement for a teenager without funds in 1928.

When I enrolled in a great university, seat of learning as they say, and in my opinion one of the best when it comes to the natural sciences—Cambridge, England—I learned the truth, according to my betters, about what I had already seen with my own eyes. It was an "eye-opener" I can tell you! I haven't got over the shock yet and, after thirty more years poking about in and observing the jungles, I am afraid that I am constrained to make a few observations.

The different kinds of what are called environments that cover the surface of our planet vary within rather wide limits. We have the Antarctic icecap, the great sand deserts, the open ocean surface, prairies and so forth. These, being surface features of our earth, are more or less readily accessible to man. However, there are other environments that are not so easily reached, such as caves, the ocean bottoms and the interiors of icecaps. Only one surface environment displays features of subsurface worlds: that of the so-called "jungles." These are vast vegetable globs hidden away in the depths of the tropical forested regions of both the New and Old Worlds. They are vast, living, breathing entities of their own, with a life of their own and laws of their own. Actually, they constitute the ultimate of life on our planet. Therein, and therein only, has plant and animal life come to its climax. This I was not told: I had to find it out for myself.

The concept of the closed-canopy, evergreen, wet, tropical forests was, I found upon inquiry, a mixed bag. No distinction was made between the primaeval, primordial, virgin, climax (or whatever you want to call it) "jungle" and the rest of the lush tropical forests and other growths. Yet, I already knew that the moment you step from one to the other—and I mean about ten paces—you pass from one world to another. I liked the so-called jungles, but I didn't much like the other types of tropical forest, though even they were, to me, infinitely better than the paltry woodlands of the temperate climes and those endless, dreary, practically sterile, coniferous forests of the north. When you enter a jungle, unless you have been conditioned against it, you start to breathe, perhaps for the first time in your life. The Nordic Caucasoids may have had their Earth Goddess, but they never knew of the existence of the enormous vegetative wombs of life. In higher latitudes people just pray that the spring will eventually come and that things will start to grow again. In jungles, everything grows all the time. I liked this idea, and I still do.

For some strange reason jungles have got an appallingly bad name among all non-jungle people. We talk glibly about "the law of the jungle" and the average person is scared stiff of the very idea of entering one, let alone living in it. And this goes for the average inhabitant of tropical forested lands just as much as it does for pale-faced visitors. This has puzzled me for years, but I suppose it must be due to the simple fact that until less than a hundred years ago our western world knew absolutely nothing about any jungle, and that those few people who began to write about the jungles had never been there and founded their accounts—as did our good friend Rudyard Kipling—on what they knew of other types of tropical forests. Thus, the initial picture we received was completely false, and this was grandiosely augmented by the movie industry. Strangely, the "Tarzan" of Edgar Rice Burroughs got nearer to the truth in his original form than almost all others but, by the time he was presented to the public visually, he was surrounded by a host of non-jungle animals and most of them on the wrong continent.

Having lived in jungles for months, I simply could not stomach this sort of "information"; and I still cannot. In my youth the tropics were dangerous places for pale-faces, for many virulent diseases were rampant and literally pounced upon sterilized foreigners—yellow fever, malaria, the dysenteries, yaws, craw-craw, elephantiasis and other filariases, and a whole host of deficiency plagues such as beriberi. West Africa, when I first visited it, was still known as "The White Man's Grave." But I knew that if you could only get away from *people* and into a jungle, provided you did not carry any disease in with you, you were in the healthiest place on earth, except for the bacteria-free air of the polar regions.

What is more, it's never too hot or too cold there; there is water, though sometimes you may have to know where to search for it; and there is food. Shelter is always to hand, and the animals simply don't bother to molest you. Bugs are there in quantity if you show a light, but even the biting ones are much less abundant in the jungle than outside it. If you discard clothes and especially footwear, you'll have few problems, and if you should get your foot 'chopped,' the antibiotic properties of the jungle soils (something discovered only a few decades ago) are so potent that your foot will heal almost while you watch. This is the terrible, dread world of bloody tooth and claw!

In other words, this is the jungle as I see it after nearly forty years of first craving for it, then living in it, and finally studying what others have said about it and making flying trips into it to check on these statements. I have had living with me many hundreds of animals caught in the jungles and have studied their personalities, food preferences, mating habits and inter-relationships. I have grown what of the jungle flora I have been able to obtain and keep alive in our miserable northern climate. My home has been a meeting place of friends from all tropical forest areas, and from them I have learned many things that I never stumbled across when I visited their countries.

These are my jungles. I only hope that you may one day be able to visit them, before they are all bulldozed or atomized, to see for yourself their astonishing plants and animals and meet their wonderful human inhabitants face to face.

IVAN T. SANDERSON

Rapho Guillumette

Dawn on the Amazon, Peru.

Part I

The Real Jungle

Djanghael to Jungle

Guises and Disguises

How Jungles Are Born

Where Are the Jungles?

Bettmann Archive

A steady hand at a supreme moment.

1

Djanghael to Jungle

ON the second-to-last day of 1865 a weak-eyed, not very robust Englishman chanced to be born in Bombay. That utterly unremarkable circumstance a hundred years ago conditions the ideas most people cherish today about jungles, for the Englishman was Rudyard Kipling, one of the world's favorite storytellers.

Like a lot of others, he wrote "jungle" when he meant any of the tropical forests which cover about one-seventh of the earth's land surface. Also, like a lot of others before and after him, he knew nothing at first hand about the most magnificent, majestic, mysterious of these forests. He took them as the setting for his stories just because he was not familiar with them and they had for him the romance of the unknown.

Why anyone would apply this word to any kind of forest is explainable only by a not uncommon English disregard for fact and logic that drives language students mad. By Kipling's time, "jungle" had been used to cover a lot of territory and was hallowed by those British Army types he so dearly loved and celebrated in his songs and stories.

As anyone who reads the tales must know, the English officer and gentleman is an ardent huntsman. His leisure at home and abroad is devoted to the chase of whatever miserable animal happens to live in the nearest countryside. Neither rain nor wind nor snow, heat nor cold, mountain nor desert can halt his pursuit of wild game. And when the devious politics of empire-building drew British military types known as "political officers" into Persia, almost the first question they asked was: "Where is the best hunting?"

The answer was that gazelles could be found among the sparse, thorny growth of the Persian plains, a near-desert for which the local name was "djanghael." Adapted to the simplicity of the English tongue, it soon became part of the common speech of these particular gentlemen, who began to talk about going for a spot of hunting in "the jungle."

Gradually their private name for a hunting ground spread until it became a mark of anyone who had served the British in this part of the world. The men who used it apparently forgot its origin, or maybe they didn't care.

The word cropped up next in the hot hills of Sind in Pakistan, to which a lot of these chaps were transferred. The terrain was very much like that to which they had grown accustomed in Persia and was inhabited by lion, cheetah and other quarry considered to be a gentleman's legitimate prey. The intrepid Englishmen hunted there happily enough, although they disliked the dust and heat and cursed the "abominable jungle."

Transferred again, many of them to India, they moved gradually southward through that varied subcontinent until they reached the Western Ghats, the range of hills stretching in both directions from Bombay. Here there is a genuine tropical evergreen rain forest of tall, column-like trees with such thick foliage at the top that it is called "closed canopy." They saw more of it as their missions of Empire took them along to southern India and Ceylon and across to Burma where some of them went to look after the teakwood business.

In all these places, they went hunting. The country could hardly have differed more from Persia or Sind, but when they became ensnarled and snagged in a lush growth of vegetable things, they damned "the jungle." Furthermore, almost every British Indian Army colonel published a book about his experience in "The East." Since he wrote a lot about his hobby, he used "jungle" over and over again as he told in great detail and with much gusto how he had pursued this or that luckless animal. Eventually the word caught on in England and spread from there all over the world.

The existence of these tropical forests had been known for hundreds of years, of course, but hardly anyone had actually entered

Bettmann Archive

Tiger-hunting in Mysore, India.

them. (The hunters knew only their fringes.) Men had passed around them and floated through them on rivers. Primitive tribes and civilized peoples had lived on the edges. But none of them knew what it was like inside. The forests were there, but that was all anyone could say, just as in another extreme of climate the icecaps are known and seen from outside, but neither the Eskimos nor European adventurers penetrated the caps.

The British hunters in "the jungle" were scarcely learned men, and their name for the forest was never adopted by science as a description of anything. Scientists, in fact, think the word is as meaningless as "dinosaur," invented by a French savant to describe any and all large fossil reptiles which are, or are thought to be, extinct. Dinosaur is simply a popular title for a host of different things, and "jungle" fell into the same class.

To men like Kipling, however, "jungle" had a romantic sound, and his readers were perfectly happy with the world of his imagination. In it he placed not only all the plants and animals he had ever seen, but others of which he had only heard, whether or not they were typical of jungles, or even could live there. In "The Jungle Book," Mowgli's adoption by the wolves begins this lighthearted catalogue of marvels. India has its wolf packs, to be sure, but they would no more enter a jungle than they would invade a crowded city, for wolves are woodland creatures in this part of the world.

Kipling's jungles were a never-never land which was so vividly described that readers took it for the real thing, and found it so fascinating and memorable that they passed the myths along to people who do not read. Perhaps some of these were the makers of the famous Tarzan films. They took much of Kipling's lore and added to it a variety of even more absurd impossibilities.

Edgar Rice Burroughs, the creator of this wonderful creature of the jungle, kept to what might have been a real closed-canopy tropical forest in the original stories. But the men who translated him for the screen completed the popular misconceptions of the jungle. Although they never specified the location of Tarzan's forest home, the best guess is that they meant it to be somewhere in Africa. Here the most surprising mixture of animals, not the least strange of them human, wander about. The Indian elephant displaces the African loxodont, member of an entirely different genus. Overhead the trees are full of monkeys hanging by their tails, although out of more than 450 known kinds of monkeys, only 22 species perform this feat, and none of them live in Africa but in the Western Hemisphere. In these films, men and beasts take advantage of or force their way through impenetrable thickets of vegetation, whereas in a true jungle there is no undergrowth to speak of at all.

Then, every once in a while, a lion is shown stalking his prey—or something. Now you only have to look at a lion to realize, unless you are color blind, that he doesn't belong in such a setting. His tawny coat is admirably adapted for his true environment, the dun-colored scrub or the brown and yellow savannah. Far from being "king of the jungle," he would starve to death if he strayed into this sort of forest.

As a matter of fact, I think I saw the only lion who ever did enter a real jungle, and the poor beast was obviously lost as well as a great deal stupider than even a lion ought to be.

Collection, The Museum of Modern Art, New York

"Jungle with a Lion." Painting by Henri Rousseau.

It happened on one of my trips to collect animal specimens for museums and laboratories. I was not very far from camp, enjoying, as I always do, a walk in the dim green light filtering through the dense foliage a hundred feet or so above my head and armed with nothing more lethal than a butterfly net. Comfort in the jungle is easy if you remember not to encumber yourself with too much clothing, and I was very comfortable this particular day in a pair of pale pink silk pajamas.

As I rounded a great supporting root which certain jungle trees develop, and which resemble the huge buttresses of a Gothic cathedral, I saw him. He was a lion, no doubt about it, and he was as frightened as I was. The poor beast was already in a funk, as all animals are when they find themselves in an utterly strange place where they cannot possibly survive. All of a sudden he was confronted, between two roots in a space the size of an average living room, by such an apparition as he never could have seen before. As for me, I was more unnerved than I would have been if I had encountered this lion on his native heath. But at least I had one great advantage over him: I knew what he was.

For a moment we just stared at each other. Then at the same instant each of us decided to get out of there. I turned and vaulted over the low end of the buttress root, running hard. As I leaped I noticed out of the corner of my eye that the lion had started off full tilt in the opposite direction.

Later I figured out how he must have lost himself. There were small strips or patches of savannah in this jungle, although the nearest such area of any size was eighty miles away, and he could have been wandering from one to another. At least I started him off in the right direction to safety, for if he had fled in the opposite direction he would have fallen into the Gulf of Guinea before he got to savannah.

When I got back to camp—in a surprisingly short time considering that I am not a champion sprinter—no one believed my story. I could not possibly have seen a lion, they said, and in their place I would have said the same. Only when I took them back to the spot were they convinced. There in the soft, moist earth were the unmistakable prints of a lion; no other cat has as big a paw. The impressions were spaced so far apart that I realized he must have been running as hard as I.

None of these remarks about the derivation and meaning of the word "jungle" is meant to detract from the entertainment value of Kipling's stories or the Tarzan movies. It is only when people get it into their heads that this is the way a jungle looks and this is what goes on in the jungle that we must take exception.

The only very popular author I know whose accounts of the jungle are first rate (no doubt because they were also first hand) was W. H. Hudson, who wrote *Green Mansions*. The title alone is a perfect description of these forests. He obviously knew and loved them. It is hard to decide whether to call him an American or an Englishman. Indeed, three countries can claim him, for he was born in Argentina and as a naturalist studied real jungles in South America. His parents were Americans but he was naturalized in England. In his best-known book, while the story is ridiculous, the glimpses of the jungle are authentic and portray the great beauty of the scene. Yet the movie *Green Mansions* hit an all-time low, even for Hollywood. European white storks posed before a backdrop of obviously artificial plants in a setting as preposterous as the plot.

The world's ready acceptance of the Kipling-Tarzan concept of a jungle is quite understandable. Until recently, almost until this century, virtually no genuinely scientific studies had been made of the interior of closed-canopy tropical forests. Kipling, for instance, was a famous writer before scholars began seriously to ask the right questions about jungles, much less find the answers. Hudson was one of the pioneers in finding some of these answers, but the facts as they became known never caught up with the fiction.

The reason science ignored the jungle for so long was that men supposed the inside must be just an extension of what they could see from outside; that, if you look at it from a river or from the edge, where this particular type of growth stops because of lack of soil or some other essential condition, all you will see is a solid green wall of dense vegetation cascading down to the ground from the tops of the tall trees. It is a thick wall, too, and lives up to the public's general idea of how tough the whole jungle is to penetrate.

The strength of the wall was impressed upon me rather tiresomely when I was utterly lost for three days in a jungle in the Guianas. Instead of sitting still and waiting to be found, which is the prescribed behavior, I wandered for miles, all over the place, until after sundown on the third day I heard a radio blaring in the still air. My wife very sensibly had kept it on full blast day and night as a beacon. I walked toward the sound for some three miles, feeling my way cautiously in the dark, before I hit the outer wall of the jungle.

I had two shots left in my gun, one of which I used to draw my camp's attention, and then I started shouting. They came immediately across the clearing to their side of the wall, and we could talk to each other almost as readily as in a small room, so you might think my troubles were over. But it took us three hours—with me hacking and crawling from the inside as they chopped from outside—to force

Pix

Jungle wall along Aeto Madre de Dios river in Peru.

a passage through the jungle wall. Yet until then, except for the darkness, I had been walking as easily as a man strolling along the platform of a railway station, meeting fewer obstacles than you would expect to encounter in an ordinary American or English wood.

Obviously when all that men knew about the jungle was the living wall, there was small reason to believe anything else was behind it. The most daring explorers were not tempted to force their way into it or follow one of the small streams that lead inside. The most obviously valuable jungle product, hardwood, was not easily transportable, and there was plenty on the fringe anyway. And the terrain did not look a likely one in which to prospect for minerals. Only recently, even more recently than our knowledge of the jungle, have scientists begun to wonder if there might not be something more inside and to experiment with ways of finding out. What has been discovered about the true jungles, what they are made of and how they grow and the myriad varieties of life they support, is the subject matter for this book. So far we have talked mostly about what the jungle is not. It is time to turn to what it is and how it got that way.

2

Guises and Disguises

JUNGLES are governed by precise laws of nature. They are what they are and where they are primarily because the earth is a sphere, because it spins on an axis tilted at 23 degrees, because of the distribution and shapes of its land and water masses. Of course, that is true of all other types of vegetation, and as far as we know the law of nature is a universal one. But in its application, there are special clauses to fit special areas.

The laws which concern us most are the ones which determine how plants grow. The study of this is called "vegetalogy." It is quite a new subject, so new that no American college or university has a chair devoted to it. Nor do we have any textbook covering it in any course of botany, of which it may be considered a branch. In England and on the continent of Europe there is a little more professional commitment in this field, but it remains neglected out of all proportion to its importance to man.

Vegetalogy is concerned with the manner in which plants are assembled and grow under various conditions. A single species may appear as a tree in one place, a bush in another, or an herb in a third. Similarly, totally different types of plants may perform the same function in different places. A pine, a palm or a hardwood tree may be the principal constituent of a forest or woodland. The innocent violet of temperate woodlands can attain the size and woody development of an apple tree in the jungle. Grasses which, if we neglect them in our backyard or a vacant lot, get to be two or three feet tall, grow as high as a four- or five-story house in the tropics.

Broadly speaking, there are twenty-eight vegetational belts or zones, each circling the earth parallel to the equator. They are by no means of uniform width. Fourteen of these belts lie in the Northern Hemisphere and fourteen in the Southern. The two sets duplicate each other as one moves away from the equator in either direction. This means that the equator itself is a double belt, so in effect there are really twenty-seven.

Moving away from the equator, the fourteen zones are: (1) tall equatorial forest (TEF for short), sometimes called closed-canopy tropical rain forest; (2) tall deciduous forest (TDF), a tropical belt dominated by trees as tall as those of the TEF but which lose their leaves more or less seasonally although it is also closed-canopy tropical rain forest. These two types of vegetation are truly jungle and the ones with which this book is concerned.

The other belts, in order, are: (3) the orchard-bush, a belt of smaller trees with grass growing between them; (4) the savannah, a grassy plain which may be dotted with trees or bushes; (5) the subtropical scrub lands; (6) the hot or true desert; (7) the temperate scrub lands, both scrub areas being distinguished by low-growing vegetation; (8) the prairies, a temperate version of the savannah; (9) the parklands; (10) the temperate deciduous woodlands, the belt of trees with rigidly prescribed seasons for shedding their leaves; (11) the boreal coniferous forests, great evergreen forests such as those of Canada and the northern United States; (12) the tundra, a belt in which only sparse, low vegetation can survive; (13) the barren lands, which might be considered the cold desert; and (14) the polar icecaps.

These belts would be quite uniform across all the land surfaces of the earth if everything were at sea level with equal distribution of light, heat and moisture. But in actuality, the vegetation in any area is modified from this theoretical pattern by several factors.

The easiest of these to follow is altitude. Moving upward every 260 feet, approximately, above sea level (the exact number varies) has roughly the same effect as moving one degree from the equator. Therefore, at 17,000 feet a mountain on the equator would be covered with snow and ice all the year round as if it were in the Arctic. If you climbed it, you would pass through each of the other thirteen belts in order as you ascended. The basic factors of light,

VEGETATION OF THE WORLD

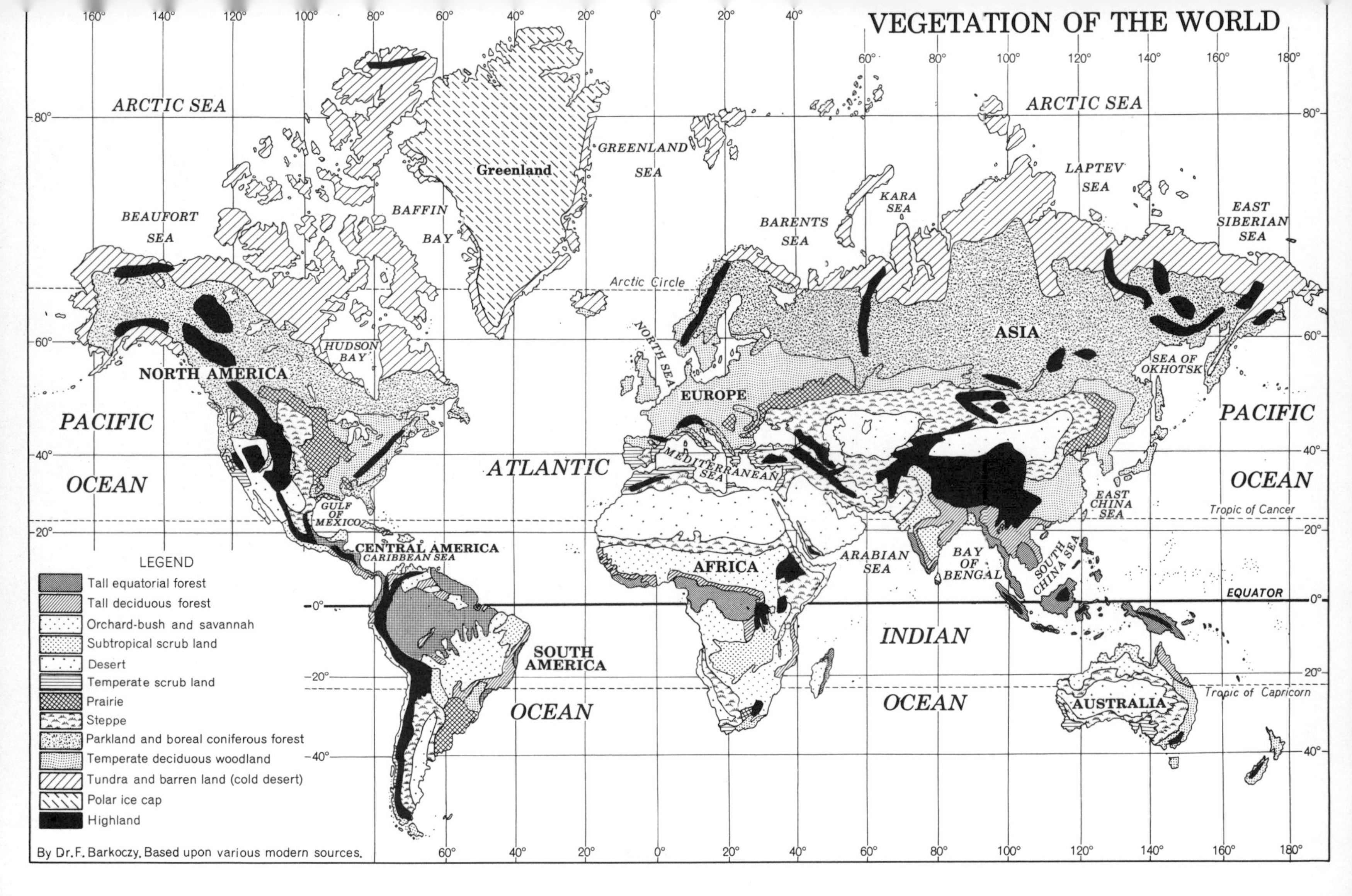

By Dr. F. Barkoczy. Based upon various modern sources.

temperature and moisture may modify the vegetation. A tall mountain in a desert will push the whole sequence of belts toward desert conditions because no moisture is available. If a similar peak stands in a jungle area, the tall, closed-canopy type of growth will tend to prevail at all levels, crowding out everything from (2) to (9)—see page 31.

A good example of all this is Mount Kilimanjaro, about four degrees south of the equator in East Africa. This enormous isolated mountain, 19,320 feet tall, rises from an upland plateau already more than 3,000 feet above sea level, which is too lofty for the real jungle. In fact, the closed-canopy forest theoretically dies away at 2,266 feet, and at 3,399 feet even the scattered trees of the orchard bush should give way to open savannah. But at a little more than 4,500 feet, *on* the equator, this in turn gives way to something else which has surprised even botanists. It is, first, a narrow belt of parklike lands and then another huge closed-canopy forest which extends from 5,500 feet to about 11,000 feet. Above this comes a zone of grasslands half that depth and then an equally wide belt of tundra. This last finally gives way to barren ground at about 16,500 feet, above which is the icecap.

Now these closed-canopy forests high above the lifeline of either the tall equatorial or tall deciduous forests are different vegetationally from both and from the closed-canopy forests of temperate climates. They are properly known as tropical montane forests, sometimes less accurately called cloud forests. They actually represent, in the general succession, the woods and forests of temperate latitudes. They also form some of the thickest tangles of vegetable growth on earth, and we shall include them in our definition of a jungle.

Of even greater effect than altitude in determining the actual location of our vegetational belts are the ocean currents. Their most significant influence is the modification they impose upon temperature and rainfall. They are, in fact, so important that they call for a separate chapter to themselves, for they are involved with all the atmospheric factors of winds, heat and cold, moisture, weather changes and so on.

The vegetation of any given region determines, of course, the

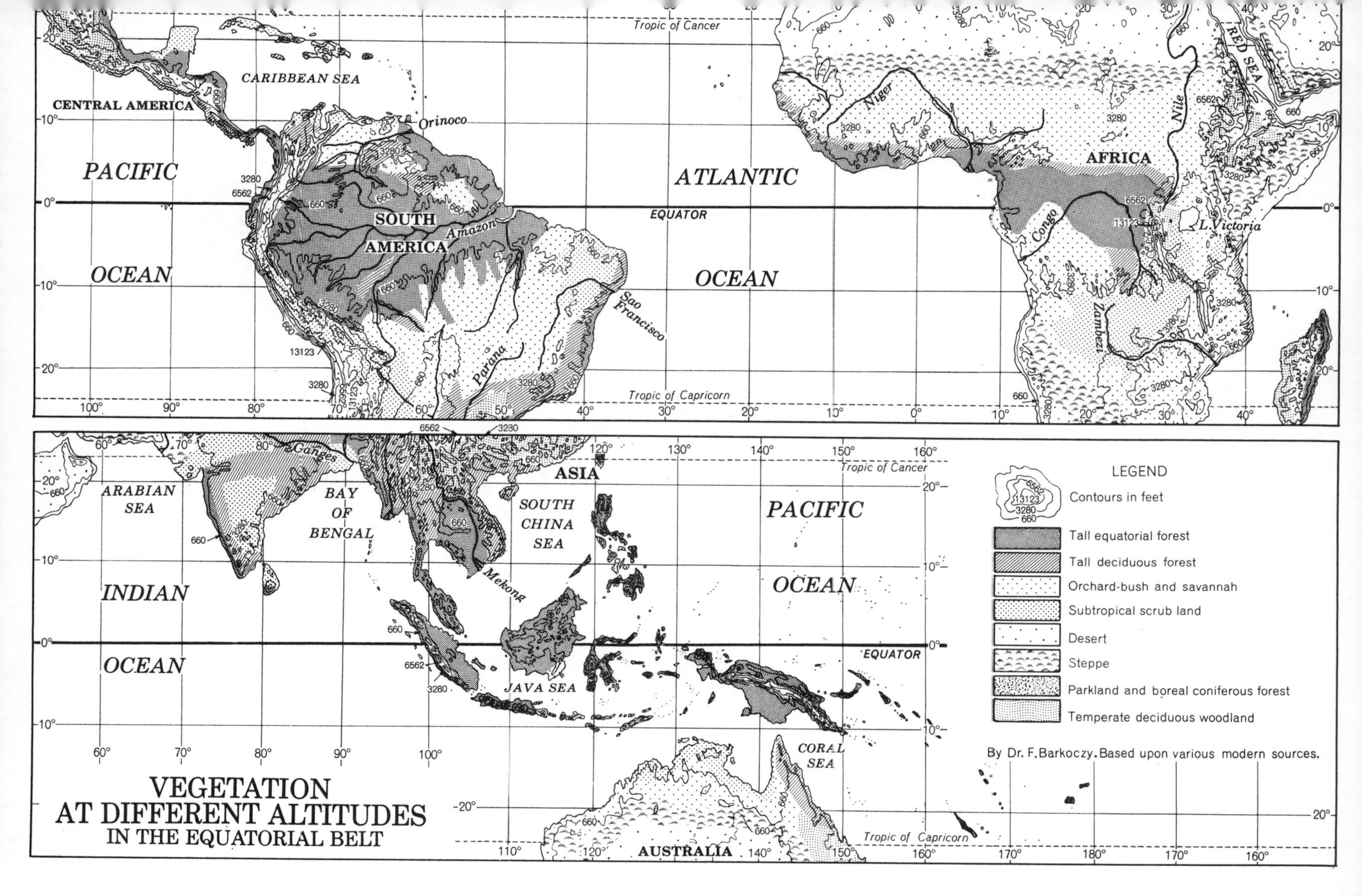

VEGETATION
AT DIFFERENT ALTITUDES
IN THE EQUATORIAL BELT

animal life that can exist there. For instance, the grasses that grow so luxuriantly on the prairie naturally support vast numbers of horned or hoofed beasts—cattle and horses, deer and antelope, buffalo and sheep. But none of these could subsist on some of the tropical grasses such as bamboo which may be forty feet tall and more suitable to use for building than for eating.

In some of these belts, men have altered the vegetational appearance by clearing land for crops, denuding forests, building cities, damming rivers, draining swamps and lakes. But they do not change the basic pattern. If they cease their activities, the area will revert to its original type of vegetation, not necessarily the same kinds of plants but the same appearance.

However, man has interfered little with true jungle. Machines that could make an appreciable dent in the jungle are very modern inventions. Here and there patches have been hacked out of jungles, mostly by primitive tribesmen but sometimes by advanced types of civilized people. When the cleared patch was abandoned, however, the jungle reclaimed the area with the same inexorable force an icecap might display.

As the geologists talk of time, the jungles are rather young, yet they may be among the older forms of life on the earth—some 70,000,000 years of age. They developed in the wet tropics and by and large are of the vegetational type most characteristic of the wet tropics. A German scientist named Andreas Franz Wilhelm Schimper coined the phrase "tropical rain forest" in 1898. That no sound scientific name was given to it until then indicates how little was known about this type of vegetation.

Ignorance of the jungle was not due entirely to the fact that few travelers had ever seen it except from the outside or as they passed through on a river boat. Professor P. W. Richards of Cambridge University, one of the great modern scholars in this field, has cited another reason, commenting sadly:

"The main source of inaccuracy is that tropical vegetation has a fatal tendency to produce rhetorical exuberance in those who describe it. Few writers on the rain forest seem able to resist the temptation of the 'purple passage,' and in the rush of superlatives they

Carl Frank from Photo Researchers

Rainforest, Guinea.

are apt to describe things they never saw or to misrepresent what was really there."

Even without that handicap, these great forests present certain difficulties to science which do not exist in other areas. For one thing, the tropics have a much greater variety of plant life than men trained on temperate zone vegetation can well believe possible. For another, the tendency of tropical vegetation toward a confusing "look alike" kinship of species, which are otherwise quite unrelated, bewilders scholars who have been accustomed to the more sober individualism of regions of the earth where relatively few species are found. They have come to expect a daisy to look like a small flower, not to suddenly sprout limbs and grow into a shade tree.

Some of the men who studied the jungles seriously came to the conclusion that all plants everywhere originated, often indirectly, in the wet tropics. While this is open to doubt, the normal rates of growth in the tropics are so rapid that they do foster unusual opportunities for mutations which could develop into new types.

Another misconception some of the early observers of jungles spread abroad, and which is only now being corrected, is that the tropical forest was a chaotic place without any of the orderly arrangement of life which had become so apparent in the less complicated temperate woodlands. Even distinguished scholars thought so when I first went into jungles in my teens. Out of respect for my elders, I assumed they knew everything that was to be known, but because I had no stubborn preconceptions, I soon noticed that the relationships between the plants follow regular rules whether they coexist peacefully and independently or depend upon each other for support and nourishment or compete with each other ruthlessly. Perhaps this is because there is so much in the jungle to be regulated. A metropolis like New York or London has to have a lot more regulations governing the behavior of its inhabitants than does a farming district or a primitive tribe. So it happens in the vegetable kingdom. The enormous plant population of a jungle must develop more strict patterns of form and structure than the less complex woods of temperate zones.

The organization, of course, is brought about primarily by the evenness of the wet, warm climate, which is the precondition of a jungle's very existence. But as a preliminary to looking more closely at the jungle's community life, whether vegetable or animal, we might consider how it gets to have a heavy, evenly distributed rainfall and an equable as well as high temperature.

3

How Jungles Are Born

JUNGLES are the offspring of the sun and ocean currents. These also provide the moist, warm incubator in which jungles grow to maturity—surprisingly fast considering their complexity. Once they have established themselves, they are virtually indestructible.

The sun provides the light and heat. The source of the water is not so simply stated. In the first place, water is a very rare commodity in the universe. The liquid can exist only within a relatively narrow range of temperatures. Below the freezing point it is a solid; 180 degrees (Fahrenheit) warmer and it becomes a gas. (Scientists prefer to use centrigrade with zero for the freezing and 100 for the boiling point, or the Kelvin scale, which begins at absolute zero, the coldest it is possible to be, which is −273° centrigrade.) There must be very few planets on which the temperature permits water. Yet water is *the* basic need of all life as we know it.

Therefore, the most important fact about our planet in this connection is its hydrosphere, the envelope of water which covers the hard ball of solid matter we call earth. The hydrosphere includes not only the oceans, rivers, lakes and ponds on the surface, but the thick crust of land which is permeated with water and our immediate atmosphere which contains moisture. All living things are born and will always live within the hydrosphere—except a space pilot, and he has to take some with him.

This essential role of water is most obvious in considering the life cycle of jungles, for it has been estimated that they require at least

Photo Researc

Areas such as this one, in French Guiana, are among the rainiest regions in the world.

80 inches of rain a year. The lowest limit of mean average temperature at which they can survive is 68 degrees. Such conditions do not prevail all over the tropics by any means. Actually, most jungles get more than 80 inches of rain and a mean average temperature of 78 to 82 degrees. (By comparison, only rarely does New York City's hottest summer month reach a mean of 78 degrees; in one recent fifteen-year period it happened only once, in July 1952. As to rainfall, Louisiana, one of our wettest states, gets only 63½ inches.)

To support a jungle, an annual rainfall of only 80 inches would have to be spread very evenly, with a minimum of 4 inches in the driest months. Large areas of the tropics know as much as 400 inches a year, and in places it may be more than twice that. But some very wet areas do not necessarily produce jungles. Where there is a definite wet and dry season with the dry one lasting for several months, jungles do not develop. In fact, a great deal of the jungle territory actually has two wet and two dry seasons, and the "dry" ones may have as much rain as the ordinary American ever sees at home.

These generalizations need a little qualification, and apply only in the long run. There are places where subterranean water supplies support jungles although the rainfall is slight. Having lived in several of these countries, I must testify that, if you keep daily records as we did for our work, the exceptions seem to outweigh the normal. I have known whole rainy seasons to be skipped, rainy seasons in the middle of dry ones, two rainy seasons running concurrently, and even droughts.

Rain, of course, develops when warm, moisture-laden air rising from the surface of land or water cools by either expansion or meeting a colder current of air. This causes condensation into clouds and then into drops of water. Since the sun is the sole source of this heat, the phenomenon is most likely to occur in those latitudes and at those times when the sun's rays are direct. That, of course, is near the equator where the sun is in the zenith longer than anywhere else.

The sun directly overhead heats the air so that during the day the warmer air is rising steadily. Since land both heats and cools faster than water, the air over the land in the heat of the day is rising and drawing in more moisture-laden air from over the sea to take its place. As night approaches, the land cools and this is why over much of the tropics one can count on a daily shower toward evening and, on the coast, a cool offshore breeze.

The steadily rising curtain of air over the broad belt around the equator is responsible for winds which have been of more interest to sailors than to landlubbers but which have some influence upon jungles too. From somewhere air must come in to take the place of that which is rising as it gets heated by the sun. But, as it is in a

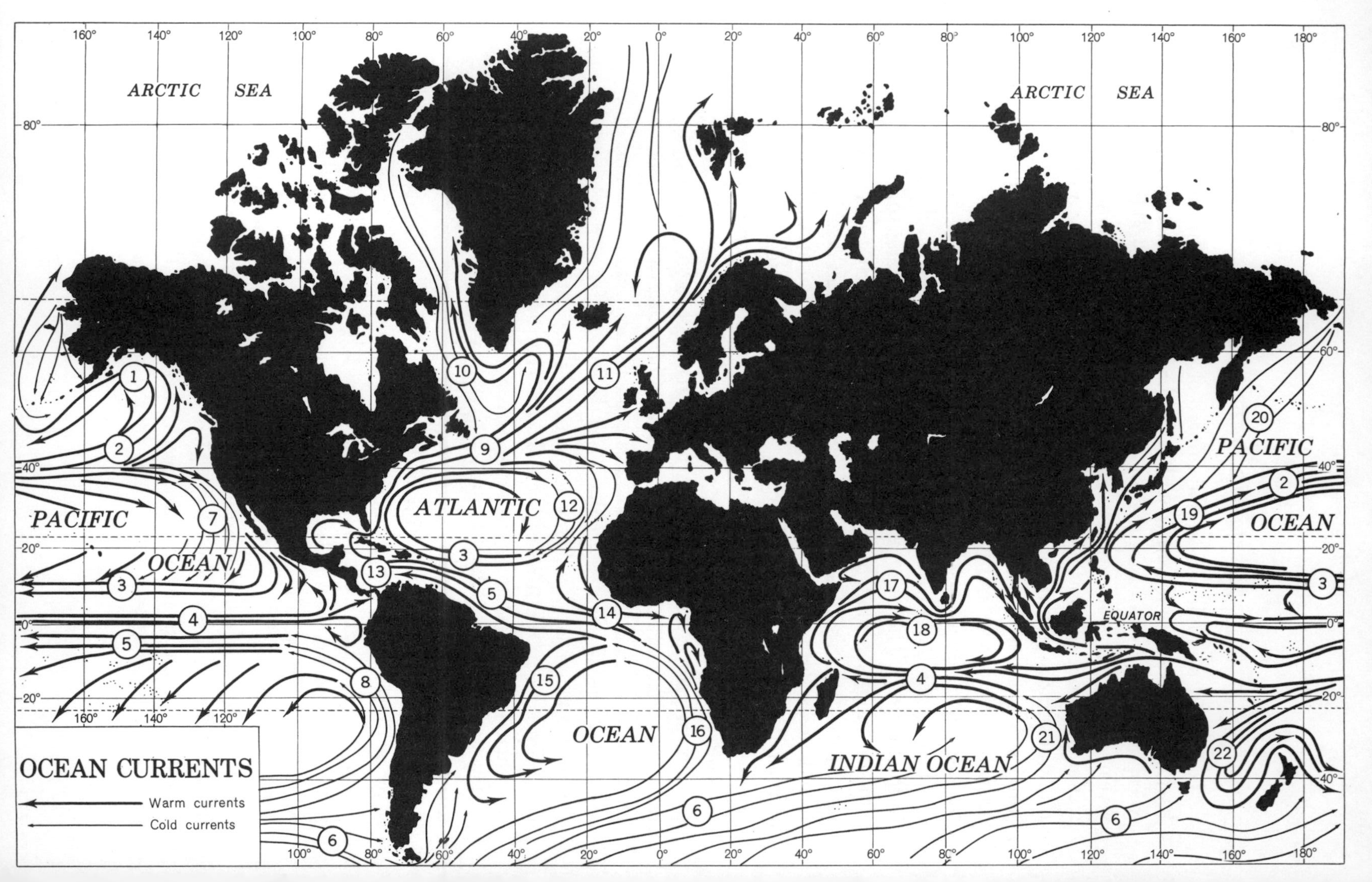
ARCTIC SEA
ARCTIC SEA
PACIFIC OCEAN
ATLANTIC OCEAN
INDIAN OCEAN
PACIFIC OCEAN
EQUATOR
OCEAN CURRENTS
Warm currents
Cold currents

belt of very low pressure, this air moves so slowly that in the days of sailing ships mariners avoided these areas even more carefully than they tried to dodge storms. These are the doldrums.

North and south of them, the air pressure increases to create two wide belts of steady air currents blowing from west to east, just opposite to the spin of the earth. These are the trade winds. They influence the movement of moisture-filled air from the sea to the land.

Tropical rainfall would be quite easy to predict and would not vary much from place to place if this were all that mattered. But, in fact, the air is subject to other forces. Mountains may interrupt the flow of air and receive on their slopes the rain which otherwise would fall in the valleys.

The principal modifier of tropical weather is the ocean currents. It may be easier to understand how these mighty governors of our climate came into being and continue to operate if we imagine that the round ball of our earth might be trying to change its shape and become a pyramid with each of its four sides equilateral triangles of exactly the same size—in short, a tetrahedron. Like a sphere, a tetrahedron looks the same from anywhere. If you were to make one out of a lump of clay or cheese and stick a hatpin into the exact middle of one of the triangular faces so that it ran through the whole body and came out at the apex opposite, it would spin on its axis, in this case the pin, like a sphere.

A round ball with a hydrosphere, such as the earth, trying to remodel itself to this shape would start by developing four pointed bumps of its solid crust sticking out of the water equidistant from each other. Then it would form ridges of land to join these bumps. The result would be four triangular islands or continents thrusting up out of the water, and they would be separated by four roughly circular oceans.

Now let us imagine this spinning sphere so placed that if it did really get to be a tetrahedron it would be in the form of an inverted pyramid rotating from left to right. The water in the circular areas would be thrown outward and around due to centrifugal force.

On the top it might be expected to become shallow and eat away at the surrounding land. This would be the broad base of the upside-down pyramid. Meanwhile on the three other faces of the pyramid, all the water would be flung to one side, but its motion would be interrupted by the triangular continents. There would be proportionately more water and thus more pressure the further south one went until eventually the waters of all three of these oceans would come together below the north-south barriers of the land and roar round and round at the bottom.

In effect this tetrahedral theory, as it is sometimes grandly called although it is just a game to help explain the idea we want to get across, describes what happens. Of course, the earth does not lose its nice round figure. But there is a shallow ocean at the top of the world around the North Pole. There are three dependent, more or less shield-shaped land masses with great circular bodies of water between them. There is a continuous ocean running around the earth south of them, and a more or less triangular land mass, the Antarctic Continent, stuck on the bottom at the South Pole.

All the oceans of the world form really one body of water in which there are islands of land, most of it in the northern half. This water is always on the move, but not always at the same speed or in the same direction.

The spin of the earth decrees that every drop of water in the Northern Hemisphere is nudged in a clockwise direction and every drop in the Southern Hemisphere counterclockwise. This becomes the route of all the major ocean currents, which may be regarded as gigantic rivers flowing along definite channels, any one of which carries more water than all the fresh water rivers of the whole world joined together. The currents take the warm water in a great curve toward the Arctic or Antarctic where it helps to melt the ice. That in turn provides some of the cold water which is carried back toward the hot latitudes.

We may consider the forces which create the major currents as starting at the poles. First, the waters of the Arctic Ocean swirl round and round, trying to spread outward. When their outer fringes find a channel penetrating the surrounding land barriers, they pour through and, being very cold, send a cold current jetting down the northwest edge of the three main land masses under the warmer surface water.

In the Antarctic, a ring of cold water also roars round the earth. But the solid land mass of Antarctica lies on its right side, and three dikes or breakwater-like snags—the southern tips of South America, Africa and Australia—on its left side. Three jets of cold water split off from the mainstream as this ocean swirls in ever widening circles until it meets the obstructions. The three curve upward or north along the southwestern faces of the three land masses. They form the Humboldt Current of the southeast Pacific, the Benguela Current of the southeast Atlantic and the West Australian Current of the southeast Indian Ocean.

Meanwhile at the equator something similar is happening. Here the surface waters run smack against a complete barrier—the right or eastern faces of the continental masses. They have to go somewhere, and they split in two with one stream going up the coast to the north and the other down toward the south. In time the water goes right around the oceans, and the great circulation system is complete.

The effect of the three cold currents in the Southern Hemisphere is virtually to eliminate rainfall along the coasts near which they pass. Take the Humboldt. It cools the air above it so that there is not enough moisture to condense even when the prevailing winds drive it against the South American coast and up the Andes where the cooling effects of altitude would normally cause rain. All along the Americas, except where the cold current flows close to the land, these winds bring rain. Even in cooler latitudes, such as southern Chile or the state of Washington, the warm winds from the Pacific cause such heavy precipitation that rain forests are created, although not jungles. But the air crossing the Humboldt has only enough moisture to produce clouds which almost never condense. Along some of the Peruvian coast the total annual rainfall is but a few inches, although dark clouds come rolling by almost every day.

Cold currents account similarly for the dry coasts of North West Africa and the arid plains and desert of Western Australia. Currents are the reason why even on the equator itself a good deal of territory which otherwise would be jungle is almost anything else.

Another meteorological phenomenon creates conditions which permit jungles to develop in some of the lands of the Indian Ocean. This is the monsoon, special seasonal winds which have only faint counterparts elsewhere. The monsoon—it gets its name from an Arabic word meaning "season"—begins with a low pressure area which develops every summer in south Asia, especially India. The warmed air rises and the low pressure draws a broad current of air from all over the Indian Ocean, several thousand miles of it. These waters, protected by the land mass of Asia from any cold currents, are uniformly warm. By the time the winds blowing across them reach the land in late summer their air is saturated. This is the southwest monsoon, and as it meets the first coastal uplands the moisture is forced out in deluges known as the monsoon rains, which last until late September or early October. In winter the wind shifts the other way and becomes the northeast monsoon.

One result is what are called monsoon forests or jungles. Most of the areas struck by the monsoon in full force are warm enough, when not too far above sea level, to support jungles. But by no means do all have enough rainfall throughout the rest of the year.

Once the sun and currents have created the warmth and wetness which jungles demand, the vegetation can hardly be checked. The combination of heat and moisture is so ideal for plant growth that no matter what sort of rock may be underneath, the great forest creates its own soil by breaking it up and by the rapid decomposition and decay of preliminary types of vegetation.

The most dramatic illustration of what ideal jungle conditions can do in a tropical land starting all over again from scratch began on a couple of August days in 1883. In the space of less than forty-eight hours the volcanic island of Krakatoa blew up in a series of explosions that literally shook the world and were heard 1,500 miles away. For days the whole west end of Java was in darkness; other volcanoes along the same mountain spine belched in sympathy, and the sea for hundreds of miles was a pavement of pumice stone. The entire earth's rainfall was altered for years, and in every climate and con-

Culver

A volcanic eruption of Krakatoa, Java.

tinent sunsets were especially lovely because of the millions of tons of dust which blew round and round the globe.

Later on there was a hot scientific argument as to whether any seed or spore or life of any kind on Krakatoa could have managed to survive. Both sides, however, agreed that if any did it was not visible to the naked eye; in fact, all life was also wiped out on two smaller islands nearby.

Krakatoa, located in the Sunda Strait between Java and Sumatra, is about five degrees south of the equator in one of the rainiest spots in the world. On August 25, 1883, it was five and a half miles long by three wide, rising to a peak of about 2,700 feet. Two days later half of it had disappeared under the sea; the mountain was split in two but the highest part remained. The entire surface was covered with a layer of ashes and pumice, a spongy sort of lava, as much as 150 feet thick.

Before this, most of Krakatoa had been covered by jungle, presumably very much like the other jungles of Indonesia, although no special studies of it had ever been made. The lowlands were tropical rain forest, shading into less luxuriant vegetational types on the upper slopes of the mountain. Nine months later one of the first visitors to this new desert island made an intensive search for signs of life, plant or animal. He found a lone spider and nothing else on the still hot, bare lava beds.

The sun baked the bare rock, and the rain—1,000 inches a year in this spot, according to Richards—cut great troughs in the volcanic deposits, washing a fair bit of it into the strait. But from somewhere—mostly wind-borne from neighboring islands but perhaps brought by birds or washed up from the sea, or from any seeds which could have survived the holocaust—vegetation appeared. By 1886 there were grasses and flowering plants on the beaches and a dense growth of ferns inland interspersed with more grasses and flowers. Remaining bare patches were covered with a green slime of algae.

In 1897 a scientific expedition found casuarina trees well established near the shores, while inland the ferns had given way to a savannah of grass more than six feet tall. Shrubs had appeared on the lower hills along with ferns and grasses.

Another group of botanists visiting Krakatoa in 1906 found the coastal terrain very like some of the shores of Java twenty-five miles away. The casuarina trees dominated closed bits of woodland; other trees, including coconut palms, had established themselves; climbers were becoming abundant. The interior was still mostly grass except in ravines where trees and shrubs were growing.

Man, in the form of a single settler who hoped to extract building stone from the island, took up residence in 1916. It was reported three years later that his stay had left few traces, but the pace of vegetational development was slowing slightly as new types had to compete with the first arrivals. Within forty years of the eruption, however, the tough aggressive climbers or lianas, which are a special jungle feature, had become so powerful that they were killing off the casuarina trees, some of which had already fallen. But forest trees which can support and live with lianas were growing tall and strong and were also invading the savannah in the island's interior. By 1927, as I can personally attest, the island and its smaller neighbors were pretty completely covered by a very fair closed-canopy forest, well on its way to becoming a true jungle.

Half a dozen years later, and only fifty years after life had been destroyed on Krakatoa, it was reported that some of the trees were 150 feet tall, and were spreading up the slopes of the mountain at least three-fourths of the way to the top, subordinating the shrubs which had been supreme there to the status of undergrowth.

The scientists who have studied the revival of life on Krakatoa believe that many more years must pass before full-blown jungle is restored. At present it is in the stage that botanists call "primary succession," meaning the first stages of new growth after an area is cleared of the ultimate vegetational type (called by botanists "climax" growth) which nature decrees for it. Yet here in the space of a long human lifetime it is possible to see one way that jungles may have originated as soon as temperature and rainfall were favorable.

4

Where Are the Jungles?

THE tropics, by definition a belt running up to 23½ degrees north and south of the equator, get more direct rays of the sun than any other part of the world, and that is where we find most jungles. However, under especially favorable conditions patches of jungle do exist outside the true tropics, but only a few degrees outside. All tropical rain forests are confined to three major areas, and neatly enough, each of these can be subdivided into three others.

The major areas are the American, the African and the Oriental. In the American and Oriental we find jungles reaching beyond the geographical tropics; in the Far East these patches occur in both the Southern and Northern Hemispheres, while in America they are only in the Southern.

The full and exact extent and location of all jungles is unknown, available information being based in part on guesswork. The jungles have not been explored scientifically in their entirety or mapped very accurately. It is a fact that despite the widely held, complacent belief that no new, untouched territory is left for an adventurous explorer, large jungle areas have never been visited by civilized men or, as far as we know, even by uncivilized men.

By far the largest continuous jungle is in the Amazon basin of South America, one of the three subdivisions of the American jungles. Continuous is only a relative term, for all are interrupted by patches of other vegetational types. Even in Amazonia, back from the endless rivers, the trees may thin out or stop abruptly, and savannahs of short grass take over. In most cases these are due to the relative absence of soil or the presence of beds of pure sand covering the surface.

This great American jungle stretches north and south of the mouth of the Amazon irregularly, and crosses the continent to the eastern

Airview of the Amazon.

or land side of the Andes Mountains. To the north it takes in the Guianas and part of Venezuela. The central portion, shaped like a great plate with a rather steep rim, was a shallow arm of the ocean not so long ago, geologically speaking. It includes the Amazon's major tributaries—the Xingú, Tapajoz, Madeira, Purús and Negro. In the midcontinent it spreads out as far south as the Gran Chaco of Bolivia, Paraguay and Argentina, and here a tongue of jungle actually reaches below the Tropic of Capricorn across the Pilcomayo River. A separate patch, commonly known as the Tupí Forest, is a strip along the eastern coast of Brazil running from just above the hump where the continent juts farthest east into the South Atlantic to a point on a level with Rio de Janeiro. Countless long serpentine belts of this jungle run inland up the river valleys.

Why it is impossible to be definite in describing the extent of these jungles can be better understood if we take a closer look at the Matto Grosso, where the British explorer Colonel P. H. Fawcett disappeared in 1925 in one of the most talked of jungle mysteries. The Matto Grosso contains, besides a lot of much more passable country, a good-sized chunk of the Amazonian jungle, although not a very big piece in proportion to all of Amazonia. In Fawcett's time its dimensions were so little known that official estimates of this Brazilian state's size varied by more than 100,000 square miles. It is now estimated to be not quite twice the size of Texas. Here were supposed to be legendary lost cities, buried for centuries in the jungle but once rivals or predecessors of the great centers of Incan and Mayan civilization. It was one of these that Fawcett was trying to find.

The difficulties such men encountered were compounded by scientific ignorance. They did not know, for example, that the foods easiest to come by in the jungle are often sadly lacking in vitamin B, and so they became ill and died of beriberi. William Curtis Farabee, who mapped large areas of South American jungle and discovered three previously unknown tribes on an expedition for the University of Pennsylvania between 1913 and 1916, lost forty-eight pounds when he contracted the disease. As late as the 1930's beriberi killed many men working for a commission seeking to define the border between Brazil and British Guiana.

The second American jungle area begins in northern Ecuador

just north of the Humboldt Current and reaches through parts of Colombia and Venezuela to the Isthmus of Panama.

The third, which may be called the Central American, is separated from the others more by a difference in types of vegetation and animals than by a break in the jungle itself. It spreads north from Panama to the eastern side of Mexico by way of the Sierra Madre Oriental up to the Tropic of Cancer. Hard pressed by desert and scrub zones, it is, for the most part, crowded into a narrow strip on the Caribbean side between the mountains and the sea. In this subdivision we may also place the jungles of the Antilles. Apart from the island of Trinidad, which is really not one of the West Indies but belongs to South America, there are real jungles there. But since the islands are mountainous and supplied with an excess of moisture, montane jungles are prolific here.

Africa presents a somewhat more manageable state of affairs. Again its jungles are separated into three areas, two wholly on the mainland and one among the islands to the east as well. For simplicity's sake we may call the two mainland blocs the West and Central African jungles.

Starting in the far west of the continent, where it thrusts furthest into the Atlantic at about the line of the Gambia River just below Dakar, we find strips of lowland jungle fringing the rivers. These strips or tongues increase in length and width as one travels south and then east around the bulge of the continent until they coalesce over the intervening higher land in Sierra Leone. They then proceed east in an unbroken blanket to the great Volta River in Togoland.

Down the valley of that river is a narrow but complete break in the jungle occasioned in part by local climatic conditions but undoubtedly enlarged and maintained by man over the centuries. To the east, in Dahomey, the jungles begin again, and they stretch—at first intermittently, and then almost continuously—across the continent for 2,600 miles to the great barrier of the Ruwenzori, the fabulous Mountains of the Moon, and south across the Congo to the west of Lake Tanganyika.

The great central basin of the Congo was, until comparatively recently, first an arm of the ocean, like the Amazon, and then a vast lake. The plants and animals on either side had time to develop along

Black Star

Dense jungle of the Congo basin near Yangambi.

somewhat different lines, different from each other and from those in the jungles on land which had not so recently been submerged.

In Central Africa a great deal of primeval forest has been repeatedly cleared in small patches for what is called "shifting cultivation," the method used by forest tribes from time immemorial. It is doubtful if in some areas any genuine primeval jungle is left; the tallest and stateliest forests really are very ancient secondary growth, creating new jungles over the once-cleared bits.

Europeans knew the Congo was there long before America was more than a vague theory, but they were much later navigating it than they were the Amazon. Ancient Egyptians seem to have been about as well informed on the Central African jungles as the men of the nineteenth century.

The first Spaniards to float the length of the Amazon made it in 1541—and gave it its name because they encountered some remarkable female warriors on the way. Henry Morton Stanley, hero of the famous line, "Dr. Livingstone, I presume," when he located the Scottish explorer as a stunt for the New York *Herald,* was the first to navigate the Congo. That wasn't until 1876–77, and Stanley thought he was on the Nile when he launched his prefabricated boat, the *Lady Alice,* west of Lake Tanganyika. He proceeded north and west for hundreds of miles before he realized he must have been on the Congo all along.

The jungles on the East African coast are extremely limited, forming a few widely separated small forests. The largest lies in Northern Rhodesia south of Lake Tanganyika; another is along the west shore of Lake Nyasa and a third in the heart of northern Mozambique. There are countless little patches in valleys at low altitudes scattered along coastal Tanzania and Mozambique, while montane jungles can be found on Elgon, Kenya and Kilimanjaro.

Related to the East African jungles is a strip on the wonderful island of Madagascar. The island itself is shaped like a huge oblong dance floor rising from the Indian Ocean and tilted somewhat toward the west. Its eastern coast is arid and sandy, but close behind this a steep, high range of mountains extends all the way from the northern

Rapho Guillumet

Jungle and mountains in central Ceylon.

to the southern tip. Jungle climbs up and over these and at the northern end straggles across to the west coast.

Associated with Madagascar are groups of small islands, notably the Comoros, lying between the northern point of the big island and the mainland, and the more distant Reunion, Seychelles and Mauritius. True jungle still exists in the Comoros; the forests of the others are montane.

The Oriental jungles are spread over a great number of islands, large and small, as well as the mainland. The first of the three blocs contains the strip along the west coast of India, the Ghats. This jungle spreads out to a considerable blob in Mysore in the south and is resumed on Ceylon, which is a chip broken off the tip of India. On this island is perhaps the most readily accessible jungle in the world, the Sinharaja Forest.

By far the largest of the Oriental jungles begins across the Bay of Bengal in Burma. On the mainland it includes the rain and monsoon forests of the Southeast Asia peninsula, which takes in Thailand, Vietnam, Cambodia and Laos, and those of the Malay Peninsula too. This subdivision also includes the Eastern Ghats, and just below the eastern slopes of the Himalayas a region known as the Khasi Hills in the state of Assam. Here an extensive lowland jungle runs up into montane forest toward China, and the jungle actually reaches as far north as twenty-six or twenty-seven degrees. It spreads into many of the Philippine and Indonesian islands, including the thousands which make up these two republics, although not extending as far to the southeast as New Guinea, of which Indonesia recently annexed a part.

Many of these islands, of course, are quite without jungles and always were. Coasts which are exposed to wind-driven salt spray do not support jungles. Volcanoes have a habit of clearing the jungle, and even when they do not, they make such fertile soil that men have pounced upon the forests at their bases and cleared patches repeatedly.

New Guinea's extensive jungles belong to the third Oriental area, the Australasian. New Guinea, second largest of all the earth's islands (only Greenland is bigger), is one of the most heavily jungled. It would have even more rain forest if it were not so mountainous; on this one island are five peaks higher than 15,000 feet. All of Africa has only four, Europe two. The tallest, Carstensz Toppen, is snowcapped at 16,500 feet, but its base is covered with jungle.

The Australasian subdivision also takes in the islands east of New Guinea—the Bismarck Archipelago, the Hebrides, Fiji, Samoa, the Solomons, where on Guadalcanal a lot of Americans learned about jungles the hard way. To this jungle I think we must add a narrow strip of the Australian mainland from above Port Douglas nearly to Brisbane. Here, protected between the Great Barrier Reef and the Great Dividing Range, pockets and fingers of rain forest flourish even to the twenty-fifth degree of latitude.

Certain lowland forests with closed canopies on Cape York are true jungles; I would include also the montane forests of east Queensland.

The Oriental jungles have had a fascination for Western man

from the earliest times and have inspired the strangest—and perhaps true—tales. The oldest come down to us by way of Persia, but with no mention of the word "djanghael," of course.

It seems that in the fourth century B.C., King Ataterxes II of Persia employed a Greek physician named Ctesias who was so impressed with what he heard of a land still further east, which we call India, that he wrote a book about it. He included fairly accurate accounts of tropical rain forests, but what future generations like best was his report on the people who lived in them, snub-nosed little black men covered with long hair, never more than three feet tall, "and called Pygmies." Except for details of his description, old Ctesias was quite right, but these jungles were so little explored that scientists wouldn't admit the existence of Eastern Pygmies until a French anthropologist, J. L. A. Quatrefages de Breau, proved it in 1887. Scholars until then had argued that Ctesias's little hairy men were Western Ghats monkeys, the wanderoos (*Silenus silenus*), which have the mane and beard of a Biblical prophet; the real Oriental Pygmy does not.

Other tall stories of the jungle have been as little credited as the ones which turned out to be true. Pliny the Elder matter-of-factly quotes a Greek historian, Duris of Samos: "That certain Indians engender with beasts, of which generation are bred certain monstrous mongrels, half beasts and half men." One reads of dog-faced men in the jungle who could not speak but could understand language, and of the Malay "orang-utan" which originally meant a Pygmy, not an ape; the first European to use the word, Nicholas Tulp in 1641, applied it to a chimpanzee.

Perhaps one of the most astonishing features of these ancient stories is that they are not very unlike those of the twentieth century. We really don't know much more about some of these jungles than Pliny and Ctesias did.

One question about jungles is whether they once covered much larger areas of the earth than they do now. The answer is yes, since they might well have covered much larger areas of tropical land surface.

Also it has happened from time to time that the crust of the earth has shifted or slipped; so that what was tropical moved into the temperate zones, and temperate zones slip into the tropics or became polar. The area of New York, for instance, appears once to have been some 2,000 miles further south than its present location. Fossilized plants and animals of a tropical appearance have been found in Greenland and Antarctica. This can mean only that both these places must have once been at entirely different latitudes.

Many people have supposed that most of the earth was covered by jungles all at once. In that age, the legend runs, the higher animals all roamed the jungles until some monkeys came down from the trees to solid ground, shed most of their hair and became men. Actually, if Greenland or even New York had ever supported a jungle in their present location, the tropics would have been so hot the water would have boiled and life would have been impossible.

Whether jungles covered more of the area within the tropics than they do now is a more tenable speculation. As the continents moved about, which they did, and the oceans rose or fell, there could have been much more or much less land in this belt, which after all is a full forty-seven degrees wide. A relatively small rising of the ocean floor would bring hundreds of miles of the continental shelf to the surface; a corresponding subsidence of land would submerge vast areas of the present continents. More or less rain might have fallen and been more or less evenly distributed throughout the year. Given favorable conditions jungles could have covered thousands of square miles now underwater or in areas now too dry or too high. On the other hand, unfavorable conditions could have restricted them even further.

The theory that jungles have been killed by major climatic changes in historical times was once fashionable in some scientific circles, but it has been pretty well discredited. What did happen was a steady encroachment upon some jungles by cultivators of the soil and nomadic pastoral tribes. Scientists are widely divided as to how extensive such reductions were. But one point can be made with confidence. The areas of jungle which to this day remain both unexplored and untouched are far greater in number than those which man, for all his efforts, has been able to eradicate.

Black Star

Rainforest, Sikkim.

Part 2

The Living Jungle

Portrait of the Rain Forest

Nature's High-Rise

The Watery World of Dry Land

Wind and Weather

The Vegetation Factory

Alma Sanderson

View inside jungle in Surinam.

5

Portrait of the Rain Forest

It is extraordinarily difficult to get a view of any jungle "in the altogether." This accounts, perhaps, for the widely contradictory, inaccurate word pictures which travelers draw; they take their individual limited points of view like the blind men describing an elephant. The airman's panorama, the view from a river or outside edge, the varied glimpses from within, are so different that even a man who has seen all of them might be forgiven for not realizing they are all aspects of the same scene. They have one thing in common, though; they are, to me at least, breathtakingly beautiful.

I have sometimes thought that perhaps this beauty is what calls forth the "rhetorical exuberance" of which my old teacher, Professor Richards, complained in even supposedly scientific writing about jungles. But another stimulus is the often eerie nature of this beauty, taking shapes and forms and colors which are not only unique but unbelievable. So when you come right down to it, "rhetorical exuberance" is an absolute requirement if you are to do justice to the subtleties and wonders of which the jungle abounds more than any other place on earth.

Look at it first as a modern traveler may see it—from the comfort of an airplane cabin. The pilot drops down to little more than the height of the Empire State Building, and you look out from your window over an endless vista of green, an undulating, slightly lumpy mattress. It stretches in every direction to the misty horizon, a green ocean without wind-waves or currents. Here and there a specially tall tree, appropriately called an "emergent" by the botanists, thrusts its green head above the surrounding giants to account for the occasional lumps that interrupt the otherwise smooth appearance of the jungle from above.

For the most part, the sea of foliage is a uniform dark bottle green, no matter what tree the leaves may sprout from. Plants in the Tall Equatorial Forest are almost exclusively evergreen. But in Tall Deciduous Forest, the beginning of a rainy season causes the canopy to burst into a riot of color. New foliage may range from almost white to various shades of pale green or pink and red. Blossoms of every color imaginable add to the blaze. I remember one West African jungle which for a time sported a parti-colored roof of green dotted with endless scarlet of flame-of-the-forest.

Only half a dozen times in half a lifetime of wandering through the great green blanket have I found a spot on land from which something like this is visible. The first was a place where men had cleared the whole top of a hill which actually stuck up far enough so I could see over the canopy. Often the only movement discernible for hours from such a vantage point is an indefinable shimmering, indefinite but persistent, that roils upward from hot surfaces. After a time, your senses reel. Then a great wave passes across the surface of the blanket, said to be produced by a wind, but somehow I have never been quite able to believe it. Winds are supposed to make a noise, and these do not.

From this elevation the stillness is absolute—most of the time. Then suddenly a raucous whoop or a harsh yell rends your ears, not like any other sound you have ever heard in clear air. It comes from within the blanket, the voice of some jungle inmate.

Perhaps you expect to see birds and bees and butterflies darting about, monkeys and squirrels clambering through the branches. If so, you are disappointed. Only after the fruits and flowers are borne is much bird or insect life visible in the jungle canopy. But always the canopy is so dense that whole troops of monkeys could go swinging by just under the surface and you would see neither them nor the branches along which they travel.

If clouds and rain obscure the sun, the sparkling dark green deepens a few tones and receives the tropical deluge as if the mattress were a sponge. Even if the rain were to be accompanied by a storm of hurricane force you might see little evidence of it. A few leaves would fly off, swirling in the wind. The whole mattress would sway a little. That is all.

But, when you descend to a river or into a clearing where the jungle ends, you have a neighbor's view of the forest. Most of the human beings customarily regarded as jungle peoples are, in fact, only the jungle's neighbors. They live outside it, even right up against it, but they are as likely to be unfamiliar with its interior as a Londoner or a New Yorker. Only rarely would you meet a member of the few tribes who actually live *in* the jungle proper, for they are as shy of coming out as their neighbors are of going in.

As you look at the jungle from the river or the clearing it seems to be at least as solid as the canopy seen from above. The phrase "impenetrable jungle" was coined by travelers who saw the forest from these vantage points. For them the two words are as inseparable as "damn" and "Yankee" to the unreconstructed Southerner. It is this density and lushness of growth that have led the same travelers to apply the phrase to woods which are not at all like a tall tropical rain forest.

As you contemplate the wall of the true jungle, a mass of vegetation seems to cascade down from the tops of the trees, a curtain so thick that the trees themselves are completely hidden. For all you can see, the foliage might be pouring over a cliff 150 or 200 feet high. Of course, a great deal of it is actually growing up from the ground, but the stems and trunks are obscured by the leaves and flowers bending outward toward the light.

Now this wall may be only a hundred yards thick, but from the river especially you might easily get the impression that this is what the jungle is like clear through—a dense, tangled mass of vegetation resembling an overgrown backyard briar patch magnified twenty or thirty times. This is what the white men who first traveled these parts believed. It explains why they did not bother to confirm their belief by actually hacking their way inside.

In fact, it is often easier to wriggle in—I have sometimes had to do it on my stomach—or to canoe down one of the creeks that are almost invisible as they emerge from the edge of the jungle. In either case you will have to cut a path for yourself with a machete until you have passed beyond the wall. Almost never have I seen paths into and through tall equatorial forest. Some do exist in the tall deciduous forest, made by tribesmen to get from one village clearing to another. But once inside, the view is completely different.

The light is strange, dim and green with only an occasional dappling of sunlight. In the tall equatorial forest you can never tell whether it is morning or noon or afternoon by looking up, for the sky is completely blotted out. Yet the visibility is surprisingly good. Whereas from outside, whether above or beside the jungle, only the surface of the wall or canopy is visible, here you can see a man further away than you can hear him. Jungle acoustics are most eerie, anyway, which accounts in part for the fact that it is often easier to signal to a companion a couple of hundred yards away than to try to call to him.

You look at him through the tall pillars of tree trunks ranging all the way from saplings an inch or two in diameter to the main supports of the jungle roof which may be as big around as a fair-sized room. In the TEF especially there is amazingly little underbrush. Over considerable areas the ground is almost completely bare and not even muddy, without the mulch of leaves or needles which carpets many temperate zone forests. Or it may be a network of the stems of creepers. Or at certain seasons it may be a matting of the most exotic fruits, juicy and sweet, more kinds than any city fruiterer carries. They will have fallen from the summit out of sight above and are so abundant that not even all the hungry little mouths in the jungle can consume them.

Looking upward, your range of vision is sharply reduced. The trees, whatever their size and variety, bear all their leaves at the top, the smaller ones in mere tufts, the larger from branching limbs which do not begin lower in proportion than the ribs of an open umbrella. The trees of medium height make a canopy of their own through which it is almost impossible, and in places altogether impossible, to see the higher canopy above. Here and there great loops of the lianas hang down; they are the cords which bind the jungle together in a single mass. Some are as thick as a man's thigh, and eventually twist their way to the tops of the tallest trees and add their foliage to the closed canopy.

Black Star

View from Maroni River in eastern Surinam.

Wherever you look you may see the oddities which for generations led botanists to think jungle plants were abnormal. The mind of an average temperate-zone gardener reels when he beholds a forty- or fifty-foot tree growing in a crotch, of an even larger specimen, half-way up to the jungle canopy. Or a thousand or so orchids of the sort he pays fifteen dollars apiece for at home.

There is still another way to look at a jungle, the way a physiologist or anatomist looks at a man on the autopsy table. A clean cut is made from top to bottom over an area large enough to give a representative cross section of what is within. The effect is very much like the revelation of life inside an apartment house when the street wall is sheared off by an explosion that leaves the other walls and floors, the furniture and inmates, undisturbed and unharmed. This multi-storied characteristic which sets tropical rain forests apart from all other vegetational formations is now visible, as it can be from no other vantage point.

The panoramic descriptions of a jungle are all very well, but they convey no idea of its infinite variety. Within the framework of the architecture of jungles there is room for bewildering but invariably fascinating combinations and permutations. Much of what one may say about one bit of jungle in detail is contradicted in another.

The ground surface, for example, is unencumbered to a surprising degree, but may present difficulties to the pedestrian just the same. Every jungle I have ever been in seemed on careful inspection to have

---

Right: Semi-diagrammatic representation of a plot (140 ft. x 15 ft.) of tropical rain forest in the wet sere, known locally as "mixed tall cohune."

Scale 5/16 in. = 10 ft. Six-foot man in halo under banak tree to right.

Trees and tall shrubs: 1. (unidentified); 2. wild coffee (*Rinorea guatelmalensis*); 3. white copal (*Protium sessiliflorum*); 4. cacho venado (*Eugenia capuli*); 5. waika plum (*Rheedia edulis*); 6. mammee ciruela (*Lucuma sp.*); 7. ironwood (*Dialium guianense*) 8. negrito (*Simaruba glauca*); 9. red copal (*Protium copal*); 10. mountain trumpet (*Cecropia mexicana*); 11. timber sweet (*Nectandra sp.*); 12. (unidentified); 13. maya (*Miconia sp.*); 14. banak (*Virola brachycarpa*); 15. matapalo (*Ficus sp.*); 16. kerosene wood (*indet.*); 17. cohune (*Orbignya cohune*); 18. monkeytail (*Chamaedora sp.* and *Synecanthus sp.*); 19. hone (*Bactris sp.*); 20. capuka (*Geonoma glauca*); 21. tree-fern (indet.).

Ivan Sanderson

been plowed in fairly straight, evenly spaced furrows by a tropical version of Paul Bunyan and his blue ox, Babe. The furrows are about forty feet wide and nearly as deep. What causes them is a mystery; they do not seem attributable to water erosion. They do not affect the even height of the jungle canopy; the trees rooted in the trough of a furrow reach as high as those on the crest.

The roots of the larger trees take forms which one does not see in other forests. The most impressive are huge buttresses, four of which may be more or less evenly spaced to support the trunk on all sides, jutting out twenty feet or more above the ground and angling out to much more than that from the base of the tree. They may be no more than two or three inches thick, great planklike flanges of solid mahogany or other hardwood. In the Central American jungle I have seen men patiently sawing them away, working in pairs, to get a slab for an enormous table. The angles between the buttresses may be big enough to park a truck. An Oriental jungle legend of the creation of the human race shows how impressive the thinness of these roots is. The story goes that a rose apple fell on the edge of one and split neatly in half. Each half fell on a different side of the buttress. One grew into a man, the other into a woman, and both were full-grown before they ever explored beyond their side of the root. Then they saw each other and mankind is the result.

Other roots as big as water mains sprawl partly above the surface. Since most jungles have shallow topsoil, the trees have to send their roots sideways rather than down. Or the roots may lift the whole tree clear of the ground, making it appear to be standing on half a dozen slender stilts. In fact, these are called "stilt roots."

Still another variant of the jungle floor is one which a party of us once encountered in the Guianas. We had come through the jungle wall by canoe along what seemed to be a small stream, but it opened out into a lake from the surface of which rose the great pillar-like trunks of the trees. At least it looked like a lake, although such bodies of water are scarce in rain forests. In reality it was a flooded area which remains covered with water to a depth of as much as six or eight feet for nine months out of the year. The ground of many jungles is so sodden all the time that it cannot absorb more rain, but

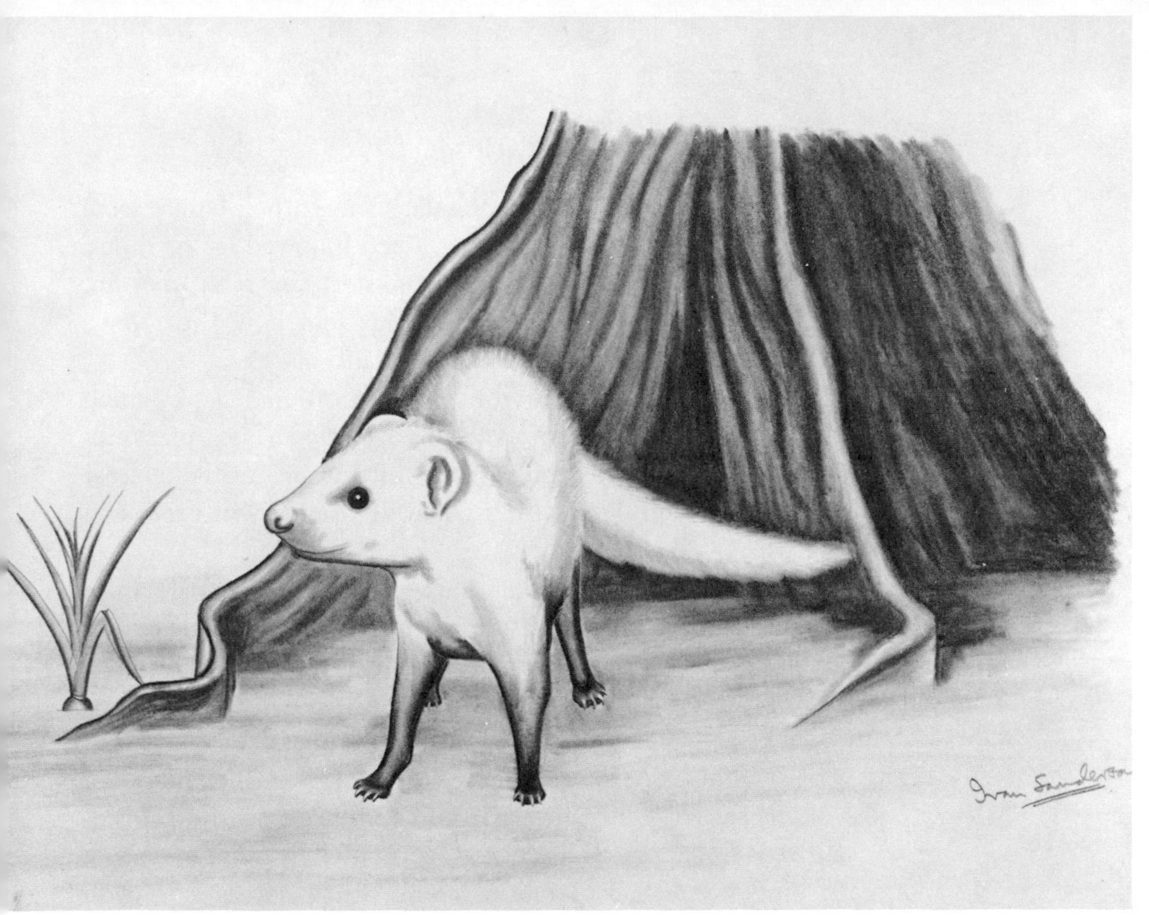

Ivan Sanderson

White mongoose near buttress roots.

this one must have been in a depression from which the water could not flow.

It was an impressive sight, a great expanse of water the color of sherry, stretching for miles. As far as we could see not a ripple ruffled the surface. All of a sudden we heard an odd sort of "whoosh," something between a deep sigh and the sound of an urchin giving his friend the raspberry. I looked around but saw nothing. Then I heard it again, and this time spotted the source, a white river dolphin rising to the surface to blow. Almost at once we were in the middle of a whole school of them, amazing creatures 200 miles from the sea, swimming happily about among the trees as much at home as monkeys and much more amiable. Some of them came so close to the canoe we could have patted them on the head. Their white bodies were scarcely more than shadows in the dark water; their babies were a delicate pink and even more shadowy. They followed us for miles.

How such a flooded forest survives is a mystery, for most trees not specially adapted to the water "drown." But somehow these have managed to convert themselves into semiaquatic plants.

More variety is added to the jungle by occasional gaps which permit the sun to alter the lower levels of vegetation. The great trees do eventually die, and may even fall, permitting for a time at least some undergrowth more lavish than usual. The hole will very soon be closed again.

Larger gaps may be gashed out of the jungle temporarily by a cataclysm such as an earthquake, although even that may leave no trace. Earthquakes have the power to rearrange the whole landscape radically. Take, for example, the description given by the famous botanist Doctor Kingdon Ward of the 1954 quake in the Himalayas. This would be beyond belief were it not from the pen of a scientist of his sagacity and sincerity, and published in the *Journal of the Royal Geographical Society*. Overnight, he relates, whole mountain ranges vanished or moved about; huge gorges and wide valleys were filled in; rivers disappeared and lakes appeared; and the whole of the vast mass of Mount Everest went up more than 200 feet. How Dr. Kingdon Ward ever got out alive was itself a miracle.

By total contrast, my wife and I once lounged in deck chairs on a grassy bank of the Rio Kuringuas in Nicaragua and witnessed one of Central America's greater recent earthquakes, the sudden leap followed by half an hour of heaving that occurred in December 1941.

We had been in earthquakes before, including a major one in Mexico City the year before. But you have little time or inclination for scientific observation when you are rocking about in a stone building with all the doors jammed while plaster and concrete blocks rain around you.

Here in the jungle, we did not know at first what was happening. We sat cleaning our guns in the soft stillness of afternoon when all of a sudden we felt peculiar and started dropping things, while the trees all began to sway, though there was no wind. Then came an errie, deep, pulsing sound; it filled our whole universe. Everything gave a terrific leap straight up, and all the giant trees were shaken like mopheads held aloft.

After that little effort, which shot us out of our chairs, the old earth really got to work. The supposedly solid ground seemingly became fluid. It not only rolled from side to side so that we could not stand up, but it started going up and down in waves just like those of the ocean. It was uncanny to watch crest after crest of these waves roll toward us through the forest, heaving the trees, some of which were 200 feet tall, into the air and then down into the troughs as if they were ships at sea. Then the waves rolled right under us so that we in turn rose some five feet as each passed. What is more, they swept on under the river in perfect order and without loss of speed, and set off again from the opposite bank until they disappeared into the jungle beyond. After about eighty had passed, the earth gave another convulsive heave, but sideways this time, and the show closed as abruptly as it had begun.

The very last act happened in the midst of the ghastly stillness that follows earthquakes. As we watched, a section of the river bank right opposite us, about forty feet high and some hundred feet long, began to give way. Slowly and rather solemnly it slid down into the water, but from the moment the crack appeared there rose a terrifying rumble. Apart from explosions, I have never heard a louder noise; it was deafening.

It was all very fascinating but, except for the noise of the slide, not at all frightening; nevertheless we might well have been obliterated. Half a mile upstream from our camp, a quarter-mile section of deep river was hurled into the air in one piece and flattened a square mile of jungle when it dropped back.

Apart from this damage and the slice of bank that fell away, the jungle emerged from this earthquake apparently in no way altered or affected. No trees fell; there were no cracks in the ground; the little streams still ran. We wandered about till dark looking for signs that such a terrific event had occurred so recently. We found none.

The reason for other cleared patches in a jungle may be more comprehensible and less dramatic. Usually a meager soil or other unfavorable conditions for the emergence of trees are obvious. One such

Molly Adams from National Audubon Soci

Jungle foliage.

patch gave me the first opportunity I ever had to climb up above the jungle from inside. It happened during an expedition to West Africa, the Mamfe district of the Cameroons and the Obubra division of southeastern Nigeria.

One day, looking for a bit of sunbathing (which is extremely hard to come by in the jungle), I encountered a clearing in which only some low shrubs and tufts of grass grew. The sunbathing was excellent. But even more unusual, I noticed on the edge of the clearing that a giant acacia, big enough to have provided the wood for the Ark of the Covenant, had so many creepers hanging from it that they formed a natural rope ladder which it was easy to ascend. From the acacia I could cross to the upper branches of an even larger "kapok" tree.

The uninterrupted view of so much forest from this angle was unique in my experience. The sun shimmered on the leaves, and shafts of glaring light reflected back from the shining surfaces. In the hot air, brilliantly painted butterflies flitted among exotic flowers. Clouds of bees hummed and buzzed while flies of all shapes and sizes darted about or suspended themselves above some tempting morsel, motionless except for the beating of wings too rapid to be visible. Birds of many colors fluttered in and out of the treetops. Hawks and eagles soared and swooped, their eyes obviously seeing things within the foliage which mine could not. I do not think I ever felt myself so remote from the world of men.

To many of its visitors, the jungle has been a place to fear. They have harped on the ominous gloom, the dripping foliage, the strange sounds, the swarms of insects. They have made much of the reluctance of primitive men to enter the jungle even to hunt when they were hungry. They have moaned about discomforts and hardships and dangers. They have told each other fearsome stories of poisonous insects, snakes and plants; of frightful tropical diseases, of impure water and wretched food.

Now it is true, of course, that a man meets some perils and discomfort in the jungle. They are a good deal less than he faces without flinching—maybe because he is not aware of them—every time he goes downtown in a big city. If he leaves his fears and prejudices behind him and does not bring any of the illnesses of his ordinary environment with him, he will find the jungle not only salubrious but pleasant, for it is the most disease-free clime outside the polar regions. There is no purer air in the world. The forest itself is cool and damp; only the clearings, where the sun gets in, give off the sort of heat which New York and Chicago are famous for in the summer, and it is not nearly as bad as in Washington or St. Louis, Missouri.

Jungles are the only places on earth where man can be almost perpetually comfortable without effort. They are the only places where neither clothes nor housing are really essential, although there is endless provision for both. Here you never need artificial heat or cooling. And here you never will be bored.

The wild animals? It may be considered an omission that this chapter, calling itself "Portrait of the Rain Forest," scarcely mentions them. The reason is that most strangers in the jungle rarely see them, except perhaps for some ants which are oblivious of the intrusion of humans. You may hear a rustling or a cry, but you will not know whether the sound was made by an animal or the faint breeze or the crack of a tree's branch. I have met forest officers, experienced men who had spent years in and around jungles, who had never encountered more than a few squirrels and monkeys.

But if you stay long enough inside the jungle and allow yourself to become attuned to its rhythms, you will probably come to the conclusion that the jungle is more than the sum of its vegetation and its animals; it is a living, pulsing entity. The individual giant trees are impressive enough, but they do not seem to be things apart. Only while operating at a dissection table do we think of the separate bones and muscles, brains and guts, of an animal or a man. When the whole organism is alive, it is exciting. So it is with the jungle; the whole is alive and therefore exciting.

6

Nature's High-Rise

FIFTY or sixty or even eighty feet up, and at night, the jungle offers another of its inexhaustibly varied experiences. The canopy, still far overhead, rustles with an unseen life of its own. The earth below is fortunately invisible in the darkness. Here in the middle layer of the forest is a world which in the ordinary course of events has almost nothing to do with the ground surface nor with the upper reaches of the jungle roof where it meets the light of day.

Normally the denizens of one jungle layer do not invade another. I, myself, had not expected to leave the surface of the earth on this particular night, but had set out with a flashlight to see what luck a couple of our African hunters were having. A barrage of shots indicated that the trophies might be interesting. As I walked toward the sound, I could hear the noise of what seemed to be a lot of animals moving through the trees overhead to get away from danger. When I shone the light upward, it spotlighted directly overhead a little object the size of a small cat and the general appearance of a teddy bear. Unconcernedly upside-down under a branch of the tree, he peered at me over his shoulder with quite as much interest as I regarded him. Slowly he licked his little pink nose with a matching pink tongue, blinked and began to move, still upside-down under the branch, toward the trunk. He was a potto, a nocturnal animal related to the lemurs and monkeys of the African jungles, and capable of surprisingly efficient progress in his oddly inverted way.

With some mad idea that I could capture the little fellow with my bare hands, I started climbing. I used one hand to keep the beam of my torch focused on him. Fortunately there were enough branches and projections on this tree, which is unusual in the jungle, to facilitate the climb. Confronting me, after swinging himself around to

New York Zoological Society Pho

Young female Congo potto.

the upper side of the branch, he lost some of his resemblance to a teddy bear. On all fours, his paws seemed large and clumsy, while his head hung down in the attitude of an angry bear, exposing a row of sharp, bony spines on the back of his neck.

As I started toward him along the branch, he reared up on his hind legs, clenched his forepaws and suddenly ducked his head down so that he was doubled up into a ball with the back of his neck toward me. If I had grabbed for him, my hand would have been gashed by the spines. I still advanced, however, whereupon he suddenly swung down under the branch and retreated out along it at a surprising rate. The limb was much too big for him to reach around it but he still clung to it, defying the law of gravity.

Naturally I followed, and he led me along the aerial highway from one tree to another. Sometimes the branches were bigger around than a man. All of them were more than ample to bear my weight, although I had to hold the flash in my mouth to have both hands free for climbing. By the time the potto got away completely, disappearing suddenly into a dense patch of foliage in a region of branches which were getting precariously slender for me, I found that I had been steadily ascending this jungle pathway. Only then, as I began to consider how I would work my way down to the ground, did I realize that I was about 100 feet above it.

Up to now, I had seen no sign of life except the potto, nor heard any either. As I contemplated the distance to earth, it seemed the better part of valor to call for help to the two hunters who probably were not far away. So I let out as loud a falsetto yell as I could—a high, shrill note travels better through the jungle than more manly shouts. The reply was surprising. It came from all around me, a great thrashing about among the leaves, punctuated with loud chirrups and cackles from dozens of voices.

I flashed the light around me and discovered that I was in the middle of a dormitory of putty-nosed guenon monkeys. The whole troop, disturbed and uneasy after my vocal performance, blinked and fussed at me, at each other and at life in general with all the peevishness of overindulged humans awakened from sleep at an unusual hour. By day these monkeys, handsome green fellows with white noses who prefer the bark of young shoots to the sweetest, juiciest fruits, flit through the branches with ease and grace, confident as a New York taxi driver threading the rush-hour traffic. Now they were clumsy, hesitant, stumbling in their uncertainty. Mothers clutched their babies and whimpered. Grown males jumped about and made a lot of noise without apparent purpose and grimaced horribly. Obviously I had seriously disrupted the sleep of the denizens of this particular jungle tenement.

The incident is related here because it was one of my earliest first-hand experiences of any jungle layers above the ordinary level of man's wanderings. For me, it has never ceased to be a revealing and astonishing adventure. Furthermore, this layer is one of the most important parts of a jungle because a considerable percentage of its life inhabits this tier. Much of it cannot be observed from a man's eye level.

This particular experience did not last long. Whether the monkeys would have become accustomed to my presence or recovered from their confusion to depart in an orderly fashion or panicked still further, I had no opportunity to learn. Our inadvertent association was cut short when, trying to inch myself to more sturdy supports than those onto which the potto had led me, I was hurled downward by the breaking of a branch which I was grasping with both hands. Luckily, a thick vine caught around my chest, and I eventually scrambled safely to the ground along its tough stem.

Since then, far more suitably equipped for climbing, I have taken many opportunities to visit what I call the Flying Continents. When a liana is not looped conveniently, a light string attached to an arrow can be shot over a big branch; rope and pulley can be hoisted after it to provide access to the heights. Once there, it is easy and quite safe to crawl or even walk along the massive limbs. I have seen them broad enough to park a Jeep.

Only after one has viewed the jungle from all its different levels can it really be seen in true perspective, for it is as clearly stratified as a layer cake. The number of layers may be five or six or even seven, each with its own distinctive character. The upper ones consist primarily of the head foliage of trees but often contain a great number and variety of other plants. Just why there should be this sharp stratification far above the ground is not known. One might expect indiscriminate gradation from the lowest to the highest, but this almost never occurs.

An ingenious, painstaking sampling method for studying the layers scientifically is known among British forestry officers as the "Burtt Davy section," after Professor J. Burtt Davy, who perfected it. A fairly level sample of jungle is selected, and one that can be located on a reasonably detailed map so that other people will be able to find it later for further comparison. It should be a rectangle 132 by 33 feet, marked off with string—the dimensions are fixed because the first samples were taken by men who used the surveyor's chain (66 feet) as their unit of measurement.

On one plan drawn to scale is marked the position and diameter of all trees or bushy stems as thick as a man's forearm. On another chart each plant more than three feet high is sketched—the exact height determined as accurately as possible. Because of the several layers, it is usually necessary to measure and sketch all those up to thirty feet first because many of them have to be cut down to get a good view of the taller ones.

There are likely to be more trees taller than thirty feet than seems possible in such a small area. On one such jungle plot, twenty-eight were counted; on another, twenty-two; on a third, fifteen, and all of them were about average for their particular types of jungle.

An accurate sketch of the foliage of the canopy is difficult—a horizontal spread of seventy feet for a single tree is common and more not unusual. It will be complicated because the chart should include all the lianas and parasitic plants of any size, and some of the big upper branches support a growth that would rival many a householder's garden, while one of the thirty-footers may spring from a crotch of its host as far as eighty feet up.

With these two plans and samples of leaves, flowers, fruit and wood from each plant, later scientific identification is possible. But the Burtt Davy section also calls for complete collections of every small plant taken from four different square-yard samples of the plot. This may seem a small chore, but the amount of little stuff on what

Hugh Spencer from National Audubon Society

Selaginella apoda, a northern representative of the *"lowly green fellow."*

appears to be a comparatively unencumbered stretch of jungle floor can be surprising. In one plot in British Honduras, where I supervised a Burtt Davy section, we counted no fewer than 2,580 ground cover plants from an area of four hundred square yards. In addition, a lowly green fellow called *Selaginella* grew there at the rate of fifty per square yard.

The process sheds some revealing light on the high-rise nature of the jungle and its components. Starting at the bottom is a subterranean world of burrowing animals, which can be a considerable population. Roots are so plentiful that any digging in the jungle is difficult, yet there is space among them for an immense variety of small beasts which can get along in perpetual darkness. Many of them never emerge at all, day or night.

The ground floor will seem sparsely furnished to anyone who

knows the more desirable upper stories. As is the case in a modern apartment house, one of the major functions of the ground floor is to serve as a lobby. The second floor is sometimes called the shrub layer because the vegetation is about the height of ordinary shrubs in a suburban garden. There may be ferns, very small trees or young palms. The plants of this tier are relatively sparse in most jungles because of the absence of sunlight. Trees about the height of a carefully kept orchard compose the usual third story—ranging roughly from fifteen to fifty feet. They may form a closed canopy bound tightly together by climbers or lianas just like the big fellows.

The next layer, middle-sized trees from forty to eighty feet tall, is missing from some TEF and most TDF jungles, especially where the giants are all or nearly all members of the same family. This fourth floor has its foliage arranged in a more nearly spherical shape than either those above or below, and also forms an almost solid ceiling at times.

The top story is composed of trees a hundred feet or more high with relatively flat crowns of foliage running in diameter up to a hundred feet or more, overlapping each other and reinforced by the foliage of the big vines. These trees, the great columns that hold up the whole jungle, have trunks as straight as pillars and in most instances four main branches spreading out horizontally. Besides bearing the tree's own massive foliage, they act as huge clothes racks on which all the lianas and other climbers hang, and on which the parasites and epiphytes grow. Higher still, the occasional emergents are free of both lianas and epiphytes.

It is characteristic of jungles that the shape of a tree's head of foliage is governed entirely by its position in the strata, not by its species. In the jungle, furthermore, the society at one level may be segregated from that of the others.

It has mistakenly been supposed that many kinds of fourth- and fifth-floor animals are rare in nature; this is because few of them are ever seen, much less caught by hunters for zoos and museums. The hunters and trappers have seldom been able to set their traps or aim their guns that high, and it is rare that they can get a shot from the ground with either gun or camera.

One of the objectives of the West African trip we have already mentioned was to bring back a specimen of a small creature related to the potto and even more elusive, the so-called dwarf bushbaby (*Galagoides demidovii*). This tiny fellow has a dark green coat with saffron belly and hind legs, a foxy face with big ears and eyes, a tail longer than its body, which is no bigger than a newborn kitten, powerfully muscled arms with long, strong fingers, and legs constructed like a bird's. He makes his home and his living in the upper apartments of the jungle where his coloring renders him almost invisible. We were especially eager to get a pregnant one for an eminent British gynecologist who wished to demonstrate a theory that this particular galago is in the direct line of human ancestry. (The name "bushbaby" has been applied indiscriminately to a variety of other small jungle animals all over the world.)

In the jungle it is never wise to ignore any story, no matter how improbable and ridiculous. One of the more implausible on this trip was told by one of our African helpers who insisted that he had seen two dwarf bushbabies sleeping in a pawpaw tree. Offhand I couldn't think of a more improbable fairy tale. Not only would no sensible galago repose where he could be seen from the ground, but there couldn't be a pawpaw tree in the jungle. This immensely useful plant, which resembles a huge cabbage on the end of a long slender pole and provides the common tropical breakfast fruit, is unknown except where it has been planted by man, and we had certainly seen no signs of human habitation during our stay in this jungle.

Therefore it was in a thoroughly skeptical mood that I followed the man along a trail he had blazed. After half an hour's walk, we ended up in a small clearing on a river whose existence I had never even suspected. And in the clearing was a lone pawpaw tree. The place must have been the site of a native settlement abandoned recently enough for the jungle not to have taken over completely. Still, the ridiculous tuft of foliage at the top of the tree seemed a most unlikely spot for any jungle animal to choose for a nap.

My companion insisted that he could see two of them, but they remained quite invisible to me. To satisfy him, I fired a shot in the hope of arousing anything that might be hidden there. To my amaze-

Ivan Sanderson

The dwarf bushbaby, known as Demidoff's dwarf lemur.

ment, a tiny galago sailed out of the tree right over my head to the lower forest trees at the edge of the clearing and on toward the taller jungle trees beyond.

This dwarf bushbaby ran as I'd never known an arboreal animal to do. Usually they leap from branch to branch, clamber along either to one side or up and then leap again. This one simply raced through space in a straight line, galloping like a horse, both forefeet and both hind feet together, as if he were on the home stretch of a racetrack. I ran after him—the jungle floor was as unobstructed as an empty ballroom—and was almost directly below him when he streaked into a clump of fernlike plants growing on a bare vine festooned between two tall trees and disappeared. But his mate was retrieved by my helper from where she had fallen out of the pawpaw tree, and she turned out to be pregnant.

On another trip, we actually lived for three weeks in the head of an emergent at just about the level of the surface of the canopy, having hoisted up camping gear and necessities and, of course, receiving regular packages of supplies from below. It was the blossoming season, and on the forest floor the usual stillness was broken only by the slow patter of bits of fruit and nuts falling from the earliest bloomers. On the ground these provided a feast for hosts of animals. But up in the canopy a tremendous activity was afoot, every animal busily engaged.

Unending troops of monkeys came crashing by to perch first upon this and then that tree to greedily devour its flowers, tender shoots or fruits. Other small animals came climbing up from below for the same purpose or to maraud the marauders. In the sky above, hawks, eagles and other predatory birds wheeled and circled, poised to swoop down upon the monkeys and others. Amid the flowers, birds great and small twittered and rustled about, while over the whole there was a blanket of endlessly buzzing, fizzing, whirring or clicking insect life. Quite apart from the ten billion bees that gathered to sample the nectar or collect the pollen of the lovely flowers, there were all manner of beetles and grasshopper-like creatures that hovered like helicopters or clacked on brittle wings from flower to flower and tree to tree.

It is through experiences like this that we have been able to learn how each of the horizontal divisions or layers of the jungle, although almost separate worlds in some ways, contribute to the sum of the whole forest.

7

The Watery World of Dry Land

THERE is still another jungle world. In part, it has been explored and described more extensively than anything else in the tropical rain forest, and that part is the rivers, which have been civilized man's principal contact with the jungle. Rivers remain the main arteries for jungle travel, even for air travel.

Another widely publicized feature of this aquatic world is rain. The almost regular showers of the tropical rainy season and the tremendous deluges of tropical storms have been so dramatically and frequently reported that they have become one of the chief images most people have of the tropical scene.

Other jungle waters have attracted less attention. The ponds and streams of the jungle have attracted few lyric writers. Lakes, marshes and swamps do not exist *in* jungles; yet from one point of view the jungle's chief tangible constituent is water. Water and heat create it, after all, and the volume of water that goes into the making of a jungle is staggering. The whole vast structure, from the foliage of the canopy to the ground below the roots, is like a great sponge just lifted out of the tub.

We have said that the tropical rain forest requires a minimum of eighty inches of rain a year. This means that every acre of jungle receives at least 2,160,000 gallons of water and usually a great deal more each year. Every drop of this water comes from evaporation into the atmosphere and the resultant precipitation through cooling.

Jungle plants, great consumers of water themselves, are in effect vast sprinkler systems with a most ingenious mechanism to maintain the circulation. The roots of the biggest trees and climbers must lift the water which carries their nourishment to a height of a hundred or even two hundred feet. Yet by the ordinary force of atmospheric pressure, water can rise only thirty-two feet. Above that it must be pumped up or sucked up, and one of these huge trees has to have it by the ton every day.

Such a tree uses several methods simultaneously. The leaves, by evaporation of moisture through their pores, or *stomata,* create a suction pressure at the top; the root system builds up a boosting pressure from below; and in between, the liquid is forced upward from one cell to the next by osmotic pressure, aided by capillary action. The net result is that in the evergreen rain forest, water is constantly being drawn upward from the ground into the atmosphere.

When that and all the additional moisture which has been absorbed from land and sea return to the earth in the form of rain, the jungles get more than their share. Tropical storms, which are often more like a waterfall than a shower, are a relatively minor source. Most jungles derive their moisture mainly from gentler rainfall, although in some, thunderstorms are an almost daily occurrence.

Really violent storms are often preceded in the jungle, as elsewhere, by still, oppressive air. A strange, ominous noise like the passing of some gargantuan Diesel train is heard, first far away but getting nearer, while the sun continues to shine. The tops of the tallest trees may sway a little and emit a gentle sigh as the light begins to fail, but the sky, if you can see it through the foliage, remains blue.

Next comes a mighty roar. The treetops wave wildly and little jets of hot air whirl down to the jungle floor, stirring the leaves gently. Abruptly the sun goes out, and all is black above. For a few moments absolute silence reigns; then comes a sound like a myriad of tiny horses clip-clopping briskly over a taut drumhead. A flicker of brilliant blue light seems to cut through the forest horizontally at exactly eye level.

This is your last chance to cover up anything you value because right after that flash comes a wind accompanied by ceaseless flickerings of light. With a roar, the whole jungle leans over in one direction; dust and leaves fly upward; the taller trees go wild, and with an

Photo Researchers

The Congo, second largest river in the world.

ear-splitting crash the heavens are rent right over your head while solid water streams down. In a moment the wind has gone; the water continues in a cascade, interspersed with thunderous crackling explosions and punctuated by the rapid flickering of the lightning. Nearly always, the rain stops as abruptly as it began.

The rains, gentle and violent, supply water enough not only to maintain the vegetation but to fill the largest rivers in the world. The Amazon and the Congo, preeminently jungle rivers, dwarf all others. The Amazon especially, with by far the largest basin of any river in the world, carries as much water to the sea as a hundred Congos or nearly a thousand Mississippis. Its true size cannot be appreciated because it can never be seen, at least in its entirety. Beginning at its mouth, you can sail upstream for five days on end before you can see both banks at the same time. The main stream is so deep, too, that

Fujihira from Monkmey

Kaiteur Falls, British Guiana.

oceangoing ships drawing fourteen feet can steam all across Brazil to Iquitos in Peru, two thousand miles from the sea. The Amazon and its tributaries drain a basin more than two-thirds the size of the continental United States, and they flow through the world's largest jungle area.

The great rivers—the Mekong, Salween, Brahmaputra, Orinoco and a few others besides the Amazon and Congo—are the veins of the jungles. Like the veins of animals, they carry away both excess liquid and unwanted residues. Leading back from them into every cranny of the forest are the streams and finally the clear rills that gurgle or trickle away between clean boulders.

Water in these tropical rain forests takes many forms, often unbelievably beautiful. The so-called black water streams are striking. They appear black because their clear water looks that way by reflected light. One of the Amazon's largest tributaries, the Negro, takes its name from this fact.

The jungle waterfall, framed in dark green all around, has a special quality of majesty that has awed many a traveler. The Kaieteur Falls on the Potaro River in British Guiana, for instance, drop over an escarpment of rock nearly five times as high as the famous Horseshoe Falls at Niagara. The Potaro River is sometimes twenty feet deep as it plunges over the cliff on a front as wide as a city block. Or consider the mighty Angel Falls in Venezuela, often called the world's highest. These falls are estimated to be up to five thousand feet, and although they start at greater altitude in the Guiana highlands than jungle vegetation grows, their feet are in a genuine rain forest.

On the Congo, the Stanley Falls are a series of seven cataracts, none very high, spread over a stretch of river sixty miles long. More than twice the volume of water of Niagara pours over them, more even than over what is generally regarded as the world's biggest waterfall, Guaira in South America. Yet the Congo at this point is nearly fifteen hundred miles from the sea and has not yet received some of its main tributaries.

Below the Stanley Pool, the wide spot where Brazzaville and Leopoldville face each other across the river, a gorge of incredible proportions and beauty interrupts Congo navigation only about a hundred miles from the sea. Here all the water of the second largest river in the world rushes in foaming cataracts to roll in one tremendous wave over a fall which does not have the drop of Niagara but carries many times its volume.

Some of the surplus water may be retained in the intermediate layers of the jungle. Little pools accumulate in holes in trees, and, in some cases, the biggest trees are literally water towers. Their hollow trunks fill to the brim with limpid water. Once when I was lost in the jungle, I could find water only by climbing fifty feet into the trees, for there were no streams or springs such as I would have looked for in temperate woods. The arboreal drinking fountains are not easily located by anyone who lacks a cat's or a monkey's footing and familiarity with the likely spots. Fortunately some of the lianas are reservoirs of potable fluid. A couple of slashes with a machete carves off a foot or so which will drip a tumblerful of clear, cool, slightly tart water. Of course, another vine of similar appearance yields a glass of clear, cool poison. But if you know which is which, you need not suffer from thirst amidst the jungle's plenty.

Of course, there is a great deal of water underground, too. Even in jungles where the floor is brittle dry, the earth a few inches below the surface is moist. Further down, seeping through the rocks or running in large subterranean river systems, there must be a great but unmeasured volume of water. Some of it may be tapped by the jungle roots; much of it surely is not.

Certain very large jungles are actually afloat. A remarkable example is the Coronie Swamp in Surinam, formerly Dutch Guiana, which lies between two great, almost parallel rivers, the Nickerie and the Coppename. Joining them is a most astonishing stream named the Wayambo. It flows both ways! As you go in at either end, you buck a strong current, but halfway along its course you find dead water. As you continue, a current begins to flow with you until you pop out into the other main river like a cork out of a bottle.

The Coronie Swamp lies between the Wayambo and the Atlantic Ocean, forming in the rainy season an extensive, almost imperceptible dome clothed in a stately jungle. If you battle your way inside, cut a thirty-foot sapling pole and start probing, you will, after penetrating

Coster from Monkmeyer

Swamp in Amazon River region.

about ten feet of matted roots and soil, break through to some fifteen to twenty feet of water. Below that you will strike firm ground. In the dry season, the whole place becomes a shallow bowl with a marshy area right in the center, about which a gigantic menagerie of wildlife concentrates. At that time of year, there is no water below the jungle floor; the whole surface of the land has simply sunk to rest on the solid ground, and you find yourself a little below sea level. The waters have been forced out into the Wayambo as if from a bladder.

A year-round swamp may hold so much water that the usual jungle plants literally drown. Also, swamps are subject to greater flooding than other areas. Marks on the trees of one Malaysian forest show that the water regularly reaches thirty feet up the trunks. Undergrowth and smaller trees die in such an environment; in a swamp with a steadier water level they may never get started at all.

The true jungles are more efficient at distributing water. The very leaves are specially adapted for this purpose. A striking botanical feature of tropical rain forests is that nearly all the leaves of trees and other growth, regardless of what sort of foliage they may produce elsewhere, are almost uniform in shape, color and texture. It is not uncommon to find twenty entirely different trees in one patch of jungle, all with leaves so alike that they could easily be taken for those of a single species. More than likely the twenty would have a typical jungle device known as a "drip tip." This is present in about nine out of ten jungle trees, but is comparatively rare elsewhere. It is an elongated, sharply tapering point which drains water off the leaf and facilitates drying after rain. Not only does the more rapid drying increase the efficiency of the leaves, but the excess water is passed along to the lower levels of the forest rather than evaporated.

But water is only one governing influence in the life of the tropical rain forest. It combines with others to make the particular and peculiar environment in which this vegetational complex can grow.

8

Wind and Weather

HOT and humid is the way most people would describe jungles. At the same time they are surprisingly equable. Their weather is not at all typical of the rest of the tropics. Yet even their extreme highs hardly ever reach those recorded every summer in most of the United States and southern Europe.

A comparison of eight different jungle areas from which extensive records are available shows graphically the jungle's wetness and warmth. Two were South American jungles, three African and three Oriental.

Rainfall and Temperature Records of Eight Jungles

	Highest	Lowest
Mean annual precipitation	164.4 inches	65.1 inches
Number of rainy days in year	212	172
Difference between wettest and driest months	41 inches	4 inches
Mean annual temperature	81°	76°
Mean of the hottest month	83°	77.5°
Mean of the coldest month	79.5°	71°

The temperature during the coldest month in the coldest of the eight was only twelve degrees below that of the hottest month of the hottest jungle in this group. The biggest spread within any one jungle was five and a half degrees. (By comparison, in New York City in one year the mean of the coldest month may be twenty-one and the hottest seventy-four.) Within these narrow limits, the temperature in all the tropics is usually a little higher in the rainy seasons, a little lower in drier ones. So on the whole, *variation* in temperature is hardly a factor in the life and growth of jungles.

Several forces combine to maintain the equable temperature. The most obvious is the direct heat rays from the sun which, in the tropics, are more evenly distributed throughout the year than anywhere else. Another is the mild influence of the oceans. About three-fourths of the entire tropical zone is covered by the sea, and water has a stabilizing effect on temperature. Finally, it has been found that the ground is hardly any cooler than the air, and may be warmer. One test in the Congo revealed that the temperature of the soil a couple of feet below the surface was actually a couple of degrees higher than that of the air above it. The reason is that some soils retain heat longer than others and lose it more slowly. In the tropical rain forests none gets cool enough to lower the general temperature of the air.

When it comes to rainfall, variation from month to month also means little, provided there is no prolonged dry season with less than three or four inches a month. In these eight jungles, the one with the largest variation between dry and wet months, located in the Cameroons in West Africa, was also the one with the heaviest annual rainfall. But the one with the least variation, which was in Malaysia, had only some ninety-five inches. Another Oriental area for which records are available is in Burma. There, with about the same perpetual warmth and the same amount of rain, we find deciduous forest and savannah. The reason? It has no fewer than four successive months when it receives less than half an inch of rain. Where jungles survive on only sixty-five inches or so of rain—the one included in this study was in the Congo—a very high humidity during the dry months, a flow of ground water, or swamps to augment the rains compensate for the relative drought. It is drought, though, only for a jungle, for there is still more rain at these times than falls on Louisiana.

The "steaming tropics," oddly enough, is a phrase often applied to places which are, in fact, comparatively dry. But jungles do have a high average humidity, frequently close to or at the saturation point for days on end, and, of course, the warmer the air the more moisture it can hold. This perhaps even more than the rain is what a temperate zone traveler notices most if he stays for any length of time. His shoes, books and clothes become moldy and rot so rapidly that he is constantly aware of the humidity. If he takes off a shirt and does not have it laundered at once but just drops it on a chair, as some people have a way of doing, he will find a nice healthy crop of "mushrooms" sprouting from the armholes in a day or two. Yet the warm air of the tropics can continue to absorb water after it has passed what would be the saturation point anywhere else. It has been estimated that a humidity of 61 percent at 80 degrees in the rain forest is the equivalent of only 6 percent at 59 degrees, the temperature of an average day in temperate climates. That is very dry indeed.

The net result of all this is that the jungle vegetation can still breathe. The moisture evaporates adequately from the leaves to complete the process by which plants take in nourishment at their roots, draw it up through the whole system and get rid of the excess through the leaves.

Winds may modify the jungle climate, principally because they increase the rate of evaporation. They can also dwarf the vegetation in very exposed spots and, if strong and steady enough, will never allow trees of great size to establish themselves. Their major influence in jungles is, of course, upon the upper canopy.

Violent tornadoes do not affect the climate specifically, but they occasionally alter the appearance of a particular section of jungle—suddenly and rapidly. These storms may do incredible damage if they can find an opening at the edge of the forest. I have seen miles of a perfectly good closed-canopy forest torn to shreds in less than an hour. No canopy remained; big trees had been blown down, and the earth was piled high with a tangled mass of limbs to a depth of some thirty feet. We were lucky to come out alive, for had we been in the middle of the three-mile-wide swath cut by the storm, instead of near its edge, we might as well have faced a mile and half of barbed wire entanglement.

In jungles, true tornadoes or twisters get started in the open places, gather force and then go whirling off across the green blanket of the forest, every now and then dipping into the forest to twist a giant tree right around on its base or suck up a mass of dead logs and rubbish or several tons of water from a river. The logs and water may be carried for miles. Startled jungle dwellers sometimes hear a terrible

Black St

Ceaseless play of cloud formations is an everpresent feature of Amazon region.

noise on a clear day and are inundated with acres of mud containing an assortment of such things as fish, turtles and plants. You can imagine the soul-searching that such an experience prompts among primitive tribesmen.

Huracán, as the Arawaks of the Caribbean called the largest cyclonic storms, are cousins to the willy-willies of Australia and the typhoons of East Asia (originally *tai fung* or big wind in Chinese). All of these are born over the oceans in the doldrums. They are vast cones of hot, moisture-laden air. The air within may travel round and round at two hundred miles an hour, the greatest velocity being near the middle around a central "eye," which is really a tube of still air that rises from the surface of the sea in the form of a funnel to the clear air above.

"Hurricanes" build up within themselves tremendous electrical storms, so that their air, which is about half water, behaves in a peculiar way, to produce extraordinary effects—curling the straightest hair, striking sparks from the most placid people. Their power can drive straws through fenceposts, and fenceposts through the trunks of palm trees. Over water, they suck up so much of it that they can dry up a shallow coast for miles, only to loose a "tidal wave" on another shore.

Such storms can make a noticeable impression on the jungles of Central America or New Guinea or the Philippines. Coastal areas may be flooded, although this will have little effect on swamp forest. Then some or many of the tall trees may be thrown down over a large area, especially on exposed ridges. Finally, and most important, really incredible amounts of water fall; it has been estimated that a modest hurricane only some three hundred miles in diameter has dumped as much as 300,000,000 tons of water in a few hours over a five-hundred-mile-long belt.

The final modifiers of jungle climate are the clouds, which are much more usual than you might expect in the tropics. Especially near the equator, the sun is behind clouds more than half the day, and the phenomenon is so pronounced that French sailors call the equatorial belt *pot au noir*. The effect is to so reduce light intensity that some meteorologists are inclined to think the solar radiation falling on rain forest areas is, on the whole, less than in temperate zones despite the much greater exposure to the direct rays from the sun. This helps to maintain an even temperature, preventing extremes which protracted periods of cloudless days might bring.

Climatic conditions on the ground in even a small patch of jungle may not resemble those above the canopy, and both may differ from what scientists call the microclimate in the middle layers. The canopy is so dense that it provides a cover within which the jungle can develop its own microclimates. Thus there may be a brisk shower at ground level while a bright sun is shining directly overhead.

The climate at the canopy's surface is the standard climate of that particular part of the world. Here the effect of the winds is felt, and the leaves are tougher and stronger than those below, partly so that they may resist being blown about. Here, too, is where dew will form and where most of the light is absorbed.

The canopy has profound influence upon the microclimates underneath. It intercepts and redirects a considerable proportion of the rain. It shelters the interior of the jungle from the wind and from other climatic changes such as rises and falls in the temperature. Radiation of heat at night is never from the ground but from the crowns of the trees. The cooling effect below comes only from the sinking of relatively cooler air through the canopy. This actually is very little, so the interior retains both a less variable temperature and less variable humidity.

At night in the jungle, humidity varies hardly at all from top to bottom, for the air is virtually at saturation point throughout. In the morning, however, the relative humidity in the canopy begins to drop as the sun comes up. Not until an hour or two later does this begin to happen on the ground, and as the day progresses, the upper air is increasingly drier than the lower. As darkness falls at ground level, the air there reaches maximum humidity well before that of the canopy.

Of all the climatic factors, the one in which canopy and interior differ most is light. The ground and first tier of the forest are bathed in a sort of bottle green fluorescence with only occasional sun flecks too small to lighten the gloom—gloom, that is, when compared to the sunlight outside. Depending on whether or not there is a second closed canopy, the light will be more or less evenly graduated from above; a second canopy will make it darker below, of course. There is some variation in the nature of the light as well as its intensity. If it is reflected from the leaves above, the red rays come down in full force. If it penetrates the leaves, the red rays tend to be filtered out.

The changes in jungle microclimates from top to bottom pose some interesting problems for the vegetation, especially the plants which germinate in one layer and must grow up through another to still a third. They must adapt themselves in much the same way as a modern factory converting from manual labor to automation. In fact, since every plant is a sort of chemical factory, processing minerals taken from the soil or each other, the study of chemistry is almost as important to an understanding of the jungle as is the study of botany.

9

Vegetation Factory

VEGETATION everywhere uses identical manufacturing processes, but has to vary the details to fit the conditions of the particular environment in which it finds itself. These conditions dictate to a great extent the kinds of plants which will grow and the form a particular plant will take—a bush here, an herb somewhere else or a tree in still another place.

Whatever the details, the process has the same purposes for all living organisms: to bring in raw material for nourishment, transform it into living tissue and get rid of wastes. For this, plants use water as a solvent and light as a producer of energy to make carbohydrates. The basic raw materials are drawn mostly from the soil, and jungle soils are quite different from those of other regions, although the rocks and other underlying minerals may be the same.

Nearly all jungle soils have a few characteristics in common. Six should be kept in mind because they are especially important: (1) Jungle soils are relatively poor, containing much less plant nourishment than fertile temperate zone soils. (2) They are acid, even when the rock from which they are formed is alkaline. (3) They weather almost entirely by chemical processes—the double decomposition known as hydrolysis, which depends upon a plentiful water supply —rather than the common physical processes such as alternating heat and cold or frost and melting which weather rocks in colder climates. (4) They are usually quite shallow, whether loam or clay, as most of them are, or sandy; the top soil is often only a few inches, sometimes a few feet and very rarely deep enough to be measured in yards. (5) They are normally rich in the oxides of iron and aluminum but poor in silica. (6) They have a comparatively small humus content.

These points, each of which plays a big role in the operation of the jungle's chemical factory, deserve a little more consideration.

That the soil of a rain forest should be lacking in plant food is surprising, because the vegetation itself is so extensive and so obviously well-fed. The fact is that the trees take up a considerable proportion of the nutritive elements before they have a chance to become part of the soil. But equally important is the action of runoff water. The ample rains insure a constant downward drainage in the jungle. Only very rarely, during an exceptionally dry period when the ground begins to parch, is water drawn toward the surface, a frequent and regular phenomenon in temperate climates. The flow carries the more soluble plant foods down to the rivers and out of the forest.

The deficiencies of these jungle soils are, of course, more obvious to man than to the jungle plants, which do quite well. Men, in fact, found out about the poor quality only after they hacked down a bit of jungle to plant their own crops. These did (and still do) rather badly. Fields are almost invariably abandoned after a year or two because they will not support more than one or two crops of any human staple—sometimes not even that many.

One of the most dramatic examples I have seen of what a jungle soil can very quickly become was at a former gold mine in the Guianas. We had reached it by way of a narrow hand railroad along which little carts could be pushed through the jungle. It was as usual silent, dim, cathedral-like. Then we emerged into a clearing, a mile by half a mile of yellow-brown absolutely bare earth where the forest had been destroyed for the mine. The mine had not been worked for two years, but nothing would grow there anymore; only around the one house on a hill, occupied by a caretaker, was there any vegetation, a really splendid rose garden blooming its head off in this unlikely spot.

Such soil as exists in the jungle is invariably acid because the drainage takes the soluble salts out of the original rocks. It has been noticed that even around outcroppings of limestone, the lime is carried off before it can have any alkaline effect on the soil. Therefore, acid-loving plants have a big advantage in the jungle.

In these forests, the ground water is highly charged with humic and tannic acid and other acid solvents—this is what makes so many tropical rivers the color of nutty sherry—and they can eventually dis-

WEST HILLS COLLEGE LIBRARY
COALINGA, CALIFORNIA

solve virtually any rock, especially one broken up by plant roots. Of course, much of the minerally enriched ground water is greedily absorbed by the vegetation before it drains off.

The only places in the tropics where physical factors assist in converting rock to soil are the rare clearings where the stone is exposed to the sun. Then the heating by day and cooling by night plus the erosion of the rain will have some effect.

Hydrolysis, however, more than makes up for it. Tropical heat, which is about the same underground as above, plus ample water are ideal conditions for this transformation of one chemical into another by the addition of H_2O. In the jungles it has been going on for countless millennia, so that deposits ought to be very thick. Yet this is so in only a few places. Accumulations of nearly sixty feet have been reported, and I personally have seen some more than half that depth—very deep topsoil by any standards. It may vanish if the protection of the jungle vegetation is removed. In one of the few places I ever saw a deep bed of topsoil—it was twenty-eight feet thick under the trees—rains washed away every bit of it before a crop could get started. It was only a matter of months before the ridges of the clearing were either completely denuded down to the surface rock—here a porous sandstone—or littered with hard nodules of iron oxide which formed while the loam was being washed away.

This sort of erosion is far more intense in hilly terrain than in the lowlands. Large areas formerly clothed in jungle have been turned into bare crags by man because one clearing has been enough to destroy them beyond any possibility of recovery, as in the Blue Mountains of Jamaica. On the lowlands, however, the jungle returns after any such clearing.

One reason that most jungle soils are shallow is that the water seldom gives them time to accumulate. They are washed away relentlessly by trickles and streams and rivers. The Amazon carries, mostly from jungles, enough silt to build islands as big as provinces in its various mouths, and still discolors the ocean a hundred miles out at sea. A comparison between the Amazon and an average European river, the Rhine, was made some years ago. From each square mile of its basin, the Amazon carries 130 times as much solid matter every year as does the Rhine.

The majority of jungles which have been studied scientifically have a characteristic red or yellow soil, more often red, which is so common that some learned writers call them "the tropical red earths." This color is due to some extent to oxides of iron and aluminum, which are relatively insoluble in water but are carried in colloidal suspension. They are readily precipitated, and so they remain behind to tint the earth as the rain drains through.

These conditions account for the remarkable uniformity of tropical rain forests growing on a variety of basic geological formations. I once watched a geological surveyor bring up from beneath an extremely homogeneous Central American jungle half a dozen varieties of rock. The same grouping of trees and shrubs grew in just the same way to the same height on shales, clays, limestones, sandstones and sundry metamorphic and even volcanic rocks.

The reason for the small quantity of humus in jungle soil is that although humus forms with greater rapidity there than in temperate zones, it breaks down even faster. This explains the very thin coating of mulch on the jungle floor. The tropical rain forest has ideal conditions for converting leaves, bark and wood litter into humus. But the same conditions facilitate an incredibly rapid decomposition of the humus into its mineral components, which, in turn, dissolve in the top few inches of soil, where the feeding roots of jungle vegetation are concentrated. They are promptly consumed by the plants, so that "soil" as we know it often has no time to form.

Scientists who first discovered these various factors in the jungle's chemistry wondered why the most magnificent forests on earth grew in quite impoverished soil, while richer but drier tropical soils grew nothing except savannah or scrub or low woods. Eventually they found out that the jungle feeds from itself, taking only a little sustenance from the deeper layers of the rocks. The speed with which it puts its own dead back into the common pot, so to speak, is amazing. I once put a wire screen around a large, fleshy green leaf that fell at my feet by our breakfast table in a jungle camp. By midday it was bright yellow; by evening it was brown and had holes in it; by midnight all that was left was a sort of filigree of its harder veins; and by next morning it was gone but for a small portion of its woody stem, which two large ants were trying to tote away. Wood and bark

Ivan Sanderson

Leaf-cutting ants of South America.

disintegrate only a little more slowly. All life, from microscopic organisms to the largest animals, helps this process. Termites are especially effective in reducing fallen logs and branches.

Most plants growing below the jungle canopy seem to make special use of carbon dioxide. While much remains to be learned about it, we find indications that the concentration of this gas in the air of lower layers of jungles can be two or three times, and sometimes five or even ten times, that outside. The chemistry involved is this: Water drawn upward from the roots is combined with the carbon dioxide taken in by leaves from the air and is converted, through energy developed from light by chlorophyll, into carbohydrates. Where the light is relatively dim, as in jungles, this basic chemical process can be facilitated by extra carbon dioxide.

Carbon dioxide is given off by all plants and animals in the course of respiration and is also a by-product of decomposition. It is half again as heavy as air, so that under the closed canopy of the jungle it tends to collect near the ground. In other forests which are more open and where the air currents are stronger, carbon dioxide is more rapidly dispersed.

Plant enzymes also require a quantity of a much lighter gas, nitrogen, and usually get it through the operation of bacteria in the soil. Long ago men discovered that the plants called legumes are especially rich in the bacteria that do the job. That is why farmers plow these plants under, or at least their roots. Or they can use fertilizers.

A German chemist, Fritz Haber, won the Nobel Prize in 1918 for discovering a method by which nitrogen could be obtained from the atmosphere, of which it forms about four-fifths. His discovery enabled Germany to fight World War I in spite of being cut off from the only previously known supplies of commercial nitrogen fertilizers, chiefly guano deposits. Ever since then, men have been able to get all the nitrogen they need from the air.

Jungles knew all about it, and about legumes too, millions of years before there were men. On soils deficient in nutritive elements, the tropical rain forest grows a great number of leguminous plants; they can be, and often are, the very biggest of jungle trees, such as the huge tropical acacias. It has been recorded that in two British Guiana jungle areas, which were either swampy and waterlogged or even

Nancy Flowers from Nancy Palmer Agency

Close-up of termite nest, Amazon, Brazil.

more badly leached than usual, more than half of all the trees were of this type. In three other areas nearby, neither as badly leached nor as marshy, the proportion of leguminous trees ranged only from 14 to 33 percent.

The jungles had also anticipated the Haber process, using thunderstorms to fix the air's nitrogen. Thunder in the tropics is accompanied by frequent and even continuous flashes of lightning. Whenever a bolt shoots from one charged cloud to another or from a cloud to the earth or from the earth to a cloud, it causes certain violent chemical reactions. One of them is the formation of nitrogen dioxide from the air's nitrogen and oxygen, and this is readily soluble in water vapor. Therefore, the rains of these tropical storms bring down on the jungle so much nitrogen dioxide that the result of a single storm has to be calculated in tons rather than just pounds.

Jungles on the whole seem to be more efficiently operated, chemically speaking, than other vegetational types, or even than our modern factories. That is why they produce plants of unexampled mass, variety and splendor.

Chester Dale Collection, National Gallery of Art, Washington, D.C

"The Equatorial Jungle." Painting by Henri Rousseau.

Part 3

Plants of the Jungle

The Book of Rules
Giants of the Vegetable World
The Weavers
Aerial Performers
The Destroyers
The Next Generation
The Lowly Things

Ernst Haas from Magnum

Boy in climbing fig tree.

10

The Book of Rules

UNDERLYING the whole functional organization of tropical rain forests is a set of precise regulations that governs all its denizens. These regulations stem from two fundamental facts. First, the jungles are extremely old vegetational complexes. Second, they are stable.

They achieve and maintain their neat equilibrium in the face of unusually lush growth and very rapid decay because, whatever alterations take place among the various plants, the functions of each remain precisely those of its predecessor. Through the ages, the forest has learned what forms of vegetation best perform the various duties required. Within rather broad limits, it develops a great number of different plants to perform each one. But it also permits the plants to have a life of their own beyond that, to express their own individuality, as it were.

It is widely supposed that this "law of the jungle" is nothing more than a ruthless competition for survival, a kill or be killed situation. In fact, people say "jungle law" when they refer to a particularly bitter fight without pity or scruple.

Of course, such competition does exist, but it is not the only rule by which jungle vegetation must live. There is an interdependence, a mutual aid as strictly regulated as that among the various parts of the human body, and without it the forest could not exist. The jungle plant, regarded from this standpoint, fights not for itself alone but for the general welfare.

You can condemn the big trees as the exterminators of hundreds, thousands, perhaps millions, of rivals for their conspicuous place in the sun. But then you will observe, too, that these conquerors have enormous responsibility for the growth and preservation of all the other vegetation in the jungle, for the orderly and systematic development of the forest itself. The straight, smooth columns of their trunks support the vast weight of lianas, flowering plants, even other trees, holding them up as much as a couple of hundred feet off the ground so that they can reach sunlight. The massive branches provide amid their own foliage both a platform for veritable gardens of quite unrelated plants and the soil and moisture to feed them.

The same dense canopy that prevents the growth of rivals for perhaps hundreds of years and destroys the lush tropical ground cover that springs up wherever sun and rain reach the surface of the earth is the benevolent guardian of shade-loving plants. Certain palms, the wild varieties of coffee and cacao, families of molds and fungi and many others rely upon screening from sun or harsh light. To them the evergreen roof of the forest is benign, as essential to them as a roof over our heads is to us.

Then there are masses of plants that live on the big trees, and even on smaller ones, too. These are the epiphytes, which are lifted up into the sun by their hosts. A single tree in the jungle may support hundreds of epiphytes, many of them quite sizable. Most of them will be invisible to an observer on the ground or even to one perched above the canopy.

Now all this spells out a rule which most people would not expect to find governing the vegetation of the tall equatorial forest. The rule is this: "The mighty shall support and sustain the weak." Its workings are so obvious that you might well wonder what perverse thinking equated "law of the jungle" with malevolent cruelty. Apparently the huge trees with their protective umbrella of foliage are a gigantic charitable institution upon which all life in the jungle depends. Like a prudently invested charitable fortune, it gives of its strength generously and still manages to grow stronger all the time.

One of the great adventure stories of the last century was the discovery of some of these true laws of the jungle by a pioneer botanist who is to the study of vegetation only a little less important than Einstein was to the study of nuclear physics. He was Richard Spruce, who spent many years in the Amazon country. In the early

Karl Weidman from National Audubon Society

Tree with masses of airplants feeding from it.

1850's he formulated some of the principles that enabled later scientists to understand the nature of the jungle as an entity.

He overcame some remarkable obstacles in order to do it. One was that he never learned to climb off the jungle floor. Another was that his generation was exposed to somewhat greater hazards than might exist today in the same areas, as he recounts in his journal of one journey down the Rio Negro.

Spruce and the four Indians who were his crew had tied up at the river bank for the night, and Spruce was lying in his hammock when he overheard the Indians discussing how they could kill him for the bundles of carefully pressed plants he had gathered, which they mistook for trade goods. They thought they could get away with it because he was alone and sick; he had been dosing himself copiously with quinine and ipecac. At last they agreed they would strangle him as soon as he went to sleep.

Spruce realized that he was lucky to be suffering from diarrhea and therefore it would not seem strange if he was wakeful. He had had to leave his hammock a couple of times even before he knew what the Indians were up to. The third time, however, he did not come back. He returned to the boat, armed himself with a gun, a knife and a cutlass, and waited behind a big bundle of papers for the attack. It did not come, although he could hear the Indians talking angrily on the shore.

At dawn, he simply told them to get aboard, all except the one he was sure was the ringleader. Spruce left him on the river bank, pretending their passport did not include him, and never heard of him again. The others, cowed, got him safely to Manaus, which he reached at the beginning of its frenetic career as the metropolis of rubber; some of his own reports, in fact, had helped start the boom.

While adventures of this sort did not deter the scientists of that day, their failure to get into the jungle canopy did hamper them more than they knew, although Spruce divined some of the need. In the same "notes" in which he tells how he foiled his greedy Indian boatmen, he writes of his disappointment "in not finding some agile and willing Indians to run like cats or monkeys up the tree for me . . . the only way to obtain the flowers and fruits was to cut down the tree." He knew he had to have these to classify his plants properly.

It took him, as it did most strangers, a long time to realize that the natives on the edge of the jungle are not familiar with its interior, while the real jungle people capable of performing the acrobatics Spruce wanted were invisible. Spruce had another handicap. As an Englishman used to the meticulously cultivated forests of his little island, he could not help feeling it was a desecration to cut down trees just to get at the fruit. But he did it, and he took some comfort from the reassurance of his Indians that the jungle would not really miss a few.

"Thus I reconciled myself to the commission of an act whose apparent vandalism was, or seemed to be, counterbalanced by its necessity and utility," he wrote.

His "vandalism" was invaluable, for it demonstrated to him how the jungle was put together. The giants brought to earth with them all the other plants they supported, and as he sorted them out, Spruce realized what an orderly place the jungle was.

Other rules, of course, apply to other constituents of the forest. The vines, creepers and lianas observe a mutual aid principle of their own. Though they sometimes strangle or squeeze to death the trees they embrace, they also tie the jungle together in a close, virtually inseparable mass which permits its giant supports to resist wind and storms. In the shallow soils of the rain forest, the biggest trees are terribly topheavy, and the mass of other plants growing on the upper branches adds to their imbalance. Even the trees with massive buttress roots would be vulnerable if they stood alone. The binding force of the lianas gives each tree the support of all its neighbors.

You can observe the principle at work with a couple of dozen kitchen matches on a table or desk. Try to balance the matches on their ends without support. You can't make them stand up, let alone resist a slight push. But place them, say, in four rows of six matches, each match half an inch from its neighbors, and wind a wire in and around them so that it loops tightly around the head of each match before passing on to embrace the next. The force required to knock them down would also smash them to splinters.

Donna N. Sprunt from National Audubon Socie

Night-smelling orchid.

Smaller plants have no such powerful role in the life of the jungle. The rules provide, however, that they shall make a contribution in proportion to their size and strength. Their function is, perhaps, no less valuable. Even parasites seem to have their duties in preserving the health and life of the forest.

The tiny life-forms called bacteria are credited with a major role in reducing all manner of raw materials to food that other plants can absorb. They account for much of the rapid decomposition of animal, vegetable and mineral compounds. And, although they themselves may be parasites, they seem to make it possible for many plants to resist the ravages of pests of various kinds. The exact mechanisms they use, however, remain obscure.

The same may be said of algae and fungi, even when these are recognized as plant diseases. The paradox here seems to be that, while they deprive the host plant of some of its food, they pay for it by assisting the host in collecting and assimilating mineral and other substances. Whatever the reason, plants infested by some fungi actually thrive better than members of the same family growing at the same level in the same jungle but without parasites.

This phenomenon has been noted relative to certain animals. Zebras, for instance, are always bloated when "in the pink" of health by a quantity of parasitic worms. But the zebra who is thoroughly dewormed deteriorates and develops all kinds of maladies that are worse for him than the bloat. It seems that the worms help the animal to digest his coarse foods, and take a little of it themselves as a commission. It is a perfectly satisfactory arrangement for both.

Even when the algae and fungi are visibly killing a plant or part of a plant, they may at the same time serve a useful purpose to the jungle as a whole. For example, algae or moss may infest a big, broad leaf to the point where the glossy green surface becomes absolutely furry with the growth. That growth may become so thick that seeds will sprout in it. Orchid seedlings are not an uncommon sight on these leaves, although, of course, they never reach maturity. Long before this is possible, the leaf is killed and falls to the ground. But it is already well prepared for decomposition and absorption as food by roots of a tree, often the very tree from which it fell, enriched by the parasites and the seedlings.

The rule here, of course, is that nothing must be wasted. In this respect the world of vegetation is something like the world of people. Among us, it is often noticed that the richest men are the thriftiest. Jungles, the plutocrats of the vegetable world, are equally thrifty.

Sometimes in the tropical rain forest you will see an apparently random assortment of leaves on the same tree ranging from pale chartreuse through a rosy pink to the usual dark green. It is far more likely in the canopy than under it. Actually there is nothing random about it; the plant is following a very common rule not only of the jungle but of nature. It is the same rule that turns northern trees and shrubs yellow, orange, flame, red, vermilion and eventually a reddish brown in the autumn. While it is true that in our climate the transformation occurs at about the onset of cold weather, it is a phenomenon having to do with light as much as heat.

Apparently the practical purpose of all this, especially in the tall deciduous rain forest, is to enable the new leaves to suck up every scrap of the sun's blazing heat that they can. Thus they can start off with some extra energy so that their little pumping pores may puff out as much inner moisture as possible to tide the whole tree over the lean period between a minimum of foliage and a new maximum. In the tall deciduous forest the effect, especially as viewed from above, can rival the beauty of the flowering season.

The rule of the jungle is quite indifferent to the identity of the species that populate it. The result is that usually no tree predominates. But a few are as exclusive as a northern pine wood. An example is the Mora Forest that stretches in a broken belt all the way from Trinidad through the delta of the Orinoco River, the Guianas and the Amazon effluence. This forest is composed mostly of a single tree, *Mora excelsa,* which grows to a tremendous height and in such close proximity to others of its kind that together they manage to keep out most other trees; indeed, almost pure stands of them are found in many places.

The Mora trees produce large kidney-shaped nuts, or beans as they are called locally. They can grow in brackish or fresh water, and the nuts can withstand prolonged immersion in either, so that they can be washed out of the great South American rivers, carried long distances by ocean currents and thrown up on distant shores to sprout and create new Mora forests. This is believed to be what happened on Trinidad. It was in a Mora forest in Dutch Guiana that we were followed by those little fresh water whales or dolphins and their baby-pink young.

This is not the only tree that achieves real dominance in the jungle. The greenheart and wallaba do it in American jungles, an ironwood tree (*Cynomatra alexandri*) and a tall, unusually low branching fellow named *Macrolobium dewevrei* in Africa, the Borneo ironwood and the kapur or Borneo camphor in the Orient.

Why this pattern should prevail in some places and not in others is not altogether clear. The trees that dominate in one forest are found elsewhere as widely scattered as any other species. What is obvious, however, is that the rule of the jungle permits such eccen-

Government Information Services, British Guiana

Mora tree.

tricities and differences as long as they do not interfere with the dynamic equilibrium of the whole.

A final factor in the regulation of jungle life that helps to achieve this balance is provided by the animals. They may have as much effect on the vegetation as beavers, for instance, do in parts of this country. The numbers of any variety may wax and wane over the centuries, deteriorating or enhancing the jungle by their digging and delving, browsing and chewing, damming and ditching.

The most controversial of all so far as influence on the jungle is concerned are men. Zoologists, anthropologists, ethnologists and even sociologists have exercised their minds for some time as to where we should draw the line between man as an "artificial" agency and man as "natural" force in the environment, just one of the fauna like any other. It has been a burning question with forest officers, botanists and phytogeographers for years, but it has not been completely resolved. My own opinion is that man is a perfectly natural biotic entity and has been playing a role in the conformity and constitution of jungles for much longer than has been supposed.

Among the major jungle belts there are the so-called secondary and tertiary forests, which are not genuine jungles but are on their way toward that "climax," as the botanists call it. The secondary forest is that which grows up at once on lands that have been artificially cleared; it is quite different from the normal regeneration of the jungle. Tertiary forest is the term sometimes used to denote the vegetation growing on land that has been cleared more than once and sometimes as that which has developed after the secondary growth. In the latter case, it is a transition between the secondary and the climax forest.

Clearing an area of jungle results in the most monumental confusion. Nowadays civilized men with bulldozers, dynamite and the other "advanced" machinery of destruction, both mechanical and chemical, can really slash into and eliminate a section of jungle in a hurry. But the local citizen, even with a store-bought steel axe and a wood saw, can do little more than clear out the saplings and bushes, kill the lianas by cutting through their bases and then ring the great trees so that they die and can be fired.

This has been the method adopted by primitive men for countless

Coster from Monkmeyer

Forest on fire in Amazon region.

millennia and is known as "shifting cultivation." It is a tremendously laborious task and may engage the whole male population of a village for years. Even when it is accomplished, the would-be farmers end up with an area of ex-jungle that is littered with vast tree trunks lying every which way, often piled thirty feet high one upon the other. Among these a whole new forest of secondary growth has already begun before the clearing of the primary jungle is finished. The new saplings may have to be cleared away before the men can plant their

Collection, The Museum of Modern Art, New Yo[rk]

"The Dream." Painting by Henri Rousseau.

humble root and vine crops wherever they can find room among the welter of fallen logs. The whole process is an endless battle.

Each village pecks away at the inexorable monster and by sheer muscle cuts out, if only temporarily, a part of it for a crop or two. Then the men move on to an adjacent area and repeat the process.

Man, therefore, cannot be considered other than a genuine biotic factor in the life of the jungle. But his lasting effects, as those of other animals, are only faintly noticeable in the reasonably level lowland jungles.

But man's effects upon the montane and other upland jungles may be disastrous. Many of these jungles grow on very steep slopes, and many seem to be not only ancient but the end result of the works of nature that began before men had even put in an appearance. Unlike the lowland jungles, however, they do not have great resilience or furious powers of regeneration. After they are cleared, the thin soil on which they grew may very readily be washed away entirely. Thus large regions that were formerly clothed in dense cloud forests have been rendered into bare rocky crags by the activities of men.

11

Giants of the Vegetable World

WITHIN the living, pulsing entity of the jungle is an infinity of smaller entities; in a way each of the millions of enormous trees is a world in itself. You can spend a long time exploring just a single tree.

The first impression of these trees is of towering height, a vast mass of foliage and relative slenderness, which often is an illusion caused by the fact that the straight, faintly tapering bole may bear not a single branch within a hundred feet of the ground. The trees also look truly indestructible. Of course, they do die, although the longevity has never been accurately calculated, but even then they are so stoutly supported by lianas and other trees that they usually do not fall until all their limbs drop off and the trunks collapse piecemeal.

What makes the special world of the individual tropical rain forest tree a world apart, even more than its great mass of foliage which may be as much as a hundred feet thick, is the hollow stem. A majority of the big trees in many of the biggest jungles are intrinsically thin-walled chimneys, the hollowness usually extending into all the major branches.

The insides of these forest giants are eerie, perhaps the oddest environment known on this planet, closer to what we have come to expect in science fiction than reality. They are, in fact, caves in the air, their strangeness surpassing even wondrous caves in the earth, for they are the hiding places and hunting grounds and homes of even more different living things than are found in caves.

Hollow trees are especially popular homesites for animals in West African and Congolese jungles. More than once we have found a whole menagerie ranging from leopards to bacteria. On one of my collecting trips in the Cameroons we took more than a thousand animals from a single tree.

We learned to adapt our hunting techniques to this structural peculiarity. One night in a British Honduran jungle, we captured a cacomistle, the tropical cousin of the ring-tailed cat of our southern and western states. After we had bagged him, we decided that his mate's probable lair was a hole that we could see high up in a neighboring tree.

Next day we went back to investigate. With ropes and a pulley we hauled ourselves up, far above the ground, to the opening that led into the hollow interior. Inside there was plenty of room for my companion to enter and look around. In fact, waving a flashlight as he went, he found he could maneuver very much like a man going down an abandoned well and with ample room on all sides. I returned to the ground to wait with a gun for whatever he might flush out of its home, and for a time heard only a great rumbling in the bowels of the tree to mark his passage.

Actually it was not the lair of the cacomistle's mate at all; in fact, we did not see one again. But as so often happens, other treasures made up for the one we had missed. This particular hollow tree was the dwelling of some big, rather special gray and white rats we wanted. Three of them dashed away from my companion and came out of a hole at the bottom of the tree—there are usually several entrances and exits. I managed to get two of them.

Often the bases of these trees have Gothic-arched entrances to the hollow column, more than large enough to hide a man. I have taken refuge in them myself so as to be unobserved as I watched the wildlife on the forest floor. Within these spaces under the center of the tree a cone or pyramid of dead wood builds up to a considerable height. A steady rain of "sawdust," chips and bits of debris, is produced by the animals scrambling about the interior, digging new homes inside the trunk or branches.

This pile of dry, dead wood can be a fire hazard, for it is pure tinder and if set alight could burn the whole tree. Invariably holes lead out far above the ground in hollow limbs or in the trunk itself, providing a flue to create the draft that sucks heat and flames upward.

New York Zoological Society Photo

Adult cacomistle.

The danger in such a situation is obvious, perhaps more so to me than to most people because I was once nearly its victim. It happened in British Honduras, just after we had set up a new camp in the jungle. While shaving one morning the same associate who had flushed the rats out of the hollow tree saw an unidentifiable creature bolt into a hole near the first fork of a giant tree close to our camp. He had only a glimpse, and the hole was as far away as the dormer window of a six-story house, but the creature sounded interesting and we set to work to get at it.

One of the simplest ways of collecting specimens from a hollow tree is to smoke them out. A little sulfur is as effective in evacuating them as tear gas is in a raid on a gangster stronghold. This particlar tree, however, had an awkard entrance. The hollow began between two of the thin buttress roots that radiated from the bases of all the trees in that forest. Then it made an almost right-angled turn into the interior. The best plan, it seemed, was to insert a pan of sulfur and a blowtorch to heat it. The sulfur fumes presumably would drive the denizens out of the hole at the fork where we would have a good shot at them.

Half an hour later we realized that this logical plan was not going to work. No smoke emerged from the hole—and, of course, no animals. Obviously the hollow was stopped up with debris at some point. However, access to the fork of the tree looked easy; many large creepers hung down one side right from the summit, sufficiently knotted and tangled to provide good holds and apparently more than strong enough to bear a man's weight.

I undertook the climb, carrying a long cord which I could lower from the fork to receive the sulfur pan and torch. However, I am not an especially eager gymnast, and I took my time, testing each vine to be sure it was not rotten or bored half-through by insects or otherwise unsafe. Also I like to pause to catch my breath at intervals, and here and there the climbers obligingly wove themselves into a sort of cat's cradle for my support. Even so I was ready for a rest when I reached the fork.

To my pleased surprise, I found that the vines had formed a spacious latticework balcony between two great branches that slanted upward toward the jungle canopy. In this natural basket dead leaves, other vines, ferns, orchids and even a few clumps of grass had accumulated into a thick, level floor as big as a small room. Gratefully I sank down upon it after making sure it was free from scorpions and other undesirables, and enjoyed a cigarette before dropping one end of the cord to the ground.

When I had hauled up the lighted blowtorch, a sulfur pan and a bottle of water, I looked around for a good perch handy to the animal I was hoping to flush. The hole was about ten feet above me on the underside of one of the large branches. A complicated arrangement of three different vines dangling from the limb enabled me to ensconce myself and my equipment opposite the opening, and a little ledge just inside held the sulfur pan conveniently so that it could be heated slowly. This was a moderately delicate operation,

New York Zoological Society Photo

Adult kinkajou.

since I wanted only to drive the animal out, not knock him out. Burning the sulfur might release so much gas that the tree's residents would be stunned and drop down into the depths of the hollow before they had a chance to run.

I had barely settled down with the pan and torch well placed when two small faces peered out at me, no more than two feet from my nose and apparently more curious than frightened. Their little round heads with neat ears set low on either side of a broad brow and their large, bright yellow eyes gave them a gentle look. They wore woolly coats and their powerful limbs ended in small clawed paws almost like hands. They were kinkajous, an entrancing arboreal denizen of tropical American jungles who is like a kitten, teddy bear and lemur all rolled into one. A chance to capture a pair of them alive was a rare bit of luck—and before breakfast, too!

A quick wave of the pan sent them back into the hollow, giving me time to knot my cord in a running noose. Then, when they started out again they emerged so close together and with such deliberation that when I jerked the loop tight, it gripped both of them at once. A twist sent them spinning out from the trunk, since the hole was on the underside of the branch, and I let the cord run through my fingers fast. The kinkajous struggled loose only just before they reached the ground, where they were promptly seized by my helpers below.

With a distinct sense of triumph I emptied the bottle of water into the hollow to damp down any sparks that might have lodged inside, and started back to the platform in the fork of the tree. The habit of caution when aloft led me to test the footing on it while I still had a firm hold on the creepers that had been supporting me. It was fortunate, for as I put my foot on the place where I had reclined so comfortably not half an hour earlier, there was a loud sharp crack and the whole mass of vegetation and woody matter dropped straight down into the wide, yawning trunk. Almost simultaneously, with a hiss and a roar, a sheet of flame shot upward almost into my face, accompanied by a shower of sparks soaring high into the foliage above.

Usually one does not think of fire as a special peril of the jungle. Furthermore, this particular forest was about as thoroughly saturated as a place can get. There had been a steady drizzle for three days, and the clear dawn had been preceded by a night as misty as the steam room of a Turkish bath. All around, the great trees still dripped. But inside, a hollow trunk can be as dry and snug as the most tightly roofed house. This one undoubtedly was so protected, and we had neglected to dampen the hollow in the base of the tree after we gave up trying to smoke it from the bottom. It had been smoldering and building up all the time I had been climbing and resting on the platform, which I now realized was the plug that contained the flames. Now that the plug was gone, tons of powder-dry tinder blazed up the shaft of this natural chimney, which was about five feet wide with a fifty-foot flue.

The intense heat sent me scurrying up the big branch. From the ground, they told me later, it looked as if I had skimmed up as swiftly as a bird for thirty feet, but I simply don't remember how I did it. I became fully aware of my surroundings only after I had reached this vantage point, if it could be called that. I was momentarily out of range of the heat and sparks, but I was also about eighty feet above the ground where the edges of the buttress roots, looking as sharp as knives, appeared even less hospitable than the inferno in the trunk.

My best chance seemed to be to make my way from the branch of this tree to one of a neighboring giant, but as I moved along a route that I thought the most feasible, the supports grew weaker and weaker and at last bent ominously under my weight. I was forced to retreat.

Meanwhile the roaring of the flames and the crackle and crash of smaller branches drowned out any shouts. I could yell as loudly as I would to those on the ground, and they yelled back, but neither of us heard anything except the blast of fire. I could see them, however, and after a moment translated into a course of action what at first seemed meaningless gestures. They had spotted a single strand of a large liana which hung beneath my branch clear of the trunk until it was fairly close to the ground. If the vine was not rotten, I should be able to lower myself to safety.

It worked, and as a reminder of my narrow escape, I passed close enough to three small holes in the main bole so that the pink tongues of flame licking out nearly scorched me as I went by. I fell the last few feet, and just in time, for within a few seconds the branch below the one from which I had descended crashed to earth, scattering us on the run and bringing down the vine that had saved me. Our luck held further, for the loss of that huge limb inclined the tree away from us, so that when it finally toppled, in a terrifying holocaust of noise and sparks, it missed our camp.

The sight of a full-grown jungle tree ablaze is almost unbelievable and always frightening, even when you are not out on one of its limbs. We once inadvertently set an even larger one than this alight in West Africa while collecting specimens by the smoking process. This giant burned for four days, lighting up the sky at night and noticeably shaking the earth four miles away when it fell.

Australian News & Information Burea

Eucalyptus regnans, pride of the Australian forests.

Aloft in one of these jungle giants, you are conscious of its size much more clearly than when on the ground, even if it is not on fire. While the tropical rain forest sets no records for either height or girth of trunk, these giants are not too far off, and the great mass of their foliage puts them in a class apart from even the largest temperate zone trees.

The subject of where the tallest, biggest, most massive trees are provided an international circus of conflicting claims until recently, especially in the United States, where we like to think we have the mostest of everything. But the records are pretty clear now, and we don't hold them.

Our biggest tree is the redwood called "General Sherman" standing in the Sequoia National Park in the Sierra Nevada. This is only 255 feet tall, having been naturally "topped," but its girth is 75 feet and its bulk is estimated at 50,000 cubic feet, apart from limbs. Our record for height is another redwood (*Sequoia sempervirens*), 364 feet tall. The all-time height record is held by a British Columbia white spruce, measured at 417 feet after felling. Next comes an Australian *Eucalyptus regnans* of 382 feet.

Jungle trees never come close to this, but when you speak of "biggest" in the ordinary sense of mass, there are vegetable things in these forests vaster than any that live outside them. The Australian eucalyptus is an immensely tall, spindly affair with a comparatively tiny crown. The great conifers of British Columbia are towering spikes. But the giant rocos and mahoganies of the jungle have massive spreading limbs and billows of foliage, so that their total bulk exceeds that of any nonjungle tree.

I have seen a mahogany, solid right through, in the Cockscomb Mountains of southern British Honduras that was more than 200 feet tall. It took twenty-four men holding hands to circle the base. This gave a basal diameter of 44 feet of solid lumber. And I have measured buttress roots from the base of a tree called terminalia that ran out more than 50 feet from the trunk. In order to encircle the four of them, you would have needed 480 men with an average armspan of six feet.

These buttresses, like the main branches of jungle trees, tend to be four in number, although there may be more on occasion—each of these roots usually being under the branches. The trunks, mostly smooth and with very thin bark, usually rise more than half their height before branching, and the branches themselves have far less subdivision than our biggest trees. Another of the odd features of most buttressed trees is that the trunk is thickest at the top of the buttresses, tapering from there both up and down.

Why most jungle trees are hollow but healthy while elsewhere most healthy big trees are solid has long been a puzzle to botanists. Now it is known that this frequently begins at birth, so to speak, and is evident when the trees are saplings no larger in diameter than your thumb. If you slash through one of them with a machete, you will see a small dark hole straight down the middle. A number of black ants may sometimes come running hysterically out of this and start milling around the cut surface or down the outside of the stem. They cause the hollowness.

The egg-laying queens of these species of ants drill a hole into a sprouting nut and ensconce themselves there. They also carry the spores of a certain fungus which go to work on the pithy center of the nut and the young shoot, turning it into a moist, mashed material suitable for nourishing the ants too. These fungi live only in darkness, so they do not rot the stem right through but keep pace with its growth and expansion according to a strict formula of size of hole to thickness of stem.

This goes on for the rest of the tree's life, so that a trunk twenty feet in diameter at the base may have walls only a foot thick. Yet so strong are the woods of these trees that they can still hold up four main limbs wide enough to park a jeep, plus half a hundred subsidiary branches each bigger than the average oak in our oldest woods. That they live and even thrive is due to the fact that all the nutrients of woody plants are carried aloft in the thin layer called *phloem* between the bark and the wood.

The extremely favorable conditions for all vegetable growth in most jungles has been believed partly responsible for the unrivaled variety of the giant trees. The plethora of different species in a single forest is quite incomprehensible to those who are familiar only with other climes. Once many years ago I was privileged to meet a rather remarkable and now famous man in the field of tropical forestry, R. D. Rosevear. Later he was Senior Forestry Officer of the Protectorate of Nigeria and the British Cameroons, but at the time I met him his duties included long tours through the jungles he administered. The only way to make them was on foot along the forest paths, with the equipment carried on the heads of stalwart local citizens after the fashion made familiar in the movies.

Mr. Rosevear told me that on one such trek he had not been able in two days of walking—a man of his experience covers about twenty miles a day—to identify the same tree twice. At the time I thought this a fable, but after some twenty subsequent years of trying to identify jungle trees, I cannot now doubt his statement.

No tree ever had a more profound effect upon humanity, in or out of the jungle, than a tall, slender variety originally called *Siphonia* by the botanists and later *Hevea,* from which the ancient American civilizations derived a product they knew as caoutchouc. We know it as rubber. When the Spanish conquistadores saw a bouncing ball, they were amused, but it was not much more than a toy until Charles Goodyear invented vulcanization.

The trees from which this sap came grew from one end of the Amazon Valley to the other, and in such profusion, although isolated individually, that more than fifty years after the boom began, astute Alfred Wallace, the British naturalist, was quite sure that Brazil could supply the needs of the world forever.

When Wallace's friend, Spruce, left the Amazon port of Manaus for the Orinoco in 1850, it was a village whose lethargy he thought exaggerated even for the tropics. When he floated down the Rio Negro back to Manaus four years later, after his adventure with the Indians who had tried to kill him, the place was a madhouse—steamships tied up to a new pier, twice as many buildings as he had remembered, men rushing about as he had never seen them do in Brazil before. Rubber went from three cents a pound to three dollars, Manaus from 3,000 people to 100,000. Rubber millionaires built a remarkable marble opera house, enjoyed the newest elegance in furnishings and fashion from Europe, imported the finest wines. Spruce, however, did not stay for all this, nor for the brutal exploitation of the rubber gatherers that accompanied it.

Some years earlier, he had tried to send a few seedlings of the trees back to England; he was so much a pioneer in the botanical classification of them that one species was named for him. But the voyage was too long for them to survive. After the boom began, the Brazilian government took stringent measures to prevent exportation of any seed or seedlings; the ban was enforced so efficiently that not for fifty years did anyone succeed in evading it. Then an Englishman named Henry Wickham smuggled out enough to found the rubber plantations of Malaya and Indonesia, which soon took the business away from the Amazon jungle trees. Manaus lost its glitter and half its population, and the jungles, unaffected by the fact that thousands of lives of volunteers, serfs and slaves had been sacrificed to tap the trees, closed over the scars.

Another jungle tree proved useful in solving the problem of transporting rubber out of the jungle. The steam vessels that brought in fresh workers by the hundred and brought out the rubber burned wood; none could carry the coal needed for such a voyage. Passengers in a hurry complained because they had to stop every day or two while the crew went ashore to chop wood. The favorite tree, which grows almost exclusively in the Amazon region, was an elegant one, frequently a hundred feet tall with foliage in the shape of a slender inverted cone and an oddly peeling bark of a warm brown color from which it takes its name, "mulatto tree." Its value for the shipmaster was that it burned well while still green. Spruce was the first man to look at it as anything except fuel, so officially it is called *Enkylista spruceana*. It and *Hevea brasiliensis* survived the boom and the age of steam.

For the average northerner the most glamorous of all tropical trees are the palms. They are synonymous with warmth, sun, a gentle, salubrious climate. Also they are the most distinctive; they seem somehow unreal in their orderliness. Few other woody things grow with any semblance of regularity or consistency of pattern. Palms have the basic geometric precision of crystals, reduplicating themselves exactly by the thousands and with a grace and beauty not seen in any other vegetation. The trunks of most of them are as straight as flagpoles, their leaves arranged in neat coronas in unvarying style, their flowers and fruits often fabulous.

Palms form quite a noticeable part of many jungles, even the major part of some. They behave like other trees in forming a solid canopy, subcanopies and subservient layers where they may flourish in deep shade. There are thousands of varieties of palms, but to most people they are either the lowly palmettos or the stately royal palms planted around our more expensive southern habitations or the coconut palms.

The coconut palm is very specialized, not only tolerating but actually liking salinity. Thus it grows best near the seashore. Its origin is unknown but it is now found almost all over the tropical and much of the subtropical latitudes, girdling every island, bordering every shore with a sandy coast. Its large, useful nuts have provided both food and drink, its leaves excellent thatching, its trunks valuable timber. Whether its exceptionally wide distribution is due to the fact that these nuts float and withstand immersion in salt water almost indefinitely, or whether men took it from place to place for their own purposes, is not known.

Many other palms also have utility for men. They are the staples of the people who live among them, but they also furnish many specialized products for our modern industries. Much of our soap comes from the oil palm of West Africa; waxes come from the carnauba palm.

Of course, not all palms are jungle plants by any means; in fact, most of them are not. But they play a rather large part in jungle economy, especially in the montane jungles. Many of these are almost pure stands of palms, and some of them produce the most delectable of all salads, called in many parts of the American tropics palm salad. This comes from the growing point of the plant that is sunk into the head of the leaf bases at the top of the tree. Like the growing point of giant bamboos, it is tender and succulent.

The eating of the salad may be the destruction of the forest. A feature of most palms is that they have no reserves for growth, only the solitary bud, and an injury to that kills the shoot. This characteristic led a more than usually eloquent botanist to write: "Like a foolhardy gambler, the palm stakes all on a single card."

I have found it a common belief that jungles are composed largely of coconut palms and bananas (of which alone there are more than eight hundred known edible kinds), but actually neither of these does or can live in a real jungle. Edible bananas are apparently as "man-made" as Indian corn. However, the banana's distant cousins—the Wahas, Sterelitzias and such—are indigenous to the borders of jungle creeks, rivers and other open places in South America.

One of the hardiest of all jungle trees, is a wing-leafed palm called the cohune. It inhabits various forests in Central and South America, and has one of the hardest woods known. If you are whacking about with a machete and the blade leaps out of your hands with a ringing "whang," as if you had tried to chop at a steel girder, you have hit a cohune palm. If it is a full-grown specimen, you would not have spotted it as a palm because its trunk resembles those of the other hardwood jungle trees, more or less smooth and unringed. Only when you look up at its immense head, spreading fronds to titanic proportions, would you recognize it as a palm.

The cohune has an interesting life story. The nut has a shell hard as stone which makes a charcoal of greater purity than even coconut hulls. The meat contains a valuable oil. The palm sprouts as a one-leafed plant of small distinction, but soon, because it tolerates shade well at this stage, it grows into a sizable tree about as big as an average fruit tree in a temperate orchard, with beautiful fronds sprouting from a little above the ground in a fleur-de-lys pattern. You might think this is the fulfillment of its maturity, but not at all. It grows taller and taller, under favorable circumstances, until at last it pierces the jungle canopy and becomes one of the pillars of the forest itself. The lower fronds disappear, leaving the trunk quite bare for forty or fifty feet or more, and only then, when its crown is exposed to the sun, can it flower and fructify.

Cohunes are part of many jungles and almost all of some. I saw one forest in Central America composed almost exclusively of these palms and tall, basket-trunked fig trees, odd and beautiful and quiet —and full of savagely biting insects, too. This, however, does not

Surinam Tourist Bureau

Wahas, distant cousin of the banana.

seem a natural climax for the forest. Apparently it was once an area of Indian cultivation during the height of the Mayan civilization. While the Mayas used the cohune nuts, they found the trunks impervious to a stone axe no matter how stoutly wielded. So the cohunes, it is thought, remained and thrived because it simply was impossible to eradicate them, and they took over almost the whole area.

Even when they die, they never seem to fall. In other jungles you see prostrate giants, often a great many of them. But even dead cohune palms stand there stubbornly. They simply stop producing fronds, and the old ones drop quietly to the ground. For years an erect shaft with a rounded point will remain projecting up into the higher foliage of the jungle, eventually crumbling away.

In the Central American jungle I mentioned, we had a practical demonstration of the cohune's vitality. In making our camp, we cut down a young one level with the ground, and it happened that our bed was placed right over it. After a few days, we were sleeping badly and grumbling about a lumpy couch. We found that the palm was sending up a sturdy cylinder right out of the center of the stump, which had grown fourteen inches and was at that point pushing right into the middle of our mattress.

Other jungle giants are the big brothers of some of our common house and small garden plants. Several relatives of the podocarpus (one appropriately named *elongata*) grow as tall as ninety feet or more in the tropics, with massive limbs and trunks to match. The periwinkle family, suitable in our climate for ground cover and ornamental window boxes, is represented in some South American jungles by a giant tree called the milkwood because of its fluid. Several varieties produce "milk" in abundance. The liquid from some is a refreshing, even medicinal drink; that from others is poison. The plant is big enough and tough enough that in a few hilly districts it has been found to dominate the whole jungle.

Violets do not attain quite this majesty in the rain forest, but their relatives are known to grow as trees in the twenty- to fifty-foot class. Daisies flower upon a woody stem of equal dimensions. And there is hardly any species of tree at all that cannot in one of the world's jungles or another attain the full size and bulk of its mightiest peers.

12
The Weavers

VINES (lianas) have been mentioned as the aerial highways facilitating entry to the upper stories of the jungle—and escape from them, too. Moviegoers are familiar with them as the apparatus for the more improbable acrobatics of Tarzan. But their role in the tropical rain forest is much more important than that. They are essential to its very existence. Jungles are not made of trees alone; the darned things are literally darned, for holes in the blanket we have described are mended by these strands; the flying continents are woven by them into an entity that trees standing alone could not achieve.

This vegetation, a mass of living and breathing stuff, lives on the trees. It binds their heads together so intricately and inextricably that you may have to cut a dozen thick boles through above the roots before any will fall. I have personally spent a day climbing along one side of the patch, hacking at tentacles for hours before the warp and woof of the great blanket weakened enough for the enormous expanse of head foliage to begin leaning over. Even then nothing fell; so tightly woven was the upper canopy, it just sagged like a bowl of jelly.

The effect seems to be largely responsible for the impression that jungles are, as some writers described them, "green hell." Yet it is the same effect which on closer acquaintance with the massive roof of foliage makes a man feel at home. One of the most dramatic chronicles of this change of attitude, from "green hell" to "green refuge," is the exciting record of Lieut. Col. F. Spencer Chapman's three years in the Malayan rain forests during World War II, *The Jungle Is Neutral.*

Left behind to join local guerillas when the Japanese over-ran the peninsula in the first months of the war in the East, Chapman had to learn about jungles the hard way. The inscrutable workings of the official army mind had selected him because he was a great outdoors man, a naturalist and a mountaineer. However, all of his experience had been in the Arctic or the Himalayas! His harassment of the Japanese, his hair-raising captures and escapes, his defeat of pestilence and wounds as well as of the enemy dims the most lurid fiction. Through it all, his opinion of the jungle underwent a marvellous metamorphosis.

Chapman's first impression was one of gloom. He hardly ever saw the sky. He complained that very little sunshine filtered through while the monotony of dark green was most depressing. Where, he wondered, were all the gay vivid, variegated colors which he had supposed featured tropical vegetation? Only later did he discover that they were out of sight in the canopy. And then, while practicing "jungle navigation," as he put it—indeed, it is hard to maintain a straight course when you cannot see the sun by day or the stars by night—he got lost and had to spend the night alone.

"At first," he confessed, "I would be overcome by panic. I seemed to be an intruder in a hostile and predatory world. The unaccountable snapping of a twig and the stealthy rustling of leaves would prey upon my nerves until I was so certain I was being followed by a tiger that a cold sweat would break out all over my body and the small hairs on the back of my neck would creep with fear, and I found myself going faster and faster until I was running."

Gradually he became accustomed to it, and then learned that the jungle, if not exactly friendly, was neutral, as the title of his book says. The saplings provided poles for huts; palm fronds, some of them twenty or thirty feet long, made the thatching; rattan bound the whole together securely. The Japanese, furthermore, did not penetrate the jungle, and indeed no one else did except the guerillas and the forest's own native dwellers, an independent people called *Sakai*. One reason, aside from the nameless terrors, was that strangers would not be able to find their way out perhaps.

Chapman's jungle travel problems become clearer when he tells of a move from one retreat to another thirty miles away. An old survey trail provided a good route most of the way, but they had to make a path of their own three miles long to get to it. The two best jungle men in camp, with Chapman holding a compass to keep them straight, needed three days to cut a track a yard wide.

The importance of the vines is brought home in his account of an adventure with elephants. One day hunting pig for dinner, he heard an elephant trumpeting not far off and managed to get very close to a whole herd of them in a jungle where, he reports, the visibility was only ten yards. The big beasts got his scent before he saw them clearly, "for after a single loud bellow, which set every leaf—and certainly myself—trembling, the whole herd began to move, and the moment I saw the undergrowth and creepers swaying I turned and ran for my life. In this part of the jungle there seemed to be only small trees, which the elephant could have trodden down without noticing them, or huge trunks which were impossible to climb; but at last I found a tree festooned with creepers and managed to run up it like a monkey. I hung there with my rifle slung over one shoulder as the herd crashed past below me, and I just caught a glimpse of a huge gray back on either side of my tree. At the time I was convinced that the elephant were hunting me, but later I discovered that I had approached from the direction of the track by which they had entered the thicket and having caught my scent, they were probably only running back by the way they had come."

By this time, Chapman had learned to make use of the peculiar vegetational features of the jungle, including the vines. The plants which bind these forests together so effectively are those known as lianas, the name given to all the innumerable species of climbers that have woody stems, as against the creepers with soft, herbaceous stems, which are not nearly so tough. Both kinds are known in our own woods, but the jungle has four or five times as many of them, and they are even larger and more fantastic than that statistic would imply.

There are four basic types of these plants, classified by the way they fasten themselves to the supports that will enable them to get off the ground—by definition these are plants that cannot stand erect on their own stems. Most of them are rooted in the ground or in the hanging gardens that thrive in accumulations of debris high up in the trees. But some simply absorb nourishment from the water running down the trunk of the tree or dangle large, fleshy roots into the air to take in moisture from the atmosphere.

First there are the scramblers. As this name implies, they simply grow out and around, looping over other plants or branches, lying across them and getting entangled in them but never clinging closely. In our gardens, rambler roses are examples of this kind. They account for more than their share of the larger and longer jungle lianas, and a smaller percentage of creepers.

Twiners, the second group, wind themselves around their host in the manner of wisteria or pole beans or the common choke vine. Such plants have a tender tip which has the ability to revolve—always in the same direction—until it has circled whatever support it can find, usually not too big around. They start their careers climbing up saplings or other vines because they can seldom embrace a full-grown tree.

Root-climbers cling to their support, which can be a cliff as well as a tree, by means of specialized aerial roots which usually are developed solely for this purpose and have nothing or very little to do with channeling nourishment to the plant. Our English ivy and Virginia creeper are familiar examples. In jungles these are mostly found among the smaller, herbaceous vines growing in the shade of the forest's lower stories. A big, woody, root-climbing vine the size of one of our really old English ivies is comparatively rare in the tall equatorial forest.

Finally the jungles are the home of a large number of vines that put out tendrils to hold them up, as do grapes and peas. Some botanists have regarded this as the most specialized of the four climbing mechanisms.

Some climbing plants are like the cautious man who wears both a belt and suspenders. They employ two methods of support. There is a jungle milkweed that twines but also develops clinging roots at its nodes, and between the two can grow to a length of several hundred feet, all off the ground. One of the climbers of the palm family,

Rapho Guillumette

Suspension bridge of lianas.

the rattan, which used to be one of the major Oriental articles of commerce and is still widely used for wickerwork and baskets as well as Malacca canes, has developed barbed tips on its leaves. These help it cling as it climbs to the top of a jungle canopy, where in many Far Eastern jungles it forms a large part of the foliage.

All sorts of plants which we never see as climbers may go off through the jungle by these methods—ferns and daisies and innumerable types that appear only as small herbs or bushes outside the jungle. The thing may develop a stem a couple of feet in diameter, rough and gnarled and as strong as the stoutest man-made cables. In fact, the internal growth of virtually all lianas of whatever species is very much like the hawsers with which ships are moored. When dissected, they look as if they had been woven in a rope walk.

The engineering feat by which jungle natives bridged chasms several hundred feet wide, though they had no metal tools, amazed the first Europeans who saw these suspension bridges. They were made from long tough lianas securely fastened at either end and floored with sticks. True, they swayed and shook horribly, but they were strong.

Then there are the philodendrons which almost all of us know as house plants, but in the jungle their pithy stems carry the fleshy leaves up the trunks of the biggest trees, and it is not uncommon for them to reach a length of several hundred feet. Infinite other forms of vines, looking more like the ones with which we are familiar, abound; many of these types are called succinctly in West Africa "tie-tie" because they are used as we use string—and are much stronger.

You seldom see the leaves of the big lianas because most of them are in the canopy. The bare, rough, elongated stems swoop down to be festooned around the trees, or dangle straight to earth, usually around or near tree trunks. But sometimes the very large ones hang in midair nowhere near a trunk. They grew on trees that have died, fallen or simply rotted completely away, but the vine remains because it has wound its upper stem securely around the higher branches of surviving trees.

Travelers on jungle rivers have cursed the lianas because they have a fiendish way of swooping down at you as you pass, delivering a nasty welt or scratch across the face or looping under your chin. On the other hand, they can be useful. In his journal, Spruce speaks of making his way in what apparently was a heavily laden boat with a roofed cabin across a flooded jungle between two tributaries of the Amazon. The water was deep enough to float the vessel, but the oars were useless because they hit a submerged obstruction at every stroke. Lianas hung down in such profusion that the crew simply grabbed handy ones and pulled the boat through the jungle.

One of the methods by which some lianas reach the sun is to fasten a good grip on a small tree and wait for it to grow up to pierce the jungle canopy, for if it can get there at all it can carry a vine with it.

Some lianas are very strange indeed. We have mentioned the ones from which the thirsty wanderer in the jungle can extract a tumbler of clear water—or equally clear poison. Others exude sticky or gummy or milky substances. I have seen one from which a fluid

Nancy Flowers from Nancy Palmer Agency

Clear water pouring from newly cut liana.

exactly resembling blood flowed when it was cut. Some of these saps are powerful medicaments.

My most vivid recollection of this last type dates from an expedition to one of the jungles of northern South America some years ago. I had been bitten on the finger by a certain small scorpion whose sting can be fatal, although it is rare for an otherwise healthy man to die from the effects. However, this time the pain was intense, and within a few minutes my hand was hard, numb and dead white. The lower arm felt as if I'd slept on it, and when I opened my finger with a scalpel where the scorpion had struck—I hoped to start drainage—no blood would flow out even when I squeezed hard. Within half an hour of the sting, the glands in my armpit were extremely tender and painful, and my mouth kept filling with saliva—the condition so graphically described as "foaming at the mouth." A most alarming situation, I hardly need say.

Fortunately a member of that particular collecting party was a Trinidadian named Vernon Dixon Capriata, the best American hunter I ever met and a man whose knowledge of his native jungles was unsurpassed. He gave me a couple of small sections of a thin creeper to chew, strongly astringent and tasting like nothing else on earth. The reaction was astounding. The pain subsided rapidly and within an hour was virtually gone. The numbness lasted longer, but the cut on my finger, which Capriata enlarged somewhat, seemed to me to heal with unusual speed. Since my heart was sound, it is probable that I would have recovered from the scorpion bite in time, but the medicinal qualities of the vine certainly hastened the process.

I think the most astonishing of all jungle lianas are the ribbon vines. Their stems, in form, are just like a vast ribbon. I have seen one more than two feet wide and only about three-quarters of an inch thick. They seem to be quite the longest growing things in the rain forest. When the Forestry Department of Surinam (Dutch Guiana) was clearing a small section of virgin jungle and doing a detailed plant-by-plant survey of it, they came across one of these vines. They tried to get it out whole, which would have enabled them for the first time to find out what the plant was like in its entirety, flowers and fruit and all. They followed one strand of it for hundreds of yards before giving up. They still had not come to the growing tip.

In sheer mass and weight of wood, therefore, some of these lianas may surpass any of the jungle trees by as much as the trees surpass the great white spruce that was 417 feet tall. Furthermore, they twist and tangle into all sorts of fantastic designs. They are sometimes protected with spines or thorns.

Among the odder forms are the climbing palms, of which there are many varieties. In some places, especially in the Oriental jungles, if you look at the great green blanket of the flying continent from above, it would seem to be composed almost exclusively of palm trees. But when you descend to the floor of that particular jungle, you may see no palm boles at all. The fronds of the canopy are the crowns of the climbing varieties.

Rattans are the most interesting of these plants, at least to civilized men, because of their commercial uses. Besides their value for making wicker furniture and walking sticks, rattans—or the fruits of some of them—exude a quite useful red resin which is known in the romantic language of Oriental trade as "dragon's blood." The ancients thought that dragon's blood had certain curative powers, and even in modern times it has been prescribed for supposed and perhaps real medicinal values. But mostly it was used for its color, in paints and varnishes, until recent years, when synthetics virtually drove dragon's blood off the world market.

Some small creepers make sure of their water supply by attaching themselves to the biggest trees, although they may never reach for the sun. During the heavy tropical rains, the giants and notably the emergents act as conduits; water runs down them in veritable cascades. Usually it pours down only one side of the bole because of some irregularity in the head of the tree; then all the climbing plants that absorb some of it as it goes by will gather on that side.

Once they reach the jungle canopy, all lianas lose their climbing mechanism. Supposedly the intense light is responsible for the change. The shade-loving shoots climb but they have little foliage. The sun-loving shoots are inspired and energized by the sun to bear leaves and fruit, but they have no more need for climbing equipment and so they discard it.

Because lianas are an integral part of the living jungle, man's attempts to eradicate them have been markedly unsuccessful. The

Fritz Henle from Monkmeyer

Lianas twist and tangle into fantastic designs.

only places where it has been tried are those hardwood forests where in the interest of better lumber the stems of lianas are severed as a routine measure of forest improvement. That makes a lot more work than the cutters bargained for, because the lianas have contributed so much of the canopy that their death lets in considerable sunlight. Immediately the growth of new climbers is enormously stimulated, and unless men keep hacking them down, they will smother the tree seedlings and saplings for whose benefit the "weeds," as a forester often regards lianas, were killed in the first place. Long before the trees achieve respectable size, the climbers take over their original place in the jungle.

13

Aerial Performers

THOUSANDS and thousands of plant species can neither survive in the shade nor fight or climb from the ground to the top of a rain forest, but they flourish in the jungle anyway. They have found ways to start their lives high up where there is plenty of light, and they simply don't bother about anything on or in the ground. Theirs is a life that relatively few plants can manage outside of the wet tropics because they need a regular year-round supply of rain and a warm humid atmosphere in which there can be relatively little evaporation. Only in the tropical rain forest do both these conditions prevail. But unless you succeed in getting quite high up in it, you will never know this vegetation is there. From the ground it is either invisible or indistinguishable from the trees and vines on which it is supported.

A sparse sampling of this vegetation can be seen in the face the jungle shows those who sail its rivers. The early explorers of these regions were usually interested solely in trade or conquest and hardly noticed. Not until botanists began to sort out tropical plant life systematically did the upper layers of the rain forest get any attention.

Spruce was the first in his field to discover these layers, and he owed a good deal of his discovery to his native boatmen. They thought him a very odd white man indeed because he was more excited by a new flower than by discoveries of gold or precious jewels. But they humored him, especially when they were paddling him upstream.

The normal difficulties of travel were bad enough, but rowing against the current was especially arduous. Spruce had his men build a cabin of poles thatched with broad jungle leaves and palm fronds where he could retire during the heat of the day while they paddled. He tells us that it was his custom to work on his papers during those

Donna N. Sprunt from National Audubon Socie

Pineapple airplant.

hours, although most men in these parts dozed. It surprised him how often his labors were interrupted by a shout from one of the paddlers:

"Patron! Here's a pretty flower."

He never could resist coming out to look, and very often it was one that was new to him; he would have to have it for his collection. Also it would be fairly high up in the jungle wall, and the whole party would rest on the shore while he and one or two helpers hacked at the supports until they brought it down. It took Spruce quite a long time to realize that he was called out to look at flowers only when it was particularly hot work at the paddles. On relatively cool days no one bothered him. Later on, when he felled a number of jungle trees, he saw that he had brought down a much greater variety of upper level plants than he had ever seen from the river or the ground.

Three main types of plant life are represented in this aerial community. First and most numerous are those called epiphytes, plants that grow upon other plants without drawing sustenance from their hosts. The name is derived from the Greek *epi* or "upon" and *phyton* or "plant." The second group are the parasites, which not only find growing room on another plant but tap that plant for some or all of their nourishment. Third are the saprophytes, plants that live on the dead. A few specimens are able to maintain themselves by using more than one of these methods at once, or separately. Mistletoe, for example, which grows profusely in many jungles, is a parasite on some trees, but if conditions are suitable, it will grow as an epiphyte. Some even have both epiphytic and parasitic roots.

If you drive down to Mexico you will see small examples of these aerial plants growing on telephone lines in the towns and way out in the desert like little fuzzes. In the jungle, they come in every imaginable shape and size, from minute stars to immense things shaped like pineapple plants with twelve-foot leaves and positively dripping with crazy-looking inflorescences. These include not only a great many orchids but all sorts of incredibly lovely blossoms, many unique to the rain forest.

The three ideal conditions for nurturing epiphytes are, first, a nice bed of aerial soil high up in or near the jungle canopy, then some arrangement for keeping that bed reasonably moist even when it is not open to the rain and, finally, the high humidity which normally prevails under the huge green blanket. The soil up there, a sort of pudding made of semidecayed wood, moldy leaves, dead insects, bits of fruit or flowers and all sorts of other particulate material, is a mixture so rich that even the most delicate orchids will grow in it. Forks and holes and crannies in the trees can fill up with this stuff, and the climbers help hold it in the natural basket woven by their stems.

In the American jungles, the epiphytes of the family to which pineapples belong (the bromeliads) are particularly common. The best known of them is Spanish moss, whose gray stems drip down in picturesque profusion from trees as far from the tropics as our own South; it used to be a favorite substitute for horsehair in upholstered furniture. Any member of its family may become so numerous it seems to take over the whole tree.

Other epiphytes are equally prolific. It is a matter of record that a single tree in a Sumatra jungle supported fifty different kinds of epiphytic ferns, all growing on its upper branches at least a hundred feet above the ground. Some accounts of the Malayan jungles describe the biggest trees as being so loaded with luxuriant plants of various kinds that their own head foliage is completely hidden.

One of the features of this aerial plant life is that it provides a home for a good many of the more important animals, even though man considers some of them undesirable. The nice moist pudding is a fine nesting place for arboreal ants and other creatures who play an essential role in the life of the whole jungle. Many epiphytes have big rosettes of leaves overlapping each other in such a way that they may hold an incredible amount of water; botanists sometimes call them "aerial water tanks" and "aerial marshes." The plants can grow upside-down and still hold water; some of their tanks are so big that a single plant may have the capacity to store more than a gallon.

These tanks or "marshes" are the breeding places of many species of frogs, mosquitoes and other insects of various kinds. A single small patch of one type of these plants may house an almost infinite variety of tiny animals. Once I brought back to camp a number of leaves of one epiphyte that is inhabited by a particular kind of long-legged, speedy wood louse I was seeking. We tore up the leaves in the middle

John H. Gerard from National Audubon Society

Spanish moss.

of a big white sheet so that we could spot the little beasts before they could get away.

We collected not only a satisfactory number of wood lice but a whole menagerie of other animals. The list included a number of small, fat, black scorpions, several dark brown flatworms with golden stripes on their backs, a pink leech, four different spiders and three types of earthworms, each of a different color. In addition, a number of other little creatures came out of the leaves, including ants—for which we had no use at the moment—and innumerable other insects.

Like so many other jungle arrangements, what at first seems an exploitation of the plants by the animals infesting them turns out to be a mutual aid society. The ants and others collect and bring home a lot of debris, and since "home" is among the roots and leaves, it is easy for the plant to use this stuff for its own nourishment. Also, the animals themselves die and their bodies enrich the aerial soil, as does their excreta while they are alive. Various scientific studies have indicated that the chemical processes in this soil are virtually the same as those on the ground.

Not all epiphytes need or even like these hanging baskets. Certain ferns of substantial size and some orchids, as well as other big herbs, will grow only on the smooth vertical trunks or the wood of the boughs. Mosses and some vines do the same. The larger plants have ingenious devices for anchoring themselves to a tree, and then develop specialized mechanisms for absorbing water. Like climbers, some of them have roots for holding and roots for feeding. Others use their roots solely as anchors. They grow tiny fibers resembling very fine short hairs on their leaves, and these hairs absorb the moisture the plant needs. Still others are aerial roots, large and fleshy, to collect water from the air.

Perhaps the most remarkable of all are the "Scotch lawyers," an amiable term for various members of the fig family of trees. They start life as epiphytes, living in this way for a long time, and may even have other trees growing on them. In their maturity, however, they are not as companionable as most epiphytes. In fact, they are such bad company that another name for them is "strangler figs."

Hugo Schroder from National Audubon Society

"Scotch lawyer."

Their life history is one of the few which fulfill the ruthlessness that fiction writers have brainwashed us into thinking of as jungle law.

Birds, small mammals and many other creatures love the fruits of fig trees, and either pick them up off the ground or snatch them as they ripen on the bough. The tiny seeds—they are characteristic of all the many varieties of figs—may be dropped as the animal munches. Or he may swallow them whole so that they pass through his digestive tract unharmed. A few of them may fall into some cranny up a tree. If a bit of soil has accumulated the fig may sprout and root itself and thrive.

Instead of halting its growth at the size of a small tree or bush, as many epiphytes do, these figs send out more roots in search of water and food. In time these envelop the supporting tree like ivy, whereupon the fig will take over like a bore in a boarding house or, as was realized long ago by British scientists, like the proverbial Scottish lawyer. This astute character had the reputation of attaching himself to you and growing rich at your expense without your feeling any pain. Eventually he strangled your business, politely paid for your funeral and ended up with his own flourishing and expanding law practice.

That is just about what the strangler fig does. He does not take anything that the supporting tree would notice or miss for a long time. He just sits on it, his long roots drinking in water that runs down the trunk along with any nourishment that may be carried in the water, while his branches reach upward to the sunlight. After a time the fig grows so big and heavy that the cylindrical cage formed by his roots begins to constrict the host's trunk. Then the fig's roots reach the ground, enter it and soon are competing actively with the supporting tree for the nutrients in the soil. Finally the tree wilts and dies because the fig has taken over completely. It may stand for years, maybe centuries, held up in the sturdy wooden basket of the fig, rotting slowly and thereby returning the rich chemicals that went into its own growth to the ground, from which the fig can now fatten complacently.

There are several astonishing plants—some ferns, a milkweed in Malaya, another epiphyte known as *Dischidia rafflesiana*—which collect and manufacture their own soil high up in the forest and seem to live in it by almost turning themselves inside-out and upside-down. Some of them produce an invitingly bowl-shaped leaf in which rain and humus are held and insects nest. Others fasten their leaves like wide brackets to the trunk or limbs of a tree for the same purpose. Then when the soil has built up in the container the plant has provided, its own roots grow around and into it.

Most of the famous jungle beauties are epiphytes. Of the 15,000 or more known kinds of orchids, the majority grow on trees; comparatively few are rooted in the ground. That is why you won't see most of them if you simply travel through the jungle by the usual river route. Orchids generally care for little sun and lots of moisture, especially in the air they breathe. They grow best, therefore, in or just under one of the jungle canopies.

They also arouse the most extraordinary rapture among connoisseurs and fanciers. It was always our custom to keep a pot of fresh flowers on our camp table in the tropics, and one day I brought back a beautiful blood-red cluster that looked like a sort of multiple tulip. I had found it growing on a tree fifty feet or so above the ground, which I climbed every morning before breakfast because I had a trap set there. The blossoms were so beautiful that my wife clipped one and pressed it in a book. Ten years later one of the world's leading orchid collectors opened that book in New York and let out a howl worth (as he put it) $5,000. That was the price he offered me for a single bulb of this plant. We had had its flowers on our table every day in that particular jungle!

On the occasion when we lived for a time in the treetops, we were surrounded by what seemed an infinity of exquisite beauty. Some orchids open only in the morning mist, others in the hot daytime sun, and still others in the evening. Some of them have flowers of the weirdest shapes, either of a curiously mechanical design or resembling animals more than plants. But there they all are, planted in a sort of natural basket by the Almighty for no one but the monkeys and kites and little jewel-eyed tree frogs.

Rich as they are in most vegetation, the jungles are relatively poor in saprophytes, the plants that live on dead matter. Even so, plenty of them can be found—fungi, ferns, mosses and even some of the handsomest orchids. (There are apparently some chlorophyll-producing plants that are saprophytes and can live only on decaying vegetable matter.) The northern woods are the great places for fungi, but the jungles have their own. There is one in the Orient that looks for all the world like deer's antlers, and is just about as tough. Other fungi weigh a ton and upheave large trees. Then there may be cascades of yellow or gold or orange or flaming tango all down one side of every tree for miles—a fungus that happens to like one wind only.

The feature that sets *true* saprophytes apart from other plants is their inability to achieve photosynthesis, the process by which light is used to manufacture carbohydrates out of water and carbon dioxide. They get their nourishment from dead stuff which already has these substances and can thrive in deep shade if they have ample and continuous moisture. It is said that in tropical rain forests which have a pronounced dry season, virtually no saprophytes are found, certainly none of the very large ones.

Jungle parasites, except for bacteria and other minute organisms, have a startling capacity to imitate their hosts. The aerial parasites especially have a tendency to grow on twigs and branches in the first-story canopy or higher, and take the form of small climbers. But they produce leaves so similar to those of their host that very careful observation is required to spot them. Often these species are identified only when they are flowering, so closely do they resemble the leaves of the tree. But when they do bloom, the colors are often spectacular, especially, for some reason, in the Malayan jungles.

No matter how they nourish themselves, the aerial plants make up the real jungle flower gardens. The trees and lianas are occasionally magnificent, but have only a brief flowering, frequently well out of sight. All this accounts for what so many travelers have commented upon as the somber appearance of the jungle. Everything, they say, is green and gloomy above and brown and bare below. But out of sight in the great hanging baskets is a perpetual riot of color, the profusion of flowers which we like to associate with a tropical rain forest but seldom encounter until we reach up to the aerial gardens.

14

The Destroyers

AMIABLE, tolerant, even benevolent—these are words that seem to apply generally to plant life in the jungle. Keen as the competition among species and even individuals may be, the forest as a whole is a much more hospitable place than men who never dwelt in it have usually supposed. Like beauty, savagery often lies in the eyes of the beholder. Men expected the jungle to be ferocious, menacing, highly dangerous, when they were entirely ignorant of what it contained. So they saw it that way when they looked, and very, very few of them ever got sufficiently familar with it to know how distorted a picture they had painted.

Distorted, but not completely false. What they feared does apply in a specialized way to one aspect of the jungle, because in these forests plants grow that are the active enemies of the animal kingdom. They are armed for attack as well as defense; some of them can be amazingly aggressive, and others just as sneaky. Their victims are insects and very small creatures; in fact, one of the technical descriptive names for them is "insectivorous." Apparently they started on this course of life when some of them, in the never-ending quest for water, developed either their flowers or special leaves into pitcher-shaped devices which they flung casually overboard to dangle in the air and catch rain for future use. If they could catch rain, why not food?

An insect catcher, known also in temperate climates, is the sundew, a low-growing plant with rosettes of innocent-looking fleshy leaves. The leaves are covered with fine but tough hairs coated with a sweet, sticky stuff. Insects coming to eat it are entangled and held in the hairs, which then excrete still another fluid powerful enough to dissolve the insect's tissues; these are absorbed as food by the leaves. Such plants get their name from the dewy appearance of

Hugh Spencer from National Audubon Socie

Round-leaved sundew.

their leaves; the fatal honeylike fluid sparkles on them as brightly as droplets of clear water.

A genus, which originated in the Oriental jungles, has received the unusually poetic scientific name of *Nepenthes* from the legendary Greek potion that was supposed to induce complete forgetfulness and banish pain—the Greek word actually means "free from sorrow." More prosaically, they are called pitcher plants because on some of their leaves they produce an appendage shaped like a pitcher or, in a few, a child's sock hung up at Christmas for the attention of Santa Claus. This handy receptacle is sometimes big enough to hold a pint of water. Glands inside the pitcher secrete a highly odorous fluid, sweet-smelling or foul, which attracts the plant's prey. This is the potion that gives them their technical name. Insects drawn by the smell fall into the liquid at the bottom of the pitcher—a sure end to their pain because the inner sides of the pitcher are too smooth, slippery and steep for them to climb out. The juices of their little bodies are then absorbed by the plant as food.

Nepenthes in a vinelike form grow as long as sixty feet in the jungle. The pitchers are often very striking—striped in almost all the primary colors or marked with bold blotches of red, green and purple. They are often so lovely that they have been brought out of the jungle to adorn greenhouses and conservatories, although here they confine themselves to a temperate size. Their flowers are small and nothing much to look at, being tiny yellowish or reddish green spikes.

These "clever" plants—there are several other genera of insect-eaters—have gone much further than the fairly simple process which gave the *Nepenthes* their name. Some have developed hairs or spines that all point inward and downward into the pitcher to make sure that any little beasts that have ventured or fallen in cannot get out. They are much like the so-called sidesaddle flowers of the United States, properly known as *Sarracenia,* which attract insects in the first place by the vivid contrasting colors of their pitchers, then lure them into a trumpet-shaped receptacle by means of a few drops of a honeylike fluid. Downward-pointing hairs prevent the victim from escaping.

Still other plants have developed neat lids which they can snap shut on their victims. Apparently the touch or even the smell of the trapped animal is enough to trigger the mechanism. One pitcher plant in the jungles of Sumatra is so active and aggressive that its movements can be detected by the naked human eye. It is a mimosa —using the word in its botanical sense to mean a group of plants that belong to the pea family and not the lovely tree that Australians call wattle.

In the tropics these true mimosas are also known as "the sensitive plant." The one of which I am speaking suddenly folds its leaves and demurely bows its head on being touched by any warm-blooded thing. It will not budge when touched by itself, another plant or, in one case, even by any cold-blooded animal. Just how it discriminates so unerringly remains a mystery. This is also true of a great many other sensitive plants that do not operate with the speed of these mimosas. There may be a clue in the fact that under the influence of chloroform, the mimosa loses the power to fold its leaves no matter what the stimulus, which suggests that it is not too unlike an animal in its reactions.

To me the ultimate in this form of plant life is a pitcher plant from the jungles of southern India which has been known to catch and digest mice. If this seems incredible, let me add that a sober account of just such a performance in a hothouse of the famous English botanical gardens at Kew has been published. I myself once had a pitcher plant from the jungles of Southeast Asia which caught a live cockroach on a television show on which I and it were appearing. Unseen by me, the plant snared the cockroach all by its little self, and an alert cameraman who spotted it put the exhibition on the air for the edification of millions.

The mimosas and *Nepenthes* and other trap plants do not have to be fed bugs when grown in greenhouses. They can do quite well with the nourishment their roots collect from a rich compost if they also are kept moist and warm. Even in the wilds, the meat course is only a supplement to their diet, not the whole meal.

All carnivorous plants digest their food very much as we do. They produce enzymes which decompose the bodies of trapped animals and convert the resulting juices into a form suitable for that plant's absorption mechanism.

Whatever terrors this vegetation may have for the insect world, it is no threat to anything much larger, certainly not to man. We are more likely to suffer from the defensive rather than the offensive weapons of the jungle, and they cannot always be avoided even by the most knowledgeable.

Of course, you can refrain from eating any fruit or nut or vegetable that you do not know to be safe. You can drink the plant liquid that you are sure is potable, no matter how inviting another may be when you are thirsty.

On the edge of jungles, moreover, you had better watch your step to avoid the fiendish plants that sometimes seem to have an almost human capacity for malicious mischief, tripping you or whipping across your eyes or stabbing you with sharp needles and cutting you

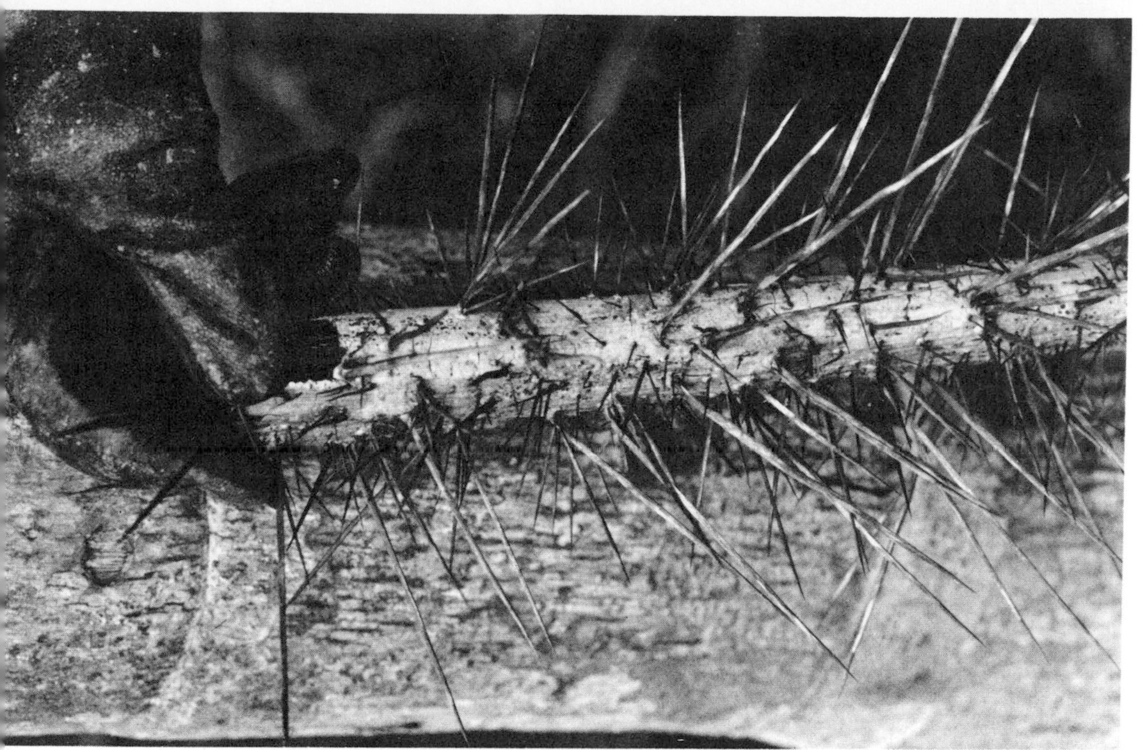

Nancy Flowers from Nancy Palmer Agency

Spiny tree branch, Amazon region.

with razors or burning and blistering you with a harsh corrosive fluid. On the edge of the jungle many vines and climbing grasses are equipped with spines or spikes longer, harder and more ingeniously designed to hurt you than the thorniest rose of our gardens. They may not be readily visible at first glance either.

Palms are especially prolific in the thrusting and cutting weapons, and as free with them as a Dumas hero. The cocorite, as it is called in some American jungles where I have had my own sad experiences of it, grows in clumps and it is not always possible to escape contact with one during hunting and collecting missions. The trunks are covered with a dense growth of needle-fine, needle-sharp, needle-hard black spikes as long as six inches. They are so barbed that they are even more painful in the extraction than in the invasion.

Lianas also may grow thorns, so that the climber in the jungle must beware just which ones he will slide down. I have encountered another reedlike plant which has a smooth stem that positively invites a handhold to help you on your way where the going is a little rough. But if you grasp it, you will find it has two sharp cutting edges on the inside which go through skin as easily as a knife through soft butter, and those edges are smeared with some chemical of its own making which will prevent your blood from clotting.

But the plant I like least of any I have encountered in the jungle is the wild tania. It is widespread in the areas it inhabits, although you may not notice it particularly until you have stumbled on it—literally stumbled or bumped or otherwise made contact with the thing.

Wild tania looks like an overgrown rhubarb plant tacked onto a palm tree's stem. Its handsome white flowers growing out of the cluster of enormous leaves are solid-looking, phallic in shape, not unlike a thick candle when viewed from three sides. But from the fourth side you can see it is merely a huge white petal curved around a vivid orange center, which it displays like a Buddha in a white wax shrine. The stem or trunk of this plant, which may be eight inches in diameter, has the solid appearance of a palm bole.

All this sounds quite pleasant, but the tania is deceptive. The hard-looking trunk is no tougher than a stalk of celery; a single slash of a machete will cut clean through it, and a blow from foot or arm will bruise it. In instant retaliation, it squirts out a fluid that stings like vitriol. If you get enough on your skin, it will raise red patches that smart and blister painfully.

In the tall tales of the jungle, which travelers exchange, you may hear of giant plants that trap men or other large mammals with as much ease as the *Nepenthes* and others catch an ant. One hears of sinister, diabolically wily lianas which twine themselves around a man like an octopus, and hold him helpless until he dies. A wonderful and frightening prospect. But, in fact, no vines have the requisite sensitivity in their stems, although plenty of them have the strength. It is quite possible to get miserably entangled in the coils of some of them, and they can be obstinate enough without any supernatural or, shall we say, supervegetable powers.

I had such an experience in Trinidad when lowering myself into a jungle ravine by means of several strong-looking vines which dangled down from a big tree on the edge. I had descended only a little way when something gave way above, sending several fair-sized logs shooting by me, followed by a great tangle of liana, which enveloped

American Museum of Natural History

"A Fight with Peccaries, Rio Trombutas, Brazil." Painting by George Catlin.

me as if in a messed-up bale of barbed wire and almost knocked me out. By the time I bumped to the bottom of the ravine, still wrapped in its coils, I had torn my hands on thorns and lost my machete, but it was the thick, resilient stems wound around me that helped break the fall. These lianas are somewhat less supple than a rope of similar thickness, and it is no easy matter to twist them away from you.

As I came down the face of the cliff, I had a glimpse of a herd of startled peccaries, the jungle pig of the Americas, staring up at me in ludicrous astonishment from the floor of the ravine and then dashing off like deer; this particular species have the legs and speed of a miniature race horse.

The incident remains in my memory in every detail because my entanglement was complicated by the fact that all the commotion had roused a pit viper, and while I normally find snakes much less loathsome and repulsive than spiders, I had heard enough about this particular breed to wish to get far away from it as fast as possible. The poison, if not fatal, is reported to paralyze the victim, who is then so helpless that ants may begin to nibble on him without waiting for him to die. While I did not exactly put implicit faith in the local stories, I dodged away from this specimen as well as I could within my cage of vines. He struck again and again, which was a surprise because nothing seemed to prevent him from simply going away and leaving me in my predicament.

Fighting against the enmeshing liana and dodging the viper, I had not noticed at first that the great vine also had imprisoned one of the peccaries. I saw him only as a mere flash going past me as he freed himself after I had made an especially violent lunge that sent me sprawling against some rocks where the rest of the vine fell around my feet. The piglike racer charged straight at the snake because that was the only way out of there. Frightened as he obviously was, he dealt the viper a resounding kick—that is the peccary's way of dealing with such enemies, I learned later. The kick sent the viper flying against the cliff while the peccary went crashing through a thick stand of saplings screaming like a terrified infant.

To my astonishment, the viper came right back toward me. But the peccary's intervention had given me time to get free from the last of the liana. Scrambling onto a pile of rocks at the base of the cliff, I threw good-sized stones at my adversary until a hit crippled him, and then I was able to dispatch him with a dead branch. I took him back as a trophy—we had not yet collected one like him—bloodied and bruised more by my encounter with the liana than by him.

15

The Next Generation

ALTHOUGH jungles are very old, very stable plant communities, maintaining their balance of life through years, centuries, even millennia, scientists are not sure how they do it, because, in actual fact, the scientists have not yet learned very much about the full life cycle of the tropical rain forest. They have been able to propound more questions than answers, and some of the answers are tentative assumptions.

The trouble is that most studies of how one generation succeeds another in the jungle have been made under conditions that do not exactly duplicate those prevailing in an undisturbed forest. Sometimes the observers noticed what happened when men or a storm made a clearing, or when a few particularly desirable hardwood trees were removed. Sometimes there was even a start from scratch, such as occurred on Krakatoa, although seldom as complete as that. But there is little reason to suppose that this is the normal process of regeneration—of old age, death and rebirth—in the absence of catastrophe.

The methods by which plants in the various jungle strata reproduce themselves vary greatly, even among those which make up the same stratum. Some trees and other plants flower and bear seed only once in their lifetime, and may need twelve to fifty years to mature to this point, whereupon some promptly die. Others seem to flower and fruit constantly without regard to season or year. In patches of jungle where the trees have been observed closely over a long enough period to permit proper records, it has been noted that some will bear fruit during as many as nine months of every year. But most of them have a longer resting period. In all of them, the cycle seems to be

Brazilian Government Trade Bur

Brazil nuts.

governed by the plant's own habit, not by what we would commonly think of as seasonal influences such as hot or cold, wet or dry.

There doesn't seem to be much difference in the survival rate between those which bear seed profusely and constantly and those which bear few seeds at long intervals. On the other hand, there are jungles where certain kinds of swamp palms are never found as mature trees but only as seedlings. The reason is that birds carry the seeds all over the forest from the adult trees in swamps. Up to the height of fifteen feet or so, they thrive in the damp shade of the swamps, but they cannot mature without better light.

That the jungle maintains itself unchanged in general appearance and vegetational essentials shows that the various patterns of reproduction are well adapted to the survival of the rain forest community, *as a community*. What happens to the progeny of the individual is less important, seemingly sacrificed altogether to the needs of the whole.

In other vegetational zones, a major force for both pollination of flowers and dispersal of seed is the wind. In jungles this is a small factor, even in the top story where there sometimes is a wind. In the still air under the canopy, of course, reliance on wind would be suicidal. At every level, plants either adapt to the intervention of animals in the reproductive process or rely upon themselves exclusively. This last is the simplest way. The more primitive types wait for the rains to wash the male sperm out of their cradles down to the female counterparts.

A characteristic of nearly all the big trees is a huge, heavy nut which drops readily through the dense foliage to rest on the ground nearby, heavy enough to settle and usually shaped so that it will roll to a flat place where soil and water are likely to be better than on a slope. The nut will contain enough nourishment to give the seedling a good chance to live until it has developed a fairly efficient root system. And sometimes the shell is hard enough to protect it from most hungry animals. If it grows near a stream, it may be floated far off to a resting place where it will even get enough light to attain full maturity.

Other trees rely upon animals not only for pollination but to transport the seed to a favorable growing site. Members of plant families that in other climates depend on the wind to blow their pollen about attract bees or flies or other insects in the jungle. This dependence, of course, helps account for the enormous insect life, which thrives on the number of plants that have a habit of flowering virtually all year round. Birds and small mammals, however, are the principal medium for getting the ripened seed to a spot where it can grow. Either they swallow the seeds whole and later eliminate them without digesting them, or they carry them away and drop a few while munching a quiet meal later. The fare is so rich that in many jungles I have had a serious problem finding anything good enough to use as bait for my traps. The fruit was so plentiful and tempting that even greedy rats disdained everything we could put before them.

The abundance of this natural feast is evident in one of the famous romantic tales of the years before the American and French Revolutions.

The story begins in 1742 when Isabela de Grandmaison, handsome thirteen-year-old daughter of Don Pedro de Grandmaison of the Viceroyalty of Peru, married Jean Godin, a member of what had been the first modern French expedition into American jungles. Seven years later he transferred to French Guiana and made the trip by way of the Amazon, 3,000 miles in four months, to test the feasibility of the route for his wife. For some reason it took him twenty years to arrange for her to follow him, but at last she started off in 1769, accompanied by her two brothers, a nephew aged twelve, three women servants, a Negro slave named Joachim, and three Frenchmen who had attached themselves to the party. A couple of dozen or more Indian paddlers, porters and guides got them down the Andean slopes to a town on the Pastaza River where the whole party was supposed to find canoes waiting for the long Amazon voyage.

They found the town burned and deserted. Survivors of a smallpox epidemic had set fire to the cursed buildings and fled. Mme. Godin's entire company of Indians promptly ran away and presumably got safely home. But she refused to turn back. Four local Indians were discovered in the forest and persuaded by payment of wages in advance to make the trip. The fifteen people and a big supply of provisions started out in a large dugout canoe and a raft. The first night they tied up on shore to avoid dangerous snags which hindered navigation in the dark, and the Indians decamped.

The remaining eleven floated on until one of the Frenchmen, steering the raft while the others slept, fell overboard and disappeared. That same evening the canoe upset just as they were preparing to tie up at the bank. They lost most of their food, and decided they needed a guide who knew the river if they were ever to get through. One hundred miles or so downstream was a mission village, so the slave Joachim and one of the Frenchmen set off in the canoe to get help while the others camped where they were.

They waited a month, the food getting scarcer, although the men hunted and managed to kill some birds. They found a few edible roots and collected some eggs. Apparently fever weakened most of them, and certainly they were plagued by insects until they scratched themselves raw. At last Mme. Godin decided that their only hope was to float down on the raft, snags or no. They barely got into midstream before the raft upset, and they struggled back to the shore minus the last of their food and too weak to seek more.

Within two days Mme. Godin was the only one alive. Later she indicated that only the stench of the corpses beside whom she lay roused her enough to get up and stagger away from the death camp into the jungle. She had hardly left when Joachim arrived with Indian paddlers and supplies; she was near enough to hear him call her name, but as she later realized, she was delirious and simply stumbled on. Already the bodies of her companions were unrecognizable, hardly approachable, and Joachim naturally reported the entire party dead.

Mme. Godin meanwhile was walking through the jungle. Alone and without anything except a machete, she made her way, trying to keep parallel to the river but far enough to avoid the tangle of vegetation along the bank. And she found food. She munched fallen fruits and nuts. She cut the tender tops off some small palm trees. After nine days she saw a fire and managed to reach it; it was the camp of some river Indians, who paddled her down to the mission.

The story of Mme. Godin was a favorite of the European salons of the 1770's. Three features of it were especially relished. How she had tramped through the jungle wearing sandals she made herself from the shoes she cut from her dead brother's feet. How she had indignantly denounced a missionary who cheated her Indian rescuers of the two thin gold chains she gave them, the last of her possessions. And finally how she, this gently nurtured lady, had fed herself for nine days in the jungle.

One of the illusions many people have about jungles is that everything in them grows very fast. A few things do, and some of them are easily seen. But, in fact, much jungle vegetation has a rate of growth that is more normally associated with the proverbial snail's pace.

There is a bamboo that has been known to grow twenty inches in length per day. Other plants have managed ten inches a day for a couple of months. In almost any new gap in the rain forest, the ground will be covered with a thick growth taller than a man within a few weeks, a period in which an equivalent temperate zone clearing

Ivan Sanders

Paca in bamboo-brake.

would develop a faint fuzz at best. Trees of the second- and third-story level may attain their full height of twenty to forty feet or so in a few years.

But all this rush only masks the much more leisurely pace of the vegetation that really dominates the jungle—the great trees and vines, and some of the epiphytes and parasites. One of the slowest growing plants known is an Oriental orchid for which you need a micrometer to measure the annual growth. It is supposed that some of the huge hardwoods required a couple of centuries or more to reach full maturity. One of the things that has not been studied very thoroughly is just how long some of these trees can remain in a sort of suspended animation, apparently without growing at all. Yet it is known that a good many species have such a facility. The seedling grows to a certain point. A sapling with a little tuft of leaves or an umbrella-like foliage, on a long, almost bare pole on a naked stem, then may stand for years. It waits for some favorable development, such as a break in the canopy; or it may just be conserving its strength for a renewed struggle among the roots of its neighbors for food in the ground and among the leaves for access to more light.

The flowering of jungle plants has some eccentricities not found elsewhere—at least they seem to be eccentric to people who are not used to them. One of them is the production of flowers and fruit directly on the trunk or old branches, although the habit of flowering only on new shoots is also observed. Many jungle plants have developed this trick—it is almost exclusively tropical—and it can be startling to the unaccustomed observer.

You walk along and see a great cluster of what resembles a bunch of overgrown grapes or ripe figs, or a corsage or perhaps an oddly shaped and colored mushroom. The natural assumption is that this must be some sort of fungus, but not at all. It is the tree's natural flower sprouting through the bark. Botanists call the phenomenon cauliflory, the production of flowers on a leafless, wood stem. Hundreds of different species in the rain forest have the quirk, but virtually all of them belong to the lower levels of the jungle. The giants which can reach the unobstructed sun for their flowering never bother with this speciality of the tropics.

At the same time, botanists have suspected that lack of light does not fully explain cauliflory. For one thing, thousands of plants that like the shade just as much never resort to it. Alfred Wallace thought that cauliflory was a device developed by smaller trees to attract low-flying, shade-loving insects who were needed for the plant's pollination. It is a fact that most of these plants do rely upon insects for their pollination, and such trees—one of the best known with this peculiarity of flowers on the stem is the cacao—often confine the blossoms to the lower part of the trunk. But others bear flowers on the bark of higher branches too. So it has been suggested that the reason may have something to do with the available chemicals in the growing section of the wood just under the bark. To the casual visitor, such speculations must remain just that; the important thing is that these odd-looking objects are really flowers or fruits.

Another lovely habit of many jungle plants is that certain species flower all at once, not just within the same general period, but literally all within a matter of hours. Some species of trees and shrubs

Ivan Sanderson

Coffee flower.

have such carefully constructed timing devices that all the individuals of one of them for miles around will blossom on the same day—and fade the same day, too. One in Java has been recorded as bursting into flower in a large jungle at exactly the same time every nine years for many generations, another in Ceylon every twelve years.

For some of these plants the stimulus to blossoming seems to be a storm. Certain orchids in the Malayan jungles, whose flowers last only a day, have been found to select the same day over a fairly wide area. Finally it was noted that this was always a certain number of days after a thunderstorm, each species of orchid needing its own particular number of days. The stimulus, first thought to be the extra rain or perhaps some electrical phenomenon, proved to be just the sudden short drop in temperature which accompanies these storms. Some coffees have exhibited the same pattern, all the bushes of the same species turning a dazzling white in the same district on the same day. All representatives of one group of trees in the Amazon jungle have been noted to blossom all at once for miles—the fact, but not the reason, was recorded more than a century ago—and by next day not a single flower can be found in the whole jungle.

Whether this habit is an advantage to the plant in replenishing itself is doubtful. In fact, it would be hard to say that any of the reproductive mechanisms have much to recommend them from this standpoint. Fortunately the survival of the forest as a living entity does not depend upon the regenerative efficiency of the individual plants. The whole process, an amalgam of waste and mystery, may seem thoroughly unsatisfactory, but it accomplishes with supreme skill one task that is far more significant than the life of any species, the immortal equilibrium of the jungle.

16

The Lowly Things

Although much of the jungle is raised high on its great wooden pillars, while the floor usually appears to be quite unencumbered, it is not entirely empty at ground level. Not only are there spindly saplings and certain shade-loving small trees and bushes, but even more lowly little plants that cling to the ground itself. Some of them make up in usefulness and interest what they lack in grandeur.

Among these are one of the most ancient and primitive of land plants, the liverworts. One of them, the *Selaginella,* may carpet a jungle floor for mile after mile. The whole plant is just little green leaves growing in pairs on short stems, sometimes a curious shimmering blue-green. They are virtually "seaweeds" that live on land, and they have a fairly close resemblance to moss, which in jungles almost never grows on soil but only on fallen logs and tree trunks. *Selaginella,* however, is actually more closely related to the ferns than to mosses, but in some respects its life cycle and reproduction are almost animal-like. It does not flower at all, but produces both male and female spores. The spores ripen and are shed, and when the male fertilizes the female, a new *Selaginella* plant is formed. In the jungle they are very much smaller and less fernlike in their foliage than their civilized cousins, creeping ground cover, which is used frequently in our greenhouses for an edging of greenery along the benches or in hanging baskets.

Even more widespread are some of the lesser fungi often referred to as molds, the sort of thing that forms a fuzzy film on shoes or books or anything kept in a damp, dark closet. The earth of the jungle floors is chock full of them. Among them are many forms related to *Penicillium* from which Sir Alexander Fleming got the substance that became the first wonder drug, penicillin.

These molds help to make the jungles healthier than any other regions on earth except for the almost bacteria-free Arctic lands. Even if you cut your foot badly when you are far from your camp and without medical aid, you need not fear infection, provided you do not wrap the wound in some dirty rag or force your foot into a leather or rubber shoe. And if it does become infected, the very best thing you can do is to smother it in the loam or mud of the forest floor.

Several years before the announcement that Dr. Fleming had discovered penicillin, we had collected jungle earths during our trips and sent them for analysis to the laboratories of Messrs. Burroughs and Welcome, one of the larger pharmaceutical companies in England. We still prize the reports they sent us in 1938—Sir Alexander won the Nobel prize in 1945—which informed us that the samples displayed outstanding "antibiotic properties."

Our research began after I had contracted an appalling case of athlete's foot in the best hotel in a certain tropical capital. It defied all treatment, and I was in agony. I could not walk and had to be carried back to my camp in the jungle. The first night there, a cloudburst washed our tent away. I had to flounder about in the dark, knee-deep in mud for most of the night, rescuing our precious possessions. And I was barefooted. The mud, of course, was soothing.

By noon the next day, all the pain had gone and the sores were beginning to heal. In four days my feet were devoid of any sign of the infection, and have remained healthy ever since.

The floors of jungles are, in effect, vast antibiotic laboratories. They are designed, after all, to reduce all dead matter that falls from above to the basically pure and fairly simple substances that are then reused by the growing plants.

Until recently it was a maxim with white men in the tropics that to insure good health they had to clear away the trees and let in the sunlight. They then had to evolve elaborate paraphernalia to avoid the sun themselves, especially in the heat of the day. After my first few stretches of living in jungles, I decided that in searching for prospective co-workers, I much preferred the sedentary type who spent his time in nightclubs to any rugged, outdoor athlete, tanned and tough. Later experience has confirmed this early impression.

The athlete is the first to succumb to the dangers to which his addiction to the open exposes him. The proper jungle procedure is to accept nature as she is, and the nightclub devotee avoids the bright sun as sedulously as any respectable denizen of the rain forest's floor. He is wise to do so because all kinds of unpleasantnesses thrive in tropical sunlight. Even many of the beneficial lowly things of the deep jungle shade adopt new ways of life in order to survive stronger light, and some of them produce effects which are dangerous diseases to us.

I should perhaps mention here that one of the greatest perils you can face in the jungle is a bath, especially with soap. The exudations of our sweat glands are themselves powerful antibiotics, and keep us free from external infections. Take a swim in a river or let yourself be rained on if you like, and you will remain both clean and healthy. Do not be afraid that you will offend. It is not perspiration on the skin that others can smell; it is dirty clothing that has absorbed stale perspiration.

This is one reason why the fewer clothes you wear in the jungle, the better. It is also why experienced people who have spent a good deal of time in the jungle customarily change their clothing three times a day; they preserve the natural oils on the skin without the risk of too much perspiration on the clothing. Experience finally taught me to abandon everything but a loincloth in the daytime—on this point the Tarzan movies are very sound—and above all to get rid of all footwear except when night hunting, for this is the time that poisonous snakes and other noxious beasts are abroad on the jungle floor. For those who must stick to shoes, a light canvas or other cloth is much better than a leather boot. The heavy breeches and leggings seen in the old pictures of explorers in the jungle are an exhausting and unnecessary encumbrance.

I have sometimes wondered how much their unsuitable clothing contributed to the dislike some eminent explorers have displayed for the jungle. When Stanley felt depressed in the Congo, it was usually when he was journeying through this type of vegetation. Fawcett often wrote such lines as "the gloom in the dark caverns under the huge forest trees weighed heavily on us." Of course, like so many Englishmen, they thought sunshine was one of the greatest boons a man could find, but their costumes, I should think, must have weighed more heavily than the shade.

Undergrowth of all kinds is so sparse in many of the tall equatorial forests that they are as easy to walk through as an open field. One need only step high to avoid tripping on a root and watch for the hole made by some burrowing animal. I have even used a bicycle to get about to my trap lines. We met one man in British Honduras, a Scot, who visited us in our jungle camp after riding twenty miles from his own on a motorcycle. He told us that he customarily took long trips through the virgin forest on this machine, looking for sapodilla or chicle trees, which provide the sap that is the basic ingredient in chewing gum, and which for some reason is more plentiful in wild trees than in any that can be cultivated.

Such undergrowth as there is turns out to be mostly woody, for that is more suitable to jungle conditions. In one Guiana jungle where fewer than fifty species of herbaceous plants were found, there were hundreds of species of trees and shrubs in the same area. To the casual observer, the reverse may seem true, because the few herbaceous specimens have a great variety of leaf form and color, while the trees and shrubs tend to look alike, although they may be quite different botanically.

Some features of jungle vegetation that have often seemed odd to students from other climates are the results of understandable and often ingenious adaptation to conditions prevailing at ground level in these rain forests. For example, the reason for cacti in jungles may be the presence of too much water rather than the plant's need to store water. A cactus is admirably suited to keeping water out as well as keeping it in.

From the earliest times, primitive man has taken out of the jungle certain smaller trees, bushes and other plants and domesticated them for his own use or enjoyment. They have given him food, stimulants or oblivion—Brazilian coffee and cacao are only two of the best known.

The cacao, a small tree of the lowest canopy story of the South American jungles where it is native, has the typical broad-leafed, widely spreading crown. It is often called the chocolate tree because chocolate is derived from its beans. The technical name for it is *Theobroma,* which is some indication of how highly the early botanists regarded it, for the word is derived from the Greek for god and food.

Cacao has often been confused in and out of fiction with a very different genus of shrubs called *Erythroxylon,* also from South America. The leaves of the most famous member of this plant tribe, *Erythroxylon coca,* were chewed by South American Indians, and the narcotic effects were so plain to white men that they promptly investigated. They discovered that they could extract cocaine from the coca plant, and it made a lot of them rich. Originally hailed in Europe and North America as an anesthetic, it has, of course, been strictly regulated and virtually prohibited under modern narcotics laws. But coca still remains a staple for a great many South American Indians, and is even cultivated today in other tropical lands.

Some of the Oriental peoples who lived on the fringes of jungles had found an equally useful commodity in one of the palm trees with the euphonious name of *Areca catechu,* known popularly as betel. It produces a nut which is the favorite chew of a good deal of the Far East. Wrapped in a betel leaf that has been smeared with quicklime, it induces a narcotic reaction—somewhat less than coca, though—and also has a cosmetic effect highly prized by its more ardent devotees. It stains the teeth black and the saliva bright red. For centuries the betel nut has been a major article of Oriental trade.

An African jungle plant that man has taken over with great success is cola (or kola), which after proving its virtues medicinally as well as in beverages has been cultivated in other tropical areas and has achieved perhaps the most respectable reputation of the three. But originally—and to this day in Africa—the seeds, known as gourounuts, were chewed for their stimulating effect, induced by the caffeine they contain. Considering the immense popularity of cola drinks in the United States, and in many other countries as well, we can safely say that no other jungle product has been sampled by so large a proportion of the world's population.

Until quite recently it was taken for granted that the relative scarcity of vegetation on the jungle floor was due entirely to lack of light. But now it is being suggested that the voracity of the big fellows is equally important in keeping down the population of low-growing plants. Their roots, it is said, take so much of the available nourishment so quickly that the little fellows cannot find food. The men who evolved this theory have pointed out that many jungle species not only tolerate but demand shade and cannot grow in strong light. Why, then, should they not grow as densely as any other vegetation? In actual fact, scattered experiments show that they do multiply enormously when the root competition of the tall trees is reduced by the process called trenching.

In spite of their relative sparseness, the low plants contribute a great deal to the special impression that true jungles make upon everyone who enters them. Unostentatious, even inconspicuous, they enhance the dim stillness between the grand columns that support the canopy. It is an atmosphere that has repelled a good many of the men whose names are most prominently linked to it. The intrepid Stanley hated the jungle; he was a lover of open spaces. The unfortunate Fawcett, his vision fixed upon the great lost cities of South America, could see no beauty in the magnificent rain forests through which he pursued his dream. But those who are temperamentally attuned to it find the jungle a place of beauty, of peace, of security and even of ease.

Just as jungles have developed their own characteristic vegetation, so they have created an animal life of their own, and a very special one too, as we would expect, since the nature of so-called higher forms, including man, is largely determined by the particular vegetational belt they inhabit. To the stranger, whether tourist or scientist or exploiter, the jungle may seem odd, unwholesome, unpleasant. But to all these other animals it is home.

Ivan Sanderson

Gorilla.

Part 4

Animals of the Jungle

The Rhythms of Jungle Life

The Daily Round

Jungle Traffic

The Flying Continents

Life Around Jungles

Life in the Jungles

Ivan Sanderso

Oil birds.

17

The Rhythms of Jungle Life

Though there are no statistics to prove the point, it is probably legitimate to say that the first response of most people to the word "jungle" is to think of animals—"lions and tigers and elephants and all that stuff!".

Yet as we have seen, jungles are essentially vegetable.

There is an even greater paradox, however, that would hardly occur to anyone not trained as a zoologist or particuarly interested in animals. This is that you see fewer animals therein than you do on an average desert—unless you are actually *looking* for them.

I will never forget an evening I spent in the home of what used to be called "an Old Coaster," a seasoned political administrator of a jungle district in West Africa. In those days before wonder drugs, the whole of West Africa was referred to as "The White Man's Grave," and indeed malaria, dysentery and a lot of other pernicious diseases were rife. Colonial officials did "tours" of eighteen months at the most and then had eighteen weeks leave out of the country. Anybody who completed more than a couple of tours was dubbed an Old Coaster. This gentleman had done more than ten such tours and was thus a Very Old Coaster. He was in charge of a district that was mostly jungle—actually tall deciduous forest—and he "toured" it, on foot, extensively.

My party had been resident near his headquarters for about ten days when he invited us to this informal social evening. We were the only Europeans in the area. This gentleman's interests happened to be intellectual rather than "sportif"—actually, he was a recognized linguist—but he had just about as intimate firsthand knowledge of the jungle as anybody in the area. One afternoon he had passed by our house on his way in from a trip and had looked with amazement upon our activity. At the time, we were training three trappers in the use of our special devices for catching small animals, and seven skinners in the preparation of our specimens. Our big catches were obtained in company with local professional providers of large "beef" as they call all animals there. Ours was a very busy household, indeed.

The gentleman forthrightly asked us where we had managed to find all these animals, adding: "I've been here most of my life and I've traveled the whole of this and other forest districts where I have been stationed, but frankly I've never seen anything much except some monkeys and squirrels." And he was being absolutely sincere. He was so intrigued, he later visited us twice a day to inspect and poke at the endless stream of new forms of life that we and our helpers brought in, for the most part, from within a mile beyond his vegetable garden.

My first sight of a closed-canopy equatorial forest was in the famous Sinharaja Forest of Ceylon. I did see a few insects, but apart from these, nothing—not even a solitary bird. Admittedly I did not penetrate very far and I was there at the dead time of day when most tropical animals are at rest before the evening uproar. Nevertheless the experience impressed me very deeply. Like everybody else, I had been brought up with the notion that the jungles were concentrated zoological gardens; I truly expected tigers to leap out at me from behind every tree. Furthermore, what I had already seen of what I call nonjungle tropical woodlands and other types of growth had only encouraged this idea, since there seemed always to be a multitude of life within sight.

When you know them, jungles are by no means dead worlds. They positively teem with life of all sizes, but the animals, like the true jungle peoples, are so perfectly integrated with their environment, having evolved in it and, in most cases, along with it, that they have achieved not just a *modus vivendi* but *a modus operandi* that is as unique as it is incomprehensible, at first, to outsiders. Once you get to know them, however, you become aware of a very discernible daily rhythm that can be divided sharply into several distinct but unequal parts.

Because this is an enormously complex subject, let me say at the

Ivan Sanderson

Black spider monkey.

outset that I must make a number of flat statements for which I can offer no supporting evidence in the form of bibliographical references. Altough a considerable amount of work has been done on what is called "biorhythms," the science of ethology of which it forms a most important aspect is itself still in its infancy. Ethology, from the Greek word *ethos* meaning custom, is, according to the standard *A Dictionary of Scientific Terms,* the "study of habits in relation to habitat; study of behavior." However, the word behavior in this context has now acquired a specialized connotation of its own and is properly reserved to denote studies of animal behavior in *un*natural surroundings, such as in full domestication, or in zoos and laboratories. Ethology, on the other hand, is now restricted to study of them in their own natural environment or in other natural ones to which they may have been transplanted. Very few ethological studies of any kind have been carried out in the equatorial closed-canopy forests, so one is forced to rely rather heavily on personal observation.

Light, for example, has a great deal to do with animal behavior. Despite the perpetual dimness and often the total absence of direct sunshine within the jungle, which one might suppose would prompt an abundance of animal activity during the day, the exact opposite occurs. All animals everywhere seek shade under trees or shrubbery or in holes in the ground. Any resident in a suburban area who tries to set up a birdbath and feeding station has noticed this phenomenon. Put these out in the open and you will get at most an occasional sparrow or starling; but put them near some thick bushes or preferably under some dense-foliaged overhanging trees, and a collection of creatures you never dreamed were your neighbors will appear. Even if you have children, dogs, cats, and a blaring hi-fi around the house, they don't worry these creatures in the least. Cover, or lack of it, is the controlling factor. Only the larger animals of the treeless prairies, deserts and Arctic tundra cannot find it. Many insects are, of course, highly active in the bright sunlight at the top of the jungle canopy, but even they, it has been found on detailed observation, buzz about only just so long before getting into the shade, literally to cool off. Desert lizards, though they bask in the sun for what seem to be long sessions, are careful to do so only until they have absorbed the right amount of heat; then, if prevented from getting out of the direct sunlight, they die in very short order.

The actual top or surface of the jungle canopy is a very busy place shortly before sunrise. The flowers attract the insects—though there always seems to be plenty of these even when there isn't a flower in sight for miles. There are nectar and fruit-eating birds as well as insect-eaters, and the sky above many jungles is patrolled by countless hawks and eagles. While the larger of these seem to stay in the air all day except after making a kill, the smaller ones make forays rather like fighter planes on missions, and then duck back into the shade of the canopy. When we lived *in* the canopy, one of our most interesting "discoveries" (to me at least, and probably because I am not an ornithologist) was that the little hawks each had a station on a particular branch to which it invariably returned. In fact, it lived on that one small section of one branch and usually slept there. The part of the tree immediately around the branch had a noticeably different small fauna from adjacent parts of the canopy. We

Ivan Sanderson

Three-horned chameleon.

feel fairly confident from the evidence we found on the forest floor beneath these perches that the birds' excrement and presumably scraps from their meals, which they seemed generally to bring back to their places, as well as fur and feathers raining down from on high, formed a very special diet for numbers of different kinds of lesser life.

In the jungle canopy dwell large numbers—though not actually a great variety—of mammals, such as monkeys, squirrels, and a smattering of rarer items, a few diurnal snakes, and occasionally a chameleon or other lizard. But all of these, apart from some monkeys, and they only for short periods, stay inside or below the "skin" of the canopy.

Apart from these forms, the jungle is by day virtually and usually absolutely devoid of animal activity from mid-morning until about an hour before sundown. There is plenty of life there during these hours, but it is all resting under bark or logs, sleeping in dense masses of vines or in the heads of palms, in holes in the ground or in the rare patches of tall ground cover consisting of large-leafed herbs, usually near water. There are a few rather mysterious birds that nest below the canopy and are active at certain times during the day. They do not constitute any one group of birds. Notable examples are some hornbills in Africa and the curassows and guans of tropical America. I have also often observed some very quiet and nondescript little birds of various kinds running about the tree boles probing for insects and flitting short distances. I did not collect birds, I never had an ornithologist with me just when I wanted one, and I couldn't identify any of these from preserved skins, so I don't know what any of them may be except for some of the easily identifiable ones like certain rifle-birds and birds of paradise which are perpetual residents of the gloom.

I should stress here that I am talking of the lowland jungles (however high they may reach up the bases of mountain ranges) and not of the montane forests. These latter are seldom, if ever, stratified, and therefore are not "hollow." They are often so dense right down to the ground that there is even less light than in a lowland, tiered jungle. Yet, in most montane forests, mammals, birds and what reptiles, frogs, and other lesser forms of life there may be—including crabs, on some occasions—seem often to be active all through the daylight hours and at all levels down to and on the ground.

It is sometimes so dark on the ground at midday, even in a lowland jungle, that one would have supposed nocturnal animals could move about in fair comfort, but they don't appear until the daytime contingent has gone to bed.

The basis of annual and seasonal biorhythms is not necessarily the coming of rain—with its almost invariable flowering of vegetation—or of a dry period, though both do provoke all seasonally breeding animals; rather, it is *any* changeover period. Thus, in some places other factors are influential, such as the seasonal drift of dust-laden air from the Sahara that descends annually upon southern West Africa for some weeks.

As we mentioned at the outset of this book, the equatorial forests and in particular the TEF have the most "temperate" of all climates on earth; the daily rhythm of day and night is virtually stable throughout the year, with darkness coming about six o'clock in the evening and daylight about six in the morning. There are rainy and dry seasons, more or less, but mostly the rain comes all the time in small or large doses. Thus, in this belt, different plants fructify at different times all through the year, so that there is a constant supply of fresh tender young shoots and leaves, flowers, fruits and nuts. The animals don't have to pace their most essential function, which is to breed and raise more of their own kind, to any one time unless they, as a species, are wholly or preferentially dependent upon some special form of vegetable life or upon some animal food essential to raising their young which is in turn dependent upon some type of tree.

In the tall deciduous forest, this is not true to anything like the same extent. While not *all* the trees shed their leaves at the same time, as do those of our northern forests, many more animals have to wait for a mass fructification of the plants—due to the more precise alternations of wet and dry seasons—than do the dwellers of the TEF. Tropical montane forests seem on the whole to be much less affected by major seasonal alternations than are the lowland or true jungles of both types. I have no record of a mass breeding season for animals in a montane forest, such as we have in our climes in the spring, and I doubt if anybody has as yet made a special study of the matter on a two-year basis. Yet every animal known seems to have a breeding rhythm, annual or of a shorter period.

And don't think that there isn't migration—i.e., a seasonal movement back and forth from one location to another—in the jungles, or that some equivalent of hibernation doesn't also occur. Many animals would appear to go into a prolonged resting phase for certain periods of each year—at least they seem to virtually disappear. Of course, they may change their habits or habitats due to short or long "migration," laterally, or vertically from below the ground up into the canopy.

In the olden days even civilized man was almost universally convinced that all animals including ourselves were strongly influenced by the moon; the idea probably stemmed from the human menstrual cycle. There then came a period when any such notion was not only scoffed at but allegedly proved wrong. However, times have changed again, and many recent studies seem to have demonstrated very clearly that some biorhythms do indeed follow the lunar cycle. To me, one of the most interesting of all is the cognizance now taken by enlightened police forces, of the fact that long-range statistics clearly demonstrate the increased incidence of certain crimes during each full moon. I don't know if this observation could possibly be tied in with one of our own—one that is known to almost all native hunters and certainly to many Western animal collectors. I long ago realized that it was practically useless to try any hunting or even "collecting" of smaller animals on nights when there was bright moonlight. Further, when collecting professionally, we customarily set up to five hundred small traps every night, on the ground, in bushes, and in each of the tiers of the jungle. Each was numbered, its location mapped, and a careful record kept of anything and everything caught in each—and we caught some funny things, I can tell you, like huge beetles and once even a fallen orchid flower that happened to trigger the setting. From these records, we were able to demonstrate beyond a shadow of doubt that as the full moon approached, the number of animals trapped fell off sharply, and as the moon waned it increased—*provided* there was still moonlight. If it was overcast or if there was a light to medium rain even on the night of the full moon, the catch shot straight up to the average for all dark nights.

Natural cycles of much longer span seem to affect animal life in the jungles, but no proper scientific studies of them have as yet been made. Native hunters, whom I tend to regard as well worth listening to, have often told me that certain kinds of game varied widely in numbers over a number of years. European residents in jungle areas, almost all of whom used to hunt (this being the only sport available) have noticed the same thing, and it was from them that I heard the suggestion that the fluctuation was cyclical. One must not forget that the white man is much more sensitive to the concept of a solar year, due to the very pronounced seasonal changes in higher latitudes, than is the inhabitant of the equatorial belt. It is possible that the true jungle peoples have no concept of it at all, so that a cycle of, say, ten years would not be noticed as such. In the very rare cases where two or more professional animal collectors, collecting the same animals, have visited the same area at different times, there is a marked difference between the number of animals they collect and the number of each kind they recorded. One collector may obtain an abundance of specimens of a particular species in one area but another, coming later, will not see a single such specimen despite intense and professional search. However, once again there are no proper records.

Within the year, there are extraordinary fluctuations even inside the jungle, which demonstrates that even if the vertebrates do not have set breeding seasons, the insects certainly do. This is one of the most impressive phenomena of the jungle.

When we were collecting professionally, it was necessary to maintain day-and-night shifts in order to keep up with the work. Traps had to be visited three times a day—at 7:00 P.M., midnight and 7:00 A.M.—for three reasons. First, one caught a different set of animals at each period—the evening contingent at 7:00 P.M.; the true nightwalkers at midnight, and the late night and early morning feeders at 7:00 A.M. Second, if you did not get your catches out of the traps as soon as possible, a large percentage would be eaten by large scavengers, then by lesser creatures such as ants, which can demolish a large forest rat in an hour; and third, anything left can bloat and start to decompose in a few hours. This almost round-the-clock activity necessitated skinning and preparing specimens from about eight o'clock in the morning until the last of the midnight catch was taken care of. Now, the jungle is alive with insects at night, and they are attracted by bright lights such as those needed for our rather fine and detailed work. But you can't comfortably work with dishes of preserving liquids under a constant and massive bombardment by insects ranging in size from four-inch water scorpions to specks at the range of vision; so, we worked in two twelve-by-eight-foot rectangular "rooms" made of mosquito or sandfly netting erected on a framework of sapling poles. To these structures, which constituted a rather novel kind of trap, the insects would come by the thousands and cling to the outside.

Even when we were not officially collecting insects, we were always deeply interested in the creatures and would go around the nets with a flashlight to see what we had as visitors. It became quite a game to see which of us came upon the most bizarre or exotic one each night. Of even greater interest was the fact that every night there appeared one or more species in superabundance. Many of these had been noted before as a few stray individuals but then would come the rush, which lasted sometimes for only one night, sometimes for a week before it tapered off. Anybody who has lived in an equatorial forest area must have noted this phenomenon, especially if they dined night after night in an unscreened house. But with a large net surface to attract the insects, the phenomenon became for me one of the most prominent features of the jungle world.

Are these breeding cycles? One hates to keep asking questions, but a zoologist living in and investigating a jungle hardly does anything else. For instance, we haven't the foggiest notion whether any one of these tens of thousands—perhaps millions—of different kinds of insects are annual breeders, or even whether they are cyclical breeders at all. We don't know how moisture, temperature or light may affect any cycle there may be. Then, perhaps there are other factors involved, such as one which may cause the remarkable variation in the lengths of time required for animals caught very close together to decompose. This rate is now believed to vary according to the amount of carbon dioxide in the air immediately above the jungle floor—high concentrations forming little meandering channels following slight depressions.

In the TDF it is more than possible that certain insects have to await the flowering or releafing of some special plant before their eggs hatch; otherwise the larvae would not have the proper specialized food available. The possibilities are endless and challenging.

18

The Daily Round

ONE biorhythm is common to all jungles—the daily one. This is not just the alternation of daylight and darkness; it is much more complex. The twenty-four hours may be divided into eight phases of unequal duration, and the best place to start is just before dawn.

Before the sun actually rises there is, of course, a period of half-light during which activity is at a very high point: the late night feeders are still about while the first contingent of diurnal animals appears. Often a mist hangs over and penetrates a little into the canopy, and apparently many animals feel comparatively safe as long as this persists. Down below it is still dark, and in very large jungles with several tiers and a level canopy, it may remain so until after sunrise when the mist dissolves. Thus, the nocturnal animals often continue to feed on the jungle floor for as long as an hour after sunrise. Dawn, therefore, may be divided into two parts, pre-dawn and post-dawn, with the night animals disappearing from the canopy down through the middle tiers by stages as the light filters downward.

Post-dawn is the best time for collecting and seems to be favored by professional native hunters who provide meat for villages at the edge of the jungle. However, and we cannot stress this too often, comparatively few hunters actually penetrate the jungle itself; they prefer the banks of rivers, small open savannahs, and other places free from the canopy, though before dawn some bold spirits will travel to such places through the jungle by recognized paths or trails.

As we have said, the inside of the jungle appears more or less devoid of life during the day, apart from that cacophony that goes on at the tops of the trees. However, there are ground-dwellers that move about all day, but I must say I have over the years become increasingly inclined to a somewhat unorthodox notion: to wit, that many of these are basically nocturnal animals, while still others can be active by day as well as by night. A good example of the latter are those delightful birds of South America known as Trumpeters, which strut about making occasional "thumping" noises that cannot be described on paper. Everybody seems to regard them as diurnal animals, and so they may be, but I have watched them thumping about at all times of the night. And this was not due to the lights we used. All of which brings up another point.

There is a tropical forest animal related to the South American monkeys proper and called a douroucouli. It lives in holes in trees and is definitely a nocturnal animal. Yet, I have encountered it catching insects during the daytime on dark days in the lower tiers of the forest. Also, I have had a number of these animals, all jungle-caught, as pets. At first they spent their days in their nest boxes and came out to leap and bang about only at night. But slowly we got all of them to shift their waking hours to conform to ours so that they slept when we did. Nor are douroucoulis the only allegedly nocturnal animals that have achieved this complete turnabout under our close observation, in captivity. I have also seen tropical forest animals believed by almost everybody to be nightwalkers meandering about *outside* the true jungle and even in brilliant, direct sunlight. In fact, the notion of a nice orderly pattern of life in the wild, on which many of us were brought up—the chorus of birds at sundown, followed by the activity of frogs, whippoorwills, owls and other night creatures till predawn—just does not hold in the jungle. There are indeed successive choruses and periods of dead silence in the jungle every day and with a pretty stern regularity, but from time to time and place to place one comes upon some sturdy individualists doing everything "wrong"—wrong, that is, according to our neat little concepts.

By the time the animals of the canopy and the lower tiers have finally gone to bed, the day creatures are abroad, but they move about only for a very short time—that is, from the first glimmering of light until a point during the morning when almost all animal activity stops abruptly, both in the canopy and below. This is siesta time for everybody, and often even the insects interrupt their constant whir-

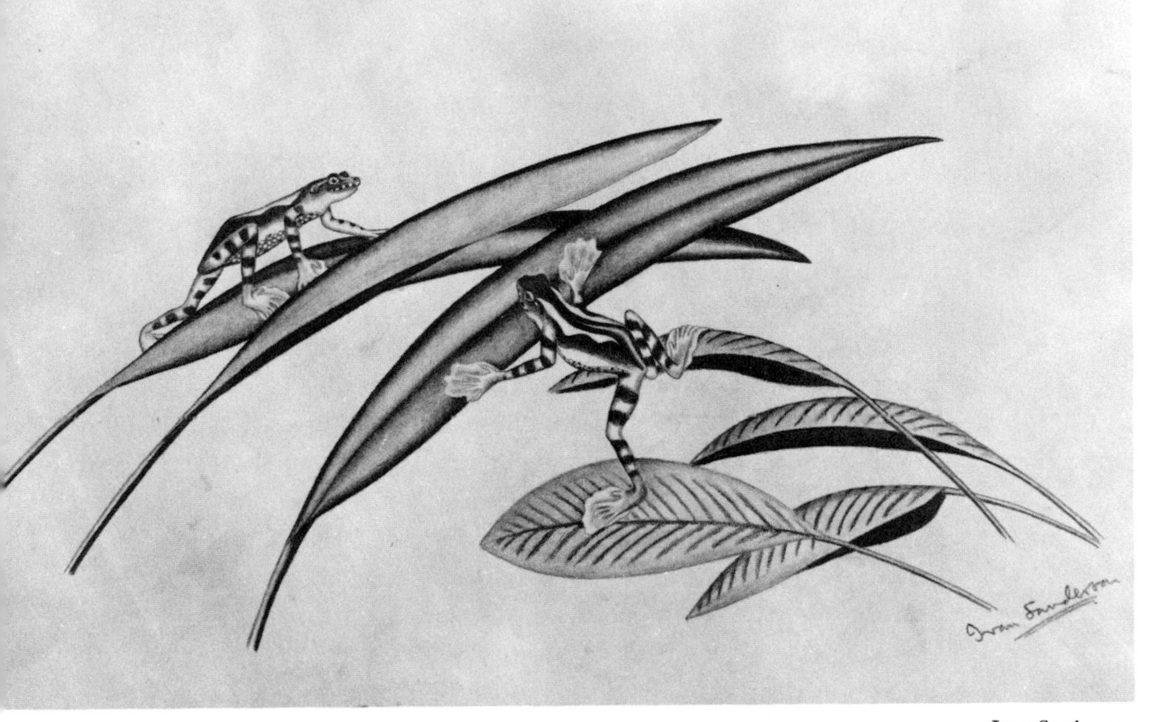

Ivan Sanderson

"Incredible frog" or dwarf leaf-toad.

ring and fizzing and are silent. This period continues until the sun begins to set on sunny days. In cloudy weather, movements and noises begin earlier and this, I believe, is due to the amount of light available. In this case the diminution of light is equivalent to an increase in "cover," though this might seem to imply that animals feel safer when they "think" they cannot be seen. Any such concept is, of course, far too anthropocentric and not valid. For every animal that normally moves about within certain upper and lower limits of light (including shade), there are predators that do the same. To beg the question, the animals become active when the physical conditions suit them, and I personally believe that the amount of light is a major factor in this. Nonetheless, the midday pause is very impressive, not only for its singular lack of movement, but for its sometimes complete silence.

After siesta the jungle comes to life again, not with the stridency of dawn, but in a gentler way. Mammals and birds begin to appear. Most reptiles and amphibians don't make any noise, but you will find that those that are residents of the jungle, like tortoises, some snakes, frogs and toads, become most active in the evening. If the weather is fine, the insects wind up again, and sundown may be an enchanting time of sound and activity. If, on the other hand, it is raining or cloudy, things are quite different. The daytime animals keep quiet though still going about their business, while the nighttime contingent gets moving early. So, instead of a myriad of insects whirring in the evening sunlight and birds and monkeys flitting or galivanting overhead, a rather somber chorus begins below. There are rustlings, croakings and thumpings in the gloom. However, the middle-tier creatures seem, rather surprisingly, to shun rain and gloom—the daytime ones retreating and the nighttime ones lying low.

Night is the time when the vast majority of jungle animals, from mammals to worms, appear and perform their appointed functions. But the night is not just one long period of darkness during which the jungle denizens gambol: quite the contrary. It is divided into three very distinct parts. The reason for this I do not know, and I don't know of anybody who has as yet offered an explanation. (This is quite apart from the influences of rain and moonlight, both of which are profound and will be discussed later.)

Before night falls, there is the somewhat fluid evening time that has a different duration, according to the weather, in the canopy, the middle tiers, and on the ground from about 5:00 P.M. until an hour after sundown when the last glimmer of sunlight has gone from even the top of the canopy. During this phase the last of the day feeders go to bed and the first night feeders make their appearance. With the coming of full darkness the truly nocturnal animals appear.

Here we witness marvelous phenomena. The canopy above is absolutely silent, but the inside of the jungle comes alive in a manner quite impossible to describe to anyone who has not been there. The cacophony of the night insects can be almost deafening, though once you become used to it, you may no longer even notice it. However, try making a tape recording of it, and you will be amazed—however low you leave the recording volume, you will want to tone down the broadcasting playback. All sorts of other noises, from rustlings to hoots, howls and wails, come with ever increasing frequency. (Sitting alone in a jungle shortly after dark, one quote always comes to mind: "Ghoulies and ghosties, and long-legged beasties, and things that go BUMP in the night.") Be assured, however, that the overall effect is in no way comparable to the ridiculous background effects used for so-called jungle films and television shows. Most of these, by the way, are recorded noises of animals that never saw a jungle, hungry animals in zoos and circuses, and fascinating ululations and other noises produced by sound-effects men and professional animal-noises specialists. Under certain circumstances, though, the jungle may be almost silent at this time. The animals are nevertheless moving about, whatever the weather.

I should mention here that I have experienced a few very exceptional brief periods when the temperature has *really* dropped in tropical areas, and even penetrated to the floor of the forest. Though on the floor it was only a matter of a very few degrees, it seemed to bring everything to a dead stop. There was a ghastly silence like that in our northern climes in autumn when the night temperature drops below 32°F. for more than two days. The effect is most singular.

If you are shivering during one of these unusual silences, which you can well do in a jungle with even a slight drop in temperature, you should not feel too alarmed; but if you are sweating, and loose papers don't move on your table, and your friends and helpers go away or stop laughing and chattering—look out! That is when, after the building up of a tension that I cannot describe, you will probably hear what sounds like a thousand diesel locomotives all roaring down-grade. Then comes the most deathly silence of all with perhaps a few flickers of lightning which, at the bottom of the jungle, produce a most eerie effect. Because you are unable to see the sky, you cannot observe any "stroke," yet the flash penetrates and seems always to be bright blue and exactly at the level of your eyes—whether you are lying on the ground, sitting in a chair, or ensconced way up in a branch of a tree. This heralds a storm, which may hit you or pass you by.

The whole thing is slightly Wagnerian; you expect to see Valkyries galloping along above. Once I saw something in one of these storms that really shook me. I was living in a precarious and very flimsy structure in the canopy and made the mistake of not going down the rope when the first bolt of lightning hit. In the foolhardiness of my youth, I wanted to see just what one of the tropical storms was like —from above. In the midst of the uproar, which took place about 4:00 P.M., I was clinging to everything available when, all of a sudden—whooosh—and half a dozen (not Valkyries) of the most hysterical birds I ever saw whirled by right over my tree. They were large vultures, apparently caught in an updraft and carried over the jungle by the storm from miles away where the orchard bush began. They were apparently completely out of control.

More sensible animals, particularly those of the jungle, know better what to do. The daytime hordes descend into the lower levels of the canopy and just hang on; the middle tier creatures stay in their holes, or descend to lower, denser levels; the daytime ground-level animals scuttle for shelter, and the nightwalkers just stay put in their holes and other retreats. Where fragile insects like butterflies go, I don't know, but they survive as well as all the rest in the great womb of the jungle.

And so comes the night, either softly, gently and silently, or with violence. Evening storms seldom last long after dark in the tropical forest areas, and once they have passed on, a positive uproar begins, mounting in crescendo. All jungle animals love rain—and its aftermath of "boiling" moisture and dripping leaves. They also like the dark, and after a storm there are usually clouds and thus real darkness for some time. Which brings me to what is perhaps the most significant feature of jungle life.

Just because *we* are day animals we have a tendency to look upon moonlight as being advantageous for nighttime peregrinations. But animals, and notably jungle animals, don't see it this way at all. They prefer the dark, and the darker the better. As we have already noted, over many years of nightly collecting in tropical forests of all kinds but mostly in true jungles as we have defined them, it has been borne in upon me that any such enterprise is almost worthless at the height of the moon in clear weather, and that the number of animals encountered and the number falling to traps increases with the waning of the moon to a high point when there is no nighttime moon, and then gradually decreases again until the next high. However, cloudy weather, particularly with a steady rain (as opposed to a flash storm), causes the count to rise to the maximum. Even citizens in northern, so-called temperate climes may have noticed that it is the dull, rainy evenings in the summer that brings out the moths. In the jungle, calm rainy sundowns bring out the insects in countless hordes; and these in turn would seem to bring out the insect-eaters; and these, in their turn, the predators, all the way up the scale to the great cats. On calm bright moonlight nights there may be not a thing stirring, and the insects are few; let there be a clouding of the moon and a gentle rain, and the whole place comes alive.

Rain causes exceptions in the nighttime jungle, but with or without rain and darkness there still is a rhythm that is clearly discernible. After the last strictly daytime animals have bedded down or disappeared, the nightwalkers are about. And the coming to life of the jungle is perhaps one of the most wonderful events that thinking man can witness. As the last rays of light go away and the crepuscular gloom descends upon the forest floor with ever increasing deepness, one hears, if one keeps quiet and just waits, little rustlings and stirrings, and an occasional howl from something going to bed or waking up. Then there is a pause—there would be a dead silence but for the whirring insects, and these one soon learns to ignore. Suddenly the hollow temple of the jungle is rent with another brief yell, and then silence again. The rustlings continue and grow in frequency and volume. Now is the time to turn on a steady light and let it beam in one direction. Very soon little "persons" will be seen moving about their normal business, quite oblivious of the light and your presence. You can even smoke or play music. Oddly enough, the animals do not seem to mind either your smell or your unusual noise.

Shortly after sundown the trees above become alive also. There, too, are rustlings, stirrings and mumblings. Flash a beam of light around and you will pick up blue eyes, yellow eyes, red eyes, magenta eyes and just plain eyes, tiny and immense.

There remain in everybody's memories a few notable things seen in one's life. One of them, to me, is a night scene in West Africa. I was lying on the giant forest floor on a blanket, being chewed up by marauding ants more or less piecemeal, but these occasional nips

Ivan Sanderson

Long-legged marsh rat.

could not distract me from the sight caught in my flashlight beam. Small mice, long-legged rats, ponderous bumping toads, delicate tree frogs, a stomping tortoise and even a busy snuffling member of the mongoose family of carnivorous mammals came by. The last was very suspicious of the light but, seeming not to understand it, marched boldly forward and started turning over dead leaves looking for things.

This early nighttime activity continues for some hours, then stops. I have observed this both in Central and South America, in Africa, and in the Orient. For some reasons, and probably all very simple and obvious ones, the nocturnal animals that start feeding and moving about at sundown go back to bed or otherwise lie low for several hours in the middle of night. This is more noticeable among the ground-dwellers and more pronounced when there is any moonlight, but it applies to most arboreal creatures too, and it seems to be universal inside the jungles. I have a strong suspicion, also expressed by many friends with firsthand experience, that the same applies to a considerable extent to the animals outside the closed-canopy forests, in the tropics. Many native hunters who worked for me on a production basis just would not work between the hours of about 11:00 P.M. and 4:00 A.M., and this ban applied to the fringe areas where they did most of their hunting as well as to the deep forest.

Whether the same individual animals come out again in the early hours of the morning or not, I do not know, but the same species may be abroad. There are other species that none of us ever found in the early night but which were abundant in the early morning, and vice versa. Here is another puzzle. Do the night animals spend two thirds of their day in retirement, resting, or do they have but one feeding period in the open and then carry on their activities in holes in the ground or hollow trees where so many of them live? And what of the larger animals that don't live in any kind of hole? Of course, I do not mean to imply in any way that *all* animals in *all* jungles just stop dead precisely at 11:30 P.M. As with everything else in nature, there are many exceptions. There are animals that may be encountered at any time, and there are nocturnal insects sounding off throughout the night. But on dark nights which are otherwise so outstandingly noisy, this midnight lull is very noticeable and sometimes quite disturbing. Often I have thought that a storm was coming, so sepulchral was the cathedral of the forest; the effect is much like that of the winter silence of the country upon a city dweller; it actually wakes you up. I have wandered for hours, night after night, during this period, and the *absence* of animal life was most impressive. Furthermore, we became so interested in the matter in South America on one occasion that we instituted an intermediate inspection of our trap lines at 4:00 A.M. to see just what the take might be between midnight and that time. My records showed night after night with not one single catch during this period.

What I call the early morning period is an altogether different matter. This is the best time both for hunting and collecting. Despite even bright moonlight, it seems that all the nocturnal animals are forced to try for a late meal before retiring while, as has been noted above, the first of the daytime feeders seem often to jump the gun. This is the time to be abroad in the jungle if you really want to see how it works.

Once again I must try to describe the ineffable beauty of dawn in the bosom of a jungle. The first light that penetrates to the floor of the forest is an almost electric blue like that given off by an arc-welder and comparable only to the color seen about a hundred feet down in the clear water of the ocean. That it is not just our eyes that interpret it as blue can be demonstrated by looking at it through camera color filters, and perhaps by the fact that a white flashlight beam appears to go increasingly deeper yellow as the daylight increases in intensity. Meanwhile, high above, the underside of the canopy slowly comes into focus as a vast jet-black latticework backed by a soft looking white semi-luminescence. This is the nighttime vapor pall that is ever present even if it has not developed into a dense mist. The contrast between the blue diffusion below and the pearly luminescence above produces a very remarkable effect and you find yourself in a sort of ethereal limbo. Though the actual dawn comes very fast in equatorial regions, this ephemeral black-white-and-blue state may last quite a long time before the sun's direct rays dissolve the mists above and unfiltered light reaches down into the great natural cathedral and the greens of the leaves and the reds, yellows and various earth colors of trunks, mold and flowers become discernible. Finally the light moves into the green bands of the spectrum and it is truly light—that much of it as there may be.

It has always seemed to me that the animals of the early morning hours, pre-dawn, and dawn, are much less cautious than those of the early night. Late-retiring night animals seem almost reckless in their rush to grab a last bite, while the emerging daytime ones flounder and crash about. I've had the impression several times that the latter are really a bit dopey, like humans on arising. Certainly the most naturally cautious of animals sometimes do the silliest of things about dawn. I will never forget one experience in Central America while we were camped by a stream in dense submontane forest.

We had two fair-sized tents, and two small ones for our local staff and the kitchen (so called). My assistant occupied one large tent which also housed our work area; my wife and I occupied the other big one, which contained personal effects, extra supplies and a large mosquito-screened double camp bed. This was a military-type double tent with a covering pent-roof that came down almost to the ground. The result was a maze of guy ropes that stretched out into the tangle all around. We had set up on a convenient small level area, a rarity in that place. I should have known better.

One morning at dawn, I awoke from a nightmare about drowning, to find myself wrestling with a seething mass of mosquito netting, a near-hysterical wife, masses of ropes and something enormous, rough and warm. At such times, awakened from sleep in the electric blue half-light, one tends to become a little irrational. I did, and instinctively resorted to clawing, scratching and yelling. Pandemonium reigned until it finally got through to me that, in addition to everything else, the tent had collapsed upon us, the mosquito bar enveloped us, and there were at least two enormous and terrified beasts involved in the tangle. Our loyal assistants came to our aid on the double and started hauling off the outer tent. As they got it free, a family party of tapirs came roaring out and charged into the stream, wheezing, panting and groaning like something straight out of Dante.

What had happened was that we had planted our tent athwart their main highway to the stream for morning dips and subsequent feeding. We had been there for two weeks during which they must have inspected us critically and finally decided that we were harmless. However, being somewhat brainless, they had just decided one morning to go back to their old ways and had come straight down their path and tried to go through the tent. Of course, they tripped on the guy ropes, rushed onward and the tent collapsed on them and us, at which point they lost whatever wits they might ever have had and started thrashing around entangled in yards of canvas, ropes, mosquito netting and two equally hysterical human beings. It must have been a ghastly experience for them.

The point is that they did this at dawn, not during the day or night when they are perfectly competent and very cautious beasts. Whether they had been resting up and were not fully awake, or confused by the increasing daylight, I do not know.

I could go on and on with other similar incidents witnessed at dawn—monkeys raiding our cookhouse and grabbing piping hot bread off a hot metal plate; crocodiles meandering out of a river and going to rest under our camp bed; crazy birds barging into camp and landing on our breakfast table to peck at fruit in a bowl, and a spotted cuscus (a strange marsupial mammal of the Australoid East Indies), of all retiring beasts, that persisted for three straight mornings in coming down out of the trees and climbing into bed with me at dawn. I may say that I was not collecting wild animals at that time and had not the heart to make a stuffed specimen of him, so I just kept tossing him out. However, I called a halt when he bit me severely on the shoulder—and in my bed!

Such is the daily round of jungle life: a curious rhythm, and not like that of any other world. Waves of activity, with different contingents of creatures going about their business, and then two flat or even dead spots, one by day, the other by night, on a beautiful, regular seesaw. Only those who actually live in the jungle, and for weeks at a time for that matter, ever sense this rhythm. I can only hope that you may be granted the marvel of going there, and living there, and seeing and sensing for yourself.

19

Jungle Traffic

ONE of the most fascinating of all the many and varied aspects of jungles is the movement of the animals, or what we call traffic.

This, like almost every other aspects of the jungles—and all the rest of nature, for that matter—is quite complex and once again there are no published studies to which I can direct your attention should you be that deeply interested. So, once more, I have to base what I say on the expressions of others with experience of the bush. These seem to confirm my own observations and what local people, native to these countries, have told me and others. In all this, exclude the montane jungles because things there are not the same and, frankly, except for a few special cases, I just plain don't understand what does go on there in this respect. I also have to exclude the expressions of the true jungle peoples this time simply because nobody has, as far as I can find out, asked them whether they are cognizant of or make any use of the facts as related by others. The jungle peoples go about their daily life in a most businesslike manner, thereby astounding outsiders in matters like tracking. But whether they have the traffic situation in their jungles sorted out, I don't know, and I don't think anybody else does. But traffic there is.

Jungle animals live in five layers—in the canopy, in the middle tiers, on the ground, beneath it, and in the waters. They move about for various, and quite separately specific, reasons. There may be those that migrate, and there may even be mass *emigrations* like those of of our northern lemmings. I have seen monstrous numbers of one kind of forest frog suddenly appear out of the jungle and go floundering about dying for miles in the surrounding open country, never to return again. There are undoubtedly those that come up out of the waters, the ground or other low places, daily or on other rhythms, and ascend the trees to feed or to mate, and then go back down again. The majority, however, at first appear just to wander about during their appointed hours, feeding; and this goes for the canopy life, the middle tier creatures, and the ground surface lot. These go, for the most part, sidewise.

I say "appear just to wander about" advisedly, because if you are a biologist and spend only a few days and nights in the jungle, you will immediately become aware of the fact that none of the animals actually do this. All of them follow absolutely precise paths and even "roadways" that are worn clear of detritus—or sometimes even of bark up in the trees.

The animals of the rivers and lakes in jungle areas—there are no such *inside* jungles, only streams and ponds—come in two categories: those that have to reside perpetually in the water, and those that can come out on land. We will ignore the former until a later chapter. The "out-of-the-water-comers," which are mostly nightwalkers, include reptiles like crocodilians and chelonians, amphibians such as frogs and toads, and such invertebrates as fresh-water crabs and others. When the night finally settles down, it is a highly enlightening experience to take a powerful flashlight and wander softly to the nearest stream or river side. Jungle streams are mostly clear and tinkling, strewn with boulders and filled with fleshy green plants; the rivers are generally muddy and turgid in rainy periods but limpid in the dry seasons and reflect light by day as if they were black mirrors. Their water is colored from the humic, tannic and other acids derived from plant roots and decaying vegetation. It may look as clear as white wine but, if you float in it and let your legs slowly sink they will—if you have a pinkish white skin to start with—appear to go gradually yellow, then sherry brown, to bronze and dark brown. Take a glass of this water and hold it to the light and it is tinted like a light sherry. At night, the water is perfectly translucent and in shallow places along the edge of big rivers, you will almost always encounter serried ranks of aquatic creatures beached like canoes along a tropic seashore. Usually a short survey will disclose muddy channels leading out of the still water by which all manner of creatures come ashore to roam the jungle floor.

There are quite a number of different crocodilians inhabiting jungle rivers, and some of these come on land at night to maraud. Some of the caimans of South America and the larger crocodiles of Africa can be a considerable menace in this respect. One is strongly advised not to get between any of the latter and the water when they are on night patrol. Crocodiles look like lumbering, slumbering beasts but they can rise up on their legs like dogs, lift their tails into the air and literally gallop downgrade into their rivers. I once inadvertently got between a batch of large ones and a sand bar, along one of their trails through tall reeds. I did something wrong and they all came charging at me. Luckily, I was born with triggered muscular reactions and a built-in panic button so that I didn't have to contemplate my footwork and became virtually airborne back down the path where I made a ninety-degree veer out of the reeds and to the right. I'll swear that the lead croc was not two feet behind me as I completed said turn. Pure kinetic energy carried the lot of them straight on into the river. Believe me, my riverside explorations were considerably more circumspect from that day on.

Crocodilians may wander a very long way from water and stay away from it for weeks. I have had a number of rude encounters in the depths of the jungle and in dry periods by arousing a large crocodile from under a bed of dry leaves. (There is a pigmy species of African crocodile named *Osteolaemus* that customarily lives on dry land and only goes to water once a year for a brief period for, it is believed, breeding purposes.) I don't like crocodilians. Of all animals, they seem to be the only really malignant ones; and they are not nearly so stupid as one might suppose. Also, they are hunters in the true sense, and the bigger ones regard us humans as legitimate food. The darned things will deliberately stalk you—and unprovoked at that. One night I was catching tidal fish and crabs with a light hand net at the edge of the mangrove swamps in New Guinea when I heard a slight noise behind me and flashed around. There was a very large croc, not creeping, but quietly walking up on me, eyes intent and mouth slightly open. I've rarely moved so fast in my life; and I never went fishing at night alone again. Yet, even with a highly competent local stalwart behind me at all times with a bright light pointing the other way, I was stalked on two other occasions on that coast. This was not strictly a jungle, but this behavior was not a local peculiarity either. I've experienced the same thing in Africa, South and even Central America. This probably doesn't happen to ordinary hunters because they pound around looking for things and moving on. An animal collector, on the other hand, moves very little, stays very quiet and keeps dowsing his lights. We are much more vulnerable.

Another group of aquatic or semiaquatic animals that come out into jungles, the various tortoises, water-tortoises, turtles, or whatever you want to call them, also follow regular pathways which can be spotted, tabbed and used as death traps by an animal collector. One might have supposed, as I initially did, in my abysmal ignorance, that the river frogs and toads would just come hopping out anywhere they could get a footing on bank, root, or overhanging branch. But no, they too appear to follow regular highways just like the crocodilians, chelonians and, I might add, well-regulated human citizens. I have seen the clear waters at the edge of a large river positively filled with frogs of several different kinds, all with eyes above water and expectantly looking toward the bank and food. Pulling back and waiting, I then observed the horde slowly begin to move shoreward, but, so help me, they then solemnly peeled off into streams of converging traffic and patiently awaited their turn to follow certain set routes to the bank. So fascinated was I with this that I took my wife, then my assistants, down to the river night after night to make them watch and confirm what I had seen—and night after night the hordes came in single file. What is more, they then proceeded along certain set routes over the ground or through the bushes for a considerable distance before fanning out vertically and/or horizontally to feed. With all the space in the world—literally—why should animals behave like people driving cars onto turnpikes? There must be practical reasons.

But, there are other lesser roads that buzz off into the jungle following altogether bizarre routes. These are animal highways and I have observed that they are followed by everybody from mice to the large cats and plodding tortoises. None of them will deviate from these paths even when being enthusiastically (though, I don't think too seriously) chased by predators. Animals are very conservative, and they are also very practical. These paths follow routes that would defy surveyors but their purpose can be seen by anybody willing to lie flat on the ground and observe the topography from mouse-eye level.

In the jungle this marvelous natural phenomenon is perhaps more obvious than anywhere else, once you get on to it. The paths are not so clearly defined as in more open terrain, but they are there, as any collector of animals very soon learns. The real jungle people seem to follow them instinctively. Non-jungle people can also be incredibly adept trackers, and it is fascinating to follow them as they work. They will go left of one tree and right of the next four; then suddenly make a right-angle turn and head up a steep bank that looks impossible. But, if you will just follow along, you will find that the course they take has a very low gradient, and all at once you are on the top of the ridge without any loss of breath. Animals travel this way too and, if you just give up all your preconceived notions of trekking (as well as tracking) and let yourself drift, you find that you are following the highways of the wild world.

Many times I have been just meandering along, especially at night, looking about at this and that on the ground or in the trees, and have come face to face with some large, startled and apparently rather peeved beast. Tapir in the Americas and in Sumatra, pigs of all kinds in Africa and the Orient and their relatives, the peccaries, in tropical America, seem to constitute your principal confrontees. These creatures are conservative to the point of stuffiness and, although the very suggestion is grossly anthropocentric, they appear to resent your presence on their highways. Nervous deer, great bumbling hippos and myopic anteaters may also be encountered. The expressions on their faces when they meet you face to face are often extremely comical. Of course, you occasionally meet a really touchy character like one of the little forest bovines, commonly called buffalo, and in Africa "Bush Cows." These animals do not give way, and if you annoy them, they may circle around and follow you and, it has been alleged, actually ambush you. This last I have not experienced but

Ivan Sanderso

Pygmy ant-eater.

I was once charged by one without, as far as I know, having caused any provocation other than being on one of its roads. Luckily it turned out to be a lone animal, and in the ensuing contretemps I won.

Leading into the jungles from surrounding land areas of other types there are also clearly discernible tracks, paths and even animal roadways, but once inside these seem to disappear. Nevertheless, after a time, you find yourself drifting along set routes, though not for any apparent reason. Somehow you find yourself instinctively going around this tree on one side and the next on the other, just like the professional hunters; and you will find yourself doing this night after night in your staked area around your camp. And it is along these unmarked "traces" that you meet the animals. You cannot predetermine your pathway in the forest and you will be sorely disappointed if you try.

I once had a most wonderful colleague who joined me in West Africa on a bet and literally at a moment's notice. I believe he had handled a shotgun once before he left England but, a few days after he reached me deep in the jungle area, he went out alone—which horrified the Africans—and pounded about half the night and came back with no less than forty animals. Where he had been, he had no idea, and how he found his way home I also cannot say; but he did. On intensive questioning we found that he had very sensibly confined his peregrinations to the edge of the jungle and along the river banks nearby. To our somewhat more experienced chagrin, he pointed out that there were little paths everywhere from which he could see the outer branches of the trees above and a lot of the ground ahead. In other words he had instinctively hit the professional, out-of-jungle, local hunters' bailiwick.

When you get to know your particular jungle you will no longer regard it at night as a fearsome place full of horrendous predators and other ghoulies. It becomes extremely friendly—provided you don't go smashing around frightening its rightful inhabitants. A startled beast can be dangerous, so the rule is *drift,* don't tramp. There seems to be a general drift of mobile life in all jungles, just as there is in shallow seas—and possibly in ocean depths. Maybe it

Ivan Sanders

Red river-hogs feeding on the jungle floor.

is caused by the regular daily "tides" but, if you move too fast or in the wrong direction, you will startle things. If, on the other hand, you stand still in an exposed position you may cause even worse alarm. (Of course, if you are in a previously constructed hiding place this is not the case.) I found very early that you could drift into a herd of animals feeding on the jungle floor, even with a light, and they would pay very little attention to you until you stopped. Then, all heads came up and around, and you were glared at; and if you persisted in staying put, panic ensued among the gathering. On the other hand, many animals, notably the great cats, are not able to define a stationary object, even if it is good food and they can smell it. The deer or antelope or man must be moving before they can get a fix on it and go after it. Yet, other animals that are normally preyed upon behave in an exactly contrary manner. You are one of the gang as long as you go along with it. It is notable that the predators tend to stay quietly waiting for their prey to drift by, so that an immobile breathing creature is regarded as a potential menace.

Drifting is just as much a daytime formula as a nighttime one, and the same general rules seem to apply in all jungles. I stress that they do not necessarily apply *outside* the jungle or in other types of vegetation. The true jungle is not comparable to the outside. It has a life, a structure, a rhythm and a set of rules of its own, and it is in all these ways stricter than other tropical forests. Herein, life proceeds on a much more recognizable pattern than elsewhere—once you get with it. I would also like to stress another point once again, even at the risk of repetition. Very few outsiders ever really go into a jungle, and if they do they take the first opportunity of getting out. Even local non-jungle people will walk miles after dark with lanterns, singing bravely, to get *through* it to the next village or clearing. Local hunters dart into its edge at dawn and then get out again. Foreigners move from one established resting place to the next and seldom bother to try to hunt in the jungle proper because they don't see anything to shoot there by day and invariably get lost by night. Only professional investigators and the wonderful little band of scientists who are described later on in this book have really lived *in* it.

Time and time again we have patiently trained intelligent local lads to help us with our collecting and then announced that we were going into the "bush" to *live* for a couple of months at a time. And that was the last we heard of them! Other times they have gone along with us but, on discovering that we were *really* going to live there, come shamefacedly to us and begged to be returned to the outside. And this went for people born and raised on the very edge of a jungle as well as those raised in coastal ports, mission stations and the so-called more civilized areas. Repeatedly I have asked them what scared them so much, but they could never answer specifically. It was some ingrained if not inborn fear just like that I witnessed among whites in World War II. Some of our GI's, nurtured on comic strips and Hollywood notions of "the jungle," would not set foot in it for love nor money, nor even their own lives, and preferred to be bombed and strafed every evening by the Japanese. The irony of all this is that in, for instance, certain western Pacific islands there were no poisonous snakes, let alone "lions and tigers and all that stuff."

For local tropical peoples, such as non-jungle South American Amerinds, Africans, Malays and Papuans, the situation is even more preposterous and futile, because the places they live in *are* often the stamping grounds of multitudinous poisonous snakes, leopards, jaguars, and all manner of other animals that can be potentially dangerous, while a few paces inside the true jungle nearby these creatures are either nonexistent or apparently just as scared as their human counterparts.

F. Spencer Chapman, in his wonderful book *The Jungle Is Neutral,* may perhaps have come closer to an explanation than anybody else. The problem is mental, for, as he pointed out, of the gang he was left isolated with in the jungle when the Japanese took over Malaya, his men died off in direct proportion to their education and mental outlook. The "ranks" went first and *in toto;* the noncommissioned officers next and more slowly. Only the officers survived.

A vast majority of jungle animals spend most of their time in holes of various kinds and dimensions. These may be rare caves, dug holes, or holes in, under, or among tree roots or fallen trunks. Holes also ascend into the air via the vast chimneys of hollow trees with which the jungles are rife. In these, there is night while it is day, and all manner of nightwalkers dwell in them—and this goes for ground-dwelling forms as well as arboreal ones. We found giant, hollow African trees inhabited simultaneously by the most incredible assortment of creatures, from leopards to flying mice (the anomalurid named *Idiurus*). These hollow-tree dwellers are actually part of the "underground," and they behave accordingly, most of them being crepuscular or nocturnal.

On the floor of the jungle there are innumerable holes, of all sizes, mostly concealed from above in a most clever manner. Curiously, very few of these are deep or of any great extent—unlike the monumental earthworks of animals outside the jungle. Poking around in these holes you can usually come upon the occupant at no great depth or distance from the entrance, and you get a lot of surprises. Large constricting snakes take up their abodes in the shallow bank pits made by pangolins and other anteaters; crazy, ground-

Ivan Sanderson

South American paca, an immense kind of guinea pig.

living birds may bed down with rats and porcupines; and on one occasion I even found a family party of the baboon-like drills ensconced in a huge hole made by some other animal. The cave dwellers are different in that even night animals don't normally go more than a few feet into the entrance, though I have found far down in caves old and sick leopards and jaguars, both alive and in the form of desiccated mummies.

Despite the apparently elaborate precautions taken by jungle animals to camouflage the entrances to their holes, there are almost invariably quite well-defined paths leading to and from them. These paths often become regular roadways, with two or three or more branches, and then they finally peter out. This is the case with large animals such as pacas in South America and pangolins in Africa. Lesser creatures are bolder in every respect. I am thinking of the famous leaf-cutter ants of the American tropics. Since this is one of my favorite topics, I had better restrain myself and refer you to a book I wrote titled *Living Treasure*.

These incredible creatures are one of the only other forms of life, apart from ourselves, known on this planet that practice agriculture (or horticulture, if you admit mushroom-growing to this category of enterprise). They feed exclusively on the exudations from the fructifications of one kind of fungus which they raise in hotbeds in holes in the ground. These hotbeds are made from a never-ending supply of freshly cut leaves and flowers gathered by the ants from the tops of the jungle trees and solemnly toted back to their nests. The fungus spores are carried by the queen and planted by special workers in these hotbeds, which are then duly aerated, moistened or dried to promote growth of the fungus *mycelia*. When these have penetrated and digested the mass, which then looks like a kind of unleavened bun, "fruits" or "mushrooms" emerge on minute stems and start exuding the food for the ants. The city economy of these insects includes all manner of other activities that cause us to boggle. But what we are primarily interested in now is *traffic* in the jungles.

These ants make regular roadways, with underpasses, cloverleaves and some other engineering (and topological) works that are still quite beyond us. Admittedly, these appear at first sight just to wander off into the surrounding forest like the paths from the holes of larger animals, but these ants have a very much more direct purpose. The paths lead to trees up which they travel in an endless stream to gather the appropriate leaves at higher altitudes. Then the workers come down again, bearing their loads held aloft like little green sails, and pound solemnly along the highways back to the nest. Traffic is superbly controlled by "police" ants at intersections and on patrol. If danger intervenes, "soldier" ants come charging out of the nest and attack the intruder, even if he be a man or other large animal—and the bigger ones can make a neat quarter-inch cut in your flesh. These roads are cleared of every bit of trash, and if something falls upon one, teams of workers are immediately organized to remove it. Thus, they are clear highways at all times. If a large log comes down, the police ants immediately set up detours and get gangs to work clearing a new route under, over, or around the new obstruction.

Is this blind instinct? I simply do not see how anybody can affirm this. Frogs coming out of a river, burrowing animals coming out to forage, even monkeys trekking through the canopy, may indeed use recognized routes following lines of least resistance, or simply their leader. That is one thing. Building highways up to lengths that are,

Ivan Sanderson

Squirrel monkey.

in proportion to the size of their builders, as much as thirty of our miles long, is quite another. There is planning here, and of a most advanced order. In fact, I was once invited, after mentioning this amazing business on radio, by the mayors of three New Jersey townships to submit my findings to their traffic engineers. I did so, but despite drawings and some photographs, nobody could figure out just how they (the ants) had designed opposing lanes of traffic under, over, and around each other without resorting to the vast "pretzels" that we have had to develop.

These Weewee Ants (the Attids) do not live exclusively in the jungle. In fact, forms of them are found over a very wide range, even up to the state of New Jersey in North America, but it is in the undisturbed tropical TEF and TDF that their activities may be seen in all their most remarkable aspects. We once lived for a month on top of one of their huge nests, about forty feet in diameter, and we devoted a considerable amount of our time both night and day to observing their activity. These creatures amaze and confound me more than any other animal I have ever studied.

There are two major sources of animal food in the jungles that seem to be completely out of place and which nobody seems to have done much about. One is snails; the other is crabs. I have said this before but I will say it again—I have never been able to get over meeting a crab in the top of a jungle tree! Where I was born, and where most of you who will read this were born, crabs come on plates in restaurants or on the beach by a sea. One thinks of them as aquatic and predominantly if not wholly marine creatures that may occasionally run out on land before ducking back into their watery element. Yet, tropical lands are littered with crabs that spend all their time out in the air, in trees, on the ground, in holes, or in and out of fresh waters. Of course, all have to go back to water to breed, but there are those that spurn streams and rivers and use instead water-filled holes in giant forest trees. I suppose I will never get used to this either, but we must admit that so-called land crabs form a very high part of the diet of a lot of jungle animals. So do snails of innumerable kinds.

Both these animals appear to have roadways also. I have watched a meticulous molluscan climber proceed up one particular liana night after night, going around one side, reaching out for the next leg of its journey, and then going mysteriously on up. I have also followed crabs in trees and observed that they too follow the leader in great masses—like the riverine frogs lining up and waiting their turn to proceed along a specific route—branch by branch, and never along any other route. There are also absolutely amazing creatures called *Platyhelminthes,* or flatworms, to which our famous high-school lab animal *Planaria* belongs, which are all over the jungles. Some of them are really enormous and colored so vividly in yellows, oranges, tangoes, reds, browns and blacks, and even iridescent blues that you can hardly believe your eyes when you come upon them gliding almost imperceptibly upon tree trunks. It was one of my duties to try to collect and preserve these creatures but the results were nearly always disastrous, as they have virtually no substance and tend to dissolve on contact. (We did finally find a method of preserving them, but in so doing they came to look like strips of old linen and all their glorious colors vanished.) The only thing to do with them is to sit down patiently and provide something that they will glide onto; then pop this into a bottle and get back to your work table as fast as possible.

In the process of doing this I learned that these strange lowly beasts were in one respect just as conservative as the monkeys of the canopy and the pigs of the jungle floor. They followed set routes. What is more, extreme patience would land more of a kind in apparently unending succession on the same route. A large platyhelminth, say six inches long, takes an hour to travel a few feet, but the darned things make it, and then come more—always along the same route. Could it be that these creatures follow a slime trail left by the fellow ahead, or do they for some reason know just what path to take? One would suppose that going aside would provide more food, since their peers have preceded them.

The greatest surprises come when you start to ascend into the galleries above the ground. There you encounter two very distinct worlds—the lower tiers and the canopy. Furthermore, the real life of the jungles begins on top and works downwards to meet the upcoming life from below, so that until we understand the activities of the canopy we cannot understand that of the middle tiers.

20

The Flying Continents

A LITTLE over thirty years ago Oxford University mounted an expedition to the jungles of British Guiana, and some members of the group—biologists—decided to try to find out what went on in the "flying continent" far above their heads. Using laborious but nonetheless practical methods, they finally attained some lofty heights and, making platforms, lived there for some time. I was intrigued to read about this on my return from an extended trip to the Orient, because a young Achinese (a fine people of Malayan origin who have inhabited northwestern Sumatra for centuries) with whom I traveled for several months in the East Indies had shown me a trick for getting aloft, though in a very crude manner. He constructed a primitive bow and arrow and attached to the latter a very long fine thread unraveled from an old piece of cloth—we had nothing else available. He shot the arrow time and time again up into the canopy until it came down over a branch. He then attached to this our fishing line and hauled it aloft; and when that was paid-out, he attached a strong strand of liana to it, and got that up over the branch and down again. Then he climbed aboard a simple sling made by a loop in this and told me to heave away.

Luckily he was much lighter than I, and he helped by pulling on the downcoming portion of the liana, so that he finally reached one of the large bottom branches. After that, by sending more lianas, partly woven, aloft and hauling both ways, I got up too. Immediately the whole world looked different.

We had been plowing through a magnificent and completely uninhabited forest for three weeks and had never seen the sun directly. Now, all of a sudden, we were up in the sky in a new world and the dim green world below us disappeared. We could see not only the afternoon sun but the great barrier of mountains far off to the south that forms the backbone of the enormous island of Sumatra. Both of us being seventeen-year-old "monkeys," we climbed all over that giant jungle tree and made side trips to adjacent ones until the sun showed signs of setting and we decided to scramble back to our Tarzan-type elevator and get down to the jungle floor to make our sketchy camp. We climbed trees on several other occasions, but we never made a project of it and we never stayed aloft, though my friend Achi told me that there were other people who spent most of their time in the trees up in the mountains, an age-old story throughout Sumatra.

This idea of getting up into the canopy of the jungle continued to intrigue me, and I made all kinds of silly and impractical plans for doing so and then staying up there, but it was many years before I was able to put the idea into practice. This was in Nicaragua, more than ten years later. There we employed Achi's technique rather than the sophisticated procedure that includes climbing irons, mountaineering ropes and ladders. This time I had a powerful store-bought bow, but I had to lie on my back, strap it to my feet, and use both hands to get the arrow with its fine line up over the lowest branch. (The power you have pulling a bow this way is quite astonishing, and I finally broke the thing in an excess of enthusiasm!) We then searched around for a good place to construct a platform, which we did with bush sticks (i.e., sapling poles), some liana rope and, I have to admit, some imported rope and large nails. To this we added floor boards ripped from our schooner by which we had reached that distant place up the Kuringuas River. On this we erected a small pup tent, a cooking platform and safe storage for our supplies. By actual measurement we were 120 feet up.

Our helpers came twice a day with supplies and water which we hauled aloft, though I have always rather felt that this was "cheating." We also sent down our duly preserved specimens. We were up there off and on for two weeks, and as we were not "exploring," but seriously trying to find out just what does go on in the flying continents, we did not indulge in any adventurous exploits; but we did eventually manage to travel in complete safety over a quarter of a mile through the treetops to a stream where our staff drew water.

Life in the canopy is a remarkable experience. Nothing one may have read or been told about it in advance seems to conform to reality, and the reality itself provides many extraordinary interludes. I never got up into the canopy in New Guinea, and I did so in Africa only by climbing for short periods to set traps or to collect small things. In South America, I had to go aloft twice a day, personally, to tend over a hundred traps, but I did not live up there. Therefore, I cannot speak for conditions in any of these other places, and it is certain that they vary. Nonetheless, I did have that one intimate view of and association with a true jungle canopy and, if conditions a hundred and twenty feet up in one tropical forest were as we observed them, it is at least possible that similar basic conditions obtain in others. From what little I have seen of others, I have a fancy that there is a certain universality to them.

I do not want to give the impression that we are the only people to have lived in the canopy: quite the contrary. Apart from the Oxford expedition pioneers, the forestry department of Malaya did a lot of botanical work in this tier, even employing trained monkeys (the Giant Rhesus) to climb aloft, pluck, and throw down flowers, top leaves and fruits of jungle trees. *Life* magazine, in its fine series entitled *The World We Live In* some years ago, ran an issue on the true jungles (in Surinam, incidentally) during the preparation of which they went aloft. Descriptive writers, photographers and an artist were hauled up and recorded the appearance, the mood and the life of the canopy. Brazilians have recorded many observations of life in this upper level, and the French, before they cleared out of Indochina, recorded a lot of biological information of their canopied jungles. Martin Johnson, sage of the early animal photography clique, reported on the Bornean jungle upper levels when he was capturing Mias (commonly called "Orang-utans"), and Tom Harrisson and his wife, curators of the national museum in Sarawak, have given us a profundity of novel information on this subject.

The most noticeable feature of the canopy, or rather, the one that finally impressed us most, was its traffic. I had always supposed that the canopy, being a continuous flying continent, since it is bound inextricably by interlocking branches and massive lianas, would

Ivan Sanderson

Two-fingered sloth makes its way in the flying continent.

present a more or less endless field for movement, at least for small animals. Not so! Just like the domain of the ground-living animals, it proved to have regular highroads with subsidiary feeder paths to food areas. What is more, all the animals seem to know, and to stick to, these highways—from jaguars and monkeys and leopards and apes, to arboreal rats and mice, snails, frogs, and insects. This was brought most forcibly to our attention when we discovered that we had built our modest platform and taken up residence at a five-way intersection.

The denizens of the canopy did not like the look or, presumably the smell of us at all, and for some time they avoided us like the plague, though we heard and saw them moving about both by day and by night just out of range. Eventually, they seem to have decided that, despite our smoke and noise-making, we were merely a novel but necessary evil and that, unless and until we made some hostile move, they might as well go back to doing what grandpa did. So after a few days, we were invaded at every hour of the day and night by various hordes of animals intent on going where they wanted to go—i.e., straight through our temporary home.

First came the tree frogs; then the snails; then the monkeys; and so on, for as long as we stayed up there. They were aggressive too. Led by one species of tree frog intent, we later learned, on streaming to the nearest ground-level water to breed at their appointed time, they came on, wave after wave. However, the most annoying were the local black and white capuchin monkeys, which marauded our very limited larder. They even filched bottles of preserved specimens and gleefully hurled them down to the forest floor. Arboreal monkeys, so extremely nervous and touchy when disturbed by anything on the ground below that might be a possible menace, behave in an altogether different manner in the canopy. If you are not sitting on one of their highways, they seem mostly to ignore you; but if you are squatting thereupon, they will approach cautiously, making their appropriate noises of alarm and spread out around you. They will not, however, digress from their regular road or make a detour, and they will often just retreat and come back another day. Eventually they seem to overcome their fear, and what one may be permitted to call outrage at this unorthodox obstruction, and just move in and stream by. Of course, if there is anything to eat or examine enroute, they will eat or inspect it. Their boldness up there is quite inconceivable to the earthbound with all our preconceived notions about the behavior of wild animals. Time and time again, I have had absolutely wild animals, including monkeys, regarded as being hypersensitive to the dangers of the world and human beings in particular, come right up to me, look me in the eye and, after making some "small talk" deliberately grab something from right under my nose and make off with it, chittering with delight. But crack one stick on the forest floor when trying to creep up on a troop of monkeys feeding above, and they will take off faster than you can run along the ground.

Just below the canopy, which is, of course, composed of mass leafage and small branches, one may encounter one of the most wonderful aspects of the jungle. This is standing water in holes

Ivan Sanderson

Black and white capuchin monkey.

between the main supporting branches. Some of these holes are veritable cisterns that go deep down into the hollow trunks, and they contain limpid pure water long after all surface water has vanished from the forest floor and the streams have dried up. Few people realize that apart from getting lost, or "bushed" as it is called, in the jungle, the greatest danger to survival is lack of water. We think of jungles as drenched, dripping places, and imagine them filled with rivers, streams and swamps. Great rivers there are, and they survive any dry season, but the feeder streams tend to dry up and the forest floor to become tinder dry. It's no good digging for water because the surface soil is usually so shallow and you almost immediately hit hard subsoil or surface rock. The only thing to do is climb trees that look large enough to have water holes aloft. It is a tedious business, but it is better than dying of thirst in a sort of steam bath with the hygrometer standing at 100; and dying of thirst in a jungle is just as unpleasant as in the middle of the desert, although you are shaded from the merciless rays of the sun. I know; I've been through the preliminary routine several times.

In these arboreal water holes one finds all manner of life. One of the most prevalent is mosquito larvae. (Incidentally, the old saw that any water in which mosquito larvae are skipping about is fit to drink is literally true in the jungle.)

Mosquitoes offer an excellent example of the fact that the animal life of the jungles is stratified. My wife happens to have been trained in medical zoology, and it was her duty to collect noxious and disease-carrying insects of all kinds, while I and my assistants got on with the larger animals, the botany, and the parasites. We had always been interested in vegetalogical and ecological matters, and so when we came to work in the jungles we naturally went up as well as sidewise. After surveying a small area of forest floor by chain and compass and examining its smaller differences, we started upward into the trees by levels of ten feet, collecting all animals that we encountered at each level and plotting them. We found some animals dwelling at each level exclusively, and others that moved from one tier to another to feed or otherwise conduct their normal lives. The animals varied from hour to hour throughout the day and night. One of my unenviable tasks was to precede my wife, divested of covering from the waist up, so that noxious and bloom-sucking insects might land on the clear expanse of my disgustingly pale skin to be captured by my loving helpmate in small glass vials. Luckily, Atabrine and Quino-Plasmoquin had been discovered by that time, so that malaria was not a problem, but I must admit to some worry about the mosquitoes of the genus *Aedes* which carry yellow fever, still endemic among the human population of that area. There was not at that time any immunization procedure for this.

As we went up the trees we began to investigate the water holes and from them my wife extracted a really remarkable series of different mosquitoes in their developmental phases—as eggs, larvae and pupae. Bringing them to ground, she then proceeded to raise them in glass jars half-filled with water and covered with cheesecloth. When the final insect (the imago) emerged she would collect and preserve it along with specimens of its pupa, larva and eggs if possible. After this material had gone off to, and been examined in, established laboratories (and I would like to acknowledge the work done on our material by the Rockefeller Institute in Panama, in this respect) a number of most interesting facts began coming to light.

In every jungle, it appears different types of mosquitoes inhabited and/or moved about through each tier or level. By hindsight, this would appear to be obvious, but until there was absolute evidence of it, the whole thing was nothing but an hypothesis. We were not the first to discover this; much work had been done on monkey malaria previously, and it had become clear that the carriers of this disease stayed up at certain levels in the trees.

I suppose that the inhabitants of the middle tiers are, in the overall, the most interesting and perhaps the most varied in the jungle. Further, they are the most neglected and the least known. Local hunters are hunting for meat, and the largest items are ground-dwelling. Casual entrants from outside travel through the jungle by day and therefore see mostly (and perhaps only) the gaudy, rowdy denizens of the canopy. The middle tier dwellers are almost exclusively nocturnal.

True inhabitants of the middle tiers also have a traffic problem.

They live in holes in the big trees, in palm heads, or in the rather rare jumbles of lianas and epiphytes that sometimes hang suspended below the canopy. There are also in some jungles rather profusely leafed saplings on their way up to the canopy which make most excellent sleeping quarters for small animals. All of these arboreal creatures have recognized paths through the trees—along one liana to a giant tree bole, up it a short way, down by another vine onto a palm head, and so on. Night after night you can sit watching one of these routes and animals keep passing, but switch your observation only a few feet and you will never see anything moving. One of the first things that intrigued me about jungle nighttime life was this roadway system, because it contradicted everything I had been taught and read and otherwise observed about animal life.

One learns that there are preyed-upon animals, and animals that prey upon these. The two lots are supposed to be bitter enemies, the former living in perpetual fear and dashing hysterically away from the latter at the slightest sight of them. But the world of wild animals simply does not work this way. First, the predators kill much less live food than was once supposed—Wells, Guggisberg and other experts on the lion (not a jungle animal) point out that slightly more than one kill per month is about the rule. James B. Schaller notes six times this figure for tiger. Second, most so-called predators are actually necrophorous or, in other words, scavengers of already dead animals. Third, it has been observed that the live victims are usually almost dead already, or young or crippled. Cheetahs, for instance, will walk boldly up to a herd of grazing antelope or gazelle and then lie down. The hoofed-animal sentinels see them plainly and appear to indicate their presence to the rest of the herd, but nothing happens. Finally, a cheetah stands up, starts advancing and then goes into his terrific rush. What happens? The herd simply opens up and one animal only takes off for the far blue yonder, but not, according to observers, apparently trying too hard. The cheetah goes right through the herd, ignoring it, and brings down this lone animal, kills it and then lets out a tiny whistling sound which brings *his* gang up to feed. These also often stroll right through the herd, which has by this time gone back to grazing placidly as if nothing had happened.

The interesting thing is that the lone animal attacked and killed appears invariably to be very young, very old or sick. Furthermore, it seems in some strange way to know that its time has come. Cheetahs are alleged to be able to hit 70 m.p.h. (though this has recently been denied rather strongly) but impala and some gazelles can certainly match their speed and perhaps outrun them. Thus a healthy antelope does not fear a cheetah, but the maimed and the old somehow know they cannot win the race, and just give up.

So it is in the middle tiers of the jungle. The traffic along the aerial ways of both the canopy and middle tiers is an extraordinary parade of hunters and hunted. In Africa, I once saw first a couple of galagos (a form of lemurine arboreal primate), then a genet (a truly fast and sharp hunter), then a number of ambling tree frogs, followed by a lot of rats, a potto (another sub-lemurine primate) and finally a small cat. If the genets and the cats are hunting why don't they just catch up with the first edible item ahead? After all, they have a very fine set of senses and cannot possibly miss the trail.

No, there is what I call a *polity of nature,* which escapes us, who for millennia now have spent a great part of our energy lashing out at our own kind, but which preserves a most conservative and most highly efficient organization. This stands to reason, for you just could not run a jungle, or any other department of nature, if all the predators were so much better equipped than their prey. They would clear out all their own food in no time at all. The vegetable feeders are preyed upon by meateaters, but everybody gets along, and there is always a plentiful supply of food for both.

A clue to this polity of nature is seen in our own countryside along the roadside or on the pavement. This gives the impression that wild animals are dying all the time all over the lot. Of course, it is manifest that all animals must die sometime but the weird thing is that you never find a dead animal in the fields or woods, or especially in the forests. The same is true of the tropics, especially of the jungles. The only dead animal I have ever come across in a jungle was an African Forest Loxodont (elephant), and, though we could not find any direct evidence to the effect, it appeared almost certain that it had been killed by hunters. Considering the sheer volume of animal life in any jungle one might imagine that the forest floor would be carpeted with dead animals. Yet, you never find *one*. Answer . . . garbage-disposal units.

This is exactly what the so-called predators are. They do not hunt live game if they can find a corpse, and often the older it is the more they like it. Even the most single-minded of all jungle hunters, the leopard, is not averse to carrion. True, they do seem to be fascinated by monkeys and domestic dogs, and will take a swipe at either and then eat them as fast as possible, but on the whole, the big cats of the jungle don't molest healthy, adult, large animals—I am, of course, *not* speaking of other types of tropical forest, or other terrain. I have been what is called "stalked" by leopards several times, and one night while cleaning a gun after midnight by the light of the moon, I suddenly became aware that a very large jaguar was cleaning itself on the ridge pole of the tent in which my wife was snoring away happily. To all of these creatures I simply said something like "Boo!" in a very loud and peremptory manner and they shoved off at the double.

The only large cat that I don't like or trust is the tiger, but then, the poor thing is not really an indigenous TEF or TDF animal, having, it appears, been evolved in the snows of northern Asia, and he appears to be as rattled by the jungle as any nonjungle man. He is an outsider, living in the tertiary and secondary forests, along river banks and around the land used by man in the thickest bush he can find. But tigers are sneaky, and there is no doubt they will jump humans with the direct purpose of eating them—in certain circumstances.

As a matter of fact, after nearly forty years of meandering about jungles under the most vulnerable conditions (when you are setting little traps your back is exposed for hours on end), I have yet to be actually jumped by anything larger than an ant. Once I shot at a pair of eyes in a tree top by mistake and with small pellets at that. I climbed aloft to see what I had hit and came face to face with a, rather naturally, peeved leopard on a large limb about eighty feet above the ground. He backed off along the branch while I returned to earth with singular aplomb. Animals, especially jungle animals, that do not know man and have not been shot at just don't seem to give a damn. However, I should insert here a fact related by an old friend, David Jordt, who spent many years in Liberia and had an animal compound there. He tells me the persecution of anything that moves in that country has been so persistent since the introduction of firearms that even the mild little forest antelopes, called duikers may attack you on sight—and they are leaf eaters!

We have long been told that we have five senses, and people still run around talking about the possibility of a "sixth sense." As of the date of writing this, we are known to have somewhere between twenty-five and thirty senses, and every year the number mounts. For instance, we have a sense of balance, of electrical flux, of thirst, of hunger, bowel compaction, and so forth. Other animals have just as many and some of them demonstrably more. On one joint of an antenna of a certain kind of fly, four different sense organs have been discovered and we don't know what any of them are for. Locusts have altimeters that outsmart any we have; horseshoe crabs have a built-in compass that does not need magnetic lines to function but only one look at the sky, night or day, to see where the rays of the sun are coming from (the basis, incidentally, of the compass used in the polar regions when magnetism does not work and there is a "white-out"). Looked at from the human point of view, all animals have supersensory-perception.

This whole matter impinges upon another one that seems to put everybody into panic. This is what is probably quite erroneously called telepathy or mental telepathy. Why this unnerves everybody so much I have never been able to fathom. If it exists, it is probably as complex as any other natural phenomenon; but it would seem to be just as amenable to pragmatic analysis, as long as one does not, in point of fact, panic. The basis of the matter is this:

We communicate certain intelligence to each other via speech and hearing, writing and other symbols. Other animals also manifestly communicate. If they did not, they would never get around to mating. So by what means do they communicate? There have been those who assert that they "talk" to each other, but everybody else denies this. Now, it is known that certain higher primates have a regular language consisting of both sounds and gestures. And massive studies have been made of many animals, both in laboratory conditions and in the wild, which demonstrated categorically that they do communicate with their own kind and even with other types of life to a more limited extent—a good example is what Julian Huxley long ago designated as "distance threat and deflection." The vital question, however, is, do wild animals use methods other than sounds, lip and other body movements, stinks and electromagnetic emanations (such as the infrared broadcasts of certain moths to attract males) for communication?

It is amazing how jungle animals seem to transmit basic and essential information to each other, and even more amazing how we humans, living near or among them, seem to be able unconsciously to affect them and their activities. Inquisitiveness seems to be an inborn feature of all mobile life. The behavior of the tapirs on the ground and the monkeys in the canopy, described above, are only two examples of this. And it is something that I have pondered for years. Inquisitive and even fearful these other creatures may be, but why do they almost invariably let the former urge overcome the latter? I can tell you that, if you are barging around hunting for meat for the pot, you will never see a tenth of the animals that you will if you are just taking a stroll with a pair of binoculars and a notebook. Of course, there is the little matter of metal that has not to my knowledge been given a proper going over as yet.

Consult any geologist, mineralogist, petrologist or metallurgist as to the occurrence of any metal in pure form on the surface of the earth. He will tell you that apart from some gold, lead and copper, metals as we know them just do not exist in nature in the pure state. They all "rust," which is the layman's way of saying oxidize, or otherwise combine with other elements to form more stable compounds that make up our rocks and soils. Thus, our purified irons and so forth are not indigenous to nature and are unknown to other animals. What is more, they stink like hell—to them. We can smell a decaying whale two miles away but never notice the smell of our own belt buckle or our gun. Animals do; and if you oil that gun with another "unnatural product," namely a petroleum oil, the stench is apparently so overpowering to a wild animal that it can spot you thousands of yards away, even upwind, at that.

In the jungle, where there is absolutely no "wild" metal, animals are enormously sensitive to this odd set of stinks. So, go out carrying a gun—no animals. But take every bit of metal off you, wash your clothes in a stream without using soap; stop washing with soap and cleaning your teeth with all manner of aromatic tainted matter; and then go wander about in the jungle. The animals will at first stay quiet, observing you, then move in to take a look, and—so help me—even move right up to you to sort of "make friends." You stink right; you have not made any obnoxious move; they overcome their fear, which I contend is very slight in the first place in wild animals that do not know man; and curiosity gets the better of them. Then, in some horribly sub-basic (and to us as yet completely inexplicable) manner you will find yourself communicating with them. Hence the "drifting" I mentioned above, or their march right through our canopy house without a "by-your-leave."

I spent ten years hauling wild animals onto television two or three times a week, and I never got bitten, scratched, or even trodden on. This was not just good luck. There was some kind of communication there. I have no idea what it was. Maybe I smelled right to them, or had the right pitch of voice, or I just didn't care!

21

Life Around Jungles

At this point you will probably be saying that this is all very fine, but just what *are* the animals of the jungles and where are they found?

Nobody knows just how many kinds of animals live on this planet, and not even zoologists know precisely how many distinct forms have been caught, examined and described. The total known is usually given rather vaguely as about a million, of which well more than half are insects. Yet the entomologists have several times made so bold as to say that we have probably not yet identified one tenth of those that exist. Even the figures given for the number of known mammals varies between 16,000 and 4500, though the major factor in this disparity is the disagreement among two groups of classifiers, called respectively the "splitters" and the "lumpers."

One fellow once split the mountain lions up into dozens of forms; another fellow lumped dozens of forms of quite distinguishably different squirrels into a single species. How to define a species is still one of the zoologist's worst headaches, and new forms of animals are constantly being discovered at the rate of about several thousand a year, though this includes protozoa and other single-celled creatures. Finally, there is still a sort of inbred reluctance to accept new forms of lower status than a species.

The classification of animals in a truly scientific sense is only two hundred years old and it began in Europe, which has a comparatively limited fauna, and so we boggle at the idea that there can be fifty species of one subfamily of beetles in one small section of Mexico, or hundreds of species of land snails on the Caribbean island of Jamaica. Yet, this great mass of different forms of animal life has now been broken down into 27 (possibly 29) groups, wildly different, each perfectly distinct and called by zoologists *phyla.* Some of these have representatives on land, in fresh water and in the sea; others are, so far, known from only two or a single one of these elements. Then there are those that move back and forth from one element to another; and finally there are many that live inside other animals as parasites. How many of these groups are represented in the jungle?

Eleven phyla are known only from salt water. This leaves us with sixteen found on land and/or in fresh water. Of these, twelve are definitely found in jungles, three very probably and one doubtfully. I will dispose of the last first, as it is a singularly unimportant group, delighting in the name of the *Entoprocta,* one species of which has been found in the central forest area of India. Of the three probables, the most likely is that of the sponges (*Porifera*) one family of which, known as the *Spongillidae,* is exclusively a fresh water dwelling and globally distributed. Their presence *in* the jungle is, however, debatable because of the difficulty in defining true jungle water as opposed to great rivers that cut through jungles, or lakes lying outside them. Another group is called the *Nemertea* or ribbon worms of which there are many land-living forms that have been found along the edges of the tropics and in upland tropical regions but which do not seem to have been recorded from inside the jungles. The last of the probables are called *Gastrotricha*—fresh water and marine minutenesses that need not concern us. Thus remaining, are twelve of the 27 phyla of animals, that are definitely known from the jungles. What are these?

First, there are the single-celled animals (*Protozoa*) that flourish everywhere there is moisture. Next, there are the *Coelenterata,* the group to which the marine jellyfishes belong and which have fresh water forms known to all high school biology classes in the form of *Hydra,* a tiny jelly-like tube with tentacles that attaches itself to water weeds. There are multitudinous small aquatic creatures called *Rotifera* that nobody quite knows what to do with in the scheme of life. But, these and another phylum called *Bryozoa* or moss-animals need not concern us. Then, there are the two great groups of true worms—the *Annelida,* which includes the earthworms, and the *Ne-*

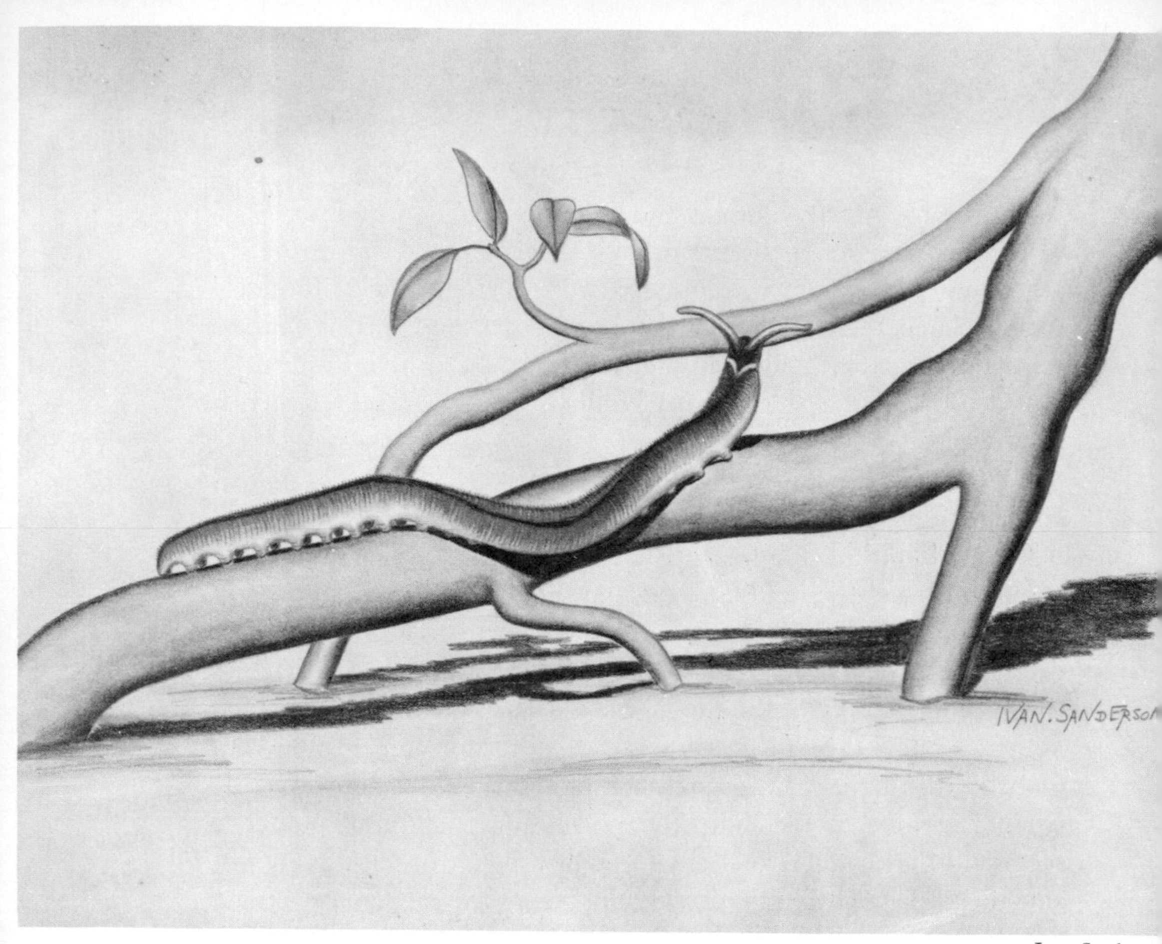

Ivan Sanderson

Peripatus.

matomorpha, or hairworms—both of which are free living; and to be grouped with them, there are three outstanding phyla that are predominantly parasitic. These are the flatworms (*Platyhelminthes*), which include, beside the parasitic tapeworms and flukes or trematodes, the famous planarian of our school laboratories. In the jungles, there are other free living flatworms of absolutely startling size and appearance which I shall refer to further again below. The other two are mainly parasitic groups, being the roundworms, or *Nematoda,* and some positively gruesome things called *Acanthocephala.*

This leaves us with the three largest and most important phyla—*Mollusca,* or shellfish; *Arthropoda,* including the insects, the spider group, the crustaceans or crabs and shrimps, and several others, among them a very strange and important small group called the velvet-worms, *Onchyophora*—i.e., the *Peripatus,* which are true "living fossils" and which appear to be links between the annelid worms and the arthropods; and lastly, *Chordata,* or backboned animals—fish, amphibians, reptiles, birds and mammals.

Out of all this mass of animals, there is no phylum that is exclusively of the jungle, nor even of the tropics for that matter; moreover, there is no phylum of land or fresh water animals that is definitely known *not* to occur in the jungles (though, unless we examine every cubic millimeter of them we can never make any certain statement about this). However, when we come to lesser groupings within these phyla, matters are quite different. You have to get right down almost to species before you can actually pin down any *exclusively* jungle dwellers.

There appear to be an endless list of genera of animals that live only in the jungle which disappear when and if it is cleared, but we must exercise the utmost caution in asserting that any of these are so rigidly confined. It is safer to put the matter the other way round and say that almost never does even an individual of any species of non-jungle animal enter the jungle—not by so much as a couple of yards. In fact, it is quite comical trying to chase a non-jungle species through the jungle wall. It will take every possible evasive action and sometimes, if cornered, will simply sit and shiver. There are, of course, innumerable animals of catholic habits, notably birds, that range over many types of vegetation including the jungle. There is also the troublesome matter of the jungle waters.

In the jungle there is very little if any standing water, in the form of ponds or lakes. By this I mean such small waters as are *covered by the canopy;* though, in the Gabun in West Africa, there are curious pools every now and then along the courses of the jungle streams on flat land. It is in these, incidentally, that the Giant Frog (*Rana goliath*) which, sitting up, is as big as a miniature terrier, is found. The tremendous rainfall on jungles, millenia if not millons of years ago, developed a unique runoff system which has resulted in a kind of giant plowed field effect, and along the bottoms of all the gutters excess water either seeps away or runs off in beautiful little clear streams. This water finally finds its way to the nearest large river.

Now, once a river is large enough and wide enough, the jungle stops short of its banks, and the canopy appears to come tumbling down to its edge. What actually happens is that by the introduction of direct sunlight, non-jungle as well as young true jungle vegetation takes hold and grows up to form a solid and sometimes virtually impenetrable wall of greenery. All of this growth has to have at least one side of its growing head exposed to the sunlight, so that the wall is never very thick, and once through it you step out into the gloom of the closed canopy forest. Are we to accept the animal life of the big rivers and its banks and enclosing vegetation walls as true jungle fauna? I contend that we are not, since the life found here almost invariably extends outward to the other forests lying around the jungle proper and/or to the shores of the seas, but does not extend inward. The only exception to the lack of standing water in jungles is the "flood forest." This is one of the marvels of nature.

In many areas, and not only on coastal lowlands, but on extended, flat bottomlands bordering large rivers, you may find that, either at certain times of the year or even, as in the Indochinese peninsula and parts of South America, all year round, the jungle trees stand in water. Coming from the so-called temperate belts we think of "drowning" trees if we flood their bases, but in the tropics many species have adapted to such a condition, just as our cypresses have. In the limpid waters of these flood forests live a very definitely jungle aquatic fauna, though some riverine animals will enter these vast flooded galleries. The most astonishing of the latter are, to me, the little fresh water whales of the Guianas and the Amazon, which we have mentioned earlier. Some river fish enter the flood forest through the small gutters that drain their waters into the rivers.

Most river fish, it seems, don't like to go into the flood forest, though they will penetrate to the headwaters of streams in areas outside the jungle whether the water is clear or turgid. Perhaps it is the excessive acidity or lack of oxygen of the flood forest waters that holds them off. Then again, the food in flood forest waters is singularly limited, while along river banks and lakes outside, it is abundant.

The fish fauna of tropical river systems is vast. One expert with many years of practical experience collecting and otherwise fishing in the Amazon Basin has declared that there are more known species of fish in it than have been described from the North Atlantic Ocean. But these are not legitimate denizens of the jungle and so constitute a vast separate subject. Yet there are those that do so enter, like the Arapaima of South America sometimes alleged to be the largest fresh water fish, though at fifteen feet it looks a bit paltry compared to the record sturgeon from Russia that measured 28 feet, caught in the Volga River. Then, there are all manner of oddities in the piscine line that also enter true jungle waters, two of which I have seen personally. One is a small armor-plated catfish with its front (pectoral) fins constructed as curved, hard scimitars with a cutting edge on the inside. These the fish can snap back against the sides of its body. But also, it has a sharp, pyramidal, poison gland in its "armpits" perforated by small channels, hypodermic-wise, the exudations from which are said to be as venomous as those of any snake. The other little horror is also South American, the Candiru. This is a minute, smooth-skinned catfish not much thicker than a pencil-lead that for some unknown reason has an affinity for mammalian urine and will enter the uro-genital openings of human beings, causing excruciating pain that can normally be relieved only by surgery due to the fact that the fish has backward-pointing spines around its gill openings.

Then, of course, there are the famous piri, or piranhas, also from South America, which have attained a worldwide reputation for pure savagery. It is true that they are carnivorous and have massive, firm-boned jaws armed with interlocking triangular teeth with razor-sharp edges which, when closed, form an almost perfect hemisphere. It is also true that coming, sometimes in the hundreds, they can demolish a large animal carcass before your eyes and before you have time to haul it out of the water. But a lot of the stories about them are exaggerated; we personally had many times to swim and dive in tropical streams and rivers filled with these fish but we were not attacked. True, many a local woman carries terrible scars or lacks a piece of the inner side of her thighs from attacks by these fish made while she was squatting to wash clothes on a river bank.

Apart from the fish, reptiles, lots of amphibians, and some mammals, such as hippos, manatees and the river dolphins, tropical rivers are most notable for their molluscan and crustacean life. There are nearly always bivalve shellfish on the bottoms of tropical waters, and they form one of the principal foods of the crocodilians and turtles. But there are also often vast swarms of all manner of fresh water "shrimps" and, on the banks, some crabs. However, the latter seem to prefer the jungles themselves, wherein they roam about on the forest floor, scuttle in and out of holes of all kinds, clank about in what caves there may be and climb trees right up to the canopy.

Then, there are the riverbank dwellers, including numerous snakes, frogs, such mammals as otters, chevrotains, monkeys of all kinds, countless hordes of insects, snails, more crabs and many other lowly beasts. In fact, the rivers and open lakes and their banks and adjoining swamps form quite a different world from that of the jungle hard by, and are inhabited by a far larger and more varied fauna. This is also where most non-jungle peoples live and do their hunting, and it is from these that foreigners think they see the jungles and their animal inhabitants. But, apart from some arboreal animals like monkeys, insects, and squirrels, and some specialized tree frogs and snakes that go up into the canopy, virtually none of these animals dwell also *inside* the jungle, and comparatively few venture into it for more than short distances. On the other hand, some jungle animals come out at night to the waters and to their verges to breed, hunt or fish.

The true jungle streams and pools—that is, those that are *under* the canopy, without direct sunlight—have a fascinating fauna all their own. There are innumerable kinds of small fish, many of most exotic design; there are some snails and other invertebrates; but above all there are frogs. The number of different kinds of jungle frogs seems to be endless. There are aquatic, burrowing, semiaquatic and climbing forms. Many of them come in exotic coloration, and most of them change color with more versatility than any chameleon. Moreover, many species also change from season to season, not only in color but in their very construction. In one species we studied extensively in West Africa (*Petropedetes johnsoni,* for the experts)

Ivan Sanderson

Water chevrotain, a small African antelope.

the males changed in one way seasonally, but differently during each of the first four years of their lives, while the females changed in another way, also seasonally, each year. Then, there are the little leaf frogs (and toads) that hop, climb or just meander about on the broad leaves of the lower tiers of the jungle. Among these are some of the smallest of all vertebrates. One of the most startling creatures I ever encountered was one of these tiny leaf toads with the name of *Nectophryne afra*. It was marked with vivid black and white stripes but had excessively large bright yellow hands and feet. At first I thought these were enveloped in some form of jelly and I supposed that the animal must have waded through rotting fungus or some other substance. However, on closer inspection, these coverings turned out to be sort of muffs extending well beyond the ends of the fingers and toes.

Another shock from which I have not recovered was the discovery of large toads in water holes a hundred feet up in trees in South

Ivan Sanderson

Brazilian otter.

America. These toads were not of the climbing variety and were in fact just as incapable of getting up more than a modest slope as our common toads are. We tried to persuade them to go up gently sloping branches, but they just fell off; and yet here they were at the tops of perpendicular giant forest trees, some even without lianas. We first traced them from extraordinary drumming sounds that boomed out in the evening from some giant trees. You could set them going by banging on one of these trees with a log or mallet. How the creatures get up there I do not know and can only surmise that they spend all their time up there and that their eggs somehow get transplanted from one water hole to another from time to time. We found none on the ground in that area, though the species is known to lead a perfectly normal toadlike life in other areas.

The waters inside the jungle are by no means devoid of lesser life, including crustaceans, aquatic molluscs, worms and such, but they are most notable for the larger creatures that go into them to feed or simply bathe. The most impressive that I know is the giant otter of South America that seems actually to reside in true jungle waters but goes out into the swamps and larger waters at night to feed. This large, sleek creature is almost as wholly aquatic as a seal.

22

Life in the Jungles

One place where the jungle really does teem with life is in the miniature world of the leaf mold on the forest floor, and under and in the rotting logs that lie on this. This world forms the basis of almost all life on the jungle floor, for most of it is either carnivorous, in the widest sense, or necrophagous.

Large herbivorous animals here are much fewer in both number of individuals and in number of kinds than outside the jungle, for the very good reason that there is really little for them to eat. Forest elephants, of course, browse, and can reach quite high foliage, but even the forest loxodont of African jungles, although resting therein by day, does most of its feeding outside. This is not to say that there are not larger herbivorous mammals to be found in jungles. Indeed no.

Going down the line of the ungulates, one should mention that the rhinoseroses of Malaya, Burma and Sumatra seem to be true jungle animals though, of course, having to stay near its edges and water courses. The same may be said of the Oriental tapir though it spends much time in and nearby rivers down to which the full sunlight penetrates. The New World tapirs are even more restricted to such areas. Likewise, the hippopotamuses are riverine or, in the case of the Pigmy Hippo, swamp dwellers and, although coming out at night to graze, do not enter the jungle but, rather, select open country.

The most typical hoofed animals of the jungles are the pigs, and their relatives the peccaries in Central and South America. These animals are to a greater or lesser extent omnivorous, not being averse to small live food of many kinds, and grubbing for roots, clearing up carrion, munching on herbs, and above all, devouring fallen fruits. In Africa there are the huge Forest Hog and the so-called Red River Hog, a bizarre looking creature with a very short chassis, bright orange in color with a white plume and long tassels on its ears. In the Oriental region there are numerous forms of wild pigs from the largest of all (*Sus barbatus gargantua*) of Borneo to the smallest (*Sus salvanius*) of Sikkim, Bhutan and Nepal. Many of these pigs, including the grotesque-looking Babirusa of the Celebes, are true jungle residents.

Another niche in the jungles is filled by small forms of deer—in South America the brockets and marsh deer; and in the Orient by the little tusked muntjacs and the swamp deer. In Africa, the equivalent is the duikers which are small antelopes with simple spiked horns. The largest, the Blue Duiker, is only about half the size of a donkey; the smallest about that of a poodle dog. There is one very remarkable one from Liberia that is striped. These little ungulates are the mainstay of the Negrillo hunters. In Africa there is also a group of large jungle antelopes—that of the bushbucks and the beautiful Bongo. Also, there dwell there the largest of all jungle herbivores—apart from the elephants—the Forest Giraffe or Okapi.

In tropical America there are giant rodents—the Capybara, the Paca and the agoutis—which fill the niche occupied by the duikers in Africa and which display a similarity in habits and even of appearance to another small group of very strange little ungulates, known as the chevrotains, which are also found in the jungles of the Orient. The general similarity in appearance between the American Paca and the West African Chevrotain is quite startling.

This roster sounds pretty impressive but, compared to the innumerable forms of deer and antelopes that dwell outside the jungle in other vegetational zones, it is really rather paltry. There are no representatives of the sheep and goat family in any jungle, and amongst the bovine beasts only the little Bushcow of Africa and the Tamarou of the Philippines are true in-jungle denizens. The Mithran and the controversial Couprey (*Bos sauvelii*) of the Cambodian-Laotian area will apparently enter jungles but are not true jungle residents.

Ivan Sanders

Babirusa of the Celebes.

The small life of the jungle floor is almost wholly nocturnal—even to the insects. If you lie on a blanket, as well protected from ants as possible, with a bright light and you are patient, you will eventually see this world at work and play. Disregarding the minutiae, I would say that the kinds of creatures you will see will be dominated by flatworms, snails, small rodents, an occasional snake and some medium-sized mammals, and according to the country you are in, mongoose, pacas and agoutis, or various kinds of anteaters. Rarely a tortoise may come stumping by. Once again, frogs and toads are very prominent. Scorpions and some spiders are on the prowl at night as are countless millipedes. (The centipedes seem to stay undercover.)

Another form of life, and one that intrigues me personally, is the opilionids, or what we call "daddy long legs," which swarm on jungle floors and come in seemingly endless forms. Watching them cranking along on their ridiculous stilt legs which they handle so adroitly that they can even lift one out of an ant's jaws before they can close, I have always had a preposterous feeling that they must have been invented by Walt Disney. They are most intriguing beasts, and one scientist has claimed to have "tamed" captive specimens to respond to calls to food and water. We once turned over an enormous slab of rotten bark on a jungle floor and found a hole about a foot deep, four feet long and two feet wide packed with a solid mass of one species. How they ever got themselves "untied" I cannot conceive, for their legs are immensely long and slender and drop off at a touch. This packing together is a habit of these creatures, but exactly what they do it for is not known; it may be some kind of hibernation or other resting period.

I cannot help mentioning again the flatworms or planarians of the jungle. You are walking along slowly, flashing your light here and there trying to discern the dull-colored forms of life on the jungle floor and the bases of tree boles when suddenly something like a glistening spear colored by a surrealist painter springs out at you. This will be gliding almost imperceptibly over a log or up a tree, occasionally raising the tip of its pointed front end and waving it about. I have seen these things of such brilliance of color and such incredibly neat patterns that words quite fail me, and I have la-

Ivan Sanders

Marmosa opossum and giant water scorpion.

mented the lack of the facilities for good night color photography, because no scientist to whom I delivered the specimens that I eventually managed to preserve (and that is a very tricky business, as I have already said, because they come apart unless handled in special ways) ever believed my color sketches of them. One I found in Central America was a vivid daffodil yellow, tangerine orange and glowing salmon pink. It had two jet black stripes down its back, and its edge all around was an iridescent electric blue. Of course, all this beauty disappeared when the creature was preserved in fluid. What do these humble creatures want all this magnificence for, since they usually move abroad by night? Nothing seems to eat or attack them anyway because they exude various secretions that seem to keep even the ants at a distance.

The small mammals of the jungle floor are particularly enchanting, though who would ever believe that any form of rat could be so?

They are all extremely busy little people, scurrying about, nibbling on things, digging and toting away stuff; but they also find a lot of time for what can only be described as play. And this goes for tiny mice, giant hopping rats, bumbling scaly anteaters or pangolins, mongoose and other civet-like animals, and even the larger cats. But the craziest thing I ever saw in a jungle at night was a sort of mating dance—at least that is what I presume it to have been—by three of the great flightless birds called cassowaries, right inside a jungle in New Guinea. I had been brought up to suppose that these were animals of the brush and open savannahs, so my surprise was unbounded. When they went into this crazy dance right in the beam of my light I could not help but burst out laughing. This startled them into immobility so that I swear I could have walked right up to them and trounced them; but then all birds are a bit balmy in my opinion and cassowaries seem to be pretty low on the avian ladder.

Moving up from the forest floor into the lower tiers, we enter an entirely different kind of world but encounter lots of the same *kinds* of animals. Among the small stuff, rats and mice, frogs, snails and crabs predominate, while a few snakes are to be found, along with other small and medium-sized mammals which would take pages just to list. Most of the last are night animals, like douroucoulis, opossums and lesser anteaters in the Americas; anomalures (called "flying squirrels," which they are not), galagos, pottos, small tree-climbing carnivores, and scaly anteaters (pangolins) in Africa; and palm-civets (musangs), lorises and so forth in the Orient. The Australasian jungles have a very different middle-tier mammalian fauna —strange creatures like cuscuses and other marsupials. Of course, several of the larger cats such as the jaguar in America, the leopard in Africa and the Orient, and rarer forms like the Clouded Leopard of the Orient, also move about by arboreal routes at night. Then there are the bats. Let us not overlook these.

Bats constitute the second largest group of mammals, and they come in an enormous variety of forms. In the jungles they live almost everywhere: in holes in trees, in what caves there are, under drooping palm fronds, and even clinging to the bare trunks of the trees. Some move about by day when the light is low. They can literally fill the air in the jungles at night, swooping down to ground level and soaring up into and above the canopy in search of airborne insect food. The Great Bats (*Megachiroptera*) normally stay outside the jungles, but when certain choice fruits ripen on the canopy great hordes of them, tens of thousands strong, may come over at dusk and descend upon the feast. Their fluttering, scrambling and chomping can become almost deafening, and a continuous shower of rinds, pits and juice comes pouring down on you from on high. Most fruit bats "smack their lips" when eating—they have to, because they are upside down and would otherwise be gagged by an excess of juice. A horde of them cleaning out a tree can be heard a mile away even though sound does not carry well in the jungle.

Most of the *Megachiroptera* or true Fruit Bats do not penetrate the jungles themselves, but there are a few forms that actually live in it perpetually. In Africa we have the incredible and quite preposterous-looking Hammer-headed Bat (*Hypsignathus*). In the Australasian region there is one named *Dobsonia,* and there is also allegedly a true jungle bat of positively enormous dimensions in the Oriental region, reported from Indochina and Java, but we don't have a specimen yet.

There are bat caves in the jungle just as there are all over the temperate world in limestone areas. Some of these that I have explored are positively fantastic. The most extraordinary I know are in Malaya, where gigantic entrances lead to even more gigantic rooms from which lead monumental galleries that go for miles. Bats dwell in many of these—by the millions. Another set of jungle caves that are of particular interest are scattered through the island of Trinidad, Venezuela, and the four Guianas. In these, in addition to countless hordes of bats, are to be found the fabulous nocturnal Oil-Birds or Guacharos, which nest in these caves and fly only by night, screeching raucously and feeding on only certain palm fruits. And it is in these caves (and countless others outside these particular jungles) that the true vampire bats (*Desmodus* and *Diphylla*) are found. These really are rather terrifying creatures, although, like almost if not all other animals, they do not mean any deliberate harm to us. They're just "sick."

Ivan Sanderson

Blood-lapping bat.

This remark is fully intended, since the blood-lapping bats are perfectly decent citizens obtaining their food by gouging little gutters in the skins of other animals with the two upper front teeth, introducing an anticoagulant into the wound via their saliva, and then lapping blood. This may sound horrid, but it is just as decent in my opinion as tearing into a three-weeks-dead hippopotamus and gorging on its rotten entrails until you can't even stand—a performance I once witnessed among human beings. These humans needed certain enzymes and protein food desperately; the bats *have* to have fresh blood because their intestines are short, straight tubes, and they cannot absorb anything else. The real trouble is that these animals are susceptible to the dread disease known as rabies; and, what is more, they are able to carry it for long periods without themselves dying. Hence, when they take one of their, to them normal, meals they may infect other animals, including men; and, since bites from these bats are very common in the tropical areas where they live (one boy was bitten fourteen times in one night in Trinidad, according to medical authorities studying the problem) human rabies is a serious problem.

The middle tiers of the jungle are inhabited by an incredible assemblage of different animals in all the three major and nine minor jungle blocks. The individual kinds are different in each, but on the whole these fauna display a certain similarity in composition. There are multitudious insects, mostly nocturnal, snails, crabs and other invertebrates on the tree trunks and in holes in them; numerous climbing frogs and toads; a certain number of climbing snakes, but very few in the jungle itself; some birds, both by night and by day, but very few at night, and numerous mammals. The last, apart from the few great cats that climb, are mostly small. Many fly: the bats; and some, like the Kobegos and the true Flying Squirrels of the Orient, the Anomalures and so-called "Flying Mice" (*Idiurus*) of Africa; and some small possums of the Australasian region, glide by means of furred flaps of skin between their limbs and sometimes extending to their tails. Many others *almost* glide in that they make prodigious leaps with extended arms and legs and have long bushy tails. A good example are the little galagos or bushbabies of Africa. There are also innumerable other small cats and civets, anteaters, porcupines, climbing rats and mice of endless varieties, weasel-like animals such as the American Tayra, the raccoon types such as cacomixtles, kinkajous and coatimundis, and various forms of marsupials. In Madagascar we have the true lemurs, which move about both by day and night in the middle tiers.

But, of course, it is the canopy that, above all, symbolizes the jungle—in fact, it *is* the jungle, for without it, these great breathing, flattened, green buns would not be jungles. The animal life of the canopy is so much more noticeable, rowdy, gaudy and exotic that, once one has got up into its domain, one gains the impression that it dominates the whole scene. I have thought about this for a long time, and have finally come to the conclusion that this is a false impression. The canopy is almost a dead place after dark. A lot of animals sleep up there but, apart from a few tree frogs and some nocturnal snakes that seem to prey upon them, there is very little moving about there at night. When we lived up there, we found that

Ivan Sanderson

Kobego.

we could attract all manner of insects *from below* at night with our lights and that many other animals awoke and became curious, but once we doused the lights, we would not even have needed a mosquito net to protect us from insects—*except for the mosquitoes!* These do abound up there, and they cause the sleeping monkeys to scratch continuously and seemingly almost automatically. It is a very wonderful thing to lie in a warm bed more than a hundred feet up in this flying continent and listen to the cacophony rising from below, while all round you is almost absolute silence. Down under, the whirring of the insects sounds like a thousand water pumps in a basement, or perhaps it is better described as the sound of the desalinaters and other machinery that run all the time while a great liner is at quayside—a sort of low mumbling and throbbing. From time to time, there will come a real noise, but not, I can assure you, in any way like anything heard in movies. The wild howls, yells, screams and so forth that are supposed to issue from the jungle day and night just plain don't.

Only in South America are you subjected to an uproar that is to me so wonderfully soul-stirring that I could listen to it indefinitely. This is the night signalling of the great Howler Monkeys. This sounds like half a dozen wounded jaguars having it out in a large, tiled bathroom. Actually, it is usually only one great bearded monkey with a goose-egg-sized, bone sound-box in his throat just simply "telling the world." All night long these giant troop leaders sound off; and when ones does, others will take it up on their adjacent territory; and then others beyond that, until, as all falls silent locally, you hear these terrific noises rolling away into the distance. Then, some local chap will start up again. Nobody has been able to make up their minds just why these monkeys do this or when they will do it but, I can assert that in one area at least it has something to do with the atmospheric conditions. I have also once personally witnessed the whole troop joining in—and what an uproar that was! It happened just before dawn and was more than memorable because the leader of the troop was of such a size as I have never otherwise seen, in the wild or in a museum. He was a pure, glistening white albino.

Shortly before dawn as we have said, the canopy comes to life.

There are those animals that start to stir while the supra-canopy mists are still thick. These are many kinds of monkeys and birds. They don't go anywhere and they don't do anything until the first rays of the sun emerge from below the rim of the horizon. Even then they may stay still and, in some cases, there may then come an almost absolute silence. And here I propose to stick my neck way out and say that I agree with certain Brahmins in India and West Africa who assert that the animals are at that time "praying." I cannot get over the sight of a huge troop of the magnificent black and white guereza or *Colobus* monkeys that I once witnessed thus engaged on the very tops of a canopy giant; all sitting quietly facing the rising sun, with heads slightly bowed and arms folded on knees. Not a sound came from them for many minutes, and nobody stirred except a few youngsters, who were then cuffed and scolded. The whole jungle was utterly silent. No insects chirped or clicked; nothing rustled. Then suddenly a crazy bird—probably a Pied Hornbill—let out a raucous yell and the whole world began to stir.

As the run rises, this great flying continent comes to life with a vengeance. First off the mark are usually birds of the parrot family, which, of course, typify the jungles as they do all tropical forests. The great macaws of the American tropics just flap about and shout, but the true parrots set out in great flocks, nearly always in pairs, squawking and, to our ears at least, carrying on long conversations in all manner of noises. Parrots I find delightful; they appear to be so cheery as well as busy, and they are certainly extraordinarily efficient creatures with their hand-like feet that can bring food up to their mouths as we do, so being able to watch for trouble while feeding.

Next come the monkeys, croaking and calling, and crashing about through the billowing foliage; and with them, the squirrels and other similar diurnal treetop creatures like the tupaias—related to our most distant ancestors but which look much like squirrels—in the Orient. The insects mostly seem to wait for the full sunshine, but then the canopy becomes a place of almost deafening buzzing and whirring. And the butterflies! Perhaps this is the most marvellous aspect of all, but one must climb to the top of the jungle canopy, preferably into one of the giant emergent tree heads, to truly appreciate it. They and the multicolored bees, and the great locust-like katydid-type of insects of the order *Orthoptera* dominate the scene, filling the air with their multifarious bright colors. Naturally, I am speaking of good weather. If it is overcast or raining, these busy, gay hordes don't appear but, instead, quite another lot emerge from the canopy and go about their particular business. These are day-flying moths and beetles, and other types that one simply does not see at other times.

The bird life of the upper canopy is often spectacular, in both sheer volume and variety of forms. The whole place sometimes becomes like a lush swamp with thick bushes in a northern spring, with tiny birds hopping and flitting through the greenery, great raucous ones smashing about, hawks sailing overhead, and what I call "the painted ones" like toucans and hornbills and curassows and all manner of shimmering pigeons dashing about as if their very lives depended upon reaching the tree ahead. In the American tropics there are also hummingbirds, and in Africa their equivalents in iridescent splendor, the sugarbirds; while in the Orient we have the honey-eaters. On the top of Oriental and New Guinean jungles there are also flitting swarms of these tiny birds, while many of the most gorgeous of all, the birds of paradise, go aloft to display. This group of birds and their relatives, the rifle-birds, are for the most part true jungle dwellers, some species being found right down to ground level in certain of the Indonesian islands.

When I was a teen-ager I went off to the Orient to collect animals and, on arrival in what was then the Dutch East Indies, decided to try and follow the footsteps of my childhood idol, Alfred Russel Wallace, whose book *The Malay Archipelago* for me came next only to the Bible. This book described his route in detail, naming even the smallest villages on each island in which he had resided. One of these was just a "place" on a creek on one of the Aru Islands, which lie in the middle of the north Arafura Sea between western New Guinea and the Kei and Timor Laut Islands. These fabulous islands are unique in many way, not the least of which is that salt-water creeks run right through some of them while jungle towers overhead. It was on one of these that Wallace resided for many weeks, and I found the creek and even, it was alleged, the house in which he had dwelt eighty years before. (Of course, the actual structure would have rotted, probably many times, in the interval, but there was still a thatched structure there that I was allowed to occupy.)

Wallace had described a great gathering of the Great Bird of Paradise one morning just after dawn in a giant tree with a few small leaves a short distance behind this house. He had been somewhat vague as to the exact time of year, but working out his itinerary, I and my young Indonesian friend managed to get there at the right time, and, by jingo, we witnessed this most marvellous thing. Literally dozens of these gorgeous birds assembled above us and, fluffing out their plumes of golden orange, bobbed and bowed and strutted about on the bare branches while the dull-colored females pecked around below in what appeared to be total indifference. I have seen only one other sight to compare with this.

This was in Surinam one morning when we awoke to a positive uproar above us and, as the morning mist evaporated, a giant tree with writhing silvery branches and very few feathery leaves came into focus, filled with red and blue macaws wandering about, flapping their wings and beating their long tails up and down. Whether they were displaying or not I do not know, but they kept up the motions for over an hour, creating an uproar such as only a couple of hundred macaws can produce.

Just as insects are more or less everywhere at all times, and the frogs and the mammals seem to dominate the nighttime jungles, so the birds dominate the daytime, notably in the canopy. My frustration rises as I face the fact that I cannot possibly give you even a pen picture of jungle bird life—there are so many, they are so wonderful to look at, and they are so remarkable in their behavior. I'm thinking of all those that I have not mentioned, like the modest little Tinamous that look like hen pheasants with their tails cut off, which meander silently about the jungle floors of South America and which seem to be related to the great flightless birds like ostriches and emus. There are also the squawking toucans with their painted bills; the megapodes or mound builders of the Celebes; the fabulous bowerbirds of the Australasian region; the screamers and the spurwings that hang about jungle waterfalls in South America; the weird frog-mouths and related goatsuckers that churr and purr throughout the forest night; and the everlasting parade of tiny winged jewels that flit all about wherever a shaft of sunlight penetrates. And then, there are the birds of the montane jungles. Here words completely fail me. There is one in the montane pine forests of Haiti (admittedly *not* a jungle in any manner of speaking) that is as large as a crow with a long tail and displays every color of the rainbow and a lot of others to boot; which, hour after hour pipes its way up a clear and true musical scale, but never hits the last note. It drives you crazy. (Birds, I find, have a maddening habit of failing to complete an octave!)

In a heavy jungle in Nicaragua we once came across a deep gully with, of all unexpected things, an open grassy area on the opposite bank. We bedded down for the night but were aroused by the strangest noises. We traced them to the grassy place, and since there was no moon that night, we centered our powerful flashlights on it. There, performing some dance, or perhaps just gathering insect food in flight, were hundreds of nighthawks flitting silently a few feet into the air and then settling again in the grass. All were churring away continuously in that eerie way common to this group of birds, and all of their huge eyes lit up like pairs of golden orbs. We spent half the night watching them and went to bed with a sigh.

There is a point that I seem to have glossed over, and this is the matter of snakes, lizards and the other reptiles of the jungle. Just as the uninitiated will cry "lions and tigers" when you so much as mention the jungle, the partly initiated will echo "Yeah, and all them snakes." I don't know which is worse, for though there are no lions in any jungle, there may be some tigers; but, the matter of snakes is far more tricky. There are jungles in which there are no snakes at all (some islands); there are others in which they are exceedingly rare. In the final analysis, however, it seems that in numbers and species the snake and other reptilian population is much smaller in all jungles than in most other types of vegetation in the tropics and subtropics, and even in the desert and scrub belts.

Reptiles are what used to be called cold-blooded, and the majority rely upon sunlight to warm them by day. For the most part, they have impervious, water-retaining skins, as opposed to the amphibians whose skins are mostly water-absorbent. On the jungle floor and below it may be found certain burrowing snakes and lizards, and there are daytime rovers, such as the skinks, among the latter. There are among the snakes, the constrictors (pythons and boas) that live either in holes in the ground by day or in trees. There are a few middle-tier tree snakes, and there are some canopy dwellers. Finally, there are the other predatory snakes equipped with poison fangs, which dwell inside the jungles and move about by night. In the American jungles we have the mapipis, the Fer-de-Lance and their relatives like the jararacussus; in Africa we have certain pit vipers; and in the Orient some true vipers. Yet, in comparison to the world just outside the jungle and to the bulk of other types of animals, poisonous snakes are really rare. Thus, another myth about the jungles should, in my opinion, be tossed out.

There remain innumerable groups of truly jungle animals that we have not had the space even to mention, but we cannot conclude this all too brief survey without giving one such group a going-over. Everybody who has heard of the apes, and particularly the so-called Great Apes, becomes intrigued with them. Since they first became known to the ancient Western world an element of doubt about ourselves seems to have crept into our thinking. Even the human natives of those countries in which the apes are found seem also to have viewed them with more than mere suspicion. They are just too like us in so many ways to be counted out arbitrarily as just other kinds of animals. Nor can they be simply classed with the monkeys. Tailless like us, they display also other disturbing anatomical characters and ethological characteristics that seem altogether too human.

Some very early writings ponder what their scribes considered to be profound mysteries regarding these "wild men." Just as our current savants, philosophers, scientists and writers, and the general public at large have no idea what to do with the reports of alleged Abominable Snowmen, so also were the ancients completely buffaloed by reports of gorillas, chimps, mias (Orang-Utans), siamangs and gibbons. Sometimes skins of these creatures turned up in places like India and China and filtered through to the then primitive

Western world. Later, live specimens of mias seem to have been brought out of their jungle homes in Borneo and Sumatra and marvelled at by the locals and yokels, by travelers and traders, and the plain curious, and some of them got shipped to civilized India. They were described, and the descriptions filtered on to the classical world of Pliny in Rome. Even earlier, the Carthaginians had reported some African ape, which has been interpreted as "gorilla" but was probably a chimpanzee. When the wonderful little Frenchman turned American, Paul du Chaillu, first described gorilla skulls that he had found on native trash heaps in West Africa and then brought back whole skins and skeletons, he was read completely out of the scientific court (as late as the 1860's) as being a liar, a phony and a nature faker. (This is standard practice for anybody who comes up with anything new but was, in his case, really a bit exaggerated since he actually *had* the darned stuff.)

The world—even the much older and wiser Eastern World—took a long time to accept the fact of the existence of the great apes, and it has not yet recovered from the shock. First, they were "hairy men of the woods"; then, they became "tailless monkeys"; next, poor Charles Darwin tried to put the concept straight, but his semantics were not of the best, so that he called one of his classics *The Descent of Man* when he was trying to say, "The Ascent of Man." This got everybody doubly confused for nearly a hundred years. Came the modern primatologists and the physical anthropologists, and the archaeologists (going backward in time with their stone, bone, and horn artifacts) and we got a fine family tree showing us as having a *common origin* with the apes.

Now everything has come completely to pieces again, since the physiologists have got into the act and shown that the body fluids of the gorillas and chimps, and the Caucasian (white) and Negroid (black, which they are not) humanoid stock, have much in common, while the Mongoloid humans, the orangs, the siamangs and the gibbons are similarly linked but are quite distinct from the former group. What are we to make of all this? (Nobody has as yet delved into these physiological esoterica among the Bushmen of South Africa, the Australoids of Australia, or the Negrillos, Negritos and other true

Ivan Sanderson

Tarsier, an Oriental primate.

Pigmy races.) Is the great Dr. Carleton Coon right in his assertion that the human stock has a multiple origin; and, if so, how far back do we have to go genetically, and in time, before its known branches link up with each other and with those of the apes?

This is not of our particular concern here. What is, is the fact that the apes are true jungle animals, though most of them are quite willing to explore outside it. The gorillas are said to come in two forms, called the Mountain and the Lowland. This is semantic nonsense, since a lot of the latter live exclusively in mountain jungles. The chimps of Africa are, however, confined to lowlands, and they prefer to stay deep in the forests. The mias of the Orient stay in the forests and prefer the closed canopy, though they are so heavy that they have to descend to lower levels to get from one large tree to another. The siamangs of Sumatra, the mainland of Malaya, and some islands near Sumatra, are also TEF dwellers, though they come to the ground rather frequently. The gibbons, which range from the eastern Himalayas to the island of Hainan and thence south throughout the Indochinese-Malayan Peninsula to the greater Indonesian Islands, are strictly arboreal animals and are confined to the closed-canopy forests.

The gorillas are not ravening beasts; they are placid feeders upon small tasty fruits and ground vegetables. They will not attack anything unless profoundly molested. If jumped by a leopard, a large male may tear it limb from limb in self-defense—they are very strong. If a man invades what a gorilla considers its feeding territory, it may rush roaring at him, gathering branches before him but, unless the puny man turns and runs, these horrendous "attacks" invariably peter out before contact is made. Gorillas are terrestrial creatures that walk on all fours. The females and young climb trees to get fruits and usually sleep up there, but the old males rest at the bottom, backs against the trunks.

Chimpanzees are of quite a different ilk. They are rowdy, boisterous extroverts who often whoop it up both by day and by night. They too spend most of their time on the jungle floor, but they climb much more often and extensively than do gorillas. They show altogether too many "human" traits for our peace of mind, and they have even been observed employing sticks as we do tools. There is a scientist of my acquaintance in this country who writes me that he is training chimps to do algebra. Don't ever underestimate the great apes!

The mias are a strange quiet lot with, one has to admit, all the passive and contemplative expression and mien of the Mongoloid human, as opposed to the ebullience of the chimps and the solemn gravity of the gorillas. They are highly "intelligent" but, I fear me, a "lost cause." How long can the few of them remain in Borneo and northern Sumatra? They lumber about their beloved jungles, following the fruiting of their favorite edibles, and they have jaws constructed like a pair of pump-pliers to crack them with—notably the massive durian, which a strong man needs an axe or machete to open. I find them "nice people," and the ones I have owned have been loving and trusting, though they do tend to be, what we call frivolously, "wolves" when it comes to members of the opposite sex of anything anthropoid!

The siamangs are very strange and rather dangerous, middle-sized apes that may be classed with the gibbons. Constructed like the latter, with excessively long arms used for brachiating through the upper canopy, they nonetheless have quite different dispositions. They have been tamed, but they are very unpredictable and irascible, and have strange notions of their own as to just how life should proceed. Their relatives, the smaller gibbons, of which there are five distinct groups—the concolors, which have several features in common with the siamangs; the hoolocks; the lars; the agiles; and the wow-wows—although less like us in bodily form, seem to me to be closest of all to us so-called humans, in mental traits.

As soon as the morning mists lift, these truly "wild" creatures go roaring about the jungle canopies, whooping and yelling like trapeze artists. They live in tribal groups and go through all the "international" problems of boundary adjustment that we do. But if you want to learn more of these wonderful creatures, please read the on-the-spot studies of Dr. C. R. Carpenter. To these I can add only my personal experiences with a silvery gibbon who traveled with me for a year in Indonesia many years ago.

Ivan Sanderson

Hoolock.

She wore a belt to which was attached a long light chain. This she gathered up and held aloft in one hand when we went abroad, while she wobbled along on her hind legs, sometimes beckoning to me if we were going into the jungle. I called her *Nona,* which is kitchen-Malay for a beautiful young girl. Her duty was to collect insects for the British Museum, for which I was on the trip, and she was superbly efficient. Climbing aboard a dead, fallen tree trunk, she would move systematically along, loosening and probing under the bark and finding all manner of wonderful specimens. Then she would grab one and hold it out to me; and she continued to do this until I closed the lid on my collecting bottle. To her this was the signal for lunch, and she would grab up and consume the remaining specimens, *of that kind*. If she came upon another species, she would hand it to me and wait! This shook me, but some of the other things she did cannot be explained—so I shall not discuss them. I am iconoclast enough without imputing actions to so-called animals which I cannot prove. Frankly, I still can't quite believe my diaries, after nearly forty years.

Perhaps it would be better, therefore, to proceed to the peoples of the jungle.

Cornell Capa from Magnum

View of Ecuador jungle.

Part 5

The Jungle Peoples

Farewell to Tarzan

The Nature of the Little People

Home Among the Hunters

The Timeless Culture

The Mystery Peoples

Photo Researcher

Pygmy in Ituri Forest, Congo.

23

Farewell to Tarzan

THE true jungle peoples, meaning those who actually live inside the tropical rain forest, are virtually all different in their normal mode of life from the humans who dwell nearest to them. They are also almost invariably of different racial stocks; there seems to be little doubt that despite certain similarities between some groups there are several such stocks.

Yet these jungle peoples almost certainly did not originate *in* the tropical rain forest; nor should they be considered *necessarily* an earlier type of man than their neighbors, who today occupy the edges of the jungles or clearings along the rivers or patches of savannah or woodland within it. However, there may be some evidence that they are indeed relics of the very early man.

All of them appear to have been originally immigrants who learned to adapt themselves to the conditions they found in this new environment. Some of them apparently went there prior to the last southward ice advance in the north. Others may not have done so until the Christian era. But, wherever they came from, they are now the only human beings who make their headquarters *in* the jungles. By this we mean people who not only live there but do so permanently, and reside nowhere else for any length of time.

In other words, they truly belong there, as opposed to other inhabitants of the tropics who live outside the jungle or in clearings in it. This has a further implication, for if you belong in the biological or ecological sense to a certain environment, you must have come to terms with that environment. This is true of mountaineers, desert dwellers, and denizens of all the other more civilized parts of the world. Thus, we are talking about only those small groups of people who actually *live* in jungles, and never anywhere else, on terms of intimacy and harmony with them. They do not upset the balance of nature by seeking to change this environment—burning it, hacking at it. They coexist with the jungle and are the masters of their environment, not its servants.

The origin of the peoples who have accomplished this is, of course, a part of the mystery that still surrounds the "descent of man," the mystery to which Darwin gave a new direction, though he did not solve it. We still do not know just how long the human race has existed on the earth, and, in fact, scientists are not in full agreement as to whether or not certain of the earliest known or suspected forms should be classified as human. Moreover, we have had to discard the old comfortable theory—comfortable because it seemed to explain everything so neatly—that man evolved from monkeys in the jungle, climbed down out of the trees, gradually became less and less apelike in physical appearance and then wandered about until his descendants spread pretty well all over the earth. Actually the earliest human beings of which fossil remains have been found were obviously not jungle animals. The earliest hominids appear to have kept out of jungles as long as they could.

Neither can we regard any other breed of men as having descended from apes. The family trees of the apes (pongids) and of the humans (hominids) now appear to have been separate for millions of years, although both belong to the anthropoid group of the Primates, meaning "the top ones," the highest order of mammals.

The hominid and pongid anthropoids are divided by such fundamental anatomical differences that talk of "ape-men" or "man-apes" is nonsense. The pongids, the true apes, are today represented by the gorillas, chimpanzees, orangutans, the siamangs and the gibbons. The hominids and pongids almost certainly did have a common ancestry; but the two branches evolved quite separately. In other words, the apes are not a halfway stage between monkeys and us.

However, it has been discovered during the last few years that the blood and other body fluids of the gorillas and the chimpanzees are like those of the so-called white race (technically the Caucasoids) and the Negroids. At the same time, the body fluids of this group are distinctly different from those of the gibbons, siamangs, orangs *and* the Mongoloid human stock! What have we here? It would seem to be a matter for the primatologists to wrangle about and it would be of no concern to us were we not confronted with the matter of these jungle peoples. Are we to assume that what we call the human race is, in fact, multiple in origin? The famous Dr. Carleton S. Coon has been roundly taken to task for expressing such an idea in his recently published book *The Origin of Races*. But he was taken to task by the new "Love Thy Brother" breed (well-meaning but not very well-informed). Unfortunately, facts are not respecters of human shibboleths. There is now growing evidence that what we call the human race as a whole *is* multiple in origin, but the split is not between what has come to be called black and white but between both of these (along with the gorillas and chimps), on the one hand, and the Mongoloid humans (along with the gibbons, siamangs, and orangs), on the other. This will doubtless infuriate segregationists and confuse integrationists. Nevertheless, we should start to face up to the facts of life as they are disclosed or even suggested to us.

Then we find that the old idea that mere monkeys gave rise to the apes, and these to men-apes, these to ape-men, and these (the Neanderthaloids) to men—but still sub-men—is no longer tenable. Out of these, it was supposed true men (vaingloriously dubbed *Homo sapiens,* forsooth) evolved. Today the whole picture appears quite different. It looks very much as if the original hominid was a ground-dwelling primate who took to running about on his two hind legs, while the first (tailless) apes took to an arboreal life. Then some hominids ventured into or were driven into the forests and adapted to that environment. These were either small of stature in the first place or diminished in size over a period of time—again in accord with this novel environment. The latter would seem to be the most likely, since Negroids, Caucasoids, Mongoloids, Amerinds and even Papuans seem to have thrown off forest dwellers that today we call "Pygmies."

The Pygmy peoples that we know today do indeed seem to have retained a number of psychological characteristics and even some anatomical and physiological features that set them apart from the rest of the human races. That the Bushmen of South Africa and the

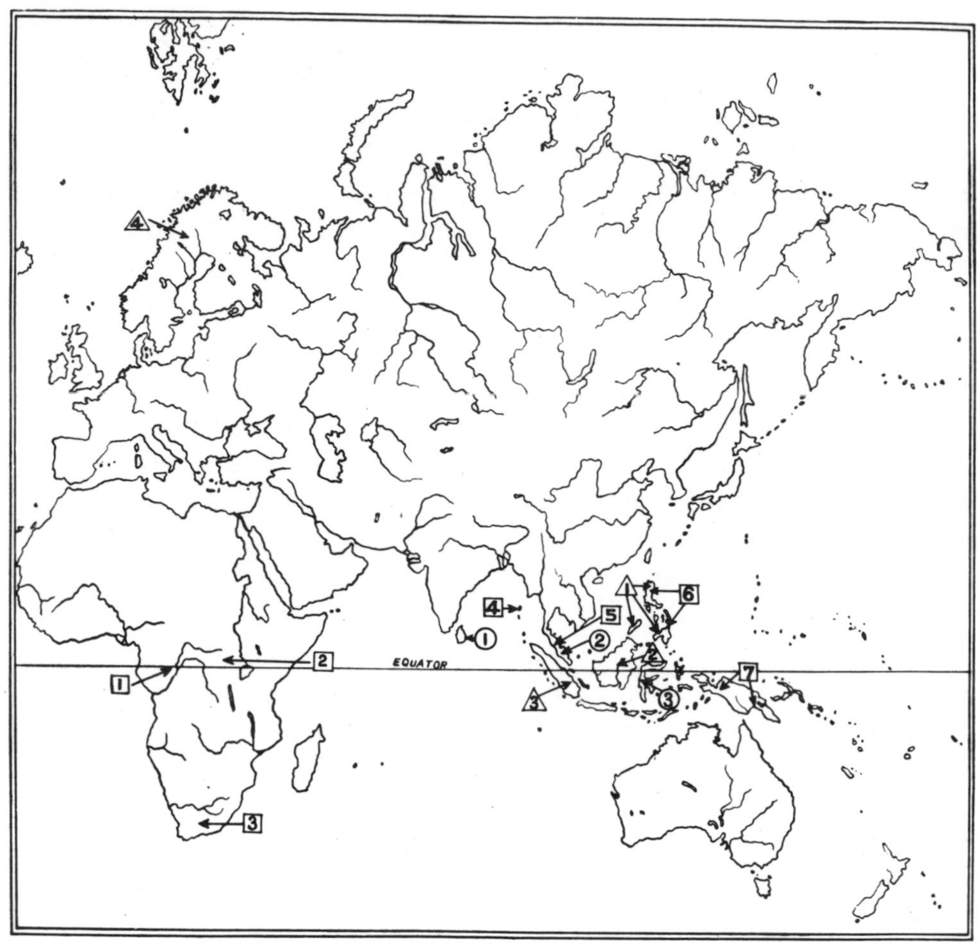

DISTRIBUTION OF THE PYGMY AND SHORT RACES OF MAN

NEGROID PYGMY TYPES

- [1] Central African Negrillos
- [2] Central African Negrillos
- [3] South African Bushmen
- [4] Andamanese Negritos
- [5] Semang Negritos
- [6] "Aeta" Philippine Negritos
- [7] Melanesian Pygmies

AUSTRALOID PYGMY TYPES

- (1) Veddah
- (2) Sakai, Senoi
- (3) Toala

SHORT MONGOLOID TYPES

- △1 Indonesians of the Philippines
- △2 Indonesians of Borneo
- △3 Indonesians of Sumatra
- △4 Lapps of Norway

American Museum of Natural History

Abo of Australia (neither jungle dwellers, be it clearly noted) display such differences can no longer be denied. The construction of the external genitalia of the former and the incredible body temperature control system of the latter are alone sufficient evidence. However, are the little African Negrillos, the Oriental Negritos and perhaps the Papuan Tapiros relics of an early offshoot of the main human stock? (Nobody knows just what to do with the "Ghosts of the Yellow Leaves" in the Indochinese peninsula; and it is fairly clear that the dwarf Amerinds of Central and forested South America are offshoots of the great Mongoloid stock.) But then, we come face to face with the question of many other far more primitive forest peoples like the Santu Sakai of the Malay peninsula and the Nittaewo of Ceylon.

In other words, the scientific problem nowadays is not so much to separate the men from the apes but the men from each other.

All this is relevant to a discussion of the jungle peoples because there has been a tendency to regard them as perhaps a "lower" rather than a different subspecies of *Homo*. Certainly this has been the view of many of their neighbors, especially the Negroes of Africa and the Mongoloid races on the fringes of the Oriental jungles. This attitude seems to have been the result of a feeling of superiority on the part of the Negro and Mongolian because they were usually bigger and always more aggressive. They had learned to till the soil and to domesticate some animals, and they had rather more efficient tools and weapons, and sometimes built great civilizations.

But most of all, their feeling of superiority stemmed from the fact that they had driven these culturally less advanced people into the jungle in the first place. They probably had the "master-race complex" of almost every organized human society, the one the white man adopted millennia later.

As for the little people, probably in order to survive and certainly in order to escape being enslaved, they retreated into the equatorial rain forests. Amazingly, and worthy of the utmost respect since many more highly regarded human types have never been able to do it, they learned not only to live but to thrive therein. Apparently, in some ways, they retrogressed in the process, at least by our standards. They lost stature, it is believed, but significantly not muscular strength nor bodily endurance. They reverted perhaps to more primitive tools and weapons; if they had ever known about working metal or stone, most of them forgot the techniques and came to rely almost entirely on wood.

True jungle peoples have been found in all the major jungle areas of the world. That there are others who have not yet been found is quite probable, judging from the fact that a few of those we do know were encountered for the first time only in recent years, while enormous jungles stretching for thousands of miles still remain completely untouched and unexplored. Myths, folklore and legends that tell of mysterious or outlandish jungle peoples are hardly evidence, but it is surprising how many times in the recent past similar local tales, at which scientists had scoffed, proved to be correct.

So far, we find that in each of the three subdivisions of the three major jungle areas—American, African, Oriental—there are three quite distinct groups of jungle peoples. This neat arrangement could easily be upset by future discoveries, but it seems probable that any new tribes will turn out to be related to the ones we already know.

The aboriginals of the American jungles are almost certainly the descendants of the peoples who migrated to the New World across the Bering Strait. These early migrants were predominantly mongoloid. Since they settled in the American jungles a relatively short time ago in terms of racial evolution, they are biologically very much like their Amerind neighbors. Their height, cranial and facial proportions and other physical characteristics do not mark them off as jungle people. Thus in South and Central America, unlike some areas of the Old World, there is no jungle race; only a jungle habitat.

Although this habitat has not affected the racial characteristics of the jungle peoples, it has had a profound influence on their culture. This culture is primarily of two kinds, each based on a different method of obtaining sustenance from the harsh jungle environment. The first method is called "slash and burn" farming. This is a very primitive kind of agriculture which is uniquely adapted for jungle life. It works like this: the entire able bodied population of a small community clears a small plot of jungle. The tree trunks and other dead vegetation are burned off. Crops are then planted among the dead stumps and charred logs.

The job is endless, because the old gardens rapidly give out and new land must constantly be cleared. The torrential tropical rains, unhindered by the jungle's canopy of leaves rapidly leach the soil of nutrients. After several harvests the garden is depleted and abandoned to the jungle. Each time a new garden is cleared, it is necessary to go farther from the village, and when the distance finally becomes very great, the entire village moves to a new area. Jungle farming communities, then, are not permanently fixed, but shift according to the availability of new land. This semi-nomadic character of jungle life insures that the community is maintained at a fairly primitive level. Even when the crops are successful, and supplemented by hunting and river fishing, there is hardly ever a large surplus of food. For these reasons the community is small, seldom measuring more than two hundred, and there are only slight differences in status and wealth. Life in these villages is relatively simple. Almost all of a man's physical efforts must be directed towards economic tasks. We should, however, discuss one important exception to this last generalization: warfare.

Prior to the pacification of much of the jungle area, warfare and headhunting were fairly widespread. The reasons for war were not to plunder or conquer neighboring tribes, but to avenge imagined wrongs and capture victims for cannibalistic rites. Among the Jivaros of Ecuador, for example, headhunting was motivated by a desire for revenge against their enemies. The best way a warrior could insult an enemy people, and gain status for himself, was to take a trophy head. When a trophy was taken, the skin was removed, the skull cleaned out, and hot sand poured in and out repeatedly to shrink the head. The completed trophy brought a great deal of honor to the successful warrior.

With the coming of the white man, warfare took on an economic character it had never had before. Captives were taken to be sold as slaves to Spanish and Portuguese colonials. Nowadays, though slavery is out of date, headhunting has been given an economic boost in some areas by the tourist demand for trophy shrunken

Rare Book Room, American Museum of Natural Hist

Brazilian Indians cooking fish, eating and sleeping in hammocks, as represented by Theodore de Bry.

heads. Many of the heads sold to tourists are actually removed from unclaimed bodies in city morgues and prepared in the traditional fashion. Some, however, are genuine Indian heads, taken, in part, for the tourist market.

The second method of wresting a living from the tropical forest is even simpler than slash and burn farming. Hunters and gatherers of wild animals and plants occupy areas of the jungle that are unsuitable for slash and burn farming, including portions of Eastern Brazil and enclaves around the headwaters of the Amazon Basin. These people are invariably nomadic and live in small scattered bands, each of which wander about their particular section of forest. Not a great deal is known of these people, because they live in inaccessible places far from the navigable rivers. One hunting and gathering tribe that is well known, however, is the Siriono of Eastern Bolivia. They were studied by Allan Holmberg, an anthropologist who lived with them for a year, and wrote of them in *Nomads of the Long Bow.* He discovered that, unlike some of the warlike agricultural people we have described, the nomadic Siriono are shy and peaceful. When Holmberg was tracking an uncontacted band through the jungle he had to shoot game with a bow and arrow so as not to frighten these people away by gun shots. When he finally located them, they were taking a siesta in a communal hut. Removing their clothes so as not to be conspicuous, Holmberg and his guide rushed into the hut and offered the Indians several baskets of meat as a peace gesture before they could grab their weapons or flee. They immediately became interested in the food, and were eventually willing to let the anthropologist remain with them and study their way of life.

The Siriono spend much of their time wandering through the tropical forest hunting game and edible wild plants and fishing. When they move from one campsite to another, they carry all their possessions, which include only their hammocks, weapons and a few crude tools. They wear absolutely no clothes, but paint their bodies and glue a few feathers in their hair. Generally they hunt and fish alone or in pairs. When the hunters return to the camp they may help the women build a simple lean-to of poles covered by leaves, a shelter which offers almost no protection from rain or stinging insects. Since it rains nearly two or three times a week during the long wet season, and the mosquitoes and flies are legion, the Siriono hardly live in a tropical paradise. Their continued existence is often threatened because game is not as plentiful in the jungle as is sometimes imagined, and there are frequent periods when food is scarce.

The danger of starvation is increased by the fact that the Siriono have no effective method of preserving food for more than two or three days. For this reason they never bother to hunt unless they are in immediate need of food. Holmberg tells, for example, of a Siriono who had caught eight large tortoises. These animals can be kept alive for about a week and eaten as needed. This fortunate hunter tied the animals up and seldom moved from his hammock until he and his family had consumed the tortoises eight days later.

The Siriono economy is extremely simple and supports only a small band which is diffusely organized and in times of stress may fragment into family groups. Their religious life is correspondingly simple. Holmberg found that they had even lost the art of making fire. The women carry firebrands from campsite to campsite, carefully sheltering them from water when it rains or when it becomes necessary to swim a river. On one occasion a small group would have starved in an area where game was plentiful because they had no fire except for the fact that they came on some of their relatives who already had one burning.

The slash and burn farmers in South and Central America, as unsophisticated as they are, are more advanced than the nomadic hunters and gatherers. Both, however, have been equally successful in adapting their way of life to their environment. The slash and burn farmer lives in impermanent, shifting settlements primarily because sedentary farming is impossible on jungle soil. The nomadic hunter and gatherer cannot farm because his portion of the jungle will not support even slash and burn agriculture. The Siriono, for example, live in an area that is too swampy for extensive farming.

Racially the people of the South American jungles are the same as their more culturally advanced neighbors. Culture and race, then, are quite distinct. Were it not for an accident of birth, we too might be living like the Siriono Indians in some part of the Bolivian jungle where the harsh environment by and large limits the people who live in it to a simple way of life.

Our present picture is not complete, however. The South American jungles are vast, and it is just possible we will one day find jungle peoples we know nothing about. In British Guiana, for example, we hear of incidents like that which happened to my friend, Fred Salazar, and three companions. They saw squatting in an Indian village a dark, silent man so completely unlike any of the local people that Fred wondered where he came from. His hair grew down on his forehead almost to his eyebrows; his eyes were small and set very close together; his arms and legs were covered with black

American Museum of Natural History

Primitives of the Matto Grosso, Brazil.

hair, a great contrast to the smooth copper skins of everybody else in the place; and he squatted on his heels, whereas the local Amerinds sat with outstretched legs.

When Fred inquired of the locals who this fellow might be, he was informed quite matter-of-factly that this was one of the forest people. They came in now and then to trade, and were obviously regarded as a lesser breed, but one to be handled warily. Fred and his companions were told to avoid the jungle area where this man and his people lived.

Throughout the jungle lands of America this same general pattern seems to prevail. There are peoples who have been in touch more or less with our so-called civilization for centuries, and these are the ones who have been studied to some degree. But over the vast area, roughly some seven million square miles, examples of true jungle dwellers keep popping up. It seems that the forests behind or around the villages of primitive Amerinds contain even more primitive bands, some of them so rarely seen that their very existence has been doubted.

Perhaps we will learn more about them as a result of the modern protection policy of some South American governments. The rubber trade is no longer as important as it once was, so there is no longer a strong economic incentive to exploit the jungle Indian. Some nations, such as Brazil, have established reservations where the Indian lives unmolested. Protection should pay off in making these people accessible for future study.

The jungle people *par excellence* are the Pygmies of the Uele District of the Congo in Africa. So well known are these delightful little people, who have been extensively written about and were a great tourist attraction before the country gained "independence," that they are popularly regarded as being both *the* Pygmies and, by inference, the *only* Pygmies. This is very far from the case, even in equatorial Africa.

First of all, there are fairly large groups of little people, well known and fully documented in official government and scientific records, from all over the closed-canopy forested area of Africa. From this, one might assume that there is a sort of relic substratum of Negroid people of diminutive stature and (to us) very primitive culture scattered all over the continent and all similar to and related to the famous Uele groups. This is a gross misconception, for there are at least three quite distinct kinds of humanoid Pygmies known in Africa.

First, there is a very large strip of forested territory along the northern rim of the Congo Basin in the districts of Ubangi-Shari-Chad of the country now known as the Congo Republic. It has been stated that there are "Pygmies" there. Frankly, after years of pleading, I have been unable to obtain so much as a single straightforward official or scientific report on them. Second, in the even more vast tracts of solid forest in the Cameroon and the Gabun, there are definitely people of Pygmy stature who are true jungle people just like the Uele lot. What is more, they would seem to be of the same stock, but this area is so little known or explored that they have never gained any popular recognition.

When we turn to West Africa proper, we find a quite different state of affairs. The Pygmy hominids reported from here fall into the category of protohominids, along with the alleged hairy little types like the Agogwe, Shiru, Sehite, Orang-Pendek and such who will be discussed later.

But this is not all. It appears from all ethnological, anthropological and even archaeological evidence that has ever come to light that a squat, yellowish-skinned group of peoples, whom Coon calls the Capsian Race, once long ago inhabited the whole of Africa north of the forests. They might even have inhabited the whole of the continent. In due course they were either exterminated or driven progressively south by the incoming Caucasoid and Negroid types from north and east. These Capsians, seen today in the form of the remaining Bushmen, were the artists who painted and engraved the walls of caves and rock shelters. As far as is known, they have vanished but for some tragic remnants in the Kalahari Desert region of South Africa. However . . . and this is a rather big however . . .

I had a very startling experience in 1932 when I was visiting a tribal group named the Akunakuna on the Cross River, which separates Nigeria on the west from what was then the British Cameroon on the east. We were on the east side. The center of the "tribe" was such a large village it might almost be called a township, and the people were absolutely delightful socially. After meeting the head chief and subsidiary chiefs and bedding down our group, who numbered just one hundred souls, we invited the whole community to a grand "opening" with all three local (drum) bands, goodies for the youngsters and general good cheer for everybody else. In due course the community assembled on the short-grass central "green," which was about the size of an average football field. The chief and his entourage were most impressive. We exchanged mimbo (palm wine) and our last supply of whiskey, and the party was on. But then I noticed something that puzzled me.

All the Akunakuna men—magnificent ebony specimens of manhood—were crowded together in one lump; their womenfolk with the children in another, as is the custom thereabouts. But then, far off to the right and completely separated (should one say "segregated"?) there was a large body of small, immensely broad-shouldered men of a brownish yellow color, with what is called perhaps rather rudely "mouse-tittie" hair, sloe eyes, high cheekbones and prognathous jaws but totally uneverted lips. A little farther removed to the right and almost in the shadows of the surrounding trees was still another lot. These were women and children, even shorter of stature and brighter yellow and all with, no less, what is called "advanced steatopygia"—to wit, enormously developed buttocks. This physical feature is, I should perhaps explain, a character of the Bushmen, as are the yellowish color, sloe eyes, high cheekbones and, in the case of older pure families, the noneverted lips.

"What be those people?" I asked the chief, and after it had been explained to him for the umpteenth time that we were *not* government officials, he looked me in the eye and told me this, and I paraphrase: "Those be slave-man." Period.

Now slavery was, of course, not allowed in that country, hence the chief's worry about our status. Nonetheless, I found that slavery, or rather bondage, has never been eliminated in that land. This does not mean that these "slave-man" were slaves in our sense of that word. It meant simply that they were a subject and subjugated people who had retained their own identity since the dawn of time and served their lordly "masters" just as the Pygmies of the Uele do theirs. They were not allowed to intermarry with or in any other way molest or associate with said masters or their families, under pain of death. They were "hewers of wood and drawers of water." But what surprised me most was that they did not live in the village but *in the nearby jungle* in their own communities, had their own customs and arts, hunted for their "masters" and obtained foods and other items

Stuart Cloete from Pix

Pygmies in Congo village.

from them in return by barter. And they were, as anybody with even a modest training in physical anthropology could see, manifestly of the Bushman or Capsian race—neither Bantu nor Sudanese like their neighbors.

How many other so-called Pygmy groups or tribes or communities in tropical forested Africa are relics of this proto-Negro race? How many are on the other hand an offshoot of the main Negroid stem? How many are true primitives with an origin more ancient? And, finally, how many, if any, are true sub-men or proto-*Homo,* maybe even relics of the little australopithecines (see Chapter 27). This has always fascinated me—perhaps because I saw it with my own eyes, but also because it fits so perfectly into theories and discoveries that have come crowding in throughout the years ever since. I don't know if any anthropologists will agree with me, but I have a fancy that some prolonged and careful study of the forest tribes of West

Africa, the Cameroons, Gabun and even other parts of the Congo would bring to light concrete traces of this substrata of primitive peoples living *in* the jungles still. Are these the little people of whom Homer wrote—or was he referring to the Uele type? Much of the later talk about them has been quite as fanciful as his, but not usually as eloquent. One may doubt that they ever really were at war with the cranes, but the Greeks had enough information about them for the poet to put them into the Iliad:

> . . . as when the cranes,
> Flying the wintry storms, send forth on high
> Their dissonant clamours, while o'er the ocean stream
> They steer their course, and on their pinions bear
> Battle and death to the Pygmean race.

It was the Negroes rather than the cranes that the Pygmies feared and fled from, at least the true jungle Pygmies. These little people are called Negrillos in Africa and Negritos in the Orient, because early European explorers thought they were all "little Negroes." Most of the other white explorers also thought this until quite recently.

It now turns out, there is every reason to suppose, that the so-called Negroes are, in fact, the latest development of *Homo sapiens,* and *not* one of the earliest. They are less like the apes than so-called whites, whose lips and hair are far more apelike than those of Negroes. Whoever saw an ape or a white man with everted lips and kinky hair?

It would appear that tall chocolate brown men turned up in Africa —probably developed there at about the headwaters of the Nile—not much before the beginning of historical times. They spread over Africa generally in the next several thousand years, reaching South Africa overland at almost the same time that the white men got there by sea, which was in the fifteenth century. In the beginning, though, the eastern Negro tribes interbred with neighboring Caucasoids to produce the Bantu and the Hamitic peoples.

As the original Negroes (technically called the Sudanese) moved west, they met the little Capsians or Bushman types, much lighter in color than themselves, less skilled in the arts of war and knowing nothing of agriculture. The warrior Negro rapidly either exterminated these little people or enslaved them or drove them into the jungle, where the black man still hesitates to venture except for hunting.

It is doubtful whether the Pygmies, prior to their immigration into the jungles, had developed technical and parapsychological skills which enable them to thrive there today while no other peoples can. Whatever knowledge of agriculture or pottery-making or metalworking any of these little jungle peoples might have had before the coming of the Negro has manifestly been lost. They learned to eat what they could kill or gather in the jungle itself, and they subsist on a wide variety of plants and animals. Never settled for very long in one place—any Pygmy woman worth having can build a house for her family in a few hours—the Uele Negrillos are the nomads of the forest, even more mobile than tribes that have flocks and herds to transport. They leave the jungle reluctantly and for brief periods only, although it must be admitted that these intervals are getting longer now for some of them. Like everybody else, they are succumbing to the temptations of modern gadgets.

Just how many jungle people there are is anybody's guess. Some authorities say that Africa holds about a hundred thousand of them. At the other end of the scale, it has been said that probably not more than three thousand to five thousand Bambuti, the generic name for all Negrillos in Africa, still roam the great jungles. The same statistical vagueness, it may be added, prevails concerning the American and Oriental jungle peoples. After all, it is hardly feasible to take a census of a population of whose existence you are not sure and to whom you could hardly send census takers or forms even if you were. Their own accounts are not likely to be of much help if it were possible to talk to enough of them, and those of the more accessible tribesmen who live near them and used to be our main source of information about them are even less reliable. The attitude of these tribesmen toward jungle people is inevitably colored by their attitude toward the jungle itself.

To the Negro the jungle is full of terrors, to some of which he gives horrendous names. To the Pygmy, on the other hand, the jungle is the source of all good—of food and drink and shelter, amusement and sport, and above all security. This is the same the world over; the neighbors of the jungle shun it on both practical and superstitious grounds; the dwellers inside it love it as home.

The neighbors, after all, lack the skills to survive in the jungle and seem also to lack the capacity to acquire those skills. They are as little adapted to it as the lion, and like him would starve to death if left there alone. As the gifted author and ethnologist Dr. Colin Turnbull points out, the Bambuti say Negroes are just too big and too clumsy to stalk game therein. They cannot find the fruits and nuts, and they cannot distinguish between the edible and the inedible. They are afraid of all sorts of animals—snakes and cats and elephants and small stinging things—which Pygmies simply ignore or avoid. So they have invented enough horror stories to fill a library about the perils and evils of the jungle. This is just as true of the average Oriental as it is of the African Negro, and has inevitably been transferred to the white men.

One result, as many observers have noted in various parts of the world, is that mothers in communities near the jungle need never fear that their children will wander off into it in search of adventure or even by mistake. By the time they can walk they are thoroughly indoctrinated with the tribal attitude toward the rain forest.

Tom Harrisson, who has studied some of these people closely and intelligently, noted in his book *Savage Civilization* that in the New Hebrides, villagers living next to the jungle let a child do anything he likes so long as he stays close to home. "Which," adds Harrisson, "he will surely do for fear of the forest. . . . The child is warned against the longer-haired, pale-skinned men, Intumbulu, who live in caves or among banyan roots; they only come out when it rains, to steal the tops of cabbage trees or to spear people on the ends of their tremendously long fingernails."

For centuries, nearly all that men from other countries knew about the forest people was what neighbors, such as these New Hebrideans, told them. Since so much of it was plainly fanciful, it was easy to reach the conclusion that the jungle people were total figments of primitive imaginations. Of course, that explains, too, why less than eighty years ago the strongholds of European and American scholarship were still insisting that there weren't any Pygmies in the Far East.

Actually there are a good many, and perhaps even more jungle dwellers who would not be classed as true Pygmies, although they are notably small in stature.

A group of related Pygmy types now are known to inhabit the Malay Peninsula, the Philippines and the Andaman Islands, which are heavily jungled dots of land in the Bay of Bengal. The seagoing natives of India named them from the Sanskrit word for "monkey people." For years South Andaman was the site of a British penal colony when the islands were an appanage of British India; now they belong to Burma. Curiously enough, *these* Oriental Pygmies superficially resemble Negroes more closely than do the African Negrillos, which is why they were initially called Negritos by the Spaniards, who saw them as early as 1521, probably in the Philippines, and long before the name "Negrillo" had been applied to the Bambuti of the Congo. But these Spaniards were sailors or adventurers—and often, it must be admitted, great liars—whose stories did not convince the learned, so for more than three hundred years the little black men of the Orient were dismissed airily as pure fables.

Then, after Quatrefages de Breau demonstrated their existence by indisputable evidence, scientists condescended to recognize them. They proved to be darker, more kinky-haired than their African counterparts. Toward the end of the nineteenth century, Sir Hugh Clifford, a distinguished British Colonial governor even better known as a writer on Malaya, described them as "like African Negroes seen through the reverse end of a field glass."

More than fifty years later, Kilton Stewart, a United States psychologist who actually lived with and was adopted into a Negrito tribe in the Philippines, wrote: "They looked like a small edition of American Negroes I had met, with the same tendency to be cheerful and jolly."

There is some evidence that at one time Negritos inhabited all of southeastern Asia, including Burma and Indochina and much of India. Those who survive have retreated into the closed-canopy primordial forests which remain on some Indian Ocean islands and in such places as the Malay Peninsula and the Philippines.

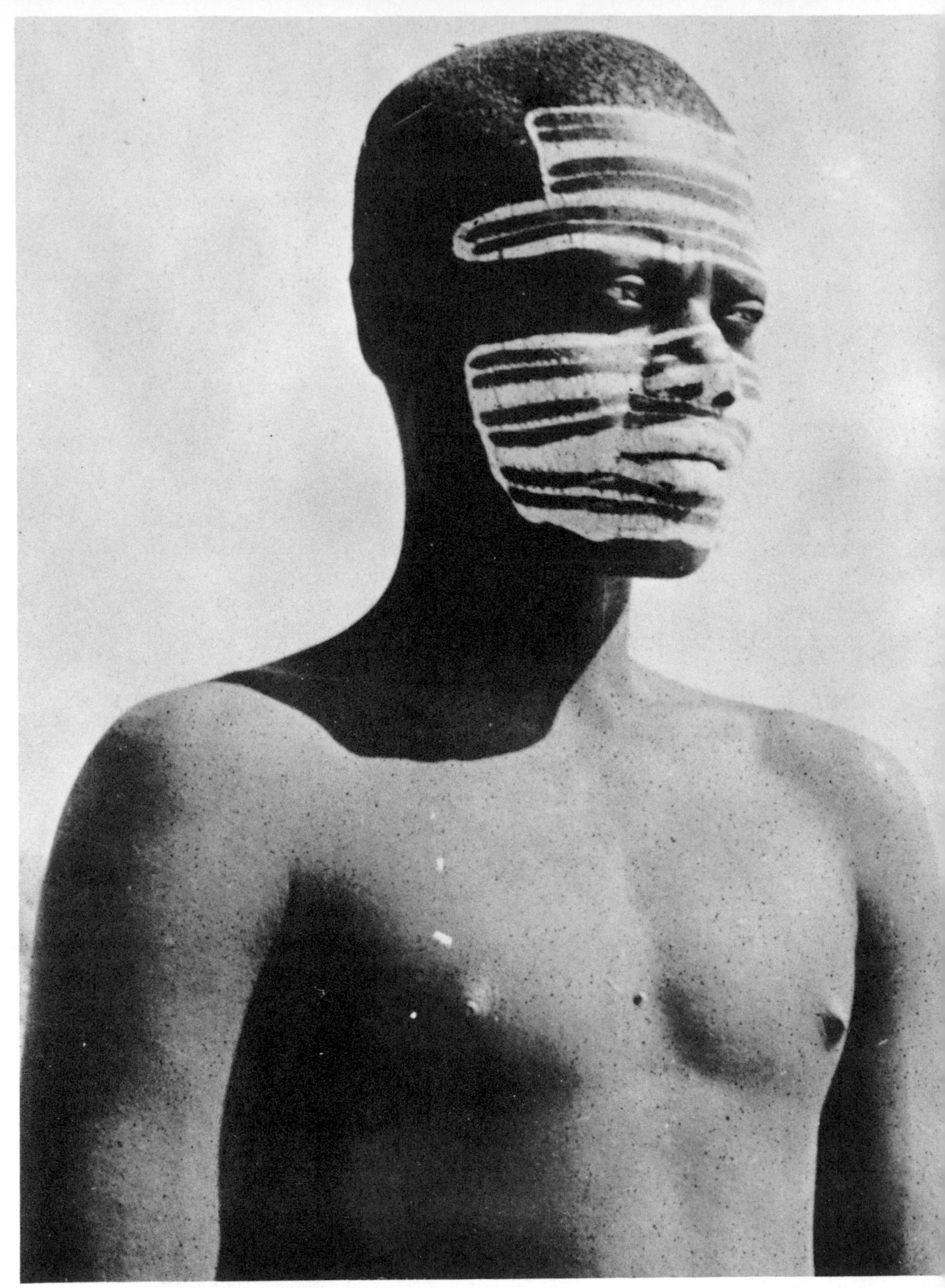

American Museum of Natural Hist

Onge tribesman from Little Andaman Island.

For such small people, they have large feet and splayed toes. Fairly thick lips and broad, flattened noses with distended nostrils exaggerate their narrow foreheads and receding chins.

The Pygmy Veddas of India and Ceylon have a quite different look, being neat, dark, Dravidian fellows with long moustaches. Still another appearance is presented by the Tapiros of New Guinea, a light brown people who are believed to be a "pint-sized" version of the Papuans. The Tapiros range in height from only four to five feet, and they were not even discovered until 1910. And finally—not recognized as really existing until even later—there are the Mongoloid-looking, beautiful and beautifully named "Ghosts of the Yellow Leaves." These people survive in the jungles of Thailand near the border of China and Laos.

When one speaks of Veddas and jungles, a brief explanation is called for. To an anthropologist, Vedda means a primitive subdivision of archaic Caucasoids found in and around the Indian subcontinent. They are apt to be short and thin, to have wavy straight hair including thin moustaches on the men, scant body hair and skin ranging in color from yellow to brown-black. In India proper they have become largely civilized, living in houses, growing crops and becoming castes in the socioeconomic order around them just like the Hindus, who arrived later than they did.

But a few of the original Veddas, apparently unwilling or unable to adapt to civilization, survive in jungle retreats in Ceylon and southern India. The men are about five feet tall, the women a few inches shorter. They seem to have been submerged by successive waves of conquerors, always driven into areas that the newcomers wanted least—the old story that has occurred on every continent except the Antarctic.

At one time, though, these small Veddic people occupied virtually all of India; apparently they drove out the Negritos who had preceded them. They, in turn, would seem to have been treated very much as the African Pygmies have been by the Negroes. Dr. Bernard Heuvelmans, who is probably the world's leading scientific investigator of as yet undescribed creatures, brought to light a number of important points about the creature called man. In his book, *On the*

Track of Unknown Animals, he tells of the declining fortunes of both the Pygmy Veddas and the Negritos, and comments: "All of these little creatures have been beaten, massacred and driven out by larger and better armed invaders."

The little people of New Guinea are dwellers in the big island's montane jungles, starting at the south central edge of the Bismarck range and trending westward. They have many features and characteristics in common with the Papuans, with whom they are usually in a state of armed truce. But for each trait of resemblance, there is another of difference. They are often lighter in color. Sometimes they appear vaguely Mongoloid or even Caucasoid, while the Papuans look more Negroid. Among the Tapiros the typical distended torso and skinny legs of the Papuan are conspicuously absent.

Not unlike them in appearance, but sturdier and more timid, are a little people on Borneo called Penans. Like the African Negrillo, they leave the jungle only to trade.

Perhaps the most mysterious and certainly the most pathetic of the known jungle people are the "Ghosts of the Yellow Leaves." Until the 1930's Europeans who had heard from the Thai woodsmen of a tiny, yellow-skinned people living in the deep jungle with no weapons at all, not even bows or spears or clubs, simply smiled at each other. The creatures were obviously figments of native mythology and superstition unworthy of serious consideration. The very name, which in the local tongue is *Pi Tong Luang,* seemed to prove that the Ghosts of the Yellow Leaves were no more real than any of the other ghosts in which simple folk believe. It was just too ridiculous to suppose that they could be anything else.

But in the 1930's, only a few years before the Japanese occupied the country during World War II, determined anthropologists, notably Dr. H. S. Bernatzik, proved conclusively that the hunters of Thailand knew their jungles better than did the skeptical Caucasians who pored over books in libraries or sipped drinks in Bangkok.

The Ghosts of the Yellow Leaves were not only real; they were quite as defenseless as the Thai woodsmen had said. The chief cause of mortality among them was said to be the tigers and leopards of their own jungles. At a rough guess, there were only three hundred

Magnum

Vedda.

to five hundred of them left. Brownish yellow and handsome, even beautiful, the tallest reach a height of five feet three inches. Somewhat Mongoloid to look at, they lack the curious fold at the corner of the eye which almost all true Mongoloids possess, and in the overall they resemble more closely the Caucasoid type. They call themselves *Yumbri,* which in their tongue means simply "the people," and indeed many primitive tribes all over the world, in and out of jungles, so name themselves.

This particular vanishing people came out of heaven knows what strange wanderings into the Asiatic jungles. It may or may not be that they brought their helplessness with them, but now they exhibit all the characteristics of any dying animal species. How long they may have been living in the jungle is pure guesswork. They themselves are reported to have no legends or traditions about their origins or their past history. Some scientists believe them to be the degenerate remnant of a once vigorous people. Others regard the Ghosts of the Yellow Leaves as a fading vestige of an incredibly ancient group which has persisted in small numbers in an even, unvarying way of life throughout many millennia.

The little that we do know about this strange, sad people emphasizes once again the degree to which the rest of mankind has avoided the home grounds of all true jungle folk. The country in which the Ghosts of the Yellow Leaves survived, in such isolation that outsiders were not easily convinced of their existence, has been one of the most frequently invaded of territories. Successive waves of immigrants passed into and over it north, east and west. The invaders are supposed to have exterminated or driven south the original Negrito inhabitants. Today a number of indigenous peoples are distinguishable in Thailand—the Thais or Siamese themselves, Malays, Annamese, Mons and Khmers.

Many of the jungle peoples we have been talking about were forced out of a previous home outside the forest by stronger tribes or invaders. But that does not at all explain how they managed to become real jungle dwellers, at home in and master of their environment. Nearly everywhere in the world the men who overwhelmed them have in turn been conquered, beaten, enslaved, dispersed, oppressed and otherwise harried at least as severely as the little folk who were there earlier. But rarely if ever did the Negro of Africa or the more advanced people of the Orient take refuge in the jungle and, more especially, remain there as comfortable, secure, happy residents.

Perhaps a single example out of many will explain our point. When Charles Goodyear invented the process for vulcanizing rubber —his patent was issued in 1844—he touched off a boom in the sap of a tree known as *Hevea brasiliensis,* as we mentioned earlier in this book, which revolutionized Brazil within a generation. The demand for rubber, then obtainable only from wild trees in the American jungles, led, among other benefits and horrors, to an incredibly brutal exploitation of the native population—incredible in spite of the fact that it had been the pattern over many centuries in many lands when the resources of a subject people could suddenly make some of the masters rich. Whole villages were wiped out by raids to impress the native rubber gatherers.

As late as 1907, Fawcett was assured when he protested at the sight of villagers being dragged off that "only the forest Indians are sold openly." The others, he was told, were simply bonded into servitude to work out their supposed debts to their captors. The Colonel heard one raiding party boast of having dashed the heads of children against trees and of dragging a woman behind their launch for miles for sport. Similar and perhaps worse atrocities, carried on throughout the rubber country for nearly fifty years, could be catalogued endlessly.

Yet the surviving victims of these horrors did not become jungle dwellers. Those who escaped retreated up the rivers or to the plains or even into the patches of savannah. Some of them learned to protect themselves a little with poisoned arrows. But in spite of their dread of the raiders and repeated losses, they seemed to have realized that they did not have the capacity to survive in the jungle, although they knew no raiding party would ever follow them there.

Halfway round the world, the inhabitants of such Oriental lands as the New Hebrides behaved in exactly the same way at about the same period. From the time Europeans first discovered these peoples, marauding white men from ships often shot up their villages. Later, and most notably in the second half of the last century, the whites

American Museum of Natural Histo

Papuan archer, New Guinea.

introduced the brutal system of labor impressment which they called "recruiting" and the world has called "blackbirding." The unwilling plantation hands were frequently abused as atrociously as any people ever were. Blackbirders murdered and stole with impunity, and one of them even wrote about it. Tom Harrisson, speaking of a specific island, quotes the fellow, one W. T. Wawn:

"The natives informed us that a schooner's crew had recently attacked Tangoa Island. [He was speaking of an incident that happened in 1878.] That having landed, they had destroyed all the canoes, burned the village, killed a score of men and had driven the remainder of the inhabitants away from the island. Luckily for us, there was no missionary in the neighbourhood to exaggerate the story and make another blood curdling atrocity out of it."

Harrisson wonders what it would take to have Wawn consider the term "blood curdling atrocity" justified. Some commentators thought African slaves had been treated better because, as one expressed it, they were "the more valuable animal."

Yet the islanders, in all their efforts to escape the rapacious invaders from the sea, fled inland only as far as the fringe of the rain forests (if there were any on their island) or paddled away to another island which they hoped would remain unmolested. They did not have the qualities needed to make a permanent home in a jungle, and apparently they never even tried.

The story is repeated in Africa. Perhaps of all the atrocities committed by white men against conquered peoples of another color, none was so widely publicized as the late nineteenth- and early twentieth-century horrors of the then Congo Free State, when it was the private property of King Leopold II of Belgium. The exploitation of mines and forests was carried out with what the most restrained chroniclers have called "barbarous cruelty." For centuries before that, slavers of various races and colors had raided Negro communities relentlessly. The Pygmies were immune to all these horrors, secure in their jungles. No Negroes sought that sanctuary as a place of permanent residence, no matter how abominable the fate that awaited them outside.

In the face of this record, a civilized man's respect for the jungle peoples mounts. What did they have that bigger men did not? What did it take to flourish in these great forests into which not even the prospect of torture, slavery and imminent death can drive supposedly more advanced peoples?

In search of answers to these questions, we may learn a little about the jungle folk as they really are, rather than as they have usually been described to us by outsiders who are sometimes friendly but usually are not. Whether the jungle people are, as many scientists think, relic survivals of the mainstream of modern man, or whether they are members of various racial groups or subgroups, they have achieved certain knowledge and acquired certain talents that we lack, for all our vaunted civilization.

24

The Nature of the Little People

PHYSIOLOGICALLY and psychologically the people of the jungle are not like other men. In becoming the masters of their environment, they have been molded by it, too, in body and mind. One would think that sensible observers of them, especially scholars, would realize that this is inevitable, but many learned men have been surprised every time they came across some evidence of it.

Physically, of course, the most obvious distinction is that nearly all of the jungle people are small in stature if not, in fact, Pygmies. The second point which has been most frequently commented upon, often with astonishment, is that most of them are also well-formed, exceptionally strong for their size, extremely graceful and sure in their movements, making them capable of swift but absolutely silent progress through the jungle.

Despite considerable differences, but no greater than those found among numbers of the so-called black or white or yellow races, there are enough physical similarities between the Negrito and Negrillo groups, wherever located, to warrant the strong suspicion that they are not examples of parallel evolution but are truly related.

This gives rise to a fine ethnological puzzle. Assuming a common origin, how did these little people get where they are today? Looking at a global map, one might at first suppose that they either originated in one place and then wandered over half the earth, or that there was once a great "land-bridge" between Africa and the Orient. Nobody seems to have even considered the third alternative; to wit, that, wherever these little people did originally evolve, they spread out from there all over the *land surface* of the earth that was suitable to them.

Indeed, there is good evidence that there was once a land connection right across the Indian Ocean but that was millions of years before man, however primitive, was evolved. However, there is equally good evidence that the lands now lying around the Arabian Sea and the Bay of Bengal were once forested and that "Little People" inhabited these areas. They may have covered many latitudes farther north in even earlier times. In fact, they may be remnants of early peoples who inhabited a very large area of the earth. There are even those who contend that several waves of real primitives inhabited the whole earth from the then subpolar regions to the equator.

That the Abo got to Australia is pretty clear evidence that "full-sized man," however primitive, used boats; otherwise, the Asiatic animals would have arrived with them over any land-bridge there might have been that late in time. The little jungle peoples are quite different; they have been there all the time—however they got there in the first place.

Important as this and certain clear physiological differences may be, true jungle dwellers of today have psychological attributes which, while perhaps not exclusive to them, are more highly developed in the individual and more common to all the individuals in the community than is the case in other societies. They are spiritually, or emotionally if you prefer, attuned to their environment. Whether their general psychological adjustment is better or worse than that of other peoples is irrelevant for the moment. The point is, it is different. Since their environment is not at all like any other on earth, it is hardly surprising that the minds of its residents should have developed in certain respects at a tangent to those of other men.

Furthermore, since adaptation to the jungle appears to have remained absolutely unchanged for thousands of years, their psychological adjustment to their environment seems to be more uniform than that of other people who are subjected to a greater variety of pressures from one generation to another. Nowhere else in the world have human beings been so little exposed to the emotional shocks of new ideas, new products, new conditions of life, and new concepts of man and the universe.

For us, the fantasy of suddenly being transported back in time to, say, the Egypt of the Pharaohs, the Italy of Romulus and Remus, the France or Germany of the Gauls or Teutons is a tremendous exercise of the imagination. We know that not only would we be in an entirely different civilization but all our feelings and thoughts would have to be readjusted radically to cope with that civilization. The true man of the jungle, dropped tomorrow among his ancestors in the tall equatorial forest of even prehistorical times, wouldn't know the difference. The houses would be exactly like the one his wife built yesterday and would be furnished in the same style with the same materials. People would be using the same tools and weapons with which he has been familiar all his life, and for the same purposes. His way of life is as immutable as the jungle itself, so it can make very little difference to him whether he goes forward or backward in time, or stands still.

The psychology of the jungle people has remained as static as their material existence, and that of itself has permitted a mental development such as our own backgrounds of incessant change would never allow. It is only recently that this has been investigated as well as appreciated.

Trained psychologists, after all, have seldom had an opportunity to study dwellers in the rain forest very intensively. One who has—and the only one who has actually done it while living among them, so far as I know—was an American from Utah named Kilton Stewart. He lived with the Negritos of Luzon in the Philippines, won their confidence sufficiently to have them take batteries of his psychological tests, shared their feasts and ceremonies and dangers. After his return to America, he wrote of his experiences in a book, *Pygmies and Dream Giants,* in which he comments, after taking part with the local shaman in what we would call a successful example of psychotherapy: "Here was a true psychology of healing which was not fifty thousand years behind Western civilization. In some respects it seemed ahead."

Stewart was familiar with modern uses of hypnosis and trances in

American Museum of Natural Histo

Negrito husband and wife, Philippines.

treatment. But he found the Negrito medicine man much more advanced than himself, and an equally skilled practitioner. Furthermore, this shaman was most successful in curing his patients of just those chronic diseases that our own medical experts find the most baffling. Stewart himself was astonished by the facile suggestibility of these people under his own hypnosis.

Many members of the first group he lived with had ringworm, which he treated by putting them into a trance and painting the cracked skins with iodine or an acid, very painful to any conscious man. But when he suggested to his Negrito patients that it would feel good, each reported on waking that that was just how it did feel.

There is no doubt in my mind that at least some of the jungle peoples, and probably all of them, have powers of extrasensory perception which most of the rest of us have either lost or never developed. Europeans and Americans for years have sneered at all accounts of even the most soberly documented demonstrations of this alleged sensitivity, refusing to believe that anything outside their ken is possible. But I know of no other way to account for undeniable facts which I have personally witnessed.

Perhaps the most curious fact about this most abstruse question is that while the jungle peoples appear to possess and exercise, practically, certain mental or psychological or parapsychological (or whatever you choose to call them) aptitudes, they are basically pragmatic people. Unlike certain primitive nonforest peoples such as the Abo of Australia, they just do not seem to have any use for or bother with what we now think of as *para*psychology. This is not to say that they lack *super*sensory perception, which is something quite else. Further, they appear to have a "going" or even what our youngsters today would probably call a "swinging" ability in the department of precognition. However, while we test ourselves with cards, and the Abo seems to know when grandma is sick a few hundreds of miles away, and a tribal African may announce the imminent arrival of a messenger long before he is even near; the jungle peoples, as far as I have been able to discover from the few serious students who have lived with them and observed them, seem not at all concerned with grandma, messengers, or face-to-face telepathy. But when it comes to natural things like weather and hunting, it is quite another matter.

Professional tracking of animals, wounded or not, is in itself an uncanny procedure, but any such exercise in a closed-canopy forest is virtually impossible. Yet the forest people can track an animal sometimes for days, and it appears they cannot even point out to an outsider who speaks their language any physical evidences—like bent or broken twigs, foot tracks, and so on—by which they do it. This may sound a bit "way out," but I can assure you that if you go and live in a jungle for any length of time without fear or cavil, you will find yourself sniffing the upcoming weather, drifting with the animals and generally slipping into a sort of vast biorhythm. I cannot, and therefore should not, proceed to say that one appears able to sense the coming of messengers or the passing of tribesmen in the night.

But when it comes to animals, words almost fail me. Having appalling eyesight but being a professional collector of animals for many years, I can only say that I stumbled across a very high percentage of the hundreds of thousands of specimens I collected through some kind of . . . what should I say? Was it supersensitivity of my other senses (and we have more than two dozen now known) or extrasensitivity, whatever that may be, or what? I do not know, but even my paid assistants constantly asked where the heck I had found such or such a specimen. Usually it was within ten minutes stroll of our camp and on territory they had gleaned as thoroughly as they could. For some uncanny reason I just went right to the animals or they came to me. There was nothing "clever" about it.

The same seems to be the general rule with true jungle peoples. But then, jungle peoples seem to have other feelings which we would call premonitions or precognition or clairvoyance, and they sometimes make those of us who cannot share in the reception of such messages uncomfortable. But our discomfort should not blind us to the reality of the experience. One which Stewart describes strikes me as typical. Because he was a trained psychologist, his acceptance of it is more convincing than it might be if related by the usual wanderer returned from far places. The adventure is told in fascinating detail in his book, but essentially was this:

One morning a young man of the Negrito tribe told of a dream he had had in which he had seen a tree demon spear Stewart. The American reacted with the indifference we would expect. In fact, he only thought of it again later in the day when a large ant bit him in the leg with a ferocity which made him think for the moment that he had been stabbed. He reported feeling "an overwhelming pang of fear" of the tree demon at that moment, but of course it passed.

Next day the tribe started for a new camping site where fruit was supposed to be more plentiful, and they left uncommonly early for travel in the cold mists of that montane jungle—the Negritos usually wait until the world has warmed a little before moving. Stewart was in no very good humor when he tore himself from his warm bedroll, and his mood became progressively darker as he plodded along among his silent companions, cold and dejected under the somber, dripping trees. They came to a canyon through which a chill wind whistled, and stopped at the face of a black cliff to appease the rock demon, to them a clear necessity but a mere addition to the white man's discomfort. From there the path climbed a ridge and descended the other side. In his growing resentment with everything about him, not unnatural considering how thoroughly miserable he was, Stewart was even annoyed when the "head shaman," an old, graying little man, dropped back to walk next to him as they climbed and started down again.

The sloping path was slippery, and at one point Stewart reached toward a tree to steady himself. The next he knew, the old shaman had yanked him back by the hair, and he was sitting on the damp ground. On the bark where his hand had reached was a large caterpillar. The Negritos showed him the thin black poisoned spines which, they told him, break off in a man's flesh and cause a nasty infection, perhaps death.

The shaman had been watching for something like this. He explained that his familiar spirit had warned him that there was danger to the white man from a tree demon somewhere on this trail. He was on the alert, therefore, and whether or not the demon actually was lurking in that caterpillar, Stewart leaves little doubt of his faith in the reality of the old man's premonition. Whether he was as convinced of the need for the small ceremony by which the Negritos propitiated the tree demon before they went on is not so certain.

It is easy to dismiss all this as mere coincidence, but then most of us are not ordinarily exposed to such dangers. In the jungle it is one of the everyday facts of life, and its people have a feeling for it that New Yorkers develop for trucks, buses and taxis. To us the demonstration of premonition or the like is an unusual event, as our dodging the truck would be to a Pygmy, for it is colored by unfamiliarity. But to the jungle people, who practice it all the time, it is no more than the normal use of their eyes or ears.

For thousands of years their survival has depended upon putting a foot down where it will not be heard and will not encounter some stinging creature. They have had to know, but without bringing what we regard as the usual senses into play, what vine or bush or branch to grasp.

Perhaps it is by their keen honing of senses *we* do not use that

Black St

Shaman driving out evil spirit with leaves.

the jungle peoples have developed their skill in psychotherapy. It has been suggested that in our society, men and women are trained to think; the jungle dweller is trained to feel instead. He becomes as far ahead of us in feeling as we are ahead of him in our intellectual processes. This explains, perhaps, why we find his perceptions so marvelous. By the same token, everything about us that strikes him as miraculous is probably the fruit of our civilization.

Successful psychotherapy, of course, is nothing more than the use of the feelings, the emotions, for healing, just as successful immunization therapy is the use of powerful serums or vaccines. We have achieved a considerable understanding of immunizers but lag in the exploitation of the emotions, and we are only just now beginning to catch up.

When Stewart put his first Negrito into a trance, he was surprised to discover that this was a recognized and quite common practice among their shamans, too. He was also struck by the way these medicine men joined him in helping the subject explore his past, and his dreams, for relevant incidents and images which would assist him in understanding the sources of his ailment—in this instance severe headaches. Stewart says he had expected much more mumbo-jumbo, since the whole community gathered around to watch the treatment. But the shamans' result turned out to be "very much like those obtained by the new psychotherapy being employed in Paris and in Vienna."

Where the shamans went beyond the best European authorities, Stewart thought, was in having the patient stay with the relevant past experience in his trance until he could give the therapist an actual representation of it in the form of a song or a dance to be performed later when he awakened. Stewart himself had been afraid to force the man to go through such a prolonged bout. It seemed, however, that any of these people not only could manage it but also transmuted the old conflict in their minds into joy, so that a headache became a song. The patient could sing the song or perform the dance from that time on instead of succumbing to the migraine. It may seem odd or even doubtful that a man would as a matter of general practice be able to remember, after he came out of the trance, the details of so complex a performance. But Stewart was reminded of the well-established fact of Western life that some gifted individuals—Beethoven was a notable example—compose music or solve mathematical problems in their heads while they are asleep, and wake up with it all so clearly in mind that they can write it down straightaway.

"But nowhere in the civilized world was this creativeness in sleep and in the half-sleep trance encouraged and guided through social cooperation to the same extent as among these pre-literate Negritos," Stewart said.

Stories of medicine men or priest doctors of other primitive peoples have given us a concept quite different from the reality of the Negrito shaman's practice. Stewart found that there was no more mumbo-jumbo about the shaman's position in the tribe than about his therapy. Anyone could become a shaman and could qualify through a process that trained him (or her, for women were not barred) as a healer. In that training, there was no passing along of recipes for magic potions or charms, no incantations, no initiation into mysteries, no ceremonies, no special costumes or adornments. The shamans were simply those who had themselves been healed and learned their art in the course of their own treatments; one is reminded that our own psychoanalysts cannot be considered trained until they have been psychoanalyzed.

In short, these little people seemed to have a practical but effective medical course as devoid of supernatural overtones as that taken by a Western psychiatrist. In the tribe of twenty-odd adults among whom Stewart first observed the Negrito psychotherapy, there were five shamans, one a woman.

A curious point about the psychology of these jungle folk was their very short memories. Stewart found that, during the tests he administered, the incidents they remembered were from the very recent past, and to a degree he felt "the Negritos forgot with a vengeance." But in a world of so little change, it could well be that there isn't very much to remember that was not exactly like yesterday or last week.

Among the Negritos, psychological adjustment to their environment seems to have been assisted by an assortment of spirits and demons which sometimes served and sometimes harassed the individual. The Negrillos of Africa achieved similar adjustment, but apparently with not nearly so great a dependence upon spirits.

Two white men, one living, Dr. Colin Turnbull, and the other dead, Patrick Putnam, probably have got as close to knowing, *really knowing,* the African Pygmies as any civilized Caucasian can. Putnam lived with the Negrillos of the Ituri Forest for many years and sent regular, scientific reports to Harvard, where he had been trained as an anthropologist. He died in the deep jungle, among the tiny people he loved, but his wife carries on his work at Camp Putnam to this day. Turnbull wrote *The Forest People,* a fascinating account of his year's stay with these little folk; and his reports on the Bambuti supplement and update Putnam.

Both of these highly trained men have indicated that the Pygmies are remarkably free from superstition. Even when they seem to tremble at the supernatural terrors imagined by Negro villagers with whom they are in contact, they apparently are merely trying to be agreeable and conform to what they consider a harmless, silly quirk. They do not really take the big men's devils seriously. Their own are neither so malevolent nor so ubiquitous, if they have any at all.

The psychological sensitivity of jungle peoples is further indicated in another feature of the Negrito psychotherapy upon which Stewart comments. He found in his own analysis of them that the shamans had a far richer, or more complicated, dream life than any of the other members of the tribe. Furthermore, the Negritos who had been or were being treated by the shamans dreamed, as Stewart puts it, "more extensively and more effectively"; the image and characters of their trances continued, even after they had awakened, to "go on working for the patient in his dreams."

More intelligible to most highly civilized observers, although equally beyond their capacity, is the ability of the jungle folk to sense the presence of an intruder long before the intruder is aware of them. This explains why the little people have survived for centuries in their great forests, often only a few miles from populated areas, without having been seen. Recent careful scientific writing has noted the ability of the Negritos, Negrillos, Ghosts of the Yellow Leaves and American jungle folk to slip away before anyone comes near them. In this, they share one of the talents of a great many jungle animals, who are so elusive that until the last few years many were known only by hearsay from the tales of the Negritos or Negrillos. Indeed, a few new ones are still being identified every year.

25
Home Among the Hunters

To the outsider, the jungle has always been regarded as a place of discomfort and danger—except for an occasional fictional character such as Tarzan or Mowgli, or such unconventional students of its mysteries as W. H. Hudson. No one "who knew better," as the phrase goes, would willingly live there. Those who do by choice were dismissed as backward, unfortunate savages doomed to a miserable existence, always haunted by superstition, fear, hunger, predatory beasts and gloomy, dripping surroundings. But the truth was well put by the African Pygmy who explained to Colin Turnbull why they were not afraid to wander about at night without weapons: "When we are Children of the Forest, what need have we to be afraid of it? We are only afraid of that which is outside the forest."

The jungle furnishes its children ample food and shelter, tools and weapons, such clothing as they need, abundant recreation and, above all, splendid protection from the world outside. Many who have known them only slightly think them incapable of really skilled work. For their part, they laugh at big clumsy clods who have neither the little people's dexterity at thatching roofs nor their techniques for gathering game and other food.

Home to the denizens of the forest is no particular clearing or space between jungle trees. A single group, seldom more than a few families and never more than a few hundred individuals, may roam impartially over hundreds of miles, guided largely by their feeling for where food will be most plentiful. We consider their mode of life to be nomadic but in point of fact it would better be called camping.

Their houses and furniture, therefore, are flimsy, easily made and abandoned without a pang. Their possessions are never a heavy

Photo Researchers

Congo Pygmies making net.

burden on the march from one campsite to another. The Ghosts of the Yellow Leaves carry this mobility to an extreme, which could be one of the reasons for their approaching extinction. They almost never spend a second night in any camp, but set up new lean-tos of poles and leaves every day.

Since the jungle folk live in the vegetational belt notable for its profusion of vines and lianas, they have learned to make great use of these natural ropes. The African and New Guinea Pygmies and some of the Amerinds are especially noted for their skill at making fish-nets and hammocks from vegetable material.

The Negrillos of Africa, who excel in the neatness and dispatch with which they can make a camp, leave the actual construction of their houses to their women. Men may help gather the broad green leaves for thatching, and any of them are quite competent at building, too, if they must. Leaves, some sapling poles and vines to tie it all together are the only building materials needed.

Uele Pygmy huts are round, roughly the shape of half a ball. They can be of any size, but a usual one for a family is six or eight feet in diameter. The women learn early to drive the pointed poles, several feet taller than themselves, into the ground without any pounding or digging tool. She jabs it sharply down, over and over, each thrust exactly in the hole left by the one before, until it sinks in far enough to hold. When she has a circle of these, a foot or so apart with a gap for the door, she bends them over and ties them all together at the top with a vine. Vines are wound about among the poles to make a sort of lattice on which the leaves are then hung, fastened by their split stems, overlapping each other like shingles. At the first rain a few leaves may be rearranged if a leak springs, but the finished job is snug and waterproof until the leaves dry out. By then the group probably will have moved on anyway. Because the jungle floor is so protected from wind, there is no danger the roof or a wall or the whole thing will blow away.

The jungle reclaims the abandoned dwelling only a little less rapidly than the Pygmies erect it. Colin Turnbull once returned to the first camp where he ever lived with them, and all he could see was a faint outline of the site. Not a vestige of any hut remained.

Most jungle people build similar abodes, neither much more nor less elaborate. Some, however, take advantage of natural shelters. The jungle Veddas sometimes live in shallow caves under overhanging cliffs in the hills. The surviving Negritos of the Andaman Islands live in semipermanent villages, their huts arranged in a circle and no more substantial than those of their African counterparts. They stay in one place perhaps because their jungle territory is not very large but also because their food supply is so plentiful that they have less need to move about.

Furniture for a jungle home is as handily constructed as the hut. A bed is not a must; in many huts a covering of leaves over a few sticks is considered ample. Others build sticks into a framework latticed with vines and set off the ground on legs. White men find them exquisitely uncomfortable, much more so than the hammock of vines which the American jungle folk have perhaps adapted from their neighbors, or perhaps took in with them.

A table is a frame similar to that of the bed, held up on four sticks,

Photo Researchers

Pygmy women completing hut.

used mostly for drying surplus meat by means of a fire built underneath—in the jungle, obviously, sun-dried meat would be impossible. A chair is a crude affair of flexible sticks, the seat and back being formed by the pressure of the body. Pygmies often use a log instead, or even sit on a big leaf on the ground. In the jungle they are a cleanly people, and they do not sit or lie on the damp earth if they can help it. Furniture for keeping or storing things, furniture for display, furniture for work, are unknown.

As for utensils, a Pygmy household is content with a few knives whose hardwood blades can be ground sharp enough to shave with, a pot or two, baskets, perhaps a mallet made out of a piece of elephant tusk lashed to a wooden handle, and a couple of pipes. The lot can be carried in the baskets without unduly slowing the progress of a family on the march from one camp to another. At each new hut, leaves serve as plates, tablecloth and napkins; sticks as spoons or forks; the shell of a large nut or the husk of a fruit as a cup.

Some other jungle folk add the refinements of crude clay pots, wooden buckets and vessels of bamboo. The Ghosts of the Yellow Leaves even have crude iron knives from metal they have smelted themselves, one reason for supposing they have retrogressed in the scale of civilization. They use these knives only as tools, never having learned that this could also be a weapon. Bamboo supplies all their other possessions. The Negritos of the Malay Peninsula also make almost everything they use from bamboo, including some razor-sharp knives, and have nothing of either stone or pottery. The Andaman Islanders did at one time make clay pots and wooden vessels but have lost the art, or given it up in favor of tin cans and other beach salvage, for they are the only true jungle people whose forests are so close to the sea that they can readily get down to the shore.

Clothing is one of the least of problems for any jungle people. A fire is better for warmth, and that has to be made for cooking in any case, so why go to the extra trouble of covering for the body? They have known for thousands of years what men like myself have discovered after long experience in the rain forest—that a loincloth is the one garment which adds to comfort and convenience. A belt to hold small objects and bags of food is the other standard feature of

Black Star

Bamboo knives are used in New Guinea to cut up pig.

any jungle costume. Anything else would be worn solely as a decoration and would seldom be so admired as a good job of painting the torso or buttocks. Pygmies who wear ordinary clothes when they come out of the jungle to the villages discard these garments as soon as they return to the forest.

In all the jungles, the main fabric is a form of cloth made from bark fibers. The relatively thin "skins" of jungle trees are soaked and pounded into soft, pliable strips which can be colored with dyes from the juices of nuts or berries. Belts are braided out of tough vines which also may be treated to make them stronger and more flexible. A feathered headdress or a cloak of bark and feathers or a short cape of animal skins would be worn only on ceremonial occasions. Kept in one of the household baskets, it would be carried about from camp to camp, but seldom brought out.

Nearly all jungle people live primarily by hunting game, which ranges from ants to elephants, and by gathering fruits, nuts and vegetables. Their ability to move swiftly and silently, their knowledge of animal habits and their uncanny faculty for looking in the right place have made them the mightiest if the smallest human hunters. The African Pygmy is as much the superior of the Negro in this field as the backwoodsman is of the city dweller.

The Bambuti are no more than fair marksmen with bow and arrow or spear. But they can creep so close to their quarry that even a poor shot usually hits the mark. They also make effective use of large hunting nets, patiently woven from strong fibers which they pull from certain tough vines. The hunters of the tribe usually string their nets together in a big semicircle, into which the women and children then drive the game, as beaters used to do for the gentry in an English wood or park in days gone by.

One of their common meat dishes is okapi, the short-necked giraffe which is so shy and elusive that until the twentieth century no white man had ever seen one. Stanley, who seems to have been the first to hear of the creature, thought the description was of a donkey. Pygmies located and killed okapi as a matter of course while elaborately equipped hunting parties of keen European sportsmen never could.

These same little people, sometimes one of them all alone, are the only foe the forest loxodonts have to fear. Only these Negrillos dare approach the lord of the jungle close enough to do him any harm, and there are two methods in use. The rarer one is to creep upon the giant and hamstring him by a spear thrust which will cut an essential tendon in one leg. No elephant can move if even one leg is immobilized, and he can then be finished off by the hunters at leisure. The more common method, but one which no other hunters apparently even try to emulate, is to crawl under the elephant and drive a spear upward into its vast paunch. The attacker slides safely away, usually, and then follows the wounded behemoth doggedly until he dies of blood poisoning, perhaps only after several days.

By whichever method the elephant is slain, the scene of his death is the group's next campsite. Their exceedingly primitive engineering

Ylla from Black Star

Loxodont.

skills have given the Pygmies no means of carting the giant home, either whole or in pieces. Therefore, the people move to where the carcass lies, and very promptly, too, before the rapid decomposition processes of the jungle begin. Elephant flesh is highly prized. The entire band can gorge themselves royally and even have plenty left over to dry and eat another day. They will remain in residence until the last of the elephant has been devoured, protecting the remains from scavenging beasts.

The successful hunter, meanwhile, will have gained enormous prestige and be very proud of it, too, prestige being the only reward Bambuti society bestows upon deserving members. He will not gain an extra ration or even the choice cut. No matter how great the hunter, his kill is not for himself alone but for the community. The meat of every day's chase is divided up, not without arguments and pleas, but not as the killer wishes either. The satisfaction of being a good provider and the admiration of his fellows are supposed to be all that a Pygmy can desire, and it seems to work out that way, too. If he can manage to be modest about his achievement, he will be regarded even more highly.

Meat provided by the men is supplemented by roots, herbs, nuts and fruit gathered mostly by women and children. Strangers in the jungle marvel at the unerring judgment of these people in uncovering an assortment of edibles, not all of which we would consider appetizing, where the uninitiated would find nothing.

According to Stewart, biting off the bodies of big honey ants while leaving the heads is considered a great jungle delicacy in the Philippines and is the equivalent of candy because these ants are sweet. Bats, rodents, reptiles and, in fact, anything that walks, flies, swims or crawls is acceptable and healthful. Nearly all jungle peoples eat with gusto a great variety of animals which even a hungry white man would gag at sampling. But the few white men who have taken up residence with the jungle folk in their own homes have learned to eat—if not exactly to relish—the native dishes.

While many items that we would normally cook are eaten raw, there is always a fire going in a Pygmy camp for roasting or stewing. Some of the jungle peoples have no knowledge of how to start a fire,

Black Star

Fire in Pygmy camp.

but many of them can do it with a couple of dry sticks if they must. All of them, especially the women, are adept at carrying a live coal wrapped in a leaf from one campsite to another. Dry wood is not always at hand in the jungle, but the people have discovered the hollow trees, and when no other fuel is available, they can always find enough bits of wood which have fallen down into the bottoms of these.

People everywhere have a taste for honey, and the jungles sometimes seem to be overflowing with that, if not with milk, because there are so many bees. Various tribes have various techniques for getting at it without being stung to death, if the bees are stingers. The nest is likely to be high in a tree and can be reached only by climbing. Some Negritos in the Orient have adopted one of the more daring methods for raiding bees. They tie a burning "tail" of dry grass and fresh leaves to themselves and ascend the tree in a cloud of smoke. The honey, they seem to think, is worth the price of a few stings when the smoke lifts a bit.

Since so much of their game never descends to the ground, and so many fruits and nuts have to be picked before they fall, the jungle folk are not far behind Tarzan in their ability to climb. Little children learn to swarm up the tallest trees and along the tough lianas at about the same time they learn to walk. Many of their games involve climbing.

Boys are initiated into the art of hunting while very young. Toddlers have miniature spears and bows and arrows, meticulously fashioned by their fathers in the exact image of the working models, although the arrows for children are of soft wood and blunt. If a piece of old hunting net is not handy, African Pygmy parents will make a small one for their son, although the preparation of the fibers and the knotting of the cords are among the most tedious chores imaginable.

Other jungle peoples vary the type of weapons and their uses, but not greatly, except for the Ghosts of the Yellow Leaves, who simply have none. The Malay Peninsula Negritos have a blowgun equipped with poisoned darts and make a bamboo fish trap for use on their streams, although they have no hunting nets on land. The Amerinds of South American jungles use a variety of weapons, as well as hunting devices (fish traps, nets), made from vegetable products. The Andamanese used to make little wooden canoes with crude outriggers to go hunting on the sea, but such craft are seldom seen now because these people no longer venture out of the jungle long enough to use boats. They do make a harpoon with which they kill the dugong, or sea cow, the big marine mammal related to the American manatee. They also barb their arrows—for the last hundred years they have made the heads out of iron salvaged from ships wrecked on their shorts. Their bows are unusually powerful and taller than the men who use them, whose height is four feet eight inches. Apparently, they never learned to make fire, but initially obtained it from a once active volcano on one of their islands—at least, this is the story.

The Andaman Negritos are among the rare jungle peoples who

Peter Buckley from Photo Researchers

Boy picking grapefruit in rain forest, Niger River region.

have a reputation for attacking strangers, probably because for a long time the only ones they saw were slavers who raided the coast, mostly coming from Malaya. They were described by the first white men who saw them as distinctly unfriendly, and they made as much trouble as they could for any shipwrecked mariner they came across. They were generally reported to be cannibals. They are not; but they did and probably still do burn the bodies of any strangers, whether killed by them or not, and this could have inspired the legend. They and the only permanent white settlement near them, the one-time penal colony at Port Blair, seem to have left each other severely alone.

The most prominent of all the true jungle people in literature is one of these Andaman Negritos, introduced by Sir Arthur Conan Doyle in *The Sign of the Four,* the Sherlock Holmes adventure which gave Dr. Watson a wife. Sir Arthur gave to his little man, named Tonga, the fierce character that English sailors had attributed to the race and also supplied him with a blowgun and poisoned darts, which not they but the *Malayan* Pygmies really do use. Even if the author knew this, he took this literary license because his plot involved the penal colony. He was astute enough, too, to permit Tonga to run barefoot about London, and the tiny prints betrayed his race to the omniscient Holmes, who thereupon read aloud this account to Watson out of what he called "a new gazeteer":

> "The aborigines of the Andaman Islands may perhaps claim the distinction of being the smallest race upon this earth, though some anthropologists prefer the Bushmen of Africa, the Digger Indians of America, and the Terra del Fuegians [Actually, the tallest race ever known!]. The average height is rather below four feet, although many full-grown adults may be found who are very much smaller than this. They are a fierce, morose, and intractable people, though capable of forming most devoted friendships when their confidence has once been gained." Mark that, Watson. Now, then, listen to this. "They are naturally hideous, having large, misshapen heads, small, fierce eyes, and distorted features. Their feet and hands, however, are remarkably small. So intractable and fierce are they that all the efforts of the British officials have failed to win them over in any degree. They have always been a terror to shipwrecked crews, braining the survivors with their stone-headed clubs,

American Museum of Natural History

Negrito man with bow and arrow.

or shooting them with their poisoned arrows. These massacres are invariably concluded by a cannibal feast." Nice, amiable people, Watson.

In the novel, Tonga misses the great detective with a poisoned dart by the proverbial hair, after killing another Englishman apparently for fun, and is shot dead by Holmes and Watson. On his own, the good Doctor calls him, "a little black man—the smallest I have ever seen—with a great misshapen head, and a shock of tangled and disheveled hair. . . . His small eyes glowed and burned with a sombre light, and his thick lips writhed back from his teeth, which grinned and chattered at us with a half animal frenzy."

Since this glimpse was obtained from the deck of a police launch as it closed upon fugitives speeding down the Thames at night, with only a lantern on the pursuing craft to shed light on the scene, the passage speaks wonders for Dr. Watson's eyesight.

Poor Tonga's homicidal temper is conspicuously absent from most jungle peoples. So far as has been recorded, they do not ever make war among themselves and very seldom upon others, even in self-defense. Their best protection, and they know it, is to disappear in the forest, which they do with ease. However, such tribes as Fawcett has reported upon in South America, the occasional Andaman Negrito and some of the New Guinea Tapiros have been known to resort to violence.

Apparently these montane jungle dwellers of New Guinea (the Tapiros) were always capable of killing any intrusive Papuans who entered their valleys. In recent years, it appears on excellent, if secondhand, evidence that certain Pygmy tribes, especially in the island's west central forests, have become extremely savage and cunning. They are the terror of the local villagers, whom they raid regularly, killing men and burning houses. That this practice may have been provoked by persecution, and is primarily defensive, seems plausible. But not enough is known about the circumstances to warrant a judgment.

These New Guinea Pygmies are unusual among jungle folk in that they cultivate the soil and have domesticated animals other than dogs. Some other jungle peoples keep dogs for food, but in New

Guinea the Pygmies also raise pigs and chickens, just like their big neighbors. They grow a few crops in jungle clearings, mainly sweet potatoes and taro, a plant with a big leaf and an edible root resembling a rhubarb. The tribes who follow this agricultural pattern are not wanderers, of course, although they are skillful hunters of the local game—cassowaries and smaller birds, marsupial opossums and other small mammals.

The poor little *Pi Tong Luang,* who do not hunt or fish, restrict their meat diet to what they can scavenge from the kill of a leopard or tiger. Mainly they subsist on what they gather—fruit, roots, nuts, insects. They drink only the standing water from hollow trees or bamboos, never going near water holes. This may stem from fear of the big cats which haunt such places, in spite of legends that these are jungle sanctuaries where no beast disturbs another.

While the jungle peoples can be entirely self-sufficient without agriculture, they have wants which their skills and resources do not satisfy, just like everybody else—notably salt. So they trade with the outside world. Always it is they who come out to the others, never the traders who go in to them.

Some of these jungle peoples are the last practitioners of the oldest and, in some ways, most satisfactory of all commercial systems, "dumb barter." There is no haggling; there are no recriminations, no disputes. In fact, the parties to such transactions never even see each other.

It works like this: A group of jungle dwellers from whatever jungle simply deposits at a convenient spot in a clearing or on the edge of the forest whatever they may have to offer. This consists of jungle products that the river and plantation folk do not have. The "sellers" put it down in plain sight and go away. Then the "buyers" come to get it and leave in trade what they think it is worth—often some food that they have grown, such as rice or manioc; a stone or metal tool; in some areas tobacco or salt. No one can get cheated more than once. If the jungle people are not satisfied with the evaluation of their produce, they do not come again.

This is commerce at its most primitive but at its most amiable. When the bargaining is done in person, the affair becomes more complicated. For one thing, the band would not think of delegating a few members to go outside the jungle on a business trip. This is altogether too complex. The whole group goes, old folks and children and all, or no one does. What happens, then, depends more on the outside villagers than on the jungle people.

The Penans of Borneo have learned that the Dyaks of Sarawak will exchange precious things such as swords, beads, cloth and salt for resins obtainable from jungle trees or a mat the Penans weave from jungle fibers. These shy folk appear and disappear at their own whim; the Dyaks never know where to find them. But one commodity they do not sell is the long blowgun and poisoned darts with which they hunt. The carefully polished tube is straight as a rifle barrel and longer than a man; it can be deadly accurate up to thirty feet or so.

The effects of trade are better illustrated in the curious relationship between the African Negrillos and the Negroes which has grown up in the course of their business dealings. It is a relationship that, with minor variations, prevails anywhere in the world between a race who consider themselves more civilized and another who would not argue the point but who do not care for civilization. In this case, of course, the Negroes with their crops and crafts are the civilized ones, the Pygmies the indifferent primitives.

With the proselytizing zeal which all human beings display when they not only are proud of their culture but can make a good thing out of it if a lesser breed is persuaded to take it on and do some of the drudgery, the Negroes try desperately to "domesticate" the Bambuti. They have never had much luck. Although they hate to leave the jungle for any reason whatever, Pygmies will visit a Negro village to trade game and honey for produce such as mealies and bananas, to drink some palm wine or beer perhaps, to acquire by barter or theft a knife or some salt or tobacco.

Each Negro chief feels that he and his village own the band of little folk who live nearest and trade regularly with that village. The big men try to put the visitors to work, boast to strangers about their serfs or slaves (as they try to make the little people appear), demand more meat and honey of them, sneer at their small stature and may even try to haze them. When the Bambuti have enough, they just vanish, whether the Negroes like it or not.

The usual result is that the villagers are in a rage. They swear at what they call the idle, worthless, lazy, cheating Pygmies, who always come out ahead in the trading, they say. The Negroes are ready to kill or at least jail the whole band, but by the time they reach this point, the band has disappeared into the jungle. The villagers are much too terrified of the innumerable devils they associate with the forest to dare follow, despite their anger. Of course, in a few weeks or months, they have forgotten their resentment, due to their desire for meat, and the little people are welcomed back, to repeat the process all over again.

In recent years the Pygmies have emerged more frequently and for longer intervals in some parts of the Congo. In a few places where either white men or Negroes have learned to deal with them sympathetically on their own terms, they may even stay for a long time, and occasionally one or two slip into the village life.

When Patrick Putnam was building his extensive camp near the Epulu River in the Ituri jungle in the late 1920's, he had so won the confidence of the Pygmies, whose ailments he treated and whose ways he both understood and genuinely liked, that they actually helped in the construction. Villages of several of the forest peoples still cluster around the site, but the Pygmies who live there are more concerned with the maintenance of the jungle animals that make up the collection of a tourist attraction called the Station de Chasse than in plantation work. But in such a setting, they are obliged to do a certain amount of farm work too. Some of them work at Camp Putnam or in the motel that came later when tourists appeared.

But most of them are not suited to anything except jungle life; they are even more subject than others to the diseases of civilization and to the unpleasantnesses that tropical sunlight breeds. Colin Turnbull's account of those he saw working in and around Camp Putnam after Putnam himself died gives an impression of a rather pitiful little people. They did the work badly, whether trying to clear a plantation for themselves or in the employ of others. They were paid little, even less than the Negroes, and were hardly treated as equals by anyone. They had no resistance to the insect-borne diseases to which Negroes had built up some immunity; they were particularly susceptible to heat prostration; the food and water did not agree with them.

Turnbull was amazed by the change in the group he accompanied when they left the villages around Camp Putnam to return to their home in the jungle. Once behind the great green wall, so forbidding to the Negro, they were not only safe but supreme. In the village they showed their worst side—sly, uncommunicative, inept, not even notably clean. But by the time they had splashed through the first jungle stream, symbolically and literally washing off the dust of civilization, they were entirely different. Now they were back in their element; they revealed their real way of life.

26

The Timeless Culture

ALL the true jungle peoples are in what *we* consider to be a most primitive stage of development. They are not civilized, their culture is comparatively simple, and they apparently are not motivated by the same urges that drive the rest of us to what we like to think of as progress. They are not, however, as is popularly supposed, in "the stone age."

The concept of the "stone age," just like that of the "cave man," is deeply rooted in our popular and scientific thinking. This idea seems to be that, as you go back in time through successive stages of culture toward the primitive, you come finally to a stone age, which goes further back with ever less efficient stone implements until you come to the dawn of human history. Somewhere along the line, as this story goes, in the middle of the stone age, men are supposed to have lived in caves—the implication being that that was the *only* place they lived. Both concepts are, of course, completely erroneous.

First of all, emerging man, and probably a lot of apes, too, must have passed through the very long period which we may call the dendritic, meaning that their tools were of wood. During this vast span of time, they developed certain skills such as weaving, basket-making, and so forth; they also learned, probably, to use the bow and arrow. Then, some of them who lived in dry areas where wood was scarce would seem to have entered the odontokeratic or tooth-and-horn culture. Others, either descended from these or on their own, began to use stones which, being less destructible, have survived in greater quantities than bone and horn implements; the wooden ones hardly survived at all. Present-day jungle people don't use stone—except in a few isolated cases, none of which have been satisfactorily documented—so they are *not* "in the stone age," while certain *non-*

American Museum of Natural Histo

Little Andaman islanders carrying palm leaf umbrella, fire container and wood bucket.

forest people, like the Papuans of New Guinea, still are. Some jungle people use bone and horn tools, but all of them are essentially in the dendritic stage of toolmaking; and this *has nothing to do* with either their primitiveness, their development or even their so-called cultural level.

Second, the hominids never as a whole passed through a cave-dwelling stage. For one thing, there are not enough caves to go around, and those that are available are primarily in areas where the surface rocks are limestones. These are comparatively limited in extent, and the very nature of limestone itself constitutes a second-rate botanical environment for the support of animal life. The notion that men did "pass through" such a stage is probably due to the fact that the best and often the only places where the remains of early man have been preserved are in caves.

Only a very small proportion of early men had the luck to inhabit caves, and they probably did so more to keep cool than to keep warm during an ice age. Also a great many of the remains found in caves seem to have been of a votary nature. Gatherers and collectors, hunters, nomad herders and settled agriculturists who lived outside caves went into them to bury their dead, perform religious or mystical ceremonies, or decorate them as holy places. Finally, I have been unable to discover one single report of any true jungle people even entering, let alone living, in caves, which are a rarity anyhow in jungle areas.

To properly place the jungle peoples in *our* scheme of things, it is necessary to list the aspects of our culture that they do *not* have. As to whether these lacks are disadvantageous or advantageous is open to the widest debate. On the one hand, these are the very aspects of their lives which have kept them where they are today. On the other hand, these lacks undoubtedly are the secret of their survival. Viewed from a purely pragmatic and biological point of view, there is no doubt that, with the possible exception of the Ghosts of the Yellow Leaves, the jungle peoples seem "happy, healthy and wise." They have also displayed a remarkable aptitude for survival. What more can you ask?

Just what is it that these peoples supposedly lack?

True, they have no written or recorded language, not even in the simplest picture form.

They know virtually nothing of the graphic and plastic arts. They paint no pictures, though sometimes, to be sure, they paint their bodies or scratch a design on a comb or other object. They make no statues and carve no figures. Some of them can draw flowers or trees or animals quite nicely when given paper and pencil, yet they seldom bother to do so for pleasure or for show.

They have no background, traditional or intellectual, that impels them to seek what we call progress for themselves or their progeny. The very concept of change in their way of life is abhorrent to them; "change" and "better" would be exact opposites in their vocabularies.

They have no law, as we understand the word—i.e., rules of conduct which a society establishes through some recognized authority and enforces by punishment or the threat of punishment if they are violated.

Yet, these limitations together with isolation are responsible for the fact that they enjoy the culture of their ancestors while all around them the more advanced peoples, who drove them into the forest, have been overrun and "improved" by the successive waves of invaders for a thousand years.

Jungle culture is old, but it has taken so long for the rest of the world to discover it that, to us, it is new—so new that we still know virtually nothing about it. The jungle peoples have been "hiders," and they resist scientific study just as they resisted enslavement, simply by disappearing into their forests.

Living in small groups, nearly all the jungle peoples have a strong sense of family, extending to cousins. But their society cannot be classed as either patriarchal or matriarchal. In most of their communities no one really has the authority implied by such terms. Decisions that affect the group are made by the group; decisions that affect the family alone are made by the family, although everyone else may feel free to offer advice.

While the community's problems are few and simple, they are not all easy. Mainly they revolve around the question of when to move the camp and where to go. The answer is worked out in a sort of New England town meeting discussion without a presiding officer. Civilized man, a highly disputatious animal, can hardly conceive of a large council which is not regulated by a code administered by an individual of high rank but in which no one speaks out of turn or too much. Jungle folk are, of course, seldom in any hurry to get it over with because it will only be followed by another meeting scheduled somewhere else. Also they behave in an orderly fashion without being regulated, whether by instinct or custom no one knows. A man of noted prowess as a hunter or sage, a woman whose wisdom is generally esteemed, may have more influence in guiding the communal decision than most, but no real authority.

Among those peoples who have a very strong belief in supernatural powers—the Negritos in Malaya are one—the shaman or

Black Star

Guest house built for pig festival, New Guinea.

tribal wizard has to be obeyed in anything that concerns the unseen. And in New Guinea the Pygmy communities do acknowledge a chief, probably because they are relatively warlike and need a leader in combat.

In ordinary matters of jungle life, such as when to move camp, there usually would be general agreement without too much argument. The most likely reason for moving is that game in the vicinity has become scarce or wary, or the best fruits and vegetables have been gathered. Where to go may present a topic for more debate; two or more opinions as to a desirable spot may be expressed. But often the group follows a traditional pattern, moving from one area in the jungle to another in a rotation that has been fixed for centuries.

About the only other decisions the group is called upon to make are when to hold a feast or a songfest, stage a ritual ceremony or embark on a trading mission. These activities seldom are fixed or dictated by the phase of the moon, the season or any special anniversary. Jungle peoples have very little sense of time anyway, because they do not plant a crop. More often than not, celebrations seem to be almost spontaneous, growing out of a sense of fun, the joy of living, a sudden inspiration, or because of a series of misfortunes or a death. In any case, they are swept along into their preparations without any special council or discussion beforehand.

Scholars used to say that no human society could exist which did not formally and as a society mete out justice or punishment to offenders. Now enough civilized observers have spent enough time with jungle peoples, especially with the Negritos and Negrillos, to establish the fact that this is not only possible but usual in these primitive democracies.

What then keeps these people from murdering each other and stealing each other blind? Certainly not the fear of a policeman, a chieftain or a tribunal of elders, because there are none. Murder within the group seems to be unheard of. Murder of a member of a nearby group becomes a matter of blood feud, not of law or tribal authority; it is regulated by custom so that it is wiped out when a member of the victim's family kills the murderer. Murder of a stranger, a wandering white man perhaps, would be harmless, if not laudable, no different than squashing a bug, for to them neither is really human. But they do not go around murdering people.

Fights occur, but when two men or two women engage in physical combat it is not the concern of society except that everybody may enjoy watching. This is a personal matter, or at most a family matter. The blows seem always to stop short of serious injury. The only interference occurs when other members of the disputants' families pull them apart.

Of course, violations of accepted behavior do occur, and the jungle peoples, although their list of crimes is far shorter than ours, condemn many of the same things we do. Theft within the group is bad; it is perfectly all right to steal from outsiders, but jungle families don't have much worth taking, since their food is in common fief. The list is pretty well rounded out by assault upon the person, incest and blasphemy or violation of taboo among those tribes who take spirits seriously. Yet no offender in most of these societies ever faces "a court," for no tribesman is empowered to judge another.

Punishment is inflicted just the same. Each individual or family, including the miscreant's own, decides for itself how to treat him. Some may refuse to have anything to do with him for a time; if the crime is heinous enough, perhaps the whole community will ostracize him.

An apology and restitution may be accepted at one time or from one person where it would not be for another guilty of the same offense. Ridicule may be meted out, and for quite serious crimes. In Africa, Pygmies so hate to be laughed at that this penalty, which is simply the spontaneous reaction of the public, is keenly felt. If the criminal is so universally condemned that he flees the community, permanent exile probably would be fatal, and stories of such incidents are told. More commonly, it would seem, the exile has a few sympathizers who smuggle food to him secretly. After a time, by the tacit consent of the community, he slips back into the group and is allowed to resume his life as before. A flagrant thief may so infuriate the group that, as spontaneously as they laughed, they will seize sticks and thrash him.

It all seems extremely slipshod, but the thing that should be stressed is that, as a system, it works.

In jungle society, women are considered the equals of men; the division of labor seems to carry no implication of inferiority. Each family has its dominant individual, but it is quite as likely to be wife as husband. Monogamy is the general rule, but some of the jungle folk are not hidebound on the subject. In any African Negrillo group, for example, a few men may have two or three wives each. There is no special prestige attached to this; the bigamist is not necessarily either stronger or a better hunter, richer or a better singer than anyone else. The arrangement is one for the man and the women in the case to settle among themselves.

Quarrels between man and wife are known to break out, of course. In fact, among the jungle folk they probably are more widely known than in most places. The construction of their homes and their proximity to each other is such that any conversation is audible to everyone. If the dispute is sufficiently serious, the woman may pack up and go home to her own people, who under most marriage customs are members of another tribe. The Bambuti are said to have the charming tradition that before departing she should take the house apart and leave her man without shelter as well as without wife. In some tribes, she may be well received by her parents, and in some coolly; certain peoples allow both man and woman to "remarry" as a matter of course; elsewhere they may be considered ineligible.

Jungle parents are generally as permissive as the most advanced exponent of "progressive" education ever was. Negritos and Negrillos both spoil their children outrageously by any other standards, yet they have as well-behaved youngsters as can be found anywhere in the world. Even toddlers are so thoroughly in harmony with the forest and its life that their worst conduct is getting in the way when mother is building a house or father is making a net, and then they may be slapped. "Don't" is a word they rarely hear.

They play all day because even the most rigorous items in the educational curriculum are games. Kilton Stewart, who administered several of our common psychological tests to five-year-old Negritos in the Philippines, thought they had about the same native intellectual endowments as Americans or anybody else. Since tests of this kind increasingly measure what the individual has learned rather than his innate capacity, the older Negrito children and the adults scored lower than those Stewart had tested in various parts of the United States.

Among some tribes youthful high spirits are encouraged. A child's practical joke, even at the expense of a respected adult, may be relished by everyone, even the victim, and in some Negrito societies the child would be praised. In others, such as the Andamanese, pranks seem to be unknown. But then, the Andamanese are a sad people, outstanding among jungle folk for their sorrowful mien and their habit of weeping bitterly when meeting friends or relatives after an absence that may have lasted only a few days. And young Ghosts of the Yellow Leaves, although plainly adored by their parents, never laugh or play games at all; they have no toys and, of course, never misbehave.

Magnum

Children in Peruvian jungle.

Geriatrics is not much of a jungle problem. The elderly are treated with respect and affection and are cared for without complaint or condescension. On the other hand, age confers no special wisdom; the aged are heard with everyone else but not deferred to because of their years.

Actually no one is likely to live very long after losing the ability to travel on his own legs. The whole group will always delay departure for an illness, but either the patient soon recovers sufficiently to walk or dies. Psychosomatic diagnosis being unknown, one cannot say to what extent the outcome is determined by the patient's state of mind, but most observers would say this is a major factor. For the primitive who is sure his time has come, death is already on the way.

Sex customs and taboos, puberty rites and initiations, courtship and marriage vary quite widely among the jungle peoples. Some of them will accept the ceremonies and the mumbo-jumbo of the outside world when they go there, but adhere to their own ways when they return to the forest.

The *Pi Tong Luang* are strict monogamists, but sex is a subject about which they seem neither to talk nor to be very well informed. Conception is a mystery to them. Marriage rites are informal, so far as could be gathered by those who have finally managed to meet them. However, they are so shy and talk so little that their customs are not at all well known.

The Bambuti at the other extreme are not at all reticent about sex nor inhibited in their enjoyment of it. Certain formalities are considered decent, certain practices discouraged. Forcible rape brings down the wrath of the group upon the man, but the girl would not be humiliated. Sex play among children is neither encouraged nor objected to, and therefore it is hard to say to what extent it is practiced.

The African Pygmies are one of the few races of human beings among whom the onset of menstruation is greeted with joy by the girl herself, her parents and the whole community. Perhaps because women have an equal status, a child's entry into womanhood is cause for congratulation, and so everyone is immediately informed. Nothing distinguishes these people more from their Negro neighbors, to whom the first menstrual blood is punishment for sin. Not only is the Pygmy

Magnum

Traditional African Pygmy courting dance.

girl proud and happy, but she and the other unmarried girls of the group are set up in a house of their own under the chaperonage of an older man and woman for a month of festivities. The girls hold court, receive expert instruction in domestic chores and celebrate with song and gladness their approaching eligibility for marriage.

Outside the house, the young men gather for flirtation and more song. At certain stages of the festival it is considered proper for a youth to fight his way inside, especially if a girl invites him—one way for her to extend the invitation is to dash out and lash him with a whip. The ceremonies, if such they can be called, involve a certain amount of rough play on both sides, and it is considered good form for the girl not to let the boy be too sure that he is welcome until she has actually marked him with the lash.

Under these circumstances, there is a good deal of premarital sexual intercourse, and, of course, it is not confined to the month of these female puberty celebrations. But, as among other primitive groups the world over, very few children are born as a result. No stigma is attached to the unmarried girl who does conceive, although she will be laughed at if the man she wants does not marry her.

The Bambuti acquiesce in the marriage customs of the people they are visiting outside the jungle, if they think they are expected to do so and if the outsiders arrange the feast. They would not look upon this as a binding marriage, however, and would repeat it all over according to their own customs when they return to the jungle. These are simple and unostentatious. The young man's family pays a visit to the girl's, and they reciprocate. The bridegroom presents her parents with a substantial quantity of meat, a whole antelope or the like, along with a bow and some arrows for her father, not as a "bride price" but to show that he and his group are good providers. Then the young couple simply walk off together to their own house.

Philippine Negritos buy their wives, and no doubt that is linked with the greater authority men have in their society. The Negritos also have many more taboos than the Bambuti; incest with them extends to a father's second cousin once removed, so that marriage virtually has to be between members of different communities. This is true of many other primitive races outside jungles.

Magnum

Pygmy dance consists of many expressive and graceful gestures.

It used to be that scholars tried to trace the origin of the jungle peoples through the tongues they speak. It is a fascinating exercise in comparative languages because, it now appears, most jungle people use the language of either the outsiders near them or a remote but obviously unrelated race. The study remains an absorbing one, but it is no longer expected to tell us where the rain forest's human inhabitants came from.

Negrillos have the same language as the Negro tribes they trade with, but they give it an accent which the Negroes often say is unintelligible and always call barbarous. The same seems to be true of American jungle dwellers. The Veddas have a few words of an ancient tongue, presumably that of their hegemony in India, but mainly speak Singhalese or Tamil. The Semang of Malaya talk to each other in a Mon-Khmer dialect indigenous to certain Mongoloid people in Cambodia and Thailand to whom they are not even remotely related and who have never been known within a thousand miles of the Malay provinces inhabited by the Semang.

The Ghosts of the Yellow Leaves hardly talk at all, often communicating with each other by small moans, soft grunts and low whistles. But when they do speak, theirs is one of the known tongues of the Indochinese peninsula. One of their peculiarities is to have no personal names; they refer to each other by the words for father, mother, child, cousin and so on. "Enemy" in their speech is a phrase translated literally as "men with hats." It derives probably from the Thais, a race with very distinctive hats, who have periodically raided the *Pi Tong Luang* to carry off the lovely young women of the jungle. And so it goes. Attempts to link all the jungle peoples together by assigning their languages a common root lasted only until white men learned what languages they really spoke. It was then easy to spot the obvious differences, but the origin remains a mystery.

In their arts, the jungle people give first place to music, and oddly enough, the most primitive of them have the most complicated musical instruments. The *Pi Tong Luang* make and play mournfully upon a sort of bamboo guitar, which seems much too sophisticated for the rest of their way of life. The Borneo Penans tootle fairly complex arrangements upon a wind instrument constructed from a gourd, bamboo tubes and vibrating reeds inside, the whole not unlike a Scotsman's bagpipes. To virtually all these peoples, dancing is the natural accompaniment of music, and they are tireless, often ecstatic and sometimes very graceful.

Negrillos and Negritos especially are lovers of song, and produce very effective singers, too; in both Africa and the Orient, the mellow male voice especially commands great respect. The common feeling for this form of expression is one of the few reasons for supposing that they are related. However, much of the Negrito singing is in prayer and mourning and supplication. Negrillo song is poured out for joy, in praise of the forest, in recitation of some happy event, in love or desire or triumph.

In both societies, the entire band joins in the singing, although an outstanding singer may take the lead. Neither have the sophisticated instruments of some other jungle people, although the Semang of Malaya have haunting little bamboo drums and the African Pygmies a great tube of bark or the stem of one of the trees with a soft pith easily hollowed out, which they play like a trumpet and call a *molimo*. It is perhaps significant that these two outstandingly musical

Black Star

Papuan musicians, New Guinea.

little people are (except for the mournful Andamanese Negritos) among the most cheerful on earth—laughing, singing, carefree souls passionately fond of their forests and completely happy as long as they are left alone there.

The Negrito music can be joyous, too, but a great many of their songs are tragic dirges in which they lament the dead at a burial ceremony, or improvised tuneful prayers to a benevolent or harassing demon, or propitiatory songs to ward off evil. They are capable of composing poems of great simplicity, genuinely moving, as the occasional visitors who have been permitted to share the intimate life of a jungle group have reported.

When the Bambuti hold a festival, they are apt to call it a *molimo,* after their musical instrument. A talented Pygmy performer can achieve quite wonderful effects with the great tube, which may be as much as fifteen feet long and usually is carried by two men. The whole group treat it as sacred; when not in use, it is kept hidden in the jungle, and women never dare to look at it, pretending to regard it as a god. Of course, they know exactly what it is, but tradition is tradition, so, as the *molimo* nears the camp, they retire to their huts and pull little doors of leaves across the opening so that they will not upset anyone by peeking.

It is interesting to note that on the Xingú River in Brazil, the Camayura have a similar practice. They construct a flute from a thick, hollow reed three feet long, and it is to them a sacred instrument. It is used ceremonially—to call for good hunting or fishing, for example. Women may never look at one of these flutes, so they are sequestered when the music starts.

Among the Bambuti, the huge trumpet is fondled, talked to, washed ceremoniously and generally treated with the kind of respect societies give to idols. But the Pygmies are very practical. Turnbull says that when he saw his first *molimo,* he expected it to be an elaborately carved and decorated affair, so reverently had the Pygmies spoken of it. But actually what the men retrieved from its jungle hiding place was a section of metal drain pipe obviously filched from some road construction project during one of the group's visits to the outside world. When he showed his surprise, they told him that this was as

Black Star

New Guinea funeral.

good as anything they could make out of bark or wood and that it lasted a lot longer!

A talented performer coaxes the most amazing music from this simple instrument. The trumpeting of enraged elephants, the cooing of doves, the snarl of the big cats or the rumbling of distant thunder is only the beginning. When the player warms to his rhythm, the big horn really sings, to any tune and in any mood he pleases. In the camp, the people listen entranced as the *molimo* circles about through the jungle, now nearer, now farther, and finally loosing a blast right outside some selected hut. The Bambuti have no higher form of expression, no clearer way of announcing their opinion of the world.

Singing and dancing are the Bambuti order of the day on almost any day—when the hunting has been good and there is lots of meat, when game grows scarce and the best fruits have been devoured by other animals in the jungle, to enliven the march from one camp to another, to lighten the task of building the new huts, while relaxing after food, to heal the sick, to rejoice in the cure, to mourn for the dead.

The pragmatic, cheerful Pygmy approach to the spirit of the *molimo,* whether the word is taken to mean a musical instrument or a festival, is characteristic of their beliefs. In this they are not typical of other jungle peoples. They are as free from superstition as almost any society on earth. Their religion is largely a simple and simply expressed faith in the goodness of their forest. Some vague acknowledgment of spirits has been detected, but it does not seem to influence them very much in their conduct nor in their observances or protestations. They do not try to embody the forest as a god in any totem of tree or animal. It is the whole magnificent jungle they mean when they sing its praises, and they do not try to shrink it to a man-sized concept. Apparently they have not found it necessary to invent devils.

They are well aware of, and have been known to use cunningly for their own ends, the superstitions of Negro villagers. When they visit the big people, they talk and act as if they were as terrified of every demon and evil spirit of which the Negroes are afraid, and these are innumerable. Negroes endow every tree in the jungle, every beast, every rock and root and vine with some sort of malevolence, and the Pygmies play up to them, no doubt to keep them out of the forest forever. But they have another reason.

Pygmies will tell elaborate stories of how some fearsome supernatural being robbed them of the meat or honey they were bringing to the villagers, or how some monster prevented them from doing their Negro master's bidding. If the tale wins them trade goods or pay, they accept it joyfully and will tell each other the story for years, doubled up with laughter at the gullibility of these oversized imbeciles who, in their dry, sun-drenched, utterly unhealthy clearings, do not understand the beneficence of the cool; damp, shady jungle.

Many of the Pygmy tribes make a point of having their sons

Pickett from Monkmeyer

Hooded figure in center of Pygmy celebration dance is witch doctor.

undergo the painful, frightening initiation of the Negroes. To the villagers, the long vigil, the scarring of the body, the hardships and ordeals are a pious necessity, ordained by unseen powers as a test to be passed before a boy becomes a man. The Bambuti don't believe it at all, but they are proud. They want to show that they can do anything the big fellows can. They do not let their sons get the idea that there is anything of a religious nature about the proceeding; it is a rough game which every boy should learn.

They have devised a wonderful sort of Hallowe'en prank which never fails to send a Negro village into paroxysms of terror. Retrieving their *molimo* from its jungle hiding place, they will circle a village in the dead of night, sending forth the most unearthly moans and howls, which the villagers talk about later as "the ghosts of the jungle." Since the spirits of the dead are as frightening to the Negroes as a maddened leopard, the effect is highly gratifying to the Pygmy sense of humor.

The Bambuti know perfectly well that they are in no danger of being found out. A Negro has not been born in one of these little Congo villages who would venture at night behind the high, thick green curtain which separates his home from the jungle. It is bad enough that some spirit, devil or monster is making these unholy noises; he does not propose to go and look at it.

Death, which brings out the superstitious fears of many quite civilized peoples as well as other jungle folk, is a matter merely of grief to the Bambuti. They mourn, and extravagantly. They weep and throw themselves about, but they make no elaborate ceremony nor do they suppose that the dead will come back if certain rites and sacrifices are not forthcoming. They profess no faith in witchcraft, curses or spells. So they bury the body very simply in a shallow grave.

Among all the Negritos, death involves much more ceremony if not more grief than the Bambuti display. The Andamanese have a system of what anthropologists call "secondary burial," which is also practiced by a number of quite unrelated peoples all over the world. This consists of digging up the bodies and reburying them at stated intervals, apparently to ward off the evil which spirits might do if the body is neglected in one place. The Andamanese not only do this, but also carry the skulls of the departed around with them from camp to camp.

The Negritos have an elaborate form of religion. Their monotheism surprises the few outsiders who ever get close enough to learn what their beliefs really are, which is not often. Reasonably, considering the prevailing jungle weather, their god is a God of Thunder, *Karei* to the Semang in Malaya and *Tolandian* in the Philippines. In both places it is significant that he is a beneficent deity, so no one is afraid when they hear his voice, except in the case of a typhoon or violent storm when it is obvious that he is angry about something. Then, or whenever any of their many taboos are violated, he must be propitiated, usually by prayer, perhaps with some small gift or offering, or even by self-flagellation.

Frank Hurley from Rapho Guillumette

Skulls of the departed, New Guinea.

The Semang carry out their observances with more formality and ritual than others. It is for this purpose, interceding with Karei, that they select a shaman, no doubt on the strength of his success as a healer, for that would indicate he has influence with the god. They obey this priest doctor in anything that concerns the unseen—when to pray, and to whom in case it is not Karei, what offering to make, when to give thanks and when to repent.

Sincere belief that the God of Thunder is all powerful does not prevent the Negrito from acknowledging a whole host of spirits and demons lurking in roots or tree trunks, in stones or the bodies of animals, in the water and the sky. When any of these has been offended, he can only be propitiated by the muttered apologies and prayers of the entire Negrito group, as Stewart watched his companions appease the rock demon and the tree demon on the march when his hand was saved.

The practice of chipping the front teeth into sharp, evil-looking points was once common among these people and thought to have religious significance. But the Negritos themselves say it is done to test a boy's willingness and capacity to bear pain, and to prove he is fit to take a full part in the community. The process is indeed painful. A sharp blow is struck on a knife edge held against the incisor while a block of wood behind the tooth keeps it from being knocked out altogether. The ragged grin of a set of chipped teeth is considered very manly, especially when the teeth are stained by betel chewing.

The Andamanese have invented even more supernatural beings to be placated and feared than have their Philippine cousins. Most of their nature spirits are evil, too, and have some association with the dead. These islanders have developed a diffuse, complex, gloomy religion quite in keeping with their mournful temperament.

The Ghosts of the Yellow Leaves have only a vestige of what might once have been a more robust religion. The remnant is a vague anxiety about ghosts or demons, which seems only to add to the terror pervading their lives. They lay out their dead on a bamboo dais covered with leaves, and place a food offering beside the body to propitiate the spirits. Then the whole band decamps hastily to avoid meeting any of the spirits who might come along to accept the offering.

The Veddas pursued a cult of the dead, who were supposed to govern all of life and nature. They had to be propitiated continuously and elaborately, thanked when the hunting or fishing was good, apologized to for all the sins of the tribe when game was scarce. These little people relied upon witch doctors to carry on dealings with the departed, but not with the same submission the Semang display.

Among Amerinds, the religious beliefs of some peoples seem clearly derived from those of the famous early American civilizations. Sun worship and a knowledge of the planets indicate this, as do some of their myths. But other jungle peoples in the Western Hemisphere have developed along different lines. One typical Amazon group believes in a god who made men from trees and created women by carving a figure and blowing smoke on it to bring this primitive Galatea to life. The god also is credited with creating all the good things of life, except that he made a mistake when he made the moon because that is held responsible for all the evil. Other groups seem to have no beneficent gods, only a vague belief in evil spirits who, in at least one instance, are supposed to be unable to see red. So these people take a lot of pains to paint themselves a dark shade of coral.

This discussion of the jungle peoples, how they live and hunt and enjoy themselves and pray, concerns only those who are best known to the outside world, who have welcomed to some extent the visits of at least a few travelers. It may seem that the sum of our knowledge about them is not very much. That is true. But there are jungle peoples about whom we know a good deal less. To get even an idea of the way they live, it is necessary to resort to speculation, inference, deduction. They are among the true mystery peoples of the world.

27
The Mystery Peoples

SKEPTICS are fond of saying that in this day and age there cannot possibly be any people alive in the world who are unkown to science. But every year new species of animals are discovered, and nearly every decade tribes or races that previously had been regarded as purely legendary or mythical are encountered by unimpeachable witnesses. In the jungles especially (although they have no monopoly on the mystery peoples) there is so much unexplored terrain and the wily folk who inhabit it can be so elusive that the real wonder would be not to find bands that have not been seen before by outsiders.

When a large herd of elephants can vanish unheard and undetected into the jungle, although their footprints are still filling up with water as men approach, the shy humans of the rain forests would have no trouble avoiding any undesired contacts. It is as great a mistake to think we know every cranny of these jungles and all the people in them as it was thirty years ago when experts said the Ghosts of the Yellow Leaves were fiction or eighty years ago when scholars ridiculed the notion that there could be Pygmies in the Orient. At the time, the pundits dismissed reports of these races as no more believable than the accounts of men whose heads were below their shoulders instead of above and whose faces were in their breasts.

Such stories never die, and they will always find both doubters and believers. This chapter will deal mainly with peoples of whom there is as much evidence as there was of the *Pi Tong Luang* before 1930 or of the Oriental Negritos before 1887. Only the mystery folk of jungle areas will be considered; there are many in other parts of the world, and I have written of them in *The Abominable Snowmen: Legend Come to Life*.

I first encountered the mystery people while searching for animals, known and suspected. One of the profitable methods of learning what may be found in any jungle is to talk long and patiently with the local inhabitants, especially the hunters. In every part of the world, I and many other naturalists have found that these people are extremely well informed about their own country's zoology and botany. They have names for every plant and animal; they know a surprising lot about the nature and behavior of birds, insects, mammals, fish—what you will. Their factual reports are usually accurate. Although a European-trained scientist may think what they describe is utterly impossible, he often finds that they speak the sober truth.

So when in British Guiana and Surinam these knowledgeable persons spoke of something they called *didis* or *dee-dees,* I refrained from scoffing. The didis were first described in English by Sir Walter Raleigh in 1595 after his expedition to this same country; he wrote of them as hairy men greatly feared by the natives. Raleigh himself did not see any, but heard of them so often he could not believe the reports were made up for his benefit.

In 1769 Edward Bancroft, a young English botanist and naturalist who later became a friend of Benjamin Franklin in Paris and spied upon him for the British government, visited the Guianas. He, too, brought back an account of the didi. Indians told him it was about five feet tall, walked erect and had a human-looking but hairy body, the body hair being thin and black.

Bernard Heuvelmans has now brought together a number of other reports ranging from 1868 to 1931. Indians who had seen didis were corroborated by a British magistrate who saw two in 1910 and by the guide to an Italian scientific expedition. This last, however, said the ones he saw left the footprints of apes. These manlike creatures have been reported from all the Guianas by the natives for centuries, the name varying hardly at all and the descriptions coinciding remarkably. The basic word is always something like didi, often with a prefix or suffix meaning in one area "nasty," in another "of the water" and so on. Over and over, it is remarked that they are seen in pairs or that they live in pairs, which is not characteristic of American monkeys of any known kind. A significant feature is that the local story never says the creature was a monkey or a manlike animal, but a wild man or man of the forest.

The accounts of the didi bear a remarkable resemblance to those which I heard in British Honduras about a little people called *dwendis*, a form of the Spanish word for goblin or elf, "duende." In the capital, Belize, it was customary when I was there for the educated city dweller to treat the dwendis as characters in a fairy tale. But men, educated as well as uneducated, who had lived and worked in the jungle areas not only believed in but had evidence of the existence of dwendis. I have talked to dozens who said they had seen these little people, and my informants have included forestry department workers who received their training in Europe or the United States.

A junior forestry officer in British Honduras told me he had on several occasions noticed two of them watching him at the edge of the forest reserve near the Maya Mountains, not far from Petén where the Maya civilization is believed to have begun. This whole area is a tangle of sharp ridges, tall peaks, deep gorges and ravines choked with tropical rain forest. Neither the jungles nor the mountains have been explored; they are not mapped, and what may be in them no man knows. This was what lay behind the reserve where the forestry officer was locating and marking young mahogany trees.

The pair he saw, he said, were three and a half to four and a half feet tall, well proportioned but with very heavy shoulders and rather long arms. They had flat, yellowish faces. So far they do not seem too unlike the Mayas themselves, some of whom are no bigger than this. But the dwendis also are always described as having hairy bodies, which the Maya do not, a common remark being that they have a thick, short brown hair not unlike a short-coated dog. Also they are said to leave very deep footprints that have pointed heels.

Usually when anyone has observed them, they have appeared suddenly out of the forest. They watch men silently but curiously from afar, never making a threatening move, although I was told they sometimes catch dogs and carry them off. The silliest thing, I thought, was that very many of my informants said the dwendis almost always held over their heads an object resembling a big Mexican hat. I heard this from half a dozen sources scattered all over that part of Central America, and I remained skeptical until later on in Africa I saw a lone chimpanzee on the ground in an open patch of jungle solemnly holding a large section of dead palm frond over his head like an umbrella, and it did look like a Mexican straw hat.

Further evidence that these "elves" did exist even if they no longer do is the fact that in many of the Mayan bas reliefs, pairs of tiny folk with no clothes except a big hat are depicted. They do not seem to have been carved small to show a low social status, because the peasants—the lowest of Mayan classes—are represented as much larger.

That there are less primitive but equally unknown people living in or among these jungles is no longer a matter of much doubt to me since I saw the evidence of their existence myself. During our stay in British Honduras, we managed to set up a camp some distance into the mountains. The senior forestry officer of the colony, Neil Stevenson, visited us there, and we took a day's collecting trip up to the top of the next ridge beyond our camp. From here we had an extensive view over territory never reached by Europeans nor by the local residents. We saw smoke rising from the forest; some rectangular areas of a distinctly different color than the rest of the jungle showed that patches had at some time been cleared for cultivation. Our companion even heard cocks crowing at dawn.

Further evidence of human habitation in that area was uncovered later when the Shell Oil Company made an aerial survey of the whole mountain block. Their photographs proved that people were living in this utterly isolated spot. A commercial air route passes over it, and from the lower slopes of the mountains, ocean liners can be seen crossing the Gulf of Honduras. Yet no one has ever been known to come out of that impenetrable land, and we have no idea what manner of men they may be—Mayas perhaps who fled there at the time of the conquest or earlier, pre-Mayan survivors of a race we do not know, dwendis who have more skills than they have been credited with so far.

It was in Guatemala that we ran across accounts of the legendary *Sisemite*. A great hairy creature much larger than human size and more powerful than any animal ever known is supposed to inhabit the montane jungles. He is not seen as often as the dwendis, nor by as reliable witnesses, and he has a fearsome reputation for tearing men to pieces and carrying off women.

One of these stories, published in 1915 in *The Museum Journal* of the University of Pennsylvania, tells how a Sisemite carried off the wife of a young farmer, who was put in jail for murdering her because his tale was not believed. At last a party of hunters captured what appeared to be a wild woman who came to a brook to drink. She struggled to get away, and all the more when a Sisemite appeared on the hillside, waving his arms and yelling.

"On his back was a child or monkey child," the hunters are quoted as reporting, "which he took in his hands and held aloft as if to show it to the woman, who renewed her struggle to be free. The Sisemite came down the hill almost to the brook; he dropped the child and tore off great branches from big trees which he threw at us."

The woman was taken before the imprisoned husband, but he simply said when asked if he recognized her: "My wife was young and beautiful; the woman I see is old and ugly." She never said a word, refused to eat and died in a few days.

The article goes on to tell more about Sisemites. Local legend had it that they are bullet-proof and impossible to trail because they can reverse their feet and run heel foremost. They desire desperately to learn the arts of speech and making fire. They assemble little piles of twigs but cannot light them; they sit by the embers of a hunter's fire until they grow cold and then eat them. They kidnap children in the hope of learning to talk. A man dies within a month if he looks into a Sisemite's eyes; a woman who sees one has her life prolonged.

The legend is old—and new. As recently as the early 1940's, in the Guatemalan town of Cobán, the police investigated the complaint of a man who charged that his son-in-law had allowed a Sisemite to abduct his daughter. Witnesses saw her carried off while the young husband sat shivering. No arrests were made; presumably he could not be blamed in view of the Sisemite's reputation.

There is an obvious relationship between these beings and similar ones reported from quite remote places. The Sisemite is kin to the *Vasitri,* which means big devil, of whom Baron Alexander von Humboldt heard on the Orinoco River more than 150 years ago. These large hairy creatures would eat men and carry off women for breeding purposes. However, Humboldt was told that they also built huts to live in, which did not prevent him from speculating on the possibility that what had been seen was really a bear. Since a bear of this size would be as remarkable in South America as the Vasitri, the explanation becomes no less wonderful than the mystery.

Kin to the little people of Central America and the Guianas, at least in the local lore about them, are the *Shiru* of the Colombian jungles. Perhaps they too are only Pygmy jungle natives who have simply retreated before the exploitation of the last 450 years and hid themselves successfully from the exploiters. They have not given rise to any fearsome tales. A well-known animal dealer of Ecuador, Herr Claus U. Oheim, once wrote to me:

> The so-called Shiru, I have heard of from the Indians and a few white hunters. . . . All reports describe the *Shiru* as a small (4–5 feet) creature, decidedly hominid, but fully covered with short, dark brown fur. All agreed that the *Shiru* was very shy, with the exception of one Indian, who claimed having been charged after having missed with his one and only shot from a muzzle loading shotgun, a weapon still used by the majority of Indians along with the blowgun. These reports were rather sober and objective, and in no way tinged with the colorful imagination into which Latin-Americans are prone to lapse.

In the Amazon basin, stories about remnants of peoples who preceded the local Indians have been handed down by generations of Europeans who believed them. Colonel Fawcett took for granted the basic truth of what he had heard of a race called by the Spaniards "the hairy ones" and by the Portuguese "the bat people." He himself referred to them as "troglodytes" and wrote that they lived in deep pits roofed with branches and palm fronds and approached by a long, sloping tunnel. They were supposed to come out of their holes only at night, hence the name "bat people," and the stories led the Colonel to believe they really were "ape-men" and also "the most barbarous kind" but with a bloodhound's sense of smell. He even met men who knew others who had seen these hairy beings in the Xingú River area, one of whom said he had been their prisoner. This Indian's story was that he was the sole survivor of a party of ten attacked by the bat people. He was spared, he said, because one of their women took a fancy to him, and eventually he escaped during daylight by

American Museum of Natural History

Drawing of the *Orang-Pendek*.

taking to the trees and swinging along the branches so that his captors would not be able to follow his trail through the forest. In this account, the fugitive even professed to know that they had tracked him to the first tree he climbed. Fawcett expected to go through the country of these people on his last trip, and he wrote that he was looking forward to the opportunity of studying them.

On the other side of the world, the existence of unknown peoples is dismissed as fable by people who have never been near their supposed haunts and is widely credited by knowledgeable dwellers in these areas. The case of the *Sedapa* of Sumatra is a good example. There is an impressive local folklore about them. Malays call them *Orang-Pendek* (Little Man) or *Orang-Letjo* (Gibbering Man), as opposed to another legendary race, *Orang-Gadang* (Large Man), and there is ample reason to believe they were not confusing all of these with apes.

Stories of the Sedapa were so widely current in the thirteenth century that Marco Polo heard and repeated them. In 1818 an Englishman, William Marsden, who lived on the west coast of Sumatra, described these little people. Definite reports of their existence have been received only in this century.

Now it is easy to dispose of the repeated stories of eyewitnesses by saying they saw an ape. The siamang of Sumatra is just such a creature as might be called Orang-Pendek, bigger than a gibbon, smaller than the great apes. While his adaptation is to life in the trees, he does descend and runs along the ground swinging his arms. But he does not leave footprints such as have been described and attributed to the Sedapas.

The evidence has left me in no doubt that such a creature is not only possible but probable. Some of the most convincing narratives come from Hollanders, particularly a timber cruiser named Van Herwaarden. In 1918 he saw some small but oddly human footprints on the banks of a creek and began making inquiries. He learned that another Hollander had seen similar tracks, and he talked to three local citizens who had had close looks at Sedapas. All three stories said the creatures were small, about five feet, their bodies covered with black hair but walking erect. In 1923, Van Herwaarden decided to wait patiently in the forest from which most of the reports came rather than try to hunt them down. He wrote a long, detailed account of his meeting with a being he thought was not at all apelike, but which he apparently was not willing to call human either.

She—"this specimen was of the female sex and about five feet high," he said—was on the branch of a tree, and when he began to climb toward her, she leaned over and looked at him. The body hair on the front was lighter than on the back; the head hair, thick and shaggy, was dark and quite long, falling almost to the waist. Dark eyes, like those of a human, and a broad but not clumsy nose, ordinary lips but a very wide mouth, yellowish white teeth with rather prominent canines, a receding chin—these were the features he observed.

"There was nothing repulsive about its face," he tells us.

He had almost climbed to the branch on which she rested when she ran to the end of it and as it bent under her weight she dropped to the ground. Van Herwaarden's account continues:

> I slid hastily back to the ground, but before I could reach my gun again, the beast was almost 30 yards away. It went on running and gave a sort of whistle. Many people may think me childish if I say that when I saw its flying hair in the sights I did not pull the trigger. I suddenly felt that I was going to commit murder. I lifted my gun to my shoulder again, but once more my courage failed me. As far as I could see, its feet were broad and short,but that the sedapa runs with its heels foremost is quite untrue.

Later reports of Sedapas have been received, none so detailed as this. That the creature should elude capture, or not be seen if it desires to remain hidden, is not surprising to one who is at all familiar with the country it is supposed to inhabit. I spent many months of my youth wandering about Sumatra accompanied by an Achinese appropriately named Achi. The forest seems endless, tall and dense in the lowlands, while the montane growth is unbelievably rich and heavy. The known population is negligible, and almost none of the swamps and jungles have been penetrated except along the rivers. A better refuge for Sedapas or any other creature wishing to avoid civilized man would be hard to find.

Across the Strait of Malacca on the Malay Peninsula, a similar situation exists. Here sixty years ago the British government decided it ought to know more about the peoples of this land, and commissioned two scientists, W. W. Skeat and C. D. Blagden, to find out who and where and what they were. The result was a multi-volumed work, *The Pagan Races of the Malay Peninsula.*

In due course the authors encountered the Negritos, who had then been known for only about twenty years. They also studied the slightly larger *Sakai* or *Senoi,* a retiring, hardy race who clear patches in the higher montane jungles and sometimes build quite elaborate, comfortable communal houses of bamboo. They have always been independent of whatever people happened to rule the lowlands. From them Skeat and Blagden heard that even higher in the more remote cloud forests were hairy, not human *Santu Sakai* or Devil Sakai, and also a larger type, admittedly wild men who, according to tradition, almost always remain in their high misty domain and were sometimes referred to as "the stinking ones."

When they do come down, the age-old story of the Sakai has it, they come to catch, kill and eat a few selected human beings, not just anyone, only thin people. Your first reaction is to exclaim, "Ridiculous!" But it has not seemed quite so strange since science has discovered halfway around the world why the "werewolves" of Norway had a craving for raw meat and an intolerance of fat. These "werewolves" were mostly boys, mentally defective teen-agers who grew up in high mountain valleys which are almost constantly misty or rainy. Misshapen of body and head, these miserable youths were found to be suffering from a deficiency of the "sunshine" vitamins. They are restricted to an almost completely vegetable diet in their valleys, and they could get the missing nutrient only from raw flesh, but fats nauseated them. Possibly the same deficiency drives "the stinking ones" to their raids, for their forests are almost perpetually shrouded in mist. When this becomes worse than usual, the need for lean meat could lead them to attack their neighbors, and dictate the selection of their victims.

This, however, is not the explanation for the appearance as recently as 1953 of a small party of unaccountable human beings in northern Malaya. At the time there was some talk that they may have been flushed from their jungle fastnesses by Communist guerrilla activities. But then it developed that there had been frequent unpublicized reports of similar creatures in the same area for some time. Piecing together the various accounts that have been published, the story seems to be this:

On Christmas Day, 1953, a Chinese girl named Wong Yee Moi was tapping rubber trees on an estate managed by an Englishman named G. M. Browne. Later, she said she felt a hand placed lightly on her shoulder, and when she turned she was confronted by a woman with a white skin, long black head hair and moustache, and fanglike teeth which she bared in a friendly grin—even in her fright, Moi thought it was friendly. The woman was clad only in a loincloth made of bark and stank as "of an animal." The Chinese girl shook off the hand and ran for the compound. As she fled, she saw standing by the river nearby two males of the same type; apparently they did not wear a loincloth.

Her story prompted Browne to call the Malay Security Guard because the whole area was in a continuing Communist emergency. A patrol under the command of a corporal soon arrived and at the river's edge saw three just such hairy people as Moi had described. As the corporal ordered his men to bring their rifles to the ready, all three dived into the river, swam underwater to the opposite bank and ran into the jungle.

Next day a Hindu working on the estate felt his neck encircled by a pair of hairy arms. He broke loose, but fainted before he reached the compound. When he revived the trio stood nearby laughing at him. That day the corporal and his patrol also saw the three again on the river bank but could not catch them.

One explanation at the time was that these were Japanese who had fled into the jungle at the end of the war rather than surrender. But Japanese could hardly have grown hair on their bodies. At the time not much attention was paid to one important point on which all those who came near these three people agreed—that there was a strong stink as of an animal. This corresponds with the traditional stories of the creatures as handed down among the Sakai for generations.

It is also significant that neither the frightened girl nor the panic-stricken Hindu worker nor the Malay soldiers thought that the strange apparitions were in any way hostile or menacing. One wonders what might have happened if the strangers had received a friendly welcome, been greeted with pardonable curiosity but not with terror and with guns. If indeed they were driven out of their secure homes in the jungle by Communist guerrillas, might they have been seeking a refuge, or perhaps just a meal? What anthropological mysteries might have been unraveled?

In Africa as in the Orient, the known existence of large apes and tiny men has strengthened the doubts that most scientists have professed when confronted with accounts of men we do not know. Yet Negrillos, gorillas and chimpanzees do not explain satisfactorily the reports of what the West Africans call *Sehite* and the East Africans *Agogwe*. At the same time, these accounts have to be examined carefully, because just as there is plenty of room in unexplored heavily forested areas for unknown races of men, so there is room for unknown apes as well. The belief of some Africans that the gorilla is a sort of degenerate human being requires care in interpreting their stories, but the care should be in interpretation; the stories should not be dismissed without investigation.

My experience of these people, especially in West Africa, is that, while they can embroider a tale with the best of the old troubadours, they are extremely factual and accurate in describing the native plants and animals. In my animal-collecting missions, I have often been startled when they told me of some highly improbable, outlandish creature, only to have them go out and produce the beast or lead me to it just exactly as they had said it would be. So I have a good deal of respect for the local "tradition" when it is presented as fact. The fellow who can spot the difference between two species of bat that even trained scientists can distinguish only after careful examination is not likely to confuse apes and men.

Furthermore, on this continent as elsewhere, the fact that some peoples, notably the Negrillos, seem to have taken refuge in the jungle and adapted their lives to its conditions would make it more probable than otherwise that others who were oppressed by stronger races did the same. The australopithecines from South Africa are just one example of such a possibility.

The first remains to which this formidable anthropological name has been given were found in a limestone quarry in British Bechuanaland in 1924. A skull embedded in a block of stone was at first thought to be that of a Bushman, a yellow-skinned people as small as Negrillos but not related to them. Then it was thought that the creature to whom it had belonged was a baboon, then an ape, something like a chimpanzee but with a much larger brain.

However, Dr. Raymond Dart, of the University of Witwatersrand, to whom the skull was sent, pronounced it an even more important find. It was about 500,000 years old, and when he examined other remains from the same area he was able to state that the *Australopithecus,* as it was named, made carefully worked tools and weapons out of bone and teeth and that he may have used fire. Furthermore, the formation of the bones and the opening for the spine at the base of the skull showed that these little people stood and walked erect as we do, and did not just wobble along occasionally after the fashion of the apes.

One theory is that these sub-men were exterminated by later races, but it is also suggested that if they were as intelligent as their brain capacity and toolmaking ability indicate, some of them might have had the wit to retreat into the jungles far to the north of their original home. Then, like the Pygmies, they might have adjusted to the new vegetational environment.

But we really do not have to go back to them to explain the Sehites and Agogwes. Extremely primitive peoples manifestly existed all over Ethiopian Africa far more recently than the australopithecines and still do. They have been hunted and enslaved by the proud, tall Negro race, who are the relative newcomers. Those who escaped enslavement would be very clever at concealment and capable of survival in areas where the Negroes would not pursue them, notably the jungle.

As to the Sehites, my own information about them is confined to vague folk tales from the area of Nigeria. These tell of the former existence of little people there, but there are definite modern reports. However, Bernard Heuvelmans received much more specific information from Professor Ledoux of the Science Faculty of Toulouse University, who in 1947 was organizing the zoological department of a new Institute of Education and Research in the Ivory Coast, then a French possession on the Atlantic coast. One of the African workers in the laboratory asked the professor about Pygmies and explained that a colleague in another department had seen one the day before. Now the Ivory Coast is many hundreds of miles and a couple of civilizations removed from the nearest known Negrillos. Yet when the astonished professor pursued his inquiries, he turned up quite circumstantial accounts of little men with reddish fur on their bodies and long reddish hair, " same like white man," on their heads, which is very different from that of the Pygmies. Some of his informants even told him that until a few years earlier, the Sehites, if that is what they were, engaged in "dumb barter" with the local Negroes, leaving fruit in exchange for manufactured articles. The full report appears in *On the Track of Unknown Animals,* and the author kindly permitted me to quote it in full in my *Abominable Snowmen.*

Heuvelmans also has presented an account of the Agogwe on the eastern side of the continent, which may be mentioned although they seem not to be jungle creatures. A 1924 article first appearing in *The Journal of the East Africa and Uganda Natural History Society* by S. V. Cook tells of a local interpreter who insisted that he and other natives were showered with stones while climbing some high hills. The missiles were flung by "scores of little red men." The writer goes on to say: "To this day even the most intrepid honey hunters will not venture into the hills."

Roger Courtenay, author of *The Greenhorn in Africa,* was informed by his guide in this part of the world that the guide's own father, a shepherd on the trail of a missing sheep, was ambushed and stunned by a blow from behind. He revived to find himself surrounded by little men who, the shepherd is quoted as saying, were as ignorant as monkeys because they did not know what his spear was for and left it lying beside him so that he could have killed a lot of them if he had been so inclined. The man's account, as given by his son, continues:

"Their skins were white, with the whiteness of the belly of a lizard, and their faces and bodies were covered with long black hair."

The most frequently reprinted evidence of the Agogwe was written by Captain William Hichens in an article in *Discovery* for December, 1937. He titled it "African Mystery Beast," and explained that the incident occurred in a forest glade while he was hunting. He wrote:

> I saw two small, brown, furry creatures come from dense forest on one side of the glade and disappear into the thickets on the other. They were like little men, about 4 feet high, walking upright, but clad in russet hair. The native hunter with me gazed in mingled fear and amazement. They were, he said, *agogwe,* the little furry men whom one does not see once in a lifetime. I made desperate efforts to find them, but without avail in that wellnigh impenetrable forest. They may have been monkeys, but, if so, they were no ordinary monkeys, nor baboons, nor colobus, nor Sykes, nor any other kind found in Tanganyika. What were they?

On reading this article, one Cuthbert Burgoyne wrote to the publisher of *Discovery* to report that he and his wife, while on a cargo boat coasting along Portuguese East Africa in 1927, saw through glasses two little brown men such as Hichens described. They walked onto a beach among several dozen baboons apparently engaged in picking up shellfish of some sort. A friend later told him he too had seen similar creatures, but was told by the native hunters not to shoot them. Burgoyne doubted that the ones he saw were really human because their presence did not disturb the baboons.

It may well prove, however, that the Sehite and the Agogwe are more closely related to the Negrillos than the descriptions of them might lead one to believe. The true Pygmies are sometimes covered with a fine, downy, yellowish hair, and they often paint themselves red or white. Once upon a time they were spread much more widely than they are now. So too were the Bushmen, who are not, as far as is known, a jungle people at all, but often are no bigger than Pygmies. They have yellowish red skins but no body hair. However, it seems quite possible that, although the Bushmen we know never dwell in the rain forest, relatives many centuries ago may have found a safe refuge there.

The seldom seen little people, one would expect, should be much more primitive than the Negrillos of the Uele District of the Congo whom Colin Turnbull knew so well. It has been suggested that the earliest types of men were not toolmakers or weaponmakers at all, not even so much as the australopithecines, who contrived clubs and other instruments from bones. The first things human beings probably used were sticks of wood. The majority of accounts we have of mystery peoples in the jungles credit them with no implements of other than wood.

All these reports have another point in common which strikes me as most significant. The creatures, whether smooth or hairy, large or small, never seem to have been located by hunters who were looking for them. That is true also of accounts of other elusive beings in different parts of the world. These mystery peoples almost invariably are seen only because they wanted to be or were indifferent to being observed.

This seems to me to explain why none of the odd strangers are captured or killed. After all, they have owed their survival to their ability to remain hidden from enemies in their forests. Undoubtedly they have developed their senses of smell, sight, hearing and a few others which we hardly use at all, so that no other human beings could match them in this respect. To some degree they are like the wiliest of animals. But, because they *are* men, although primitive, they bring to the use of their senses an intelligence that no animal has.

I suspect that when civilized investigators do make the aquaintance of the mystery peoples, it will not be by rushing about in the jungles with fancy equipment or new gadgets or trained dogs. We will not find them at all, but we will let them find us. We will encounter them by sitting still and appealing to the inquisitiveness that is such a powerful influence upon all the races of men and almost all other mammals.

T. Hearn del J. Caldwall sculp

In Testimony of Esteem & Regard to Joseph Banks Esq. President of ye Royal Society
Who thirsting after Knowledge, left the Enjoyment of
Opulence and Ease, to sail round the World.
This VIEW of DORY HARBOUR on NEW GUINEA, is inscrib'd by his most humble Servt
Thos Forr.
Publish'd as the Act directs Jan. 20. 1779, by Capt. T. Forrest.

Rare Book Room, American Museum of Natural History

Part 6

Discoverers and Explorers

The "Lost Civilizations"
The Wisdom of the Ancients
The Age of Discovery
The Great Precursors
The Lonely Genius
Strange Adventures
A Naturalist Trio
A Knightly Trio
A French Trio
Livingstone and Stanley
Scientific Progression
The Tragic Adventurer
A Pair of Moderns

Marc & Evelyne Bernheim from Rapho Guillumette

Mayan jungle ruins, Tikal, Guatemala.

28

The "Lost Civilizations"

THE fragile document was 150 years old, the writing crabbed, faded, almost unintelligible. But it described with a wealth of mouth-watering detail the splendid ruins of a deserted city once inhabited, (the not very well educated author thought) by a race from whom the Inca civilization sprang. He was sure that the remains he had seen were far older than anything in Cuzco. Protected by sharp, steep ridges and set in the midst of what still could be seen as once cultivated fields, the city was, according to him, isolated from all the world by the mighty Brazilian jungles. The writer's story was that he had led a party of eighteen in search of legendary mines. Criss-crossing the wilderness for ten years, they had found the mines, when they found the city. He then went into the details of what he had seen, but he never did say just where all this was.

It was a walled city of wide streets lined with two-storied houses built of great slabs of stone cunningly joined without mortar and roofed with stone—those which still had roofs. An entrance of three great stone arches led through the wall to the main avenue, at the end of which was a huge square with what had been a magnificent palace on one side and a temple on the other. In the center of the square a huge column of black stone still stood, surmounted by a perfectly preserved statue of a man with one hand on his hip and the other pointing north.

The palace had some of its great square columns intact, and frescoes and carvings could still be seen in what must have been the main hall. Over one doorway was carved the figure of a youth carrying a shield and wearing what the discoverer took for a wreath of laurel. Here, and on the city's entrance gate, were carved symbols which seemed to be the characters of a written language, but one strange to the party, although they thought it resembled Greek. At the far side of the square, remnants of a broad promenade bordered a placid river some 150 feet wide which flowed through the fields outside the city and disappeared into the jungle.

All about were the tumbled carved blocks and broken columns of past magnificence; obviously the place had been abandoned many centuries earlier. A single gold coin or medal was picked up; it bore on one side the likeness of a youth kneeling, on the other a bow, a crown and a musical instrument.

The author of the old document thought he saw all the signs of a frightful earthquake. He supposed that this would have led the surviving inhabitants to abandon their city forever. Now it was the dwelling place of millions of bats, and of course, there were no traces of any furnishings that may have been used; these would have rotted long ago.

Across the river on a slight rise mounted by a flight of broad stone steps of many colors was a surprisingly complete building of fifteen chambers opening off a great hall, ornate with carvings and inscriptions. In each room a serpent's head of stone still spouted a thin stream of water which fell into a basin formed by another serpent's open mouth.

Men have risked death on the basis of such stories. The Brazilian who wrote this one planned to go back to the fabulous city and get rich. Whether he tried or not, no one knows, since there is no further record of him. But we do know that more than 150 years later his story was the inspiration, in part at least, for another trip into the jungle from which no one ever returned.

Legends of cities buried in jungles are only a little less common than stories of lost civilizations in mountains or deserts. A supposedly eyewitness account, but third or fourth hand to be sure, describes a place very much like the Brazilian's mysterious city. The big difference is that this one was inhabited; from the surrounding ridges the observer saw Indians walking around in the plain, and he was afraid to go nearer. In another jungle there is rumored to be a stone tower lit up like a New York skyscraper in the winter dusk; the lights were said to burn all night so that every one of the many doors and windows was illuminated.

A letter written in 1924 by Colonel Fawcett, about a year before his last trip, tells of two cities, not one. Of the first, he said Indians by a river—he does not say which river—had offered to take an army officer and a Brazilian gentleman to a "lost civilization" if they were willing to brave "bad savages" on the way. The letter continues:

> The city, said the Indians, had low stone buildings with many streets set at right angles to one another, but there were also some big buildings and a great temple, in which was a large disc cut out of rock crystal. A river running through the forest beside the city fell over a big fall whose roar could be heard for leagues, and before the fall the river seemed to widen out into a great lake emptying itself they had no notion where. In the quiet water below the fall was the figure of a man carved in white rock (quartz, perhaps, or rock crystal), which moved to and fro with the force of the current.

Fawcett went on to say that his forthcoming expedition should take him near the place, and he might visit it; he does not seem to have questioned its existence. Then the letter resumes:

> My ranching friend [a gentleman Fawcett already had quoted in relating other tales of the forest] told me he brought to Cuyabá an Indian of a remote and difficult tribe, and took him into the big churches here thinking he would be impressed. But the Indian said "This is nothing. Where I live, but some distance to travel, are buildings greater, loftier, and finer than this. They too have great doors and windows, and in the middle is a tall pillar bearing a large crystal whose light illuminates the interior and dazzles the eyes!"

Earlier Fawcett himself had put his finger on the flaw in these Indian tales of lost or hidden splendor. The reliability and accuracy of these people in identifying things in their own country have been proved by many a naturalist. But when it comes to something that lies over the horizon where they have never been, their stories are complicated by the common human tendency toward exaggeration and their own special disregard for time and distance on any scale larger than their daily activities involve. Thus it is probable that the description of an Inca city could travel the whole South American continent, certainly all through the Amazon valley, and the city could still be located "over that hill" or "not far beyond the river." While Fawcett recognized this trait, he thought that he had learned how to discount it and interpret the tales so he could find the site they described.

Are there really no fabulous cities in the jungles to justify the library of fiction about them? Is there no Shangri-la protected by the rain forest rather than mountains? No pre-Incan El Dorado hidden under the massive vegetation or enclosed by it?

I think the best answer is given by the well-known archaeological remains of two widely separated peoples. Many hundreds of years ago they built great cities which thrived for centuries but sank back into the jungles when they were abandoned. These peoples were the Khmers in Southeast Asia and the Maya in Central America. They have left us the plainest surviving records of what happens in one area of competition between nature and the works of man.

The most famous example is Angkor, both the great Khmer temple of Angkor Wat in Cambodia and the nearby capital of the old Khmer Empire, Angkor Thom. The temple is supposed to have been built in the twelfth century, while the city goes back to about the ninth. Angkor Thom remained the capital until about the middle of the fifteenth century.

Without doubt it was one of the most splendid cities men ever made. They were men who, judging by all that remains of their civilization, could not bear the sight of a stone that was not carved into a figure or adorned with a bas-relief. On the walls of their buildings they reproduced by the hundred human faces six feet high, and they carved elephants not only life-size but in herds. It is estimated that at the peak of the Khmer power, Angkor Thom had a million inhabitants and perhaps covered an area of twenty square miles, although only three and a half were within its massive walls. Its towers were as tall as those of the European cathedrals of the Middle Ages.

During the era of their finest architecture and sculpture, the

Photo Researchers

Detail of relief at Bayon, Angkor Thom.

Khmers were at the peak of their military power. Their armored battle elephants seem to have acquired in their day something of the reputation of German tanks after the fall of France. But other peoples learned to deal with them, and gradually the Khmer Empire shrank; Angkor was sacked and finally abandoned. The details of the decline are not known, but it would appear that for nearly five hundred years there was no resistance to nature, and the jungle began its inexorable return unopposed.

Although Angkor is only about three hundred miles from Saigon and even less from Bangkok, the city faded from human memory. By the time the French were asserting their protectorate over Indochina in the nineteenth century, much of the Khmer Empire's past was so confused with myths and legends that many people of the relatively

Unes

Tree growing on stones at Preah Khan Temple, Angkor.

few who had heard of Angkor nevertheless doubted that such a city had ever existed.

Then a French naturalist, Henry Mouhot, penetrated the Cambodian jungles on a plant collecting trip in 1861. When he came to the ruins of Angkor Wat and Angkor Thom, the jungle had encroached upon, split up and grown over and around a large part of the ancient city and temple. But great splendors still remained. Some of the towers were more than a hundred feet high and still stood under the jungle's canopy. The vegetation had buried whole sections of the old city, but not all of it. M. Mouhot was understandably overwhelmed by the acres of massive buildings, hundreds of huge stone figures and bas-reliefs, elaborately adorned terraces, gates sixty-five feet high, avenues lined with gigantic stone heads. His account of what he had seen, published in the *Tour du Monde* in Paris, caused these ruins to be hailed as one of the great archaeological finds of all time.

The French government acted more promptly than officials usually do in these matters. A careful and extensive program of preservation and reclamation was begun at once under scholarly auspices. The advance of the jungle was checked, and a great many of the ruins were gradually disentangled from the vegetation. But much of Angkor still remains under the control of the forest.

Angkor, of course, deserves to be one of the earth's greatest tourist attractions, and no doubt will be when, if ever, peace is restored to that troubled part of the world. It can now be reached by passable roads, and there are hotels not far from the best sights. But the jungle is felt as well as seen. Even at the temple of Angkor Wat, which was a distance from the city, many of the sculptured treasures are overgrown with vegetation. Only the major ruins have been saved from the jungle. But it is possible to walk beyond these and see what the whole place looked like a century ago.

Lianas loop around the fragments of sculpture and blocks of stone that remain among the tall pillared supports of the jungle canopy. The vegetation has found cracks in pavements and walls, in stone steps and pyramidal structures. The workers at Angkor say that a great deal of the old city is now inhabited by monkeys and gibbons—indeed, you can hear them—while leopards are said to prowl among old shrines.

One scholar who has spent some time among the ruins of Angkor described in a single paragraph the fantastic effects that the jungle's recapture of the proudest works of man can achieve. He was Martin Birnbaum, writing in the magazine *Natural History:*

> Sometimes the destructive fig trees reach dimensions paralleled by the ceibas of the West Indies [these are among the true tropical giants though there are no true jungles in the West Indies]. One celebrated specimen seems almost to have been planted purposely by some prehistoric botanist who knew what its roots were capable of doing. It sprouted on the roof of a small architectural gem known as the Neak Pean, built in the center of an artificial pool. At low water you can see the ever-present stone nagas [serpents] guarding the steps of the tiny island on which the shrine is built. The roots of the huge tree growing on the roof almost completely hide the building and allow only the doorways and some of the sculpture to

be seen. The spreading branches shade the entire pool to its artificial edge, and should a powerful tropical storm ever strike it down, the lovely temple in its toils will be doomed.

Some of the Maya ruins have survived the onslaught of the jungle even longer than Angkor, and they show it. Inside the buildings, pottery and even carved wooden beams remain, but the main structures have been much more damaged externally by time and the vegetation than those in Cambodia. Nevertheless, there remains enough left to have added enormously to our knowledge of these people, most of the new finds having been made in fairly recent years.

A most exciting reclamation of the Mayan ruins is currently being undertaken at a place now called Tikal in Guatemala, although what the original inhabitants a thousand years ago called it we do not know. It was the largest and probably the oldest of the classic Maya cities of which we have any record. The earliest of its stone monuments are believed to date from about 1400 B.C., the latest about A.D. 800, although Tikal was inhabited for longer than that. It is now believed the quality of the civilization generally, as well as the power of its rulers, declined during several generations before the city was abandoned.

A Spanish priest who stumbled on the remains of this great city at the end of the seventeenth century is believed to have been the modern discoverer of Tikal. He was making his way from what is now called Guatemala to Mérida in Yucatán; got lost and, in his wanderings through what is a thoroughly representative Central American jungle, came to great pyramids overgrown with trees. One or two of the structures were even higher than the jungle canopy. He eventually reached Yucatán safely and, it is supposed, the place he described was Tikal. No one bothered to try to confirm his account.

Indians, however, continued to tell about the stone city in the jungle, and at last in 1848, the governor of the province in which it was allegedly situated undertook an investigation. He pushed northward from Lake Peten and rediscovered the ruins, which about this time began to be called Tikal. During the last half of the nineteenth century, they were visited by a succession of European and

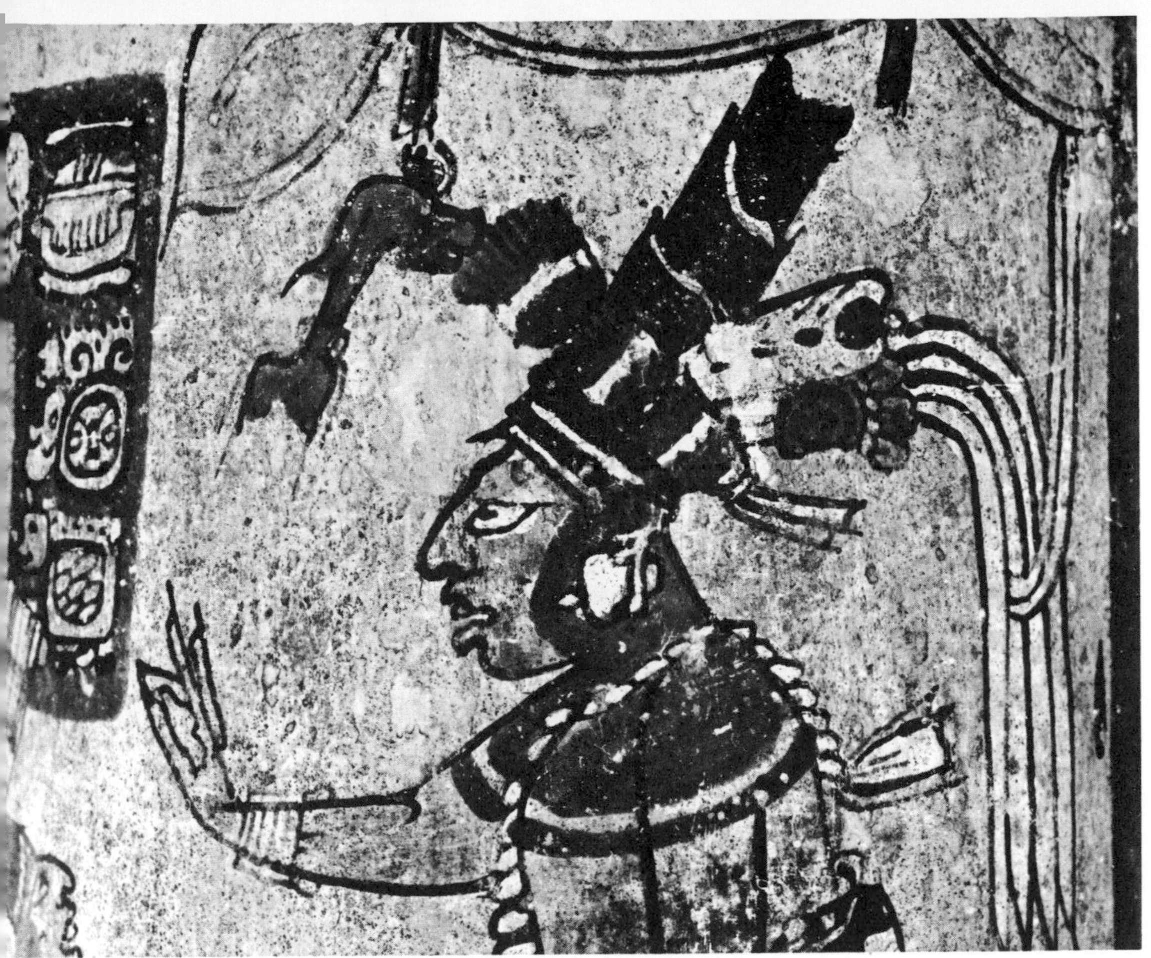

Photo Researchers

Detail of polychrome vessel found in Maya ruins at Tikal.

American archaeologists who accumulated a considerable body of observations and some "souvenirs," we are unhappy to have to say.

The jungle covered the site so thoroughly that anyone passing a few hundred yards to one side or the other could not even have seen it. Tall trees grew upon the high terraces and from the sides of the pyramids. One structure, now called "the five-storied temple," is 229 feet high, a record for Mayan architecture anywhere. The early scientific visitors found that it was easier to climb to the top of such buildings by means of exposed roots, vines and tree trunks than to risk the crumbling, overgrown steps. Roofs and the tops of walls were gay with orchids and other epiphytes which seemed to be as much at home in crevices of the stone as on the branches of trees.

Inside, however, the great beams made from sapodilla trees still bore their extraordinarily fine Mayan carving virtually undimmed by time. Vessels and figurines of pottery, including elaborate hollow statuettes, with the colors still visible have been brought to light within the upper chambers of the temples.

Over the years, archaeologists were able to trace the outline of the city and its main buildings, streets and plazas from what remained, much of it scattered on the jungle floor.

Each party of scientists did some cleaning and scraping to expose outlines of monuments, the bas-reliefs on them, the walls of the temples. But by the time the next group arrived, the jungle had obliterated the traces of their predecessors. For a hundred years the only approach to Tikal was by a long day's journey through the jungle from a camp which, after World War II, could be reached by air from Guatemala City. Kenneth L. Gosner, a member of the scientific staff of the Newark Museum, was there in 1947 and again in 1949. He made the day-long trek on muleback and explored Tikal carefully. He later wrote that although he knew many had preceded him, he "found the entire city in what seemed to be an essentially untouched state," so quickly had the jungle returned.

Finally, in 1956, the University of Pennsylvania undertook an excavation and restoration project at Tikal. The vast mass of vegetation is being removed bit by bit from the tops and sides and bases of the major buildings, and the city of the Maya has begun to resume its shape of a thousand years ago. The jungle which had almost succeeded in hiding it completely from mankind is being forced back, and no doubt will be held in check once the job of reclamation is complete.

Colonel Fawcett was regarded by many as a "crackpot" because of his theories as to where the sundry Amerindian peoples of South America came from. However, he *did* receive the Gold Medal of the Royal Geographical Society of London, and was most highly regarded by most South American governments as a competent surveyor and scientist. They even *paid* him—and year after year—to survey their messed-up boundaries! Yet, Fawcett had a bug in his head. He was convinced that the account given at the beginning of

Photo Researchers

Archaeologists of University of Pennsylvania at work in Tikal ruins.

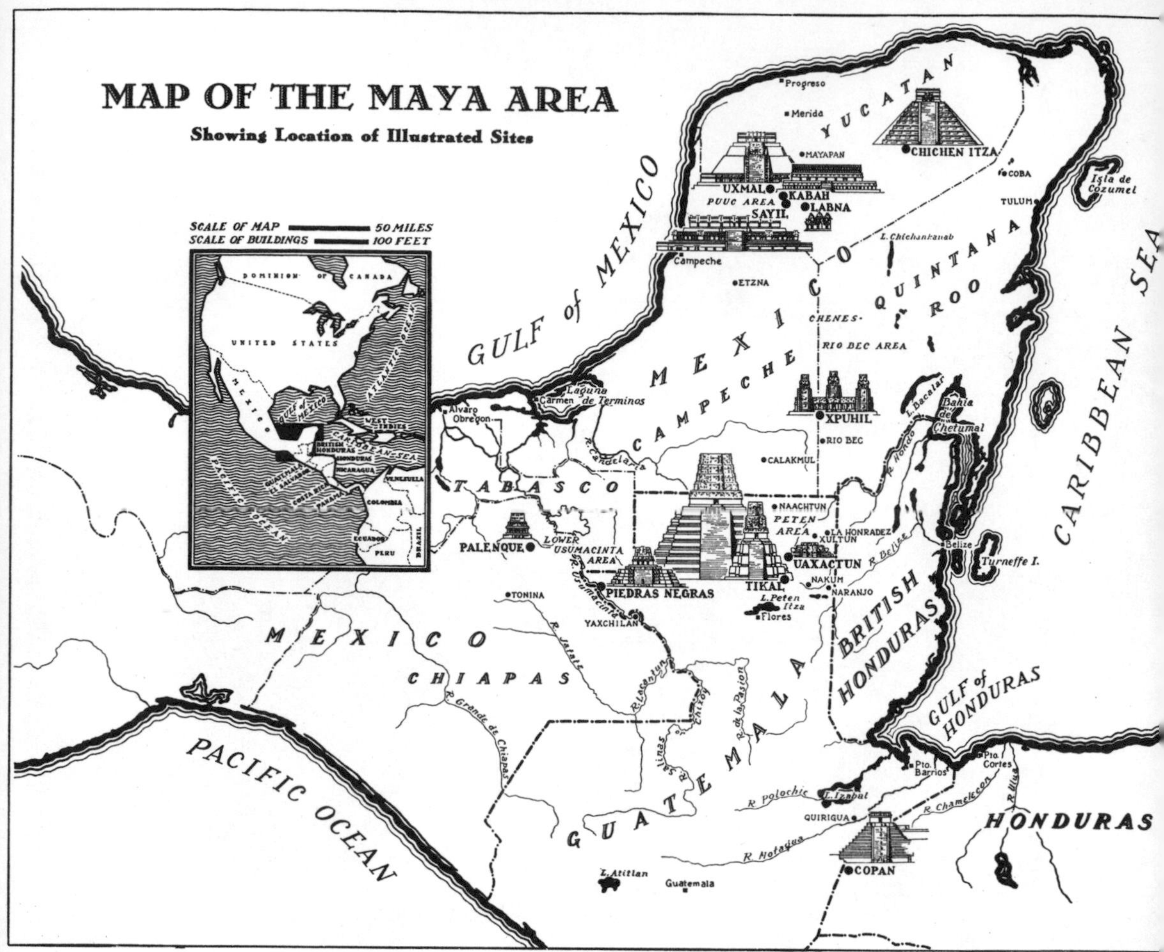

American Museum of Natural Histor

this chapter, which he stumbled across in some old archives in Brazil, indicated the prior existence of some great cultures in the forested parts of unexplored Brazil. He never gave up this belief and it fired both his imagination and his enterprise for many years.

Colonel Fawcett was honest enough (in his diaries, as edited by his son Brian, *Lost Trails, Lost Cities,* Funk & Wagnalls Company, N.Y., 1953.) to state that he did not find one, or more than second hand evidence of their prior existence. Colonel Fawcett disappeared into the Brazilian jungles in 1924, along with another of his sons and an English assistant. Nobody has really heard of them since, though not a few expeditions have gone to look for them or traces of them, and a whole library of speculation has been written on their demise. Yet, perhaps, Fawcett has been at least in part vindicated by a most extraordinary happening in Paraguay in 1946.

This was reported in *The World Almanac,* no less, of 1947. This is not a fly-by-night publication. In fact, it is a very serious compendium of world events and it does not publish facts unless there is a *very* solid basis for them. In this issue appeared a tiny four-line squib, under the general heading of "Leading Archaelogical Discoveries of the Year," at the bottom of a page, and read as follows:

> An ancient wall, four thousand five hundred feet long and at least 120 feet high, was unearthed within the heart of a mountain ridge in northeastern Paraguay.

Who are we to say just what is and what is not in the jungles? I further most strongly suggest that we stop opinionating about the subject, and get down to a litttle real search. The true jungle peoples never, as far as we know, built an advanced culture; but what of the near-jungle dwellers. If the Khmers and the Mayas could do so, others also could have done so. Just because we have not found any evidence that others did, is no possible reason for asserting that *no* others did.

29

The Wisdom of the Ancients

THE sages of the old Mediterranean civilizations left us a legacy of subtle and profound speculations on the nature of the universe as well as their observations about the parts of the universe they knew. Jungles were apparently not known to them *by sight* but they were familiar with stories about the animals and the men of the rain forests which, apparently, interested them much more than its vegetation. They imagined a great many wonders when they wrote or depicted the vast *terra incognita* to the south and to the east of their homelands, but of the vast equatorial forests with their dense canopy and gigantic pillars, they seem to have had no inkling.

It is remarkable that they recorded as much as they did, especially about the people. While they encountered Pygmies (presumably the Negrillos) in Africa, some of whom lived on the Nile in early Egyptian times, the Negritos of the Orient were known only at second hand to westerners. In general, the ancients seem to have assessed rather soberly the reports their travelers brought back from far places.

The Egyptians were capable of expeditions to the south, and may even have reached the jungles or the edge of them. Certainly they traveled among, traded with, and fought people who had. At times the Egyptians must have gone in sufficient force to capture some of the forest people or little folk just like them. Pygmies are pictured in the accounts of Egyptian triumphs, true Pygmies who are recognizable because their captors were able to reproduce their huts in drawings. These are exactly the same as the huts Negrillos make today.

One of the literary riddles of the ages is how Homer learned about these people. Since we really know very little more about him than about the Pygmies of his day, we are not likely ever to get a true

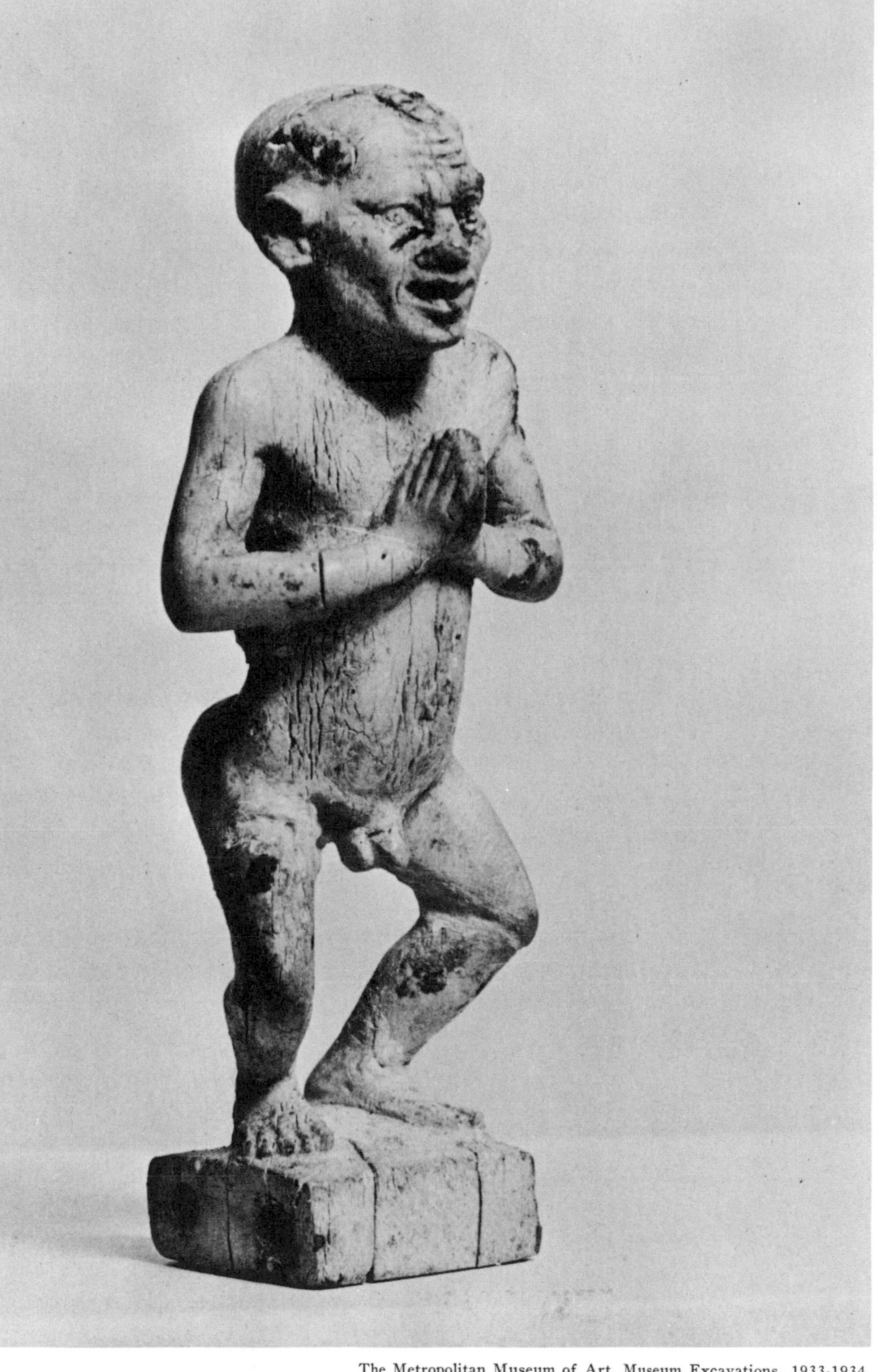

The Metropolitan Museum of Art, Museum Excavations, 1933-1934

"Dancing Pygmy." Egyptian sculpture from Lisht, Tomb of Hepy.

answer. It is now pretty well established that he lived before 700 B.C., but just how long before and exactly where is a guess. Yet the Greeks of his time had some knowledge about parts of Africa far beyond the limits any recorded voyage of theirs had reached.

However, there were more adventurous and more widely ranging traders than the Greeks in those days. The Phoenicians were the master mariners of the Mediterranean, and by the time Homer lived they were also quite accustomed to navigating the outer oceans. In fact, in the century during which Homer probably flourished, a Phoenician fleet is believed to have circumnavigated all of Africa. The voyage is supposed to have taken two years or more because the crews stopped once or twice to plant and harvest crops. The returning mariners might quite well have brought back tales of the peoples and the animals of the jungles, and it is probable that these stories spread quickly over the whole Mediterranean world, for which the Phoenicians were the great carriers of trade.

Most of what is conjectured about this African expedition derives from another, about a hundred years later, in the sixth century B.C. This one was commanded by a Carthaginian navigator named Hanno. Carthage was, in its beginnings, a Phoenician outpost and her seamen inherited the skill and seagoing ability of its founders. What is generally believed to be the account of this voyage survives in a Greek translation in which it is reported that the original was inscribed on tablets in a Carthaginian temple. It was an uncommonly large expedition, if the translation is accurate, for it is said to have consisted of thirty thousand men and women, embarked on sixty great oared ships. It was customary to pack people pretty closely in those days, but accommodations for an average of five hundred apiece on the vessels of those days does seem a little too much.

However, there is no doubt that Hanno did make a voyage and did return, although he did not duplicate the earlier feat. He sailed out through the Straits of Gibraltar and around the coast as far as the westernmost point of the African continent's bulge. Then he turned east for some distance. This seems clear, say the seamen who have examined the account, because he apparently sailed to within less than ten degrees of the equator. The western bulge of Africa is well above that.

Culver

Hanno approaching the "Island of Wild Men."

Hanno was the first to bring back to the Mediterranean first hand reports of what probably was a chimpanzee. The Carthaginians thought the creature was human, although strange and savage and very hairy. They were amazed at the way these "people" fled over cliffs, grabbing at holds too difficult for any sailor. The Carthaginians captured a few of the "women," but these could not be subdued by any means. Finally they were killed and the chronicle says their skins were brought back to Carthage.

So Phoenician and Carthaginian stories were prevalent in the Greece of the Golden Age. Herodotus knew about the supposed circumnavigation of Africa, but did not believe it. His clinching argument in explaining why it could not have happened was that the Phoenician sailors were reported to have said they saw the sun in the north. Herodotus thought people who made up "such obvious nonsense" of this kind could not be believed about anything. Of course, later scholars are inclined to think this is one of the most convincing bits of the story. The sun really *is* in the north at noon south of the equator, and how would these Northern Hemisphere sailors have known that unless they had been there?

Neither of the two great seagoing nations followed up these voyages. The Phoenicians and their Carthaginian colonists were businessmen—not scientists or philosophers. The trade possibilities of the coasts they had seen did not promise a rich commerce, so they began to look east for new markets.

The Phoenicians also found markets in the east, which is how the Greek physician Ctesias came to be employed in Persia where he heard about the strange little people who lived in the Oriental forests. Ctesias and his Greek successors in that part of the world seem to have repeated these tales, though it is not certain that what they reported was not embroidered later by translators and others. Their own writings have not survived, though extracts purported to be from a book by Ctesias were reprinted a thousand years after he had lived!

It would seem to be in order to give at this point a word of explanation on the Phoenicians. These have been the "mystery people" of history, but modern research is finally bringing to light something real about them. It appears that they were originally a Semitic people centered somewhere around the Gulf of Persia and that, about 2000 B.C., some of them moved overland to the eastern Mediterranean, establishing on the coast of Palestine (now, in part, Israel) a number of port cities—Arvad, Tyre, Sidon, and others known to history. From there they seem to have moved out into the Mediterranean, primarily as merchant-seamen.

Currently, there is some lingering debate about their relationships with the Cretean and associated Minoan civilizations of the Aegean, and it has been pointed out that the languages of the two peoples seem to have much in common. In fact, they may have exercised a common culture, but whether this was resident or came from the east in the hands of the so-called Phoenicians has not as yet been decided.

Nevertheless, said Phoenicians appear to have founded trading outposts, and subsequently settlements or what we may call "colonies," all around the Mediterranean. A fine example is Carthage. But there were others in Sicily, Sardinia, and on the southern coasts of what we now call France and Spain. The fabled Tartessus was probably one of the latter. What is more, these strange sea-people, coming from the Persian Gulf and the Indian Ocean seem to have brought great expertize in seamanship—fin-keels, fore-and-aft sails, and possibly even in-ship rudders as opposed to steering oars. They certainly boated, and they certainly traded; and they seem to have gone out through the Strait of Gibraltar into the Atlantic, at a very early period. There are now scholars who have stated categorically that they may have reached the Americas before 1200 B.C., and then carried on over-ocean trade therefrom until as late as 400 B.C. But, though this last is not of our story, it should be mentioned that these extraordinary mariners may have reached the great tropical rivers of South America and Africa, and thus have brought back to Europe some solid accounts of what they found there.

There are some very strange publications by one Professor Ramos of Brazil that I personally cannot discredit out of hand. Herein, allegedly, are transcripts of petrogylphs found on the upper Amazon, in *both* Phoenician scripts, talking about gold mines, and floods, and annual packet-boats from the Old World. Professor Ramos' works have been mightily "discredited" by Anglo-Saxon scholars, but I am afraid I just cannot count them all off as lies or the ravings of some lunatic. (I happen to be able to read Portuguese, and I have examined these records, and I solemnly state that I think they are worthy of most careful study.)

My point is that, if there is anything in all this re-discovered history of the Phoenicians, we must look to them as the first explorers of the jungles that we so far know of. Unfortunately, the Phoenicians themselves, and their colonists like the Carthaginians and Tartessians, have not left us any written records. We have to work backwards, as it were, and try to reconstruct just what they *did* do. Phoenician inscriptions on rocks far up the Amazon were anathema fifty years ago: now, we are not so certain.

Bettmann Archive

Pliny the Elder.

Rome was the next Mediterranean power to have contact with peoples who could have known the jungles. This was especially so in Africa, because the southernmost boundaries of the Empire were in Nubia. Roman remains have been found along the Nile as far south as the new Aswan Dam. But, in the reign of the Emperor Diocletian, who ruled from A.D. 284 to 305, the frontier was pulled back, and Rome lost contact with the peoples to the south. Romans, who had ventured to these outposts of Empire and beyond, added little to their world's information about "jungles." Their chief contribution in this respect was to assemble and preserve some of the data from more ancient sources. For example, in the first century A.D., Pliny the Elder recounted in Latin some of the Greek reports by Ctesias and others.

Pliny especially liked the one that certain half-men, half-beasts of India were the result of natives copulating with animals. At least he spares us the theory that the animals were monkeys or apes! Another of the Greek stories had it that some of the little forest people—the ones Ctesias said were less than three feet tall—had such long hair that the men did not wear clothes but simply wrapped themselves in their beards.

The temptation to smile at these exaggerations, repeated by wise men of the past, lessens a bit if one reflects that even in our own time wise men have erred in the opposite direction. Skeptical by habit, they have rejected a great many truths about the jungles and their inhabitants because the truth did not fit a preconceived theory.

30

The Age of Discovery

When Europeans, two thousand years later, began to be as adventurous on the open oceans as the Phoenicians had been, they found their way in considerable numbers to the areas of the world where there are jungles. The tropical rain forests of Africa had previously been beyond the range of any voyager; America was unknown; the Orient had been visited only by the occasional wanderer, never by fleets or expeditions. So the opening of the jungles had to be preceded by exploration, colonization and settlement in the vegetational belts where such forests grow.

The great navigators, however, had very little to do with jungles directly. Some got close enough to look at them, and their tales inspired curiosity and wonder in folks at home. Others got not only close enough to look, but close enough to trade with the near-jungle peoples, and this inspired a great cupidity in the people at home, which led to an expansion of European horizons beyond all precedent. Even the smallest countries could become great empires.

The first was Portugal. A tiny kingdom wedged between the mountains and the sea on the Iberian Peninsula, she was blessed in the early fifteenth century with a young man who had a passion for ships and, being a king's son, the means to indulge it. He is known as Henry the Navigator, although he never went to sea. In 1416, when he was only twenty-two years old, he founded a school to which he brought everyone he could find who might help improve the seaworthiness of ships and the quality of seamanship—Italian sailors, Spanish shipbuilders, Arab map-makers and mathematicians, Jewish astronomers. Among them they developed the West's first true navigational instruments so that the shipmasters could find their way.

Bettmann Archive

Henry the Navigator. Facsimile of rare seventeenth-century engraving made in Holland.

By the end of the century the Portuguese were getting rich on the wood, ivory, gold and slaves from Africa. When Bartolomeu Dias rounded the Cape of Good Hope in 1488—he called it Cape of Storms but his king, who had not been there, thought "Good Hope" would attract more imitators—Portugal was well on her way to primacy in the Oriental trade. Vasco da Gama insured this expansion a few years later when he found a more reliable way around this Cape to India—by sailing west to Brazil and then east, using the southern westerlies, south of the Horse latitudes.

Meanwhile Columbus's "discovery" of America, though it was the basis for a great Spanish Empire, did nothing to diminish Portugal's commercial supremacy. When the latter's captains and colonizers gave her Brazil as well as the best trading posts in Africa and the East, her prosperity rose to its peak. The other great explorers—French, English, Dutch, and Italian—opened the way for colonists and traders and missionaries who provided the coastal bases from which Europeans eventually penetrated the jungles themselves.

The explorers had seen only as much tropical rain forest as was visible from their ships or within a very short march from the harbors they charted or rivers they penetrated. Pedro Alvares Cabral, who claimed Brazil for Portugal on his way to India—he actually got there—seems to have had a glimpse of lowland jungle.

What these navigators did do was to set the stage for the conquistadores; who in turn gave the impetus to the first important jungle expedition ever made by Europeans, the descent of the Amazon by a contingent of Francisco Pizarro's men. This exploit, which took over ninteen months during 1541 and 1542, actually began earlier than this, as an expedition which Pizarro dispatched over the Andes under the command of his brother Gonzalo in 1538 to discover the land of cinnamon reported to be of easy access in the interior. By the time the party reached the headwaters of the Amazon, they were in trouble and realized it was impossible to proceed further overland. One of the captains, Francisco de Orellana, was commissioned to float down the river to seek help. The men built a boat which the chronicler of the expedition called a brigantine, and Orellana set out with fifty-six companions, a few of whom followed the boat in canoes.

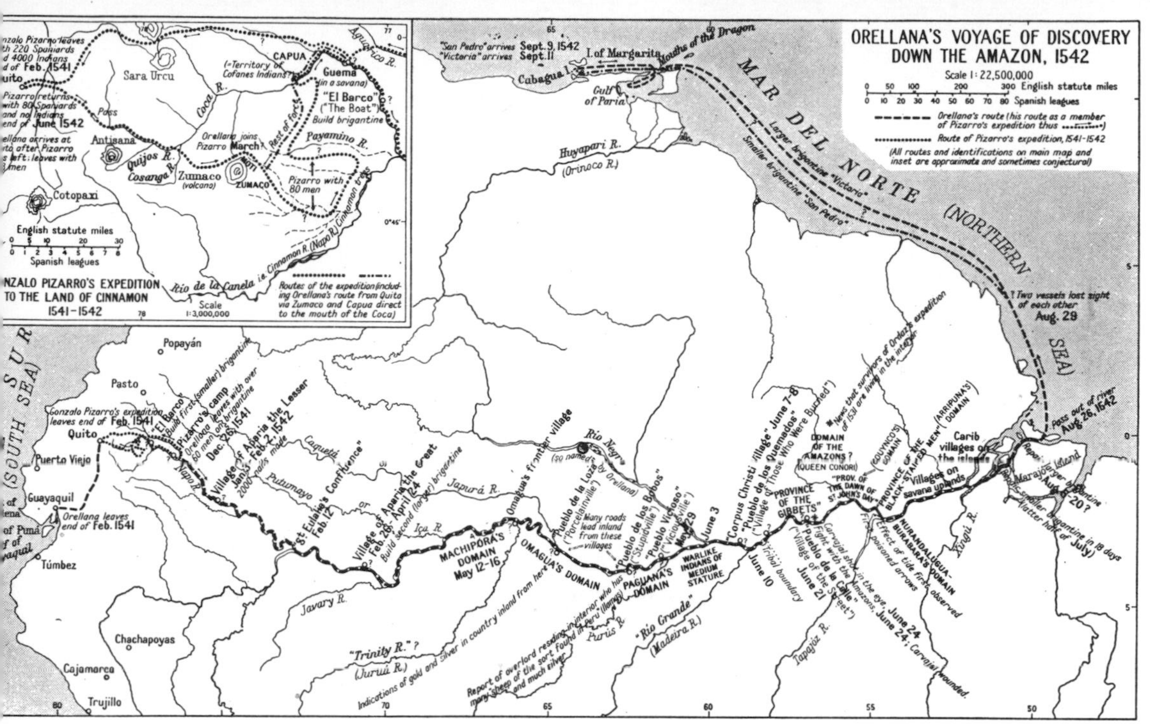

American Museum of Natural History

Orellana's voyage of discovery down the Amazon.

In the group was a Dominican Friar named Gaspar de Carvajal, a rugged thirty-seven-year-old friar from the Spanish province of Estremadura. His "Account" of the voyage is virtually our only source of information about it, but it has the ring of truth. The marvels, hardships, agonies and dangers are all set down in scrupulous detail. Exaggeration seems to be confined to what others told him, not to his account of what he saw or experienced himself.

The party had not proceeded very far before Carvajal became aware of Orellana's intention to float down the river to the sea and not to return to Gonzalo Pizarro. The captain was unmoved by arguments that this was a betrayal, and the majority of his men clearly preferred the unknown dangers ahead of them to the hunger and suffering they had left behind. (Two years later, Gonzalo and the remnant of his band managed to struggle back over the Andes to Lima.)

Orellana and his men, the first Europeans to navigate a great jungle river, were equipped with noisy but not very accurate harquebuses and a supply of powder which was often too damp to fire. But their crossbows were deadly. Carvajal thought they would never have gotten through without this efficient weapon, which outranged the common Indian bow, for their relations with the natives, especially during the last part of the trip, were on a shoot first and palaver afterward basis.

For weeks on end they floated downriver with the jungle walling them in on either side, and never a sign of life. They heard birds and monkeys but shot no game, gathered hardly any fruit or nuts, and were either very poor or very unlucky fishermen. They were ravenously hungry nearly all the time. Whenever they saw an Indian village, they were generally in no mood to parley very long. If the villagers seemed reluctant to share their stores, the Spaniards opened fire, cleared out the village and helped themselves to all the food they could find. Where the Indians were friendly enough to trade meat and fish and fowl, fruit and meal for items of clothing or trinkets, the travelers gorged themselves. At one such village about halfway down the Amazon, they paused long enough to build a second "brigantine" from the huge hardwood trees, a job that took five weeks, although Carvajal says none of his companions were skilled shipbuilders.

From this point on, the party gave up canoes, which Carvajal thought just as well, because the stout sides of their vessels afforded them some protection when they fought the unfriendly natives. The jungle inspired no praise from them. They had never seen such trees, such dense masses of foliage, green and absolutely motionless in the still air which was disturbed only by occasional thunderstorms. They seem not to have speculated on what might be behind that impenetrable mass; presumably they supposed it just went on that way indefinitely. Carvajal went into detail only when there was a break in the forest, a stretch of savannah, for example. At one point, looking inland across some fields and grasslands, he saw several large "cities" gleaming white in the sunlight—they were probably groups of big communal huts or thatched houses which many of the Indians built. However, the party never landed to try and get a closer look; they were too wary of being attacked to come ashore for anything except food.

Carvajal called the river the Orellana after his captain, but the name the world now uses is taken from a part of the narrative describ-

Rare Book Room, American Museum of Natural History

Theodore de Bry's view of Brazil jungle at Tammaraka.

ing an incident that occurred after the Spaniards had been nearly a year and a half on their journey. The friar wrote that they were looking for a peaceful spot in which to celebrate the feast day of Saint John the Baptist, June 24. They rounded a bend in the river and found themselves in what the narrator called the land and dominion of the Amazons, although presumably he did not know this at the time but only learned it later.

Great crowds of Indians jeered at the white men. When Orellana ordered the two boats beached so the party could forage for food, the natives loosed a shower of arrows, and the fight was on. The Spaniards usually warded off these attacks without difficulty because they were well protected by great shields and body armor, and could keep the Indians at fairly long range. But this particular contingent of natives was more determined than most, Carvajal says, and he attributes their persistence to the fact that they were the minions of the Amazons. He adds that they had sent to their rulers for help and that ten or twelve female warriors had responded. They served as captains of the Indian squadrons, fighting like ten men each and keeping the men keyed up to battle too. In fact, Carvajal reports that whenever a man turned his back on the fight, one of these women would brain him on the spot. This particular engagement lasted for more than an hour—in sharp contrast to the usual hit-and-run Indian tactic—until seven or eight of the Amazons were killed along with great numbers of their native men. Five Spaniards were wounded, including Carvajal, who was struck in the side by an arrow. When the Indians finally faltered, Orellana ordered his men back to their boats, and just in time, because massive reinforcements for the natives were seen to be arriving.

Carvajal describes the female warriors as very white, tall and robust with long dark hair wound around their heads in braids. They fought naked except for a bit of cloth covering their genitals.

This is all he says about them, but one of the Indians captured during the fight told the Spaniards a great deal more, and Carvajal repeats what the prisoner reported. The man said he knew the Amazons well because he went back and forth to their city carrying the tribute which his own overlord was obliged to pay. The women lived seven days journey back from the river with a great wealth of gold and silver treasure, much of which they dedicated to the worship of the sun. They dressed in woolens (like those of the Incas) and dined off silver and gold plates. When roused by sexual desire, they did not simply seek out men but marched off to war against a particular people who lived not far away. Any prisoners they were able to capture were brought back to serve as lovers. After the women became pregnant, the men were sent home. Boy children resulting from these unions were either killed or given to their fathers; girls were raised as warriors.

The Indian prisoner's story so fired the imagination of contemporaries that Carvajal's name of "the Orellana River" won no supporters. Reports of the warlike women of the jungle have been repeated ever since along the Amazon, and they are believed by many Indians.

Men who had never been on the river, however, scoffed at Carvajal's credulity, and to this day learned writers suggest that in the heat of battle he mistook long-haired men for women. But the fact is that the Spaniards had been fighting nothing but long-haired men for months. Experienced wanderers in and around the South American jungles are not so skeptical. That there could have been women warriors such as those Carvajal described is quite possible, and since he says he saw them, as did the other Spaniards, there doesn't seem to be any reason to doubt his word.

At any rate, the Amazon River got its name as a result of that fray on or about the feast day of Saint John the Baptist. The weary victors, too tired to man their oars, simply drifted with the current. They were hungry, too, and when they came to what seemed a deserted village, Orellana consented to land in search of food. It proved to be an ambush, however, and Carvajal was shot through the eye by an arrow. The party embarked immediately. And it is interesting to note that although his wound was excruciatingly painful, Carajal continued to write his notes.

Two months after the battle with the Amazons, the party reached the mouth of the river. Carvajal recorded with amazement that it must be 150 miles wide and that its waters colored the sea for 75 miles into the ocean, so great was its flow. Still rowing, the men made their way up the coast to Nueva Cadiz, where Orellana left to return and report to his king. He came back four years later to explore his river from its mouth, and died there. Carvajal returned to Peru, wrote his narrative, became an important figure in his order, received the title of Protector of the Indians and died near Lima at the age of nearly eighty, forty-two years after the battle with the Amazons.

He recorded perhaps the most remarkable feat of river navigation in history, nearly four thousand miles through totally unexplored country with only the certainty that every river comes someday to the sea—a truism Orellana's men may well have begun to doubt long before their voyage ended. They had made the largest of jungle rivers the first to be known in Europe. The next largest, the Congo, was not navigated for its full length until more than three hundred years later. The third great jungle river, the Mekong, wasn't even known to Europeans.

31
The Great Precursors

Two eighteenth-century aristocrats, one French, the other German, laid the foundation for the true scientific study of jungles. From the days of the fifteenth- and sixteenth-century navigators, a vast amount of lore and legend had been poured out in Europe concerning all the new discoveries. Sailors and soldiers, businessmen and civil servants, pirates and adventurers, and even some scholars and clergymen, had written books about the tropics, had described their own experiences, and had repeated stories that they had heard. Some of these accounts contained a great deal of sound, scientifically accurate information. But real information about the true jungles were yet to come.

It would be hard to estimate how many men have made substantial contributions to our understanding of the tropical rain forests. Every student of the subject will have his own favorites among these, and it would take an encyclopedia even to summarize the work of all of them. Here and in the succeeding chapters we are not attempting a complete catalogue; nor are we suggesting that the men of whom we write were more important than any others. What we have sought to do is to convey some impression of the variety of talents that have been involved, the nature of the manifold tasks that were faced, and the sort of adventures that were encountered. We have tried to select men who are representative; but we have had to omit many whose achievements were just as great.

Anyone who has ever engaged in scientific work in the jungles will assuredly acknowledge a debt to two aristocrats—Charles-Marie de La Condamine and Alexander von Humboldt, for they brought to the study of these vegetational complexes the cool objectivity and enthusiastic curiosity of European Enlightenment. It is said that La Condamine was the first genuinely scientific student of the jungle.

American Museum of Natural History

The son of a very rich man, he grew up in the early days of the reign of Louis XV. He was a junior officer, eighteen years old, when he met a Spanish soldier who had been in America. The man's stories of the Andes captured La Condamine's imagination, and he longed to see this continent for himself. But he had an orderly mind and a purpose which led him to study geodetics and mathematics in preparation for travel. In 1730, when he was twenty-nine, the French Academy of Sciences elected him to membership. Five years later it appointed him to head one of two scientific expeditions being fitted out to settle perhaps the keenest controversy of the age—to wit; exactly what shape is the earth? Round, of course, and no doubt slightly flattened at the poles? or at the equator? Each school of thought had its ardent proponents. The French Academy proposed to settle the argument by actual measurements. One expedition would go as near the pole as man could get. This was Lapland. The other would go to the equator.

King Louis provided ships to take the scientists across the oceans, and gave some money, too. La Condamine himself made a princely contribution to the equatorial mission, which he headed—100,000 livres—although his biographers have made it clear that this did not influence his appointment. He sailed from La Rochelle in May 1735 with a party of ten scientifically trained gentlemen, and he spent ten years in accomplishing his task.

The actual measurements were made in Ecuador where La Condamine, during nine years of work in which he established a complicated series of triangulations over more than three hundred miles of difficult territory, confirmed the measurments of the Lapland expedition, which got through first. Both proved that the earth is indeed an oblate spheroid, a fact that Sir Isaac Newton had already announced theoretically. Most of the survivors of the expedition—three had died—scattered, but the leader decided to return home by Orellana's route, down the Amazon.

He was fortunate that it was a much more peaceful trip than the one two hundred years earlier or than it would have been two hundred years later! Missions, established by Spain and Portugal all along the river, helped the travelers get paddlers and food. There was no fighting with Indians, and the whole voyage took only two months. La Condamine himself wrote that the trip was mainly tiresome because of the sameness of the scenery. He occupied himself with measurements—the speed of the current, the width and depth of the stream, the rate of the river bed's fall—and with observations of the jungle. He experimented with curare, with which Indians for centuries had poisoned arrows, and learned that sugar was a quick antidote. He also noted how the Indians fished by "leaves or roots which when thrown into the water have the faculty of intoxicating the fish," which was the discovery of rotenone, better known to us as a major chemical weapon of the modern exterminator. He described the trees and the vines. He explained more clearly than anyone before him the remarkable role that lianas play in the make-up of a jungle. He had already collected samples of rubber and quinine: now he noticed that the trees from which rubber was derived grew wild in the jungle. He made a waterproof rubber covering for his scientific instruments from this material and he brought with him to Europe the first practical specimens of the stuff. Finally, La Condamine's observations enabled him to make the first reasonably accurate chart of the Amazon's course from source to mouth and of the points at which it was joined by its principal tributaries.

On his return to Paris, La Condamine wrote his account of the descent of the Amazon which was published in English as early as 1747 under the title *A Voyage Through the Inner Parts of South America*.

One of the important results of his writing was its influence upon young Friedrich Heinrich Alexander Freiherr von Humboldt, born in Prussia in 1769 and reared in an atmosphere of learning which was encouraged at the court of Frederick the Great where the boy's father was a respected military figure. Alexander and his brother had a tutor who had been the translator of *Robinson Crusoe*. He regaled his charges with tales of tropical adventure which imbued one of them with a taste for travel to far places. As a matter of course the boys learned French, English, and Spanish. Alexander preferred all his life to write in French, as did his Prussian king, but he grew up with so little feeling of national patriotism that he was able to pass through the whole era from the French Revolution to the upheavals of 1848 without becoming politically embroiled.

He was a man so devoted to science and so indifferent to war that he was equally comfortable in the Paris of the Jacobins, the Bourbons, and of Napoleon, in the Russia of the Czars, the Spain of the almost imbecile Charles IV, and at Monticello with Thomas Jefferson. He acquired his early training at the best German universities for the physical sciences, and continued his studies, preparing himself throughout his twenties to explore the unknown world beyond the seas.

He seems not to have been particular where he went just so long as it was across the ocean. His first ambition was to join an expedition around the world which was being organized in Paris in 1798. The leader accepted him, and he was all packed to go when Napoleon postponed the project. Humboldt's next project, an exploration up the Nile from Egypt, was canceled by Nelson's victory at Aboukir.

In the interval, Humboldt made the acquaintance of Aimé Bonpland, a French physician who was too interested in botany to build up a medical practice and who also had been accepted for the round-the-world voyage. The two had a common passion for scientific observation in uncharted parts of the globe, and otherwise complemented each other nicely. Humboldt was small, neat, graceful and socially accomplished. Bonpland was large, blunt, vivacious and unambitious. They thought they might still get moving with the Egyptian adventure by running the British blockade, and in 1799 they went to Spain for that purpose. A passage to Egypt was not easy to arrange. But why not, someone suggested, a passage to America? There was plenty to be learned there.

Humboldt remembered La Condamine, and Bonpland was enchanted by the prospect of all the unrecorded American botany. Through a friend of his family, the young nobleman obtained an audience with the king of Spain, who, in a moment of easy geniality, gave Humboldt a letter requiring all Spanish authorities in the New World to assist him and his companion in their travels and studies. Such an unconditional passport had never before been issued to a foreigner.

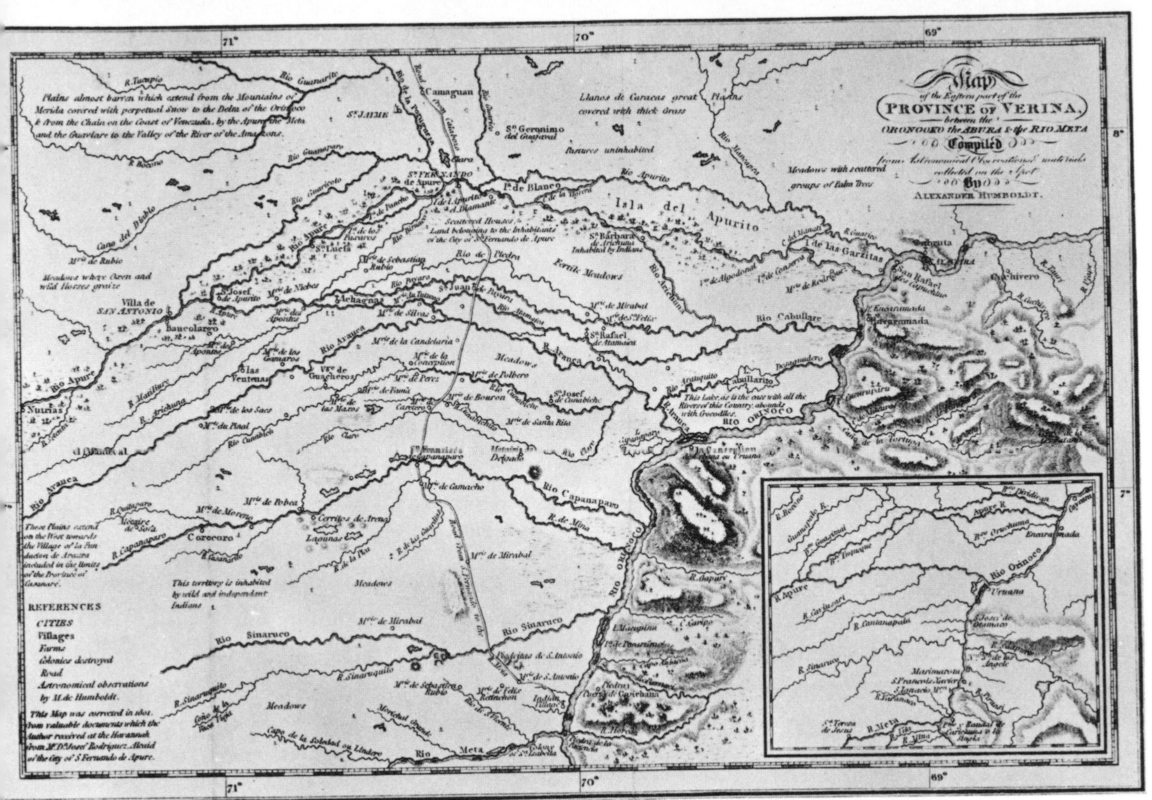

American Museum of Natural History

Von Humboldt's map of the Province of Verina, on the Orinoco.

In June 1799, the most widely known of all scientific expeditions to America was launched from the port of La Coruña when two unknown young men embarked on a ship named *El Pizarro*. They were the entire expedition, but by the time the twenty-third volume of their *Voyage de Humboldt et Bonpland* had been published thirty-five years later, they were famous, and the way to scientific understanding of all new territories was greatly advanced.

The expedition that brought them to the jungles was their first, inspired by Humboldt's desire to elaborate a conclusion reached by La Condamine. The Frenchman had written that he was certain a water connection existed between the Orinoco and the Rio Negro. Meanwhile other scholars who had never been in America and a few who had were saying this was impossible. The only party ever sent to find out had failed to reach the upper reaches of the Orinoco and lost 312 of the 325 men who started. Humboldt's opinion was not that La Condamine needed verification but simply that it would be an amplification of his work to locate the link between the two rivers.

Like La Condamine, Humboldt and Bonpland were helped by the missions and by Indian paddlers as they journeyed up the Orinoco in a canoe about two and a half feet wide. Bonpland collected botanical specimens by the hundred and Humboldt took observations. Eventually they found the strange little Cariquiare River, which does indeed connect the Orinoco and the Rio Negro which is a tributary of the Amazon, and were almost arrested by the commandant of a Portuguese border garrison who took them for spies. Their story—to wit, that they were looking for a river link—sounded fishy to him. Didn't everyone know it was there? But he let them go at last, and they were able to look into another old story that was not so greatly supported by local gossip. In Europe, however, it was as old as Raleigh's voyage, and told of a huge mythical lake at the headwaters of the Orinoco. Humboldt was able to assure friends at home that it did not exist.

Long before he returned to Europe, his letters had made him famous. He sparked his correspondence with exact accounts of eels five feet long, boa constrictors big enough to eat a horse, a little woolly monkey which eventually got his name, tapirs, manatees, strange cats and weird insects.

The work for which he became best known was, however, done on the western side of the continent, although at one time he came east of the Andes again to spend a few days in the vicinity of the spot where La Condamine had started down the Amazon. In the Andes and on the Pacific shore, Humboldt established the relationship and influence of altitude to latitude on vegetation, showing how a few hundred feet of altitude equals one degree of latitude. He ascended Mount Chimborazo to a point higher than any man had ever climbed any mountain. He calculated his ascent at 19,286 feet which, if correct, was within about 1,200 feet of the top. He expanded the world's knowledge, by the most exact archaeological observations then made in South America. And, finally, he explained the action of the great ocean current that bears his name and its effects upon climate, vegetation and animal life. It is from his work in part that men now know why jungles are where they are.

After five years in America, Humboldt and Bonpland went home.

Bettmann Archive

Von Humboldt on the shores of the Orinoco.

The publication of their findings was largely Humboldt's work, and he became the grand old man of science, for he lived to be ninety. Bonpland had a fantastic career as a gardener for the Empress Josephine at Malmaison, as an author of works on botany, as a prisoner for ten years of the half-mad *El Supremo* of Guayaquil, the Dictator Francia who kept him virtually enslaved as an agricultural expert despite protests from great men in half the civilized world.

La Condamine and Humboldt taught later scientific investigators many valuable lessons. One, which is imperfectly learned by some even now and is particularly applicable to any inquirer into the many remaining mysteries of the jungles, is this: Do not scoff at the accounts given to you by simple or untutored men who have been there. Rather, preserve an open mind, although the story may appear to be ridiculous or improbable; and go see for yourself. That is what La Condamine and Von Humboldt did, and they are revered for their achievements to this day.

32

The Lonely Genius

A MAN who learned the lesson of La Condamine and Humboldt extremely well was one Alfred Russel Wallace, who started life as a poor, obscure schoolteacher. The world owes him a great scientific debt for his part in establishing the science of vegetalogy. It was his work in the jungles of America and the Far East that proved the decisive role of vegetation in determining the nature of animal life in any area. He systematized animal geography, a science in which he was a pioneer, and the practical value of his achievement is commemorated in what scientists call "Wallace's Line," which divides the Asiatic forms of life from the Australian through the islands of Indonesia. (This is not the only "line" nor is it absolute since some Asiatic forms slip over into the Austral Province.)

Wallace was one of a new breed of naturalists who developed mostly in England during the nineteenth century. They were in a sense the first professionals in their field. Neither rich nor influential, without patrons or institutions or governments to finance them, they not only made a living from their work but trained themselves in their specialties, many of which were new. Their economic achievement was hardly less remarkable than their scientific one, and Wallace was unsurpassed in both.

Born in 1823, he was employed in a school in Leicester at the age of twenty-five, but nursed a passion for botany and zoology which the English countryside stimulated without satisfying. With no special scientific education, as we would use the term, he knew he had no chance of being subsidized or asked to join an expedition. But he thought he might support himself on a plant and animal collecting journey by selling duplicate specimens to museums, universities and private collectors. Another teacher in the same city,

American Museum of Natural History

"Entrance to Lagoon Shore," Lagoon of the Amazon. Painting by George Catlin.

Henry Walter Bates, two years his junior, was as keen as he and as frustrated in his ambition, which was gathering and identifying insects. They decided to join forces in an expedition to the Amazon, which seemed to them to be the most likely source of previously uncollected specimens.

Wallace later explained that they selected these jungles only after reading about them in a short book, *A Voyage Up the River Amazon,* published in 1847. They went down to London to meet the author, an American of their own age named William H. Edwards, who had actually been only as far as Manaus, but was as enthusiastic as if he had been Carvajal himself. Edwards had made the people sound so hospitable and the cost of living so low that Wallace and Bates set off for the Amazon almost immediately. It would appear, however, that their readings in Humboldt and in Darwin's *Journal* which described the voyage of the *Beagle* were great factors in their decision.

Wallace spent four years in South America, leaving the main

Amazon to Bates, while he took on the Rio Negro and its tributaries. And when he reached the Negro's headwaters, he followed Humboldt's trail to the Orinoco. Many of the animals and plants he collected he was able to send home, but the best he kept with him, and they were an impressive lot. During this trip he contracted malaria, and toward the end of the four years a friend who met him at the little town of São Jaoquin, where the Rio Uaupés joins the Negro, thought him so wasted and yellow that he must be dying. But Wallace was as full of enthusiasm, talking vivaciously about his finds in the jungle, as any healthy man.

He had never allowed these spells to prevent him from appreciating jungle life. He was one of the few men to find the jungles comfortable although he was not, of course, born in them. He always declared they were pleasant and healthful. The solemn columnar trees with their festoons of lianas, he wrote, "produce feelings in the beholder of admiration and awe." And he liked the "fine, naked, independent forest dwellers."

However, after his worst bout of fever, he decided it was time to go home with his specimens. Seven hundred miles east of Bermuda the brig *Helen* on which he was a passenger caught fire, and those on board were lucky to get away in the boats. Wallace's tremendously valuable collection went down with the charred hulk. The survivors were picked up after ten days by a vessel bound for London.

Neither the memory of illness nor the hunger and thirst of those days in an open boat nor the loss of his priceless specimens dampened Wallace's enthusiasm for scientific inquiry in the field. But he did not return to the Amazon. Instead, he headed east to study the vegetation and animals of the Malay archipelago. During the rest of the 1850's, after visiting a number of the islands, still amassing specimens, he had ample leisure in his lonely life in and near the jungles to form a philosophy as well as a collection.

He once explained that when he was in South America he was "bitten by the passion for species and their description," an occupation which he came to think of as "comparatively profitless work." His principal observations in the Amazon jungles were of the immense number of different trees, so that it was usually hard to find two of a kind close together; in his old age he modified this to say that three features of his South American journey still remained impressive:

> The first was the virgin forest, everywhere grand, often beautiful and sublime; the second, the wonderful variety and exquisite beauty of the butterflies and birds; and the third, the meeting and living with man in a state of nature—with absolutely uncontaminated savages. The true denizen of the Amazonian forest, like the forest itself, is unique and not to be forgotten.

In the Far East, however, solitude combined with the occasional illnesses which he counted a part of normal tropical life led him to some profound, novel and interesting conclusions. Nearly fifty years later he explained:

> At the time, I was suffering from an attack of intermittent fever, and every day during the cold and succeeding hot fits had to lie down for several hours, during which time I had nothing to do but to think over any subjects then particularly interesting me.

The subject of his feverish reflections for a long time was the why and how of animal adaptation to fit the environment. The vastness of his own collections gave him clues to the fact of the adaptation—after three and a half years in the Orient he drew up for Bates a list of 8,540 species of insects he had gathered—and he thought deeply about the origin of species. He knew now that species did change, but the cause and the process remained mysteries. He applied Malthus's theory that population tends to outrun food supply, and saw that the fittest of the population survived under these circumstances. This would improve the breed by perpetuating changes that would help the animal in getting along where it was, and so a new species would originate.

At last, in a thatched, unwalled house on the edge of a Borneo jungle, he wrote a paper which he titled *On the Tendency of Varieties to Depart Indefinitely from the Original Type*. He mailed it to an English naturalist, whose work he had admired since his schoolteaching days, who had been all around the edges of South America while Wallace was still a schoolboy and who, unknown to the lonely author in Borneo, had been developing a similar theory for a dozen years. Charles Darwin received Wallace's paper one morning at his London home with a covering letter which requested him, if he found the contents had merit, to send the document to Sir Charles Lyell, an eminent professor of geology whose chief work, published in the early 1830's, had been a valuable part of both men's educations.

"I never saw a more striking coincidence," Darwin wrote to Sir Charles; "if Wallace had my own sketch, he could not have made a better short abstract."

"I was, of course, very much surprise. to find that the same idea had occurred to Darwin," Wallace remarked, "and that he had already nearly completed a larger work fully developing it."

Later commentators have compared this coincidence with the simultaneous invention of calculus by Newton and Leibnitz. In this case, although Darwin was well aware of the kudos that come with being first to announce a scientific discovery or theory, he took the unusual step of reading Wallace's paper at the same meeting of the Linnaean Society that heard his own. Darwin went on to develop the theory of what both men called "natural selection" in his famous book, *On the Origin of Species,* while Wallace settled down to the vegetational theory which led to the delineation of Wallace's Line and his own pioneer book, *The Geographical Distribution of Animals.*

Wallace enjoyed the Eastern jungles quite as much as he had the South American, although he continued to be loyal to the beauty of England in spring. He had uniformly happy and friendly relations with the local peoples, even when he became exasperated with individuals, perhaps because he liked and paid a lot of attention to their children. He spent a month in the home of a Dyak family in Borneo, and wrote of his amazement when he tried to teach his host's offspring how to make a cat's cradle: they dexterously showed him how to twist the bit of string into figures he had never seen. No wonder he never felt in any danger. He became the first European

American Museum of Natural Histor

Alfred Russel Wallace.

to live alone in New Guinea, and had a wonderful time there. He was so little dependent upon others that he wrote to friends:

"You cannot perhaps imagine how I have come to love solitude. I seldom have a visitor but I wish him away in an hour. I find it very favorable to reflection."

At one of his camps, Wallace enlivened his solitary life by trying to raise a baby orangutan. He cared for it lovingly, preparing a sweetened and progressively thickened formula of rice-water which he fed to it in an ingeniously contrived nursing bottle. He brought in a monkey named Toby to play with it and keep it company, and spoiled it outrageously. He extolled its good and amiable qualities in a long, jocose letter to a friend in England, dwelling on the strength of its fingers and toes, its intelligence, its pretty little hands and feet. He ended his account with a parody of the rhapsodies with which, no doubt, his friends had written to him of their young:

> Of course baby cannot walk yet, but I let it crawl about on the floor to exercise its limbs; but it is the most wonderful baby I ever saw, and has such strength in its arms that it will catch hold of my trousers as I sit at work, and hang under my legs for a quarter of an hour at a time without being the least tired, all the time trying to suck. . . . From this short account [Wallace had written about the equivalent of four pages of this book] you will see that my baby is no common baby, and I can truthfully say, what so many have said before with much less truth, "There never was such a baby as my baby."

During his years in the Orient, Wallace remarked over and over how very similar in appearance the jungles there were to those of the Amazon. The most striking superficial difference he could see was that there had been many more butterflies in America. When he came to Malacca and heard native helpers he had hired speaking Portuguese, he says he thought he was back in Brazil. This resemblance is all the more remarkable because at the same time he was learning the subtle differences that distinguish the vegetation and the animals found on opposite sides of a single river. When he wrote to admonish his scientist friends in other parts of the world to be sure to say from which bank they took a given specimen, he explained that he had himself been at fault. A critic had pointed out to him that in his writings on the Rio Negro palm trees he had been guilty of this omission, and he admitted cheerfully that he had then been ignorant of an important truth. This willingness to confess error was one of his most appealing qualities.

Wallace's years in American and Oriental jungles and his important findings were chronicled in a series of scientific works, mostly written after his return to England. He lived there for fifty more years before his death in 1913, in the English countryside which he had so stoutly insisted was in its own way as beautiful as any exotic, tropical paradise.

33

Strange Adventures

BEFORE men like Wallace could pursue their studies in peace and security, more "adventurous" types had to pave the way, or in some cases find the way. The scientific investigation of jungles was preceded by the experiences of pioneers who could be described as empire builders. Two whose dramatic careers were preliminary to sober inquiry in the interior of Africa and the Far East were Mungo Park, the Scots doctor-explorer, and Sir James Brooke, "the white rajah."

Mungo Park's share in all this began one evening in 1788 when a dozen curious London gentlemen turned the conversation of their Saturday dining club to the lamentable lack of knowledge about the "dark continent," still in the state of which Swift had written:

Geographers in Afric maps
With savage pictures fill their gaps,
And o'er uninhabitable downs,
Place elephants for want of towns.

One of the diners on that particular Saturday was Sir Joseph Banks, who had been bitten by the botany bug as an Eton schoolboy, organized fellow students at Oxford to hire a lecturer on the subject, and gone on Captain Cook's famous *Endeavour* expedition around the world at his own expense to collect biological specimens. He had been a Fellow of the Royal Society at twenty-three and its president at thirty-five; for the next forty years he was the chief influence there and at the Kew botanical gardens. Possessor of a large fortune, he was regarded as a leading patron of science and learning. Largely through his leadership, the Saturday diners formed themselves into an "Association for Promoting the Discovery of the Inland Parts of the Continent of Africa."

Culve

Mungo Park.

Since England's interest was largely trade, the new association decided that knowledge and commerce might both be served by prospecting the route of the Niger River, which was known to Europeans only as Arabs told of it. No one knew where it went after passing Timbuctu, but perhaps it would serve as a highway to the interior. Two of three explorers who were sent to find out how best to get to the upper reaches of the river were killed on the way; the third scarcely got started before he turned back.

The association was hard put to find a willing fourth, until a young ship's surgeon returned from a voyage to Sumatra, a journey he had been able to make through Sir Joseph's recommendation of him to the East India Company. He was Mungo Park, son of a Scots farmer, who preferred travel to practicing medicine. He had also been interested in botany, which was how Banks had heard of him; he was now twenty-two years old with an itchy foot. He was also strong, tough and did not flinch when Sir Joseph told him he was being considered for the Niger River project because perhaps a rugged young man might get through where more experienced travelers had failed. He was cautious, however, and took two years to prepare himself for the venture. Finally with two hundred pounds supplied by the association he set off to learn how the Niger might be reached and where it went.

His first trip was one of the great adventure stories of the age. The hardy Scot, six feet tall, fair and with a bush of whiskers which so impressed Africans that they still called him "Big Beard" a century later, made his way through fiercely hostile country until he actually reached the headwaters of the Niger, having entered the continent from its western bulge. He was robbed and had to beg his way, starving and thirsting to the point where he considered it a favor to be allowed to drink from a trough along with the cows; he was insulted as a "Nazarene" and held captive in a Moorish camp where he owed his life to an immensely fat queen named Fatima; he finally escaped on a half-dead horse with no equipment and not much clothing except a cloak, which was promptly stolen.

Nearly a month after his escape, on July 21, 1796, he actually reached the Niger, barefoot and so ragged "that I believe the very

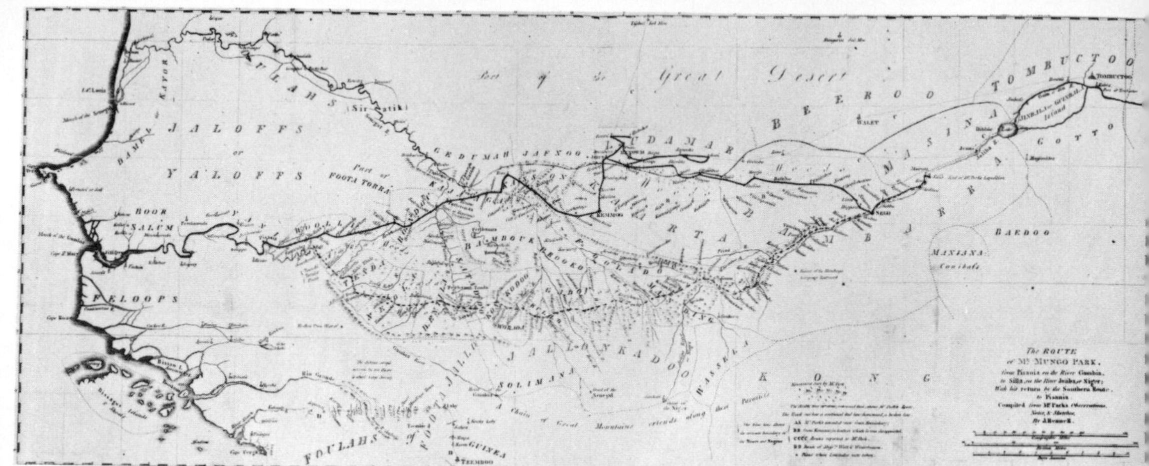

American Museum of Natural History

Route of Mungo Park.

slaves were ashamed to be seen in my company." He had traveled part of the way with a coffle of seventy slaves being marched to Morocco, "tied together by their necks with thongs of a bullock's hide, twisted like a rope; seven slaves upon a thong, and a man with a musket between every seven." Then after seven months of fever and delay, living in a hut on the bounty of a Negro who had never before seen a white man, he was taken back to the coast in the train of another slaver, whose human merchandise was driven so hard that when a woman could not keep up, she was simply cut out of the coffle and left to die. Slaves were one of the three great commodities that England sought in Africa—gold and ivory were the others—and some of Park's backers were in the slave trade themselves.

Park got back to England in November 1797, after the association had presumed him dead. His account, written with the assistance of a gentleman whose style was pompous even for that era, was so successful that Park cleared one thousand pounds, a fortune in Scotland. All England exclaimed over his narrative. He also introduced a phrase to the language, "mumbo jumbo," a term used among the Kaffirs (this term—originally "coffre," or coffee-colored was then applied to all peoples south of the Sahara much as we use the loose term "Negro" today) to describe "a strange bugbear employed in keeping their women in subjection." It was a husband, or friend of a husband, disguised as an avenging spirit come to punish an objectionable wife. After scaring all the married women in the village, the mumbo jumbo indicated the culprit, who was stripped and beaten by everybody, especially by the women who were relieved that they were not the victim.

"Daylight puts an end to this indecent and unmanly revel," Park (or his collaborator) added.

Mumbo jumbo went through various transmutations to its present meaning of superstitious confusion. It was Park's contribution to literature, but the spur he gave to African exploration can hardly be exaggerated. The Niger had been visited; now the British government decided it would like to know whether the river petered out in the sands of the interior, flowed into some great lake or was the upper waters of the Congo. In 1805, Park set off again, with a captain's commission and official support, to navigate the full length of the Niger. He himself thought that after flowing east it turned south to either the Congo or the sea. (It is actually the sea.)

This time he took a force big enough to prevent robbery or even insult—thirty-four British soldiers, four carpenters (to build boats) and three officers, including his brother-in-law. Fever and dysentery reduced this party to six soldiers, one carpenter and two officers besides Park by the time they reached the Niger. The carpenter, three soldiers and one of the officers, their leader's brother-in-law, died before a boat could be built. The survivors put together a flat-bottomed forty-foot craft from the sound parts of two big native canoes; Park grandiosely called it "His Majesty's schooner *Joliba*." With three slaves and a guide-interpreter to augment his four white companions, he launched this vessel on the Niger in November after sending his last letters home. In one of them he gave the first clear report of the river's bend to the south; his informants, however, had never seen its mouth.

The rest of the story emerged in bits and pieces, the first of which came to light only five years later. Apparently he went down the river for a thousand miles, fighting off hostile natives or perhaps firing on peaceful natives because he was afraid they were hostile. One more soldier died of fever. The guide left at a point where it

Bettmann Archive

Sir James Brooke, Rajah of Sarawak.

had been agreed he might turn back. Shortly after this, some five hundred miles from the sea, the *Joliba* met a force of Tuaregs (not the people of that name from the Central Sahara, as recognized today, but obviously "Arabs" from the north) too powerful to overcome, even though each of Park's men had fifteen loaded muskets. Two of the slaves were killed by Tuareg missiles, whereupon Park and his lieutenant, each clasping a soldier because these men could not swim, leaped into the river and tried to get away underwater. All four were drowned. This was the account told by the surviving slave located years later by the guide.

Subsequent explorers were surprised that the party got as far as it did. The Niger was not navigated its full length until 1896, and by then the legend of Mungo Park was firmly fixed among Europeans who had African ambitions. His failure inspired so many later adventurers that, in a sense, the discovery of the inland parts of Africa really was initially promoted by his short, tragic career, though he probably never saw a real jungle.

History offers few sharper contrasts to this tale than the life of James Brooke. He was born in Benares in 1803, the son of a rich British civil servant. Too restless or too unorthodox for the English school to which his father sent him, he joined the Army as a cadet when he was sixteen and served for six years in the East. Then in 1825, during the first of England's three wars with Burma, he was so severely wounded in the lungs that he was invalided out of the service.

This, plus an inheritance of thirty thousand pounds, sent him traveling about the islands of Indonesia between visits to London, where he talked about possibilities for expanding the Empire. The government was not eager to back him, so he outfitted an armed yacht of 142 tons, named her *Royalist,* and sailed for Borneo, which he had settled upon as a likely sphere of British influence and trade. When he arrived at the port of Kuching in Sarawak, the northwest portion of Borneo, he found a languid civil war in progress. Taking sides with the traditional ruler, the Sultan of Brunei, Brooke brought ashore the six cannon from his yacht and inspired the Sultan's troops to the unorthodoxy of actually attacking the enemy.

The rebellion was crushed, and the Sultan rewarded his white friend with the gift of Sarawak—about twenty-eight thousand square miles of it with perhaps thirty thousand Malays and an unknown number of Dyaks. Rajah Brooke, as he was called thereafter, settled down to govern his domain on what in the first half of the nineteenth century were highly enlightened principles. Not yet forty years old, he ruled the mutually antagonistic Malays and Dyaks with no greater outside force than a shipwrecked Irishman who served as aide, an English doctor who never learned to speak the local tongue, an interpreter from Malacca and an illiterate servant. He stamped out piracy with the help of a British naval contingent and discouraged Dyak head-hunting. Both segments of the population trusted him, which was the secret of his success, and when he went back to England to be knighted, Queen Victoria asked him how he had succeeded in controlling all those wild people.

"I find it easier to govern thirty thousand Malays and Dyaks than to manage a dozen of Your Majesty's subjects," he replied.

Once settled in his capital, the Rajah began to explore his country. He traveled inland, mostly along the rivers, and made notes about the jungle. He brought back a collection of plants and animals and a realization that there were people other than the coastal folk in his dominions. However, all his writings and most of his possessions were burned when the Chinese residents of Sarawak rebelled against him. The Chinese had been in Borneo since long before white men knew the island, had their own colony and formed a powerful element in the community. They seized Kuching suddenly, Rajah Brooke barely having time to escape from his "palace" by a back door and get away by swimming the river. The Malay and Dyak population remained loyal, so he won back his capital, but his home and all its contents had been destroyed.

Except for this incident, Sarawak had been a place where men could come to study the jungle. Alfred Wallace was the most notable, and he was lavish in praise of what the white rajah had accomplished, both for his people and for the visiting naturalist. After fifteen months in Sarawak, Wallace said it was a marvel that Sir James, a white man among foreigners, "rules over two conflicting races—a

American Museum of Natural History

Dyak blowing the sumpitan, a kind of blowgun which discharges arrows.

superior and an inferior—with their own consent, without any means of coercion, but depending solely upon them both for protection and support." He added that both were well on the way to regarding their white rajah as God. In the history of science, Sir James would have an honored place if only for the help he gave in furthering Wallace's work.

34

A Naturalist Trio

JUNGLES have held a special fascination for naturalists ever since they learned that the tropical rain forests have the richest, most varied plant and animal life on earth. Three English professionals of the last century illustrate this preoccupation. They are Henry Bates, Wallace's early partner; Richard Spruce, one of the greatest of botanists; and Thomas Belt, an engineer turned scientist. Bates and Spruce are famous for their work in the Amazon, Belt for his in Central America.

Spruce was born in 1817. The son of a Yorkshire schoolmaster who encouraged his early interest in botany, he had virtually no formal education. While still in his teens, he collected and listed plants he found on the moors. His father was unable to finance further study for him, so he reluctantly became a teacher of mathematics in a school in the city of York. Hating every minute of it, he devoted his spare time to reading and thinking about botany. He wrote a few articles which were published in scientific journals, but his real release came when, in his twenty-eighth year, the school closed and he was out of a job.

Some of his articles had been admired by members of the staff of the Royal Botanic Gardens at Kew, which had just been presented to the nation by the young Queen Victoria. When Spruce visited London after he lost his teaching post, Sir William Hooker, one of the staff at Kew, took a liking to him. So did George Bentham, nephew of the famous Jeremy, and between them they suggested to Spruce that he might try collecting for sale to museums and collectors. Bentham told Spruce that carefully preserved, accurately identified dried plants would have a ready sale, and that Spain would be a good place to start. Bentham also offered to act as the young man's agent, and advanced traveling expenses.

Two years of work, from 1844 to 1846, proved Bentham right and made the Yorkshireman's reputation as a botanist. He wrote a well-received book, *Notes on the Botany of the Pyrenees,* and both Hooker and Bentham urged him to try South America, which he already had begun to think of as a botanist's paradise. He prepared himself by long study at Kew, and then with Bentham's help lined up eleven collectors who agreed to purchase his specimens. Again Bentham advanced expenses, and Spruce sailed for Brazil in June 1849. Interestingly, one of his fellow passengers was Herbert Wallace, on his way to join his older brother, Alfred.

South America was Spruce's home for the next seventeen years, if the word "home" can be used to mean a wandering existence from Belém at the mouth of the Amazon to Guayaquil on the Pacific. Soon after his arrival, he met Wallace and Bates at what Spruce's account makes clear was a fine hilarious party in the home of an old Scots trader in Santarém. The host, Spruce says, received English newspapers in great bundles and was an avid reader of them, but with such a disregard of chronology that he confused Napoleon I with Napoleon III. During all his forty-five years in this river port, it had been his custom to pick a paper out of the pile at random, so by now it might be forty years old or more. With three eminent scientists at his table, plus all the other Englishmen in Santarém, he served his best brandy and port lavishly. From the first, Spruce and Wallace took to one another and their friendship was to last a lifetime. It was one of Spruce's most memorable evenings in Brazil.

But such interludes were rare for him. Mostly he lived and traveled alone, though he did make a few trips with Bates and, in the beginning, with a young English helper. Spruce was very tall, lean, blue-eyed, with a light brown beard and a natural courtesy which went over well in the Amazon. The few who passed him on the river never forgot the Yorkshire jigs he played on his bagpipes, sounds like none others heard in the jungle before or since.

More important, he brought to the collecting of jungle plants an orderliness and attention to detail which greatly enhanced the value of his work for his clients. In all, he sent back to England no fewer than thirty thousand different plants picked up and carefully preserved in the course of ten thousand miles of travel on South American rivers, mostly the Amazon and its tributaries. For each, he recorded the date and place where he found it, and the name by which it was known locally—before he was done he had accumulated sizable vocabularies in twenty-one different Indian languages. He also took great pains to note what properties the local people supposed a plant to have; he learned to respect their knowledge, and whenever possible he tried out the fruit or leaf or flower on himself.

Not far above Santarém, which was as much of a headquarters as Spruce permitted himself, the Trombetas joins the Amazon from the north. Spruce spent some time here and decided that this must be where Orellana's men had battled the Amazons. He carefully read what Carvajal claimed to have seen and the very similar report that Orellana had made on his return to Spain. Spruce put his own observations and research into an article—published after he died—in which he concluded that there was a good deal of substance to the Amazon story. He was not alone in this conclusion. A great many eighteenth-century missionaries had repeated it because Christianized Indians frequently mentioned in confession that they had gone off to be with "the women who live without men."

Spruce thought reasonably accurate the version of an old man who said no one could doubt that the Amazons had, and still, existed. This old man explained that after whites established their missions along the main stream, the women warriors withdrew from the neighborhood of the Trombetas to the basin of the Negro. There was no longer talk of their capturing lovers in battle; meetings were prearranged on a more amicable basis, and it was part of each man's story that when he was dismissed, he received a present of gold and a precious green stone. Europeans bought the green gems for talismans in the eighteenth century—they became quite well known as "Amazon stones"—and every Indian who sold one said he had gotten it as a gift from an Amazon. Spruce kept looking for the stones but never saw one. However, he was sure that "the women without men" did exist, even if they did not live in the magnificent cities of some of the legends.

Spruce was a keen observer of much more than botanical specimens. His journal was rich in notes about the way tall stories get started. One night he and another man went out over some treacherous ground to see if the main channel of the river was open. They cautiously approached the brink of a low cliff and looked over.

"And what saw we at the foot, creeping gently along, and apparently about to ascend? A troop of tigers! Involuntarily we each seized an arm of the other and fled with no tardy steps."

After he had run a little, he decided tigers were impossible; they must have seen herons. So they went back and looked again; the "tigers" were thick masses of scum gliding and twisting on the current. Spruce supposed it would be easy for less reasonable men to have started quite a story about big cats.

He was also still enough of a schoolteacher to try to enlarge the horizons of people he met, and good-humored enough to be amused by his failures. In his journal he says:

> I once took some pains to describe the ocean to a lot of Indians, telling them of the immense extent and almost fathomless depth—how long it took to cross it, and how it had the Old World on one side of it and the New World on the other. They listened eagerly, giving vent to occasional grunts of admiration, and I thought them intelligent. When I had done, a venerable Indian turned to the rest and said in a tone of wonder and awe, "It is the river of his land! What is this little river of ours" (pointing to the Amazon) "compared to *that!*"

Unfortunately for Spruce's fame, he did not publish very much during his lifetime. When he returned to England in 1866, his fellow botanists praised his collections to the skies. They all agreed that he had done more than any other man in their field to familiarize scientists with the vegetation of the Amazon. But the best they could get for him as a material reward was an annual pension of fifty pounds a year (then about $250). Because Spruce had lost his savings in the failure of a business firm, he lived, after a period of employment at Kew, until his death at seventy-three in a one-room cottage in Yorkshire. Years later, in 1908, his notes and letters, edited by his friend Wallace, were published, and they remain one of the most widely quoted of sources on the jungles.

Spruce's work in botany was closely paralleled by that of Bates in entomology. Jungles, as we have tried to stress, are a lush breeding ground for insects; Bates caught fourteen thousand different species, eight thousand of them previously unknown, in eleven years on the Amazon. An example of his powers of observation was his description of the recreation of army ants, which, until then, were believed to be always at work. He wrote:

> They seemed to have been all smitten with a sudden fit of laziness. Some were walking slowly about, others were brushing their antennae with their forefeet; but the drollest sight was their cleaning one another. Here and there an ant was seen stretching forth first one leg and then another, to be brushed or washed by one or more of its comrades, who performed the task by passing the limb between the jaws and the tongue, finishing by giving the antennae a friendly wipe . . . the conclusion that the ants were engaged merely in play was irresistible.

Similarly, he reported on leaf-carrying ants, and was first to learn that the ones called sauba do not use the bits of leaf as food but rather to thatch the domes over their subterranean dwellings which protect them from the rains. This was not true, for a few years later, Belt, another self-taught naturalist, found something that even Bates had missed.

Working in the Nicaraguan jungle, Belt completely excavated a big "formicarium," which Bates never had done, and discovered that the bits of leaf were made into a sort of compost in which the ants raised a fungus which was their principal food. The hill he dissected was at least twelve feet deep, more than two-thirds of it below ground, and was a maze of passages and chambers. In the lower ones, the fungus grew in spongy masses as big as a man's head. It was one of the mutually profitable arrangements sometimes found in jungles; apparently this special fungus can grow only in that particular kind of leaf mold, and the ants, Belt demonstrated, eat nothing but an exudation from this fungus.

Belt's *A Naturalist in Nicaragua,* published in 1874, was regarded for more than half a century as one of the half dozen most valuable

American Museum of Natural History

Henry Bates with curl-crested toucans.

works on the natural history of tropical America. To him the leaf-cutting ants, each with a little slice of green larger than itself, were "a mimic representation of a moving Birnam wood." He watched hummingbirds long and closely enough to tell that while they did suck honey from flowers, their principal food was insects. He dissected enough of them to prove it, and then elaborated a theory that their long bills were "a delicate, pliable pair of forceps, most admirably adapted for picking out minute insects from amongst the stamens of flowers."

Bates and Belt were among the early accurate chroniclers of that most implacable, almost invincible creature, the army ant. Bates found ten different species in the Amazon, eight of them previously unknown, varying in size and in their manner of foraging—some in thin columns, some in massive phalanxes several feet wide. All, however, were meat eaters, and no creature in the jungle disputed their right of way. Larger animals ran or flew away. Although Bates said he never found a human home into which they had moved, he heard that when this happened, the occupants left cheerfully, knowing that when the ants had passed, there wouldn't be a single cockroach, mouse, lizard, snake, centipede or other vermin left.

Belt reported that the army ants displayed a "sympathetic help such as man only among the higher mammalia shows." He tested this quality by covering one of the ants with a bit of stone or encasing it in moistened clay. The first ant to come along promptly summoned help. A whole gang would come running and push at the stone or bite out pieces of the clay until they had released the prisoner.

"The excitement and ardour with which they carried on their unflagging exertions for the rescue of their comrade would not have been greater if they had been human beings," he wrote.

The excitement and ardor with which the new breed of naturalists represented by Spruce, Bates and Belt carried on their meticulous observations were their new, unique contribution to science. They were willing to devote themselves entirely to a specialty, and their single-mindedness resulted in achievements that could not otherwise have been recorded. Yet there was still a place, and a great place, too, for still another breed of "explorer."

35

A Knightly Trio

A BUSINESSMAN, a writer-traveler and a painter would not offhand seem to have much in common, and in many ways Sir Stamford Raffles, Sir Richard Burton and Sir Harry Johnston were as different as three Englishmen could be. One is remembered chiefly as the founder of Singapore, one as translator of *The Arabian Nights,* one as Special Commissioner of the Protectorate of Uganda. Yet they were alike on two counts. By the exercise of extremely diverse talents, they helped us to know more about jungles, and all three served the British in official posts abroad.

Raffles, the eldest, born in 1781, was the earnest, industrious son of a Micawberish shipmaster whose most brilliant achievement was to get the lad a job as office boy in the London headquarters of the East India Company. Raffles was fourteen years old then, a notably hard worker with an odd taste for reading natural history after his long day's work. A junior clerk at nineteen, he was appointed at twenty-three assistant secretary to the company's office in Penang on the Malay Peninsula—Singapore was an unregarded island then.

Unlike the average Englishman on this sort of foreign duty, Raffles became fascinated by the language, customs and history of the native peoples. He ventured into the countryside, even into the jungle, and began collecting plant and animal specimens. (He had the instincts of a naturalist to such a degree that in later years he was one of the leading organizers and first president of the Zoological Society of London.) For all these outside interests, he was so devoted to his work that, although without influence, he earned several promotions. In 1811 he drew up the plan by which England seized Java, the island then being under French control because Napoleon's brother had just been made king of Holland. Raffles governed the

Sir Thos. Stamford Raffles, Knt. F.R.S. & A.S.

Lieut.-Governor of Bencoolen, &c.

Culver

place with great success until Java was restored to the Dutch after the wars, and then he was rewarded with the post of governor of Benkoelen on Sumatra, where the British maintained control for a number of years.

On Sumatra, Raffles was able to indulge his taste for jungle exploration and collecting. He traveled in comfort, too, especially when his wife was a member of the party, proving how easily one could pass through these forests. On such occasions, fifty porters carried the camping equipment, food and drink. Raffles made careful drawings of what he saw, pressed flowers and leaves in paper, preserved or skinned animals. His specimens and letters to such eminent gentlemen as Sir Joseph Banks led him to be referred to as "one of the first authorities on matters scientific, historical or philological." His botanical interest is commemorated in the scientific name of one of the gaudiest jungle flowers known, a parasitic plant which the local citizens called the devil's betel box—islanders carried betel in highly ornamental little containers, much as Europeans of that age carried snuff and some now carry pills.

Raffles and his health officer, a Dr. Arnold, who shared his chief's scientific interests, were the first to describe the devil's betel box for civilized savants. A full-blown flower may be three feet across, weigh fifteen pounds and have a six-quart capacity inside huge petals half an inch thick. Even the unopened bud is a foot in diameter. The full flower, much too big to be preserved in the supply of alcohol Raffles had with him, was purple and yellow and red. It was the most ostentatious of Sir Stamford's finds, and its scientific name is *Rafflesia arnoldi*. He was also the discoverer of one of the insectivorous pitcher plants which has become popular in America, *Nepenthes rafflesiana*.

The true value of the Raffles collection and drawings will never be known. Like Wallace's first, they were lost in a ship's fire at sea while Sir Stamford and his wife were returning to England in 1824. Eighteen months after he got back to London, he died of a stroke on his forty-fifth birthday, July 5, 1826.

At about that time, growing up in a well-to-do English family that was wandering about Europe in search of health for the ailing head of the house, a precocious child was developing a taste for travel and adventure. Richard Burton was only five years old, but already remarkable for his ability to learn what pleased him and to resist any subject that did not. This characteristic stayed with him through a brief career at Oxford, where he was frustrated in his desire to study Arabic, and from which he succeeded in getting himself dismissed by attending a forbidden horse race. At this point his father permitted him to join the Indian Army, and the career of the century's greatest traveler was launched.

In the East, besides seeing all those places where the word *djanghael* was being pronounced jungle, the young officer became so proficient in native languages that within five years he was able to pass for one of the local people. This facility led to a journey as a Mohammedan pilgrim to Mecca and Medina, from which he returned with information that enabled the Royal Geographical Society to fill in some large blank spots on the map of Arabia.

An exploit in 1853 when he was thirty-two years old, and the book he wrote about it, made him famous in England and led to the travel that linked him to the jungles. This was an expedition to discover the sources of the Nile. For all its fame in history, the Nile was still an enigma to European scholars. One of the great unanswered questions of the age was where the water came from. A popular opinion was that the river flowed from a huge lake; some maps represented the lake as very like the Caspian Sea. Financed by the Royal Geographical Society, Burton was invited to find out, taking as second in command Captain John Speke, a man of some experience and a skilled map maker.

In nearly three years, 1856–59, the two accomplished a considerable part of their mission. Together they discovered Lake Tanganyika and disproved the existence of a single large inland sea. Speke went on alone, while Burton was convalescing and writing up notes, to discover one of the sources of the Nile, Lake Victoria. He also thought he had seen the legendary Mountains of the Moon, but he placed them overhanging the northern end of Lake Tanganyika.

By the time they got home, the two explorers were bitter enemies. Speke was sure he had discovered the sole source of the Nile. Burton was not sure he had discovered anything except a large body of

Bettmann Archive

Richard Francis Burton.

water. When Speke went ahead to London to announce his find and be acclaimed a hero while Burton was delayed by fever at Aden, the breach was complete. Each sneered at the other, and each had some advantages. Speke made better maps, but Burton turned a better phrase. Refusing to allow his lieutenant any claim to new discoveries, he quipped, after Speke drew his fabulous mountains where none were to be found:

"Probably his Sources of the Nile grew in his mind as his Mountains of the Moon had grown under his hand."

Actually there was plenty of credit for both. Speke went back in

1862 and proved that the Victoria Nile does flow out of the lake. Burton was credited by many with opening the way for such men as Livingstone and Stanley.

Sir Harry Johnston is listed in our catalogue of eminent jungle figures for the faithfulness with which he represented both the clear-sightedness of modern naturalists and the "old school tie" tradition of the Victorian gentry, who took the manners and customs of the London élite society to the outermost corners of Empire. He belongs in both worlds, for he was born in 1858 and made his career in Africa during the reign of Victoria.

Johnston went to "the dark continent" on a shooting trip in 1882 and stayed simply because he wanted to paint pictures and see the country, not explore for new routes or opportunities for trade. He met the great Stanley, who invited him to paint his way several hundred miles up the Congo. On this trip he saw his first patches of jungle and learned how much cooler and easier to live in they were than the savannah or orchard bush country. A couple of years later he was selected to head a naturalist expedition sent by three learned societies to East Africa. As a result of this venture, he obtained a post of vice consul in the Cameroons and the friendship of the aging Sir Richard Burton.

Johnston's advancement from an obscure post in the Cameroons to administrator of Uganda was a part of the keen late nineteenth-century British interest in Africa, which has been compared to the preoccupation of Spanish conquistadores with America. In all his posts, he was an avid collector and explorer, from the higher slopes of Mount Kilimanjaro to the Congo jungle. Several plant species he discovered bear his name, *johnstoni*. He collected animals for the London Zoo, and his home, a thatched bungalow without any glass in the windows, had its own zoological garden where he kept monkeys, cats, snakes, baby elephants, chimpanzees, eagles, and zebras. He accepted animals in lieu of taxes. He used to allow one of the baby elephants into the drawing room for tea, where it behaved well, drinking milk from its own bottle and helping itself to jam sandwiches from the plate. The commissioner took some of his pets along on his exploring expeditions, so that his brother, who was also secre-

Culver

Sir Harry Johnston.

tary and zoo keeper, thought they resembled a traveling circus. Writing of their last major trip into the jungle, the brother wrote:

> Harry was inexorable on his traveling staff appearing in full evening dress [at dinner] . . . Conversation and cards were then encouraged by the campfire, the smoke of which somewhat mitigated the swarms of night-flying insects, whose object in life seemed to be to commit suicide in the soup. . . . The Press was quick to appreciate the meaning of Harry's table in the wilderness, realizing that when white men abandon the symbols of civilization in the tropics they tend to lose its substantial and spiritual gains.

While Johnston was an Englishman of legend who dressed for dinner in the tropics, he was one administrator who thought administration should be as much for the benefit of the native peoples as for their masters. He had his own quaint ways of expressing belief in racial equality; he required his staff to wear canary yellow waistcoats with their black and white evening dress to symbolize the black, white and yellow races. But he made genuinely humanitarian gestures, too. On this particular journey, Johnston rescued a band of Bambuti Pygmies from a German who had kidnapped them for display at the Paris exhibition. Returning them to their home in the rain forest was rewarding, for it enabled him to complete his most important jungle quest.

For years, Sir Harry had been one of the few Europeans who believed in what was called the African unicorn. While he did not think it was exactly the one-horned beast of mythology, he did suggest that the jungle might harbor a horned animal something like a horse. Only the Pygmies had ever seen it; they described it as a striped creature like a zebra and they called it *okapi*. Even on this trip, Johnson was frustrated. His Negro escort was so terrified of the jungle that as the party advanced through the damp gloom, the men kept blowing their bugles to scare away evil spirits. They certainly scared any game, but the Pygmies were so grateful to him for getting them back home to their jungle that they later sent him a complete okapi skin and two skulls. He was, therefore, able to describe

American Museum of Natural History

Okapi.

and identify the animal as the short-necked giraffe which, ten years later, finally was seen by white men.

At the end of his life, Johnston emulated his friend, Burton, by becoming a best-selling author, but his most popular works were novels, of which *The Gay-Dombeys* is still remembered. His career in Africa, which ended in 1901, was an important part of a century of progress in jungle science.

36
A French Trio

ENGLISHMEN and Americans often have a hard time understanding why the language of so many new African nations in the Congo basin is French. The travels of Britishers who wrote books obscured for their countrymen and the Americans who read them the fact that exploration was far from a British monopoly and that colonization in the vast Congo region was even less so.

One of the Frenchmen who played a role in all this compounded the confusion by getting naturalized in the United States and writing his books in English. He was Paul du Chaillu, born about 1831, perhaps in Paris but possibly in West Africa. Certainly he spent his boyhood in the Gabun, where his father was an agent for French commercial interests, and there began to be consumed with a desire to know more about the country and the animals back of the coastal towns. Paul was sent to a Jesuit school and seems to have encountered teachers who fostered his interest in the natural sciences.

Receiving little encouragement for mad adventures from his family, he crossed the Atlantic when he was about twenty-one and found the Philadelphia Academy receptive to his ideas. The learned members of this society undertook to finance a four-year expedition by the persuasive young Frenchman, so that he was able to cover some eight thousand miles of inland territory between 1855 and the end of 1859. He discovered exactly which rivers between the mouths of the Congo and the Niger were coastal and which ran inland. From the interior he brought back some important zoological specimens, including a number of small mammals and birds that were previously unknown. But the most exciting was the first gorilla ever seen in America.

Royal Geographical Society

Paul du Chaillu.

His book, *Explorations and Adventures in Equatorial Africa,* was published in 1861 and upset a great many cherished ideas about the nature of the lands through which he had traveled. He was ridiculed as a believer in native fairy tales about cannibals and big apes, and denounced as an ignorant faker for saying a lot of things which turned out to be true. Forty years later the most enterprising of women travelers in the same region, Mary Kingsley, refrained from repeating her own adventures, similar to those of Du Chaillu, because he had been so fiercely attacked for recounting his.

Some of the most venomous sarcasm centered on Du Chaillu's stories about Pygmies. They lived, he said, in the forests of the Ogooué River basin not far from Lambaréné, famous a century later as the home of Dr. Albert Schweitzer. Pretty well authenticated reports of these little people had been cropping up for a couple of hundred years or more, ever since Andrew Battel, an English sailor kept prisoner for eighteen years by the Portuguese when they held their monopoly of African trade, published an account of them in 1625. Yet scholars were skeptical, even after Du Chaillu went back in 1862 and proved his tale. During the rest of his life—he died in 1903—he wrote and lectured on equatorial Africa, and more popular with audiences than many of his critics, he added to the sketchy knowledge Americans had about Africa.

Meanwhile much of what he had written in the 1860's was confirmed, especially by a naturalized Frenchman named Pierre Paul de Brazza in the 1880's. Miss Kingsley, who followed in the footsteps of many African explorers a few years later, thought that De Brazza was the greatest of them all. Certainly he was responsible for the fact that a great deal of the Congo became French. It was he who made it possible for those who came after him to explore and explain the jungles.

De Brazza was born in Italy in 1852 but was naturalized in France. He joined the navy, and in 1875 when his ship was off the Gabun, he got leave to do some exploring up the Ogooué. In so doing, he located two other streams, the *Alima* and the *Likona,* which he realized were tributaries of the Congo. He brought back from this trip some Pygmy skulls which remained on exhibition in Paris for many

American Museum of Natural History

Hunter killed by gorilla, as depicted by du Chaillu.

years. He also succeeded in diverting some of the official French ambitions from the Niger to the Congo.

In 1880 the government commissioned him to explore the region further with a view to establishing a French claim to the territory. On this trip he laid the basis for what became known as the French Congo. Recruiting a group of Gabun natives, he proceeded up the Ogooué and then crossed over to the Congo well above the Stanley Pool. Following the north bank of the big river toward its mouth, he made treaties with as many local chiefs as he could, including the paramount "king" of a very large area inhabited by the people known as *Bateke*. These documents placed vast, but of course not precisely defined, territories under the protection of France. Early in November, De Brazza had passed the Stanley Pool, pausing at a village there called Ntambo by its citizens. A few days later he heard that a party of Belgians was building a road around the cataracts below. He scribbled his name on a bit of paper and sent it to the leader of the road builders, who turned out to be the Congo's first navigator, Stanley. Stanley entertained De Brazza's party for two days and then helped him on his way down the river without *either* one learning exactly what the other was doing in signing up tribesmen for France or Belgium.

In 1883 the French government commissioned De Brazza to establish a colony, and he selected for its headquarters the village of Ntambo, which he purchased and which came to be the city of Brazzaville. Within three years, the French Congo was important enough to rate a commissioner general as its ruler, and De Brazza was appointed. He remained at this post until 1897, carrying on systematic explorations of the territory, which was mapped as French Equatorial Africa with the thoroughness Miss Kingsley so admired. His administration made it possible for men of the twentieth century to carry on genuinely scientific investigations in the jungles with a reasonable degree of security. De Brazza himself, after seven years of retirement in France, returned to the Congo to look into serious charges of cruelty to natives. He died in Dakar on the way home on September 14, 1905, without having had a chance to make his report.

Our third Frenchman is one of the many great scientists and scholars who have furthered our knowledge of jungles without ever having seen one. Theirs, of course, have been adventures of the mind, but they have sometimes been as exciting and certainly as important as those of the men who fought their way through terrible dangers and hardships. Jean Louis Armand Quatrefages de Bréau, Professor of Anthropology at the Museum of Natural History in Paris, made his contribution by the study of what other men wrote or drew, by the careful analysis and interpretation of specimens others had collected. In his early manhood—he was born in 1810—he specialized in marine biology, but later he became one of the leading anthropologists and ethnologists of his day. He published in his eighty-two years nearly 150 important books and scientific papers.

In the very early 1860's, just about the time Du Chaillu's book was being ridiculed, Quatrefages began to interest himself in what he called "the small black races." He read the works of others, pored over pictures, measured skulls, examined artifacts and relics, and finally decided that he should "gather and unite these materials in a book which should present a sort of monograph of this human type, very curious for more than one reason." *Les Pygmées* was published in 1887, and since that date it has hardly been possible for even the most stubborn pundit to doubt the existence of Oriental Pygmies.

Quatrefages also marshaled the evidence to indicate that the Negritos had been very much more widely spread over the islands and the mainland, although "today almost everywhere scattered, separated, and often hunted by races larger and stronger." He noted, too, that "one finds the little blacks located in the least favorable localities of the country where they live." He meant the jungles, and his remark is more the cultured European's thought than the Negrito's opinion. But he did realize that being hard to find was what preserved them in the Philippines, the Malay Peninsula and the Andaman Islands. Elsewhere, he deduced, they had been exterminated by "the murderous instincts" of the Malays and other big people.

The book assembled an impressive body of facts about the customs and behavior of the Negritos. The reputation of the Andamanese for killing shipwrecked strangers was set forth, along with the explanation that for centuries the only outsiders they had contact with had been Chinese and Malay slavers. He believed the islanders to be more primitive than Negritos in the Philippines. He thought the latter were hunters and gatherers only because they were afraid to stay in one place long enough to plant bananas or yams, while the Andamanese didn't know how. No one as yet had realized how secure from their enemies these little people were in the true jungle. Because his theory really did not explain why the Andamanese failed to till the soil, he wrote:

> Living upon the shores of a sea filled with fishes, close to great forests where boars run at large, and which furnish them besides honey and fruits, they have not felt the necessity of wringing by labor from the soil a supplement to their food supply; and this very luxuriance of food, perhaps, has been of influence in keeping them at the lowest point in the social scale.

The writer did understand, as many of his generation did not, that simplicity of apparel and shelter does not necessarily imply cultural inferiority. He commented that in the tropics "clothing is more often inconvenient than useful." And, while Negrito huts were flimsy by temperate zone housing standards, they had advantages which many Frenchmen eighty years ago could well envy. Citing a traveler's description of one jungle dwelling, Quatrefages added:

> It is certainly anything but luxurious; yet it presented this peculiarity—a flooring two feet above the ground. Most peasant houses *here* have only bare earth for floor. The poor savage has been able to place himself in better hygienic conditions than the European.

At the time Quatrefages was writing, no outsider trained to scientific observation had studied the Pygmies at home, much less lived with them there. The accuracy of his account, therefore, is amazing. His was the type of cool, observant intellect upon which true knowledge of the forest and its components depends.

37

Livingstone and Stanley

ONE of the most famous confrontations in history has been kept fresh in the minds of men for nearly a hundred years because of Henry M. Stanley's oddly stilted greeting of Dr. David Livingstone near Lake Tanganyika. But few who have repeated it ever read it in the context of what Stanley actually wrote. He was so excited, he says, that he wanted to turn a somersault, bite his hand, slash at a tree. And he goes on:

> I would have run to him, only I was a coward in the presence of such a mob—would have embraced him, only, he being an Englishman, I did not know how he would receive me; so I did what moral cowardice and false pride suggested was the best thing—walked deliberately to him, took off my hat and said:
>
> "Dr. Livingstone, I presume?"
>
> "Yes," said he, with a kind smile, lifting his cap slightly.

It was a meeting of opposites, and yet Livingstone and Stanley had two things in common. They had been born on the same island, Livingstone in Scotland, Stanley in Wales. They had been miserably poor as children, Livingstone working in a textile mill in 1823 at the age of ten, Stanley an illegitimate workhouse brat who ran away at fifteen in 1856 after kicking back at a brutually sadistic schoolmaster.

Livingstone had worked, read, studied and at last become a Presbyterian medical missionary in South Africa. By the time he was fifty he had gone beyond setting up remote missions and was opening roads into the unknown interior of the southern half of the continent so that other less hardy souls could follow and establish more missions. He had mapped a good deal of that part of Africa, discovered

American Museum of Natural Histor[y]

Manyuema hunters, from sketch by Livingstone.

and explored the Zambezi River, written some cogent books and articles condemning the slave trade.

The combination of his zeal and experience led the Royal Geographical Society to commission him to clarify the nature of the country between Lakes Tanganyika and Nyasa, hinted at by Burton and Speke. Livingstone left England in midsummer, 1865, on this mission, and eighteen months later some of his porters reached Zanzibar with word that he was dead. His friends doubted the report, and they were proved right when letters trickled out from Livingstone dated as late as July 1868. Then a long silence.

It was supposed that these communications indicated he was on his way home, so the eccentric James Gordon Bennett of the *New York Herald* ordered one of his star reporters to Aden to intercept the missionary-explorer and get his story before all the world heard it. The reporter was Stanley, aged twenty-seven, who had enough experience already behind him for a couple of novels. After escaping from the workhouse, he had held a number of unsavory jobs, signed on as a cabin boy to America and jumped ship in New Orleans, been befriended by a prosperous businessman whose name he took—he had been christened John Rowlands, after his supposed father—and finally turned journalist after deserting from the armed services of both the Confederacy and the Union during the Civil War. Stanley spent his twenty-eighth birthday in Aden, waiting for Livingstone, and then moved on to other assignments.

He was covering a civil war in Spain in the autumn of 1869 when the younger James Gordon Bennett summoned him to Paris and reassigned him to the Livingstone story. Was he alive or dead, and where? Bennett sent Stanley off with a phrase that became famous in journalism, "Find Livingstone." He also had told the reporter to cover quite a list of other stories first—the opening of the Suez Canal, happenings on the Upper and Lower Nile, Jerusalem, Constantinople, the Crimea, Persia, India and finally the Euphrates Valley Railroad. Only then was he to go after Livingstone. Stanley got his orders in Paris on October 27, 1869; he reached Zanzibar, the outfitting place for expeditions to East or Central Africa, on January 6, 1871. No one had heard from Livingstone yet.

Four months and a thousand miles later the "rescue" expedition came to the missionary at Ujiji on the eastern side of Lake Tanganyika. When he saw the venerable doctor, gray-bearded, in tweed trousers and a red-sleeved waistcoat and looking only a little pale, Stanley wondered if he needed or wanted rescuing. It turned out he desired only more supplies, which Stanley arranged to send him, and to have a box of his papers taken to England. Stanley and Livingstone traveled together for four months, after which the missionary continued his explorations until he died in the field on May 1, 1873. His body was returned to England for burial in Westminster Abbey.

Stanley, acclaimed as a hero, was also reviled as a faker in London and criticized as a bad lecturer when he took to the plaform. He was not a nice man in many ways—tactless, arrogant, touchy, ungenerous, unforgiving and greedy for fame and fortune. Yet when he heard of Livingstone's death, the only man he ever seems to have got along with, he wrote in his notebook:

"May I be selected to succeed him in opening up Africa to the light of Christianity! My methods, however, will not be Livingstone's."

The note, meant for no other eyes but his own, was doubtless sincere. Immediately after Livingstone's funeral, Stanley arranged with the *London Daily Telegraph* and the *New York Herald* "to solve, if possible, the remaining problems of the geography of Central Africa; and to investigate and report upon the haunts of the slave traders," as the *Daily Telegraph* announced it.

The expedition of more than 350, thirty-six of them women, left Zanzibar in November 1874 with unusually complete equipment, including a forty-foot portable boat in five sections called the *Lady Alice*. Three young Englishmen—Edward and Francis Pocock, who knew a lot about small craft, and Frederick Barker, a hotel clerk—were the other white members of the party, but Edward Pocock and Barker died of fever fairly early.

In the next two years, Stanley circumnavigated Lakes Victoria and Tanganyika, never done before, making the first fairly accurate maps of them, and explored part of Uganda. Tracing the course of the Lualaba River was his main object because Livingstone had begun it. Both had believed the river flowed north into the Nile, but all anyone knew was that it was broad, mysterious, heavily forested and disappeared into a land inhabited by cannibals.

The Lualaba, originating far to the south, had been traveled by Livingstone as far as Nyangwe, almost the dead center of the continent between the Atlantic and Indian Oceans, some four degrees south of the equator. Livingstone had never been able to get anyone to go with him further north. Even the most daring and violent slave trader of the age, Tippoo Tip, who lived at Nyangwe, dared not try. Tippoo Tip, an Arab, had by might and guile built up a great fortune and immense power in Central Africa. He allied himself with one Negro tribe after another, offering to help it conquer its enemies. The surviving enemies became his slaves. He looted their ivory, and then turned on the victors and treated them the same way. As a result he obtained quantities of both "black gold" and "white gold" at no greater cost than ammunition for his men's muskets, so his profits were enormous.

When he heard that Stanley was determined to head north, Tippoo Tip agreed to accompany him with seven or eight hundred

American Museum of Natural History

Dr. Livingstone's last mile.

of his own people for sixty days at a fee of five thousand dollars. They started on November 5, 1876. Within two weeks, they found the trees of the jungle too close together for the men carrying the sections of the *Lady Alice,* so Stanley launched her on the river and went aboard while the rest continued to travel by land.

For the first few days they had passed only deserted villages; their people fled at the approach of white men and Tippoo Tip, leaving behind fresh skulls and gnawed human bones as proof of their cannibalism. Toward the end of the month the expedition was frontally attacked. Then, for a month, it marched and fought. Christmas was spent about halfway between Nyangwe and the series of seven cataracts, now called Stanley Falls, which mark the beginning of the Congo proper. Smallpox broke out, killing forty-five and incapacitating many more, who were sent back with Tippoo Tip's forces just before the first of the year. Then, embarked on the *Lady Alice* and a flotilla of captured native dugout canoes, Stanley, Frank Pocock and 200-odd surviving Zanzibaris continued the voyage alone.

Stanley's narrative, written from notes meticulously kept all through his travels, is our only source of information about this period. He was amazed by the almost uniform hostility of every native people he encountered in this part of Africa. He thought it was because they regarded him and his party as merely meat on the hoof. (His story helped create the general opinion in England and the United States that all Africans were cannibals.) By February 1877, when he reached the land of the relatively advanced Basoko tribesmen, who made elaborately carved ivory idols and had iron tools and ornate wooden masks, he had been in twenty-eight battles, losing thirty-three men killed. Nearly all had been wounded except Stanley, who thought he bore a charmed life. The Basoko put up one of the hardest fights, and the account of it is a good example of the explorer's style. He tells how he anchored his flotilla in the broad river to receive the attack of a fleet of native canoes. Then:

> There are fifty-four of them! A monster canoe leads the way, with two rows of upstanding paddles, forty men on a side, their bodies bending in unison as with a swelling barbarous chorus they drive her down toward us. In the bow, standing on what appears to be a platform, are ten prime young warriors, their heads gay with feathers of the parrot, crimson and grey; at the stern, eight men, with long paddles, whose tops are decorated with ivory balls, guide the monster vessel; and dancing up and down from stem to stern are ten men who appear to be chiefs. All the paddles are headed with ivory balls, every head bears a feathered crown, every arm shows gleaming white ivory armlets. From the bow of the canoe streams a thick fringe of the long white fibre of the Hyphene palm. The crashing sound of large drums, a hundred blasts from ivory horns, and a thrilling chant from two thousand human throats, do not tend to soothe our nerves or to increase our confidence.

The expedition's guns, forty-eight of them at this stage, gave an ample margin of victory in this as in all their other pitched battles. Stanley found that the cataracts were more trouble, for it had taken a month to work around Stanley Falls.

By the time of his fight with the Basoko, he had realized that this river was not the Nile because he was too far west, but he was not sure whether it was the Congo or the Niger. A few days more and the course trended a little south as well as west, and for the first time they met people who were willing to sell them food instead of regarding them as food. After Stanley Falls, their progress was rapid, so that only a few days after meeting friendly tribes, they were fighting new enemies, armed with old Portuguese muskets although they never had seen white men. Fortunately the natives had only bits of wire and iron to put in the weapons, and the voyagers were reasonably safe behind their shields and bulwarks if they did not let the warriors get too close. Stanley recorded the last engagement, his thirty-second, on March 9, and on the twelfth the *Lady Alice* floated into what looked like a lake, Stanley Pool. The explorer wrote in his notebook that he had covered 1,235 miles from Nyangwe in a little more than four months, an average of almost ten miles a day.

They made no such fast time thereafter. Below Stanley Pool is the famous series of cataracts where the second biggest river in the world, the Congo, plunges through narrow gorges, which Stanley named Livingstone Falls. The first thirty-four miles took them thirty-seven days, and then they had to go even slower. The *Lady Alice,* the canoes and all the supplies had to be coaxed through slower shallow water near shore or hauled over portages by a painfully reduced crew, fewer than a hundred able-bodied men by now. Eight were lost when one canoe was swept over the falls, and Frank Pocock was killed attempting to shoot the rapids. Lack of food—the local people had little more than they needed—weakened both healthy and sick, so at last on July 30 Stanley decided to abandon the river and head overland for the sea; he knew now he must be close to it. Getting from Stanley Pool to the latest cataract had taken longer than all the rest of the trip from Nyangwe. Ironically this one, Isangila Falls, marked almost the end of the dangerous water.

Leaving the *Lady Alice* high and dry, they started to walk. Stanley found he was in "civilization" now. Rum had been introduced to the local citizens and become the currency of trade. They would not give food in exchange for his remnants of wire and cloth, but on August 4 he persuaded a reluctant chief to send a messenger to the nearest European settlement with a letter. His men were so hungry and desperate that, he wrote in English, French and Spanish: "The supplies must arrive within two days or I may have a fearful time of it among the dying." A line of porters reached him in just two days, bearing food and rum to finance him the rest of the way.

Culve

Stanley's escape from wounded elephant.

In only a few more days, the navigation of the Congo was complete. The party numbered eighty-nine, of whom seven died within the week. Twelve of the survivors were women and six were children born en route.

Stanley's exploit did more than make him a hero again. His report of the easy navigation of the Congo from Stanley Falls to Stanley Pool, his notes on its tributaries and people and possibilities, all set forth in two volumes called *Through the Dark Continent,* inspired great commercial and political activity. Stanley himself went back as agent (in effect) for King Leopold of the Belgians, and in five and a half years he laid the foundations for that monarch's private empire later known as the Belgian Congo. Although not the sole author of the European rush to exploit equatorial Africa, as he and some of his biographers have thought, Stanley certainly was a leader in that development. In 1877 only a fifth of the continent was claimed by European nations. When he died in 1904, virtually every bit of it was under the sovereignty, suzerainty or "special sphere of influence" of one or another of them.

Stanley had been very much the European of his day in hating jungles. He traversed part of the vast Ituri Forest three times, and called it a "region of horrors." He "found it difficult to accustom myself to its gloom and its pallid solitude. I could find no comfort for the inner man or solace for the spirit." The Pygmies shot poisoned darts at his men, but he impressed the rare ones he could catch to serve as guides. One of his biographers summed up his view of them as "living out their lives in terror, pain, and dark superstition. Dying they leave behind no monument, no progress, no history, no hope. Pygmies, the ugly and diminutive Negrillos, here live out their secluded, furtive lives."

It is hard to believe these are the same people of whom Colin Turnbull wrote. But obviously Stanley, overdressed and miserable, was transferring his own superstitions and disgusts to the little people of the forest. Marching through the jungle with tons of equipment and scores of unhappy men is not the way to see it. Also, it must be remembered that he was writing for an audience that would have been disappointed by anything pleasant found in a tropical forest.

38

Scientific Progression

EXPLORERS always had an exciting tale to tell the public when they came home from the jungles. Scientists, too, have had exciting tales, but usually they excited only other scientists. Their accounts of tracking down some elusive species of fungus or insect, or the evidence of why plants and animals are found where they are, never had quite the drama of Orellana among the Amazons or Stanley relieving Livingstone. But let us look briefly at the achievements of a few, remembering that many more have done equally important work.

The brothers Schomburgk, for instance, have no rivers or mountains named for them. Yet they gave men who studied the vegetation and the animals an understanding of the jungles of British Guiana that has been acknowledged in dozens of technical works. They were born in Prussia, Robert in 1804, Richard in 1811. The elder took the lead in natural sciences. In 1835 he was asked by the Royal Geographical Society of London to undertake an exploration of British Guiana and make a botanical survey at the same time. He was so successful that the British government commissioned him to determine the colony's boundary with Venezuela. This time he took his younger brother along, but they worked quite independently of each other, carrying out the best scientific studies of Guiana jungles made up to that time.

Robert not only defined the boundary—it used to be called the Schomburgk Line—but made extensive notes on the vegetation of the frontier area. Furthermore, he was a very tactful man. One of his finds was an especially gorgeous lily. He brought specimens back to London in the early years of the young queen's reign and named it *Victoria regia*. One is not surprised to learn that he was knighted for his services to science and diplomacy.

American Museum of Natural History

View of Guiana village visited by Robert Schomburgk.

Richard Schomburgk traveled over even more of the country, up and down rivers mostly, but also across mountains and through the jungles. He seems to have been an even keener observer than Robert, but he wrote in his native language and his *Reisen in Britisch Guiana* was little known outside Germany. He had the patronage of Humboldt, and was acclaimed in zoological circles for his descriptions of a good many animals previously unknown or very sketchily identified. One of his admirers has said he wrote in more or less detail about every mammal, bird and reptile, and fish in British Guiana, which is a perhaps pardonable exaggeration. He ended his career in Australia, where he lived for more than forty years, most of them as director of the Botanical Gardens in Adelaide. Sir Robert held several British consular posts which enabled him to continue his botanical work until his death in 1865.

Another German botanist, Georg August Schweinfurth, sent to explore jungles by the Humboldt Institute in 1863, published the first authoritative accounts of African Pygmies. He made his most serious study of them on a trip which took him into their forests for two years, from 1868 to 1870, and he described it all in *The Heart of Africa.* He had been fascinated in North Africa by stories of dwarfs living far to the south who had beards down to their knees. They sounded to him like the fairy tale dwarfs of the Baltic regions, where Schweinfurth had been born in 1836, and he believed them to be just as imaginary. But as he traveled south, he met men "who averred that with their own eyes they had seen this people of immortal myth." He was inclined to believe that there was only an occasional midget as occurs in Europe, but at last in the Congo he saw them himself. His account of them is marred by the fact that he never observed them in their own homes, only when they came out of the forest to trade meat to the Negroes for beer, wine and meal. They never told him where their huts were, much less took him there, so he was not aware either of their skill in building nor of their full prowess as jungle hunters.

A Swiss scientist also had a prominent share in recording the vegetational complex of the jungles. He was J. F. Dieffenbach, and his name has been given to one of the common tropical plants grown in temperate zone houses, *Dieffenbachia.*

Almost as well known is William H. Hudson, the native of Argentina who wrote the poetic prose of *Green Mansions.* Born in 1841 to parents who had gone to South America from Massachusetts, he moved to England when he was twenty-seven years old, and never went back to South America, although he lived to be eighty-one. As a naturalist, he is best known for his work on the birds of the pampas, the great plains far south of the jungles; but, he wandered about in the rain forests enough to put the impossible story of his famous novel in a realistic setting. And in that novel, a great many English-speaking readers have found their only accurate information about jungles. Yet, his finest work *Far Away and Long Ago,* was written in his old age.

A man from whom scholars have learned more, perhaps, than any other traveler was Andreas F. W. Schimper, who in the closing years of the nineteenth century went beyond Wallace in pointing the way

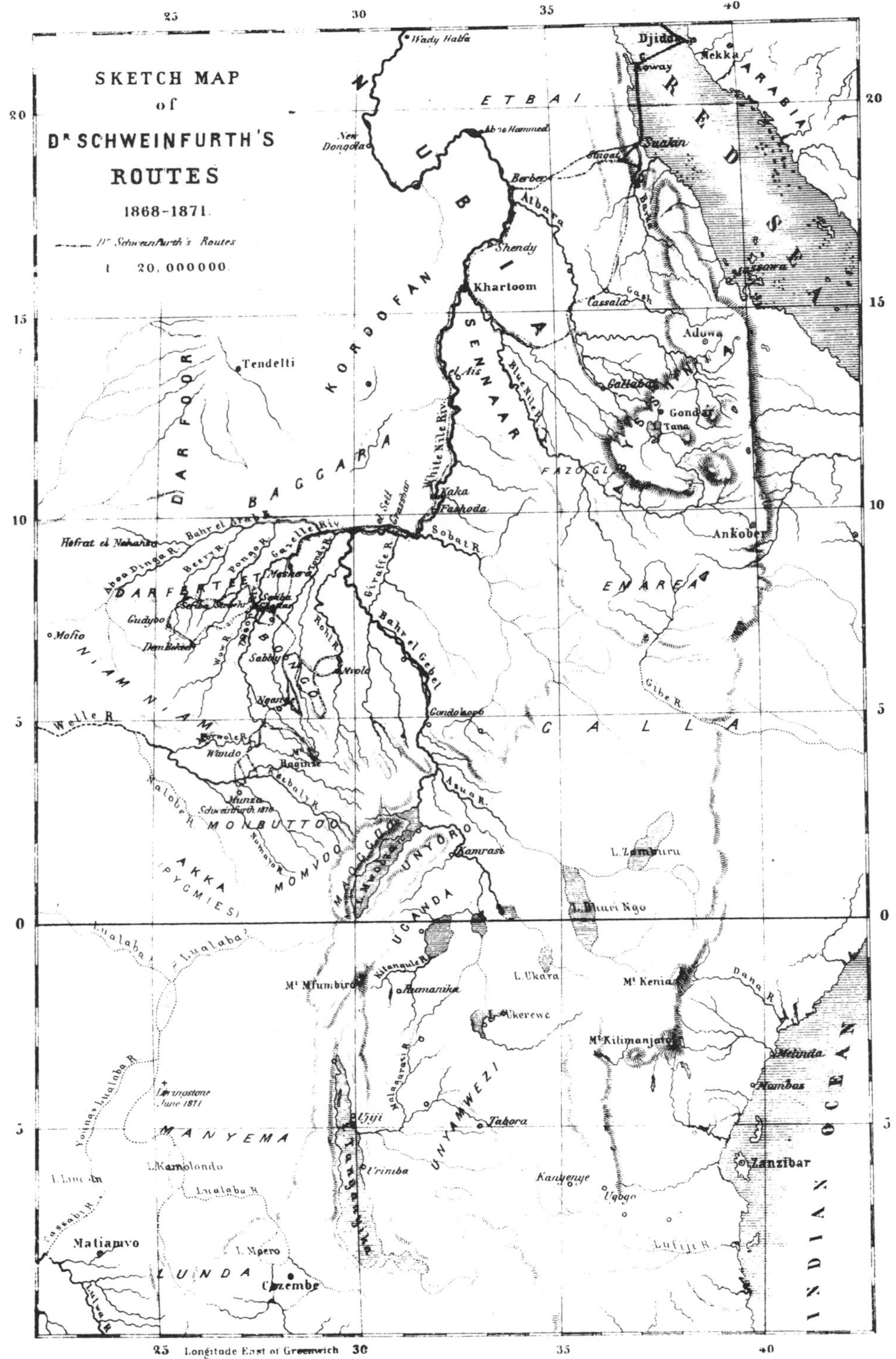

American Museum of Natural History

toward the science of vegetalogy. Schimper, best-known member of a famous German family of naturalists, was a pioneer in what has come to be known as plant ecology. His most famous work, published in English as *Plant-Geography Upon a Physical Basis,* was finished only three years before he died in 1901 at the age of forty-five. He based his book to a great extent on field trips into the jungles of the Orient and the forests of the West Indies. It was in this major work that Schimper applied to these particular vegetational complexes the phrase "tropical rain forest," the first time a scientifically appropriate name had been found for them.

In the progression of scientific understanding about jungles, the men who have studied its peoples are among the latest arrivals. A good representative of them was the American archaeologist, William Curtis Farabee, who during a well-organized South American expedition from 1913 to 1916 collected the basic information on the Amerinds of the Amazon basin.

Farabee, born in 1865, taught at Harvard and then became curator of American Anthropology at the University Museum of the University of Pennsylvania. This institution placed him in charge of the Amazon expedition. Farabee mapped some of the unknown parts of British Guiana on his way, then worked along the Amazon and its main tributaries. His later studies—he died in 1925—were among Andean peoples, but his writings on the Amazon have been credited with being among the first, if not *the* first, that told about these folk as they really are, not with a mixture of fairy tale and speculation.

39

The Tragic Adventurer

Of all the men who have been sacrificed in attempts to unravel jungle mysteries, none has attracted more notice in this century than Percy Harrison Fawcett. Perhaps because he was himself something of an enigma, and a rather famous one, his disappearance in the unexplored Amazon world with his son and his son's friend inspired a tremendous volume of speculation, legend, rumor and debate. The facts were romantic enough, for Colonel Fawcett was the possessor of the 150-year-old document summarized at the beginning of Chapter 28, and he vanished in the Brazilian wilderness on the trail of that "lost city."

He was no ordinary fortune hunter. An artillery officer in the British Army from the time he was nineteen, he had served in Ceylon, North Africa, Malta, and Hong Kong, as well as the home islands. He was basically an engineer, surveyor and geographer, and he got only a taste of these occupations as an artilleryman. In his diary he once wrote: "Much as I loathed army life, it had the merit of leading up to the work most attractive to me."

That work came to him in 1906, when he was thirty-nine years old, a major with a reputation for careful attention to detail, a yachtsman who had designed improvements for racing cutters, and a lone wolf, as he admitted. The occasion was the still active rubber boom in the Amazon basin, which had led to much acrimonious debate over the unsurveyed corner where Peru, Bolivia and Brazil meet. Bolivia asked the Royal Geographical Society in London to nominate a British army officer to make an impartial determination, warning that it would be dangerous. The society selected Fawcett.

His three-year stint, filled with adventure and hardship, led to a request by the President of Bolivia that he undertake a four-year mis-

Royal Geographical Society

Colonel P. H. Fawcett.

sion to settle the whole Peruvian boundary, which would involve an exploration of the virtually unknown River Heath, hitherto considered impassable because of the reported savagery of the natives in the disputed territory. Fawcett retired from the army, since he could not obtain a leave for another four years. He gave up his commission gladly, but resented a reduction in pension decreed because he was serving a foreign country.

On this mission he encountered the primitive, hairy people called the Maricoxis in the jungle. He also heard legends of lost cities hidden in the forests or mountains, stories of remains of civilizations rivaling that of the Incas. He was supremely indifferent to the primitive people he actually saw, although he dutifully recorded details of their customs and behavior; he was irresistibly drawn by tales of cultured peoples he never did see.

After World War I, Fawcett felt that the future of the world lay in the Western Hemisphere, especially South America. He failed to interest the British government or the Geographical Society in his plans to track down the lost cities. At last, sneering at the English preoccupation with expeditions to Mount Everest and the Antarctic, he went to Brazil on his own, and after many months won the backing of that government for an expedition into the states of Bahia and Matto Grosso.

In organizing this trip, he had the assistance of one of Brazil's most remarkable men, a jungle expert who had reversed the accepted method of treating native inhabitants. General Candido Rondon, himself born in Matto Grosso, grew up in a world where, as he once put it, the rubber collectors customarily shot anyone who didn't wear pants. Between 1905 and 1910, Rondon led a movement which made Brazil a model to other nations in the protection of their indigenous populations. He and a devoted body of men under him lived, and sometimes died, by a new slogan: "Die if you must, but never shoot an Indian." In 1920, General Rondon was fifty-five years old, and a great expert on the interior of Brazil where he had located fifteen sizable rivers previously unmapped.

Fawcett appreciated the general's help, and after a round of festivities in Rio de Janeiro and São Paulo, he headed for the Matto

Grosso. Again his wanderings were epic; everywhere he went he picked up new versions of the fabulous cities of the past—and present, for some of them were supposed to be populated still. He noted a "Ciudad de los Césares" in Chile, said to be paved with silver, roofed with gold and peopled by a race of Utopians. He heard, too, of the less glorious "Grand Paititi" in Brazil and finally of a magnificent lost city which he called simply "Z" and which he at first calculated was somewhere in the six- or seven-hundred-mile area between the Xingú and São Francisco Rivers. He emerged with some excellent maps, further notes on Amerindian customs, and a fanatic, all-absorbing determination to locate "Z." He wrote:

> I found enough to make it imperative to go again. The hints that follow may be sufficient to indicate the extraordinarily interesting nature of the research. With the right companions, the right organization, and knowledge of the right way to go, it can, I am confident, be brought to a successful conclusion. I have probed from three sides for the surest way in; I have seen enough to make any risk worthwhile in order to see more, and our story when we return from the next expedition may thrill the world!

The "hints" were summaries of all the evidence that had convinced him that "Z" existed, although not on the Xingú nor in the Matto Grosso. During three years of heartache and disappointments he sought in vain for backing in England. At last in 1924 he raised the money in New York, in large part an advance from the North American Newspaper Alliance for the right to his story. Then he set off with his son Jack and Jack's young friend, Raleigh Rimell. Fawcett wrote:

> Our route will be from Dead Horse Camp, 11° 43′ south and 54° 35′ west, where my horse died in 1921, roughly northwest to the Xingú, visiting on the way an ancient stone tower which is the terror of the surrounding Indians, as at night it is lighted from door and windows. Beyond the Xingú we shall take to the forest to a point midway between that river and the Araguaya. . . .

Then, after further details, almost impossible to follow even on a good map, he went on:

> There are curious things to be found between the Xingú and the Araguaya, but I sometimes doubt if I can stand up to that journey. I am growing too old to pack at least forty pounds on my back for months on end, and a larger expedition costs a great deal of money and runs greater risks—besides, all the men who go *must* be picked men, and there is probably not more than one in a thousand who is fit for it.
>
> If the journey is not successful my work in South America ends in failure, for I can never do any more. I must inevitably be discredited as a visionary, and branded as one who had only personal enrichment in view. Who will ever understand that I want no glory from it—no money for myself—that I am doing it unpaid in the hope that its ultimate benefit to mankind will justify the years spent in the quest?

On May 29, 1925, Fawcett, Jack and Raleigh—the last with an infected foot—were at Dead Horse Camp, where the peons who had been hired for the first leg of the adventure were to turn back. In a letter to his wife, he said he and the two young men would move in a few days, adding:

> We go on with eight animals—three saddle mules, four cargo mules, and a *madrinha,* a leading animal which keeps the others together. Jack is well and fit, getting stronger every day even though he suffers a bit from the insects. I myself am bitten or stung all over the body by ticks—*piums,* as they call these tiny ones. Raleigh I am anxious about. He still has one leg in a bandage, but won't go back. So far we have plenty of food, and no need to walk, but I am not sure how long this will last. There may be too little for the animals to eat. I cannot hope to stand up to this journey better than Jack or Raleigh, but I had to do it. Years tell, in spite of the spirit of enthusiasm.

That was the last word ever heard from any of them. Time after time rumors came from the jungle of an aging, and then of an aged, white man held prisoner by Indians, of his ruling over them as a god, of his having been murdered, of relics having been found. A rescue expedition organized by the North American Newspaper Alliance found nothing in 1928. A journalist, Albert de Winton, tried in 1930, but was killed in the jungle. For a quarter of a century more the stories continued, but of evidence—nothing. That the "lost cities" were not where Fawcett expected to find them has been proved; the area has been crossed so often by planes that no such collection of buildings could have escaped notice.

The colonel would have counted it a failure not to come back with tangible proof of the reality of his dream. But he has left his mark on the history of man in a way that, perhaps, he would have scorned, for his discovery and description of the hairy Maricoxis may have an importance beyond his conception of them.

Few scholars agreed with Fawcett's interpretation of the legends—doubtful documents and cultural remnants of some Amerindians. Yet none of his critics ever questioned anything Fawcett said he himself saw. They quarreled with his speculations, but they acknowledged that he was a keen, sober observer, meticulously truthful. So, though Fawcett did not attain the goal for which he strove so determinedly—proof that there were other rich American civilizations many centuries ago—perhaps his discovery of the Maricoxis, those dark primitive people who cannot by any stretch of the imagination be considered Amerindians, is even more significant in increasing our knowledge of man.

40

A Pair of Moderns

WITHIN our time, many have become familiar with jungles in ways which the most accomplished scientists of earlier generations could not, because we have enjoyed the benefits of the trails they blazed for us—literally and figuratively. Since I first encountered the great green blankets of the tropics when I was still in my teens our understanding of them has been increased by scores, probably hundreds of pragmatic, clear-thinking men and women. Two of the modern greats in the field have been Pat Putnam and Colin Turnbull. Their careers sum up current progress in jungle learning admirably because the younger man knew and followed the elder's work in the same area, the great Ituri Forest.

Patrick Tracy Lowell Putnam, son of a distinguished American surgeon, was graduated from Harvard as an anthropologist in 1925 and immediately joined a two-year expedition sent by that institution to the East Indies. He had already been smitten by what, I suppose, one can only call "jungle fever," for the rain forests held a great and abiding fascination for him. He had hardly returned from the Orient before he set off in 1927 at the age of twenty-three to study primitive peoples in Africa for Harvard's Peabody Museum. He spent the rest of his life in Africa, mostly in the Belgian Congo, with remarkably few trips back to the United States or Brussels or London. Before he was thirty, he had settled on the place and the people for his life work.

In the Ituri Forest the Bambuti not only were available for scientific study but needed a friend. The Pygmies appealed strongly to Pat, himself a long, lean New Englander without the obvious ebullience the little people display when they are at home. He spent some eight months in Brussels arranging to be appointed as a government

American Museum of Natural History

Pygmies at Putnam's camp.

agent sanitaire, a sort of health officer without a medical degree, which gave him a modest subsidy. Then he went out to the jungle again, and on a relatively high spot on the banks of the Epulu River, about as close as you can get to the geographical center of Africa, he built Camp Putnam.

His big house, a frame of posts and lattice walls plastered with layers of mud until they were several inches thick, became a sort of hotel. He ran it as a guest house, partly because the paying customers, who ranged from European royalty and American tycoons to truck drivers, helped finance the nearby hospital. His establishment grew considerably; in the hospital he eventually had fifteen beds. But in the jungle, beds are not the measure of a hospital's capacity. In at least one emergency, Pat cared for more than two hundred people at a time, in sheds, office, hallways—anywhere. Negroes as well as Bambuti came to him from miles around. He was perhaps the best untrained physician of his generation. With the latest in modern drugs and what he picked up out of books and experience, he was able to treat successfully the principal diseases and injuries of his Pygmy patients.

His reports to Harvard were a great addition to scientific knowledge about the little people, who gradually established an almost permanent village near him, and could always be enticed over to stage dances for a visitor. Although he himself never wrote for a popular audience, the things he told and showed the men and women who did write found their way into many books of general circulation. For sportsmen, scientists, professional authors and just plain tourists, Camp Putnam soon became easily accessible, as the main Congo highway passed within a mile of it.

Like everyone I know who likes the jungle and its people, he always had a lot of its animal life around him. On his first trip back to the United States from Africa, he brought along a chimpanzee, an affectionate and generally well-behaved companion but a little startling when one encountered it unexpectedly in his doctor-father's Park Avenue apartment. At Camp Putnam he had a corral and cages for a constantly changing zoo, and his pride and joy was a real live Okapi.

Of all the outsiders who knew Pygmies up to his day, Pat Putnam was probably the one who had learned the most about them and who was most trusted by them. Certainly no other trained anthropologist of his generation or earlier could be compared to him in this respect. His wife, an American painter who shared the last eight years of his life in the Ituri Forest, has given a clear record of his human achievement in a book, *Madami, My Eight Years of Adventure with the Congo Pygmies*. His contribution to science was recognized by his colleagues, who generally agreed that he was the world's greatest authority on the little people.

During World War II, he organized the collection of wild rubber, a matter of great urgency after the Japanese captured the plantations of the Far East. At this time he contracted a bad case of Malta fever, and he never threw it off. By the end of the 1940's he was frequently so crippled that he was confined to a wheel chair, and at best had difficulty walking. Yet he kept up his work at his hospital as if he were as fit as ever, even when he had to be carried there. He died at Camp Putnam in December 1953, and although communication with the outside world had been improved during his quarter of a

American Museum of Natural History

Colin Turnbull.

century in the Congo, it took more than two weeks for the news to reach his parents in New York. He was only forty-nine years old.

Two years before Pat's death, a young Londoner named Colin M. Turnbull, an anthropologist, too, came to Camp Putnam, simply because of curiosity, he says. He had studied philosophy and politics at Oxford when World War II interrupted his career; then he spent two years on a research project in the Department of Indian Religion and Philosophy at Benares Hindu University. That led him to return to Oxford for anthropological training, and he decided to specialize in Africa.

His 1951 visit to Camp Putnam and the glimpses of Pygmy life he had seen there determined him to come back for a closer look, which he was able to do in 1954. Pat had recently died, but the Pygmies were still there—as they are today. Turnbull won their confidence to such an extent that he was allowed to attend the rites by which some of their sons were initiated into adult society. The Negroes, whose rites they were and who believed in them more sincerely than did the Bambuti, were not happy about a white man witnessing this debut, but the little folk had adopted him and insisted he had a right to be there.

Turnbull's thorough knowledge of them began then, but he laid a more solid foundation for it with another two years of study at Oxford. With that preparation, he wrote:

> I felt ready to return to the Ituri to try and understand just what it was that made the People of the Forest what they were, what made them so very different from the villagers all around them, what made them seem to adopt village ways with such enthusiasm, only to abandon them with utter unconcern the moment they left the treeless confines of the village and returned to the forest.

He actually acquired that understanding during 1957 and 1958 when he lived with the Pygmies in the jungle. That was the experience which led to *The Forest People,* published in 1961, a work already cited in these pages. The great merit of his book is that the author was at once a thoroughly trained anthropologist and an unusually graceful, skillful writer. For example, he helps explain the limited horizons of the little people when he tells us that they had the same word for "forest" and for "world." He had a feeling for the virtues of the jungle as well as for the features which had given it such a bad name in the tales of earlier visitors.

Colin Turnbull became a New Yorker after he left the Ituri, but a peripatetic one. He joined the Department of Anthropology of the American Museum of Natural History. His knowledge of Africa outside the jungle led to a second book. *The Lonely African,* in 1962, a volume shedding considerable light on the nature and problems of the emerging independent countries. At this writing, he is in his favorite continent once more, on an expedition for the museum which is expected to keep him there until the latter part of 1966.

It is fitting to end this narrative with our pair of modern greats, not only because they bring us up to date, but because they exemplify a truth which has not been much appreciated except by the true jungle peoples, all of whom are too primitive to write books. It is simply this: the jungle can be a friendly place, comfortable, healthy, attractive, where a man can find peace and friends, too. It is a world of such fascination that those of us who have really known it are drawn to it irresistibly—again and again.

Index

Index

Index

Index

Index

208371

COALINGA STACKS
208371
574.909 SAN
Ivan Sanderson's book of great jun